Macintosh®
Programming
Primer

Inside the Toolbox Using THINK's LightspeedC™

Dave Mark   Cartwright Reed

Addison-Wesley Publishing Company, Inc.

*Reading, Massachusetts   Menlo Park, California   New York
Don Mills, Ontario   Wokingham, England   Amsterdam   Bonn
Sydney   Singapore   Tokyo   Madrid   San Juan*

To Kate and Deneen

Many of the designations used by manufacturers and sellers to distinguish their products are claimed as trademarks. Where those designations appear in this book, and Addison-Wesley was aware of a trademark claim, the designations have been printed in initial caps or all caps—for example, Macintosh, THINK C.

Library of Congress Cataloging-in-Publication Data

Mark, Dave.
    Macintosh programming primer.

    Includes index.
    1. Macintosh (Computer)--Programming.
2. C (Computer program language). I. Reed,
Cartwright. II. Title.
QA76.8.M3M368 1989   005.265   88-34992
ISBN 0-201-15662-8

DEFGHIJ-AL-93210
Fifth Printing, July 1990

Contents

4 The Event Mechanism   **103**

5 Menu Management   **143**

6 Working with Dialogs   **197**

7 Toolbox Potpourri   **263**

Acknowledgments

WE'D LIKE TO thank some of the people who made this book possible:

Deneen Melander and **Kate Joyce**, who waited patiently for us to return;

Fred Cole: Without his support and guidance, this book would not have been written;

Dr. Oleh Tretiak, director of Drexel University's Image Processing Center, who gave us the time to do a better job;

Steve Baker, **Bill Wagoner**, and **Dave Frazier**, ATU personnel nonpareil;

Julie Stillman, **Debbie Cook**, **Perry McIntosh**, **Judy Ashkenaz**, and **David Ershun**, who kept this book on track to the end;

Jim Friedlander, our technical referee, who managed to squeeze a move to Paris in between chapters;

Steve Chernicoff, who was there at the beginning;

Stu Mark, who was like a brother to us!

Jacob Joseph Taber. This was why I missed your first birthday party. Hi, Lori. Hi, Ralph.

Hayward, **Mary**, **Brian**, **Erik**, and **Chris**, and **Amy**, the best kind of kin;

Karen Elizabeth Ann Swartz: the newest member of DATOM Enterprises;

the great **DD**: **Ross** and **Chris Bartell**, **Mike Poreda**, **Jeff Sesler**, **Denis Roark**, and **Steve** and **Linda Schnetzler**;

Erik and **Deb Hardy**, and **Allen Lang**, the folks at NASA HQ; and the entire gang in LA—thanks, guys!

and finally, our parents, **Murray** and **Trudy Mark**, and **Ogden** and **Nancy Reed**, who gave us years and years.

Source Code Disk
for the Primer

IF YOU WOULD like the source code presented in the *Macintosh Programming Primer* on disk, please send in the coupon on the last page.

In addition to the source code presented in the book, we also include the HyperCard XCMD source code and libraries. These were made available to us by Symantec, the publishers of THINK C.

We hope you like the *Macintosh Programming Primer*. If you have any comments or suggestions regarding future editions, you can reach us at this address:

The Mac Primer—Comments
2534 North Jefferson Street
Arlington, VA 22207

Foreword

Stephen Chernicoff

EVERYBODY REMEMBERS How revolutionary Apple's Macintosh computer was when it first appeared in January 1984. One look was enough to tell you that this was something new. The bright, lively screen, the high-resolution graphics, the multiple fonts and type styles—not to mention that funny little gadget with the button on top and the roller ball on the bottom—all served notice that this was not just another boring old computer. Here at last was a machine that met you on *your* terms instead of its own.

Gone were the days of enigmatic prompt characters, cryptic command sequences, and incomprehensible error messages. In their place was a new vocabulary of concepts, novel and yet reassuringly natural and intuitive: windows and scroll bars, pull-down menus and dialog boxes, check boxes and radio buttons, icons and desk accessories. Using a computer was suddenly easy, comfortable, and above all *fun*. For most of us, it was love at first sight.

But as great a boon as the Macintosh was to ordinary users, it held an unprecedented gift for programmers as well. An integral part of the system was the User Interface Toolbox, a body of tightly engineered, lovingly handcrafted machine-language code built into every Macintosh in read-only memory (ROM). By implementing the features of the standard user interface, the Toolbox gave programmers all the support they needed to produce finished-quality software with the distinctive Macintosh "look and feel."

Unfortunately, even with this considerable helping hand from Apple, learning to program the Macintosh remained a formidable undertaking. All

ix

that increased freedom and convenience for the user imposed a heavier burden of discipline on the programmer, who had to master a new and perhaps unfamiliar "event-driven" style of programming. The original Toolbox included more than 400 different routines, and the latest models add even more. Apple's own epic reference work on the Toolbox, *Inside Macintosh,* was a prodigious brainful for any programmer to digest.

It was to help readers come to terms with this mass of material that I wrote my *Macintosh Revealed* series of books back in 1984. My aim was to present the fundamental ideas underlying the Toolbox in a more readable, accessible way, along with an extensive, fully developed example program showing how to put those ideas to practical use. I hoped to give my readers a compass with which to chart their own course through the labyrinth of *Inside Macintosh.* Still, the sheer scope of the subject remained daunting. What was clearly needed was a good introductory book that could serve as a stepping-stone to the level of *Mac Revealed* and *Inside Mac.*

Now, Dave Mark and Cartwright Reed have filled that need with their *Macintosh Programming Primer.* Starting from the most basic concepts, they take you by the hand and lead you step by step into the brave new world of the Toolbox and event-driven programming. Instead of a single, all-embracing programming example, Dave and Cart have taken a more gradual approach. A series of smaller, more manageable programs focus on specific aspects of the Toolbox: drawing simple text and graphics, displaying and maintaining windows on the screen, defining menu commands, managing scroll bars and dialog boxes. By the time you've worked through all the examples, you'll be ready to combine the concepts to build full-scale application programs of your own.

One of the great strengths of this book is its emphasis on the use of *resources* as a way of structuring Macintosh programs. The Macintosh Resource Manager is perhaps its boldest and most innovative contribution to the state of the programming art, an idea whose versatility and power are only beginning to be fully realized. Right from the start, Dave and Cart show you how to use resources as a central organizing principle to make your programming easier, cleaner, and more modular. Their chapter on Apple's on-screen resource editor, ResEdit, is the best discussion I've seen on this important program development tool.

If you're interested in learning to program the Macintosh, there isn't a better place to start than with the book you're holding in your hands right now.

Stephen Chernicoff
Berkeley, California
December 15, 1988

Introduction

Macintosh Programming Primer *is a complete course in the art of Macintosh programming. With this book and Symantec's THINK C, you can learn to program the Macintosh.*

NO OTHER COMPUTER is like the Macintosh.

The Mac is a new kind of computer. It's fast. It's different.

The Mac plays by a new set of rules. To program it, you need a new rulebook. That's what the *Mac Primer* is.

At the heart of the Macintosh is the Toolbox, a collection of over 700 procedures and functions that give you access to the Macintosh interface. The *Mac Primer* will teach you how to use the Toolbox, to add the power of pull-down menus, windows, and scroll bars to your programs.

This book serves as a bridge to the Macintosh way of programming.

The Macintosh Vision

Nowadays, the Macintosh line is successful, highly praised, and much emulated. When the Macintosh was introduced in 1984, however, people were perplexed: It was like no computer they had ever seen—a beige box with a little screen and a mouse. People called the Macintosh a toy because it had a graphic interface, and graphics were not the way normal computers operated.

It was no sure thing.

At first, Apple did everything wrong. Macintoshes were incompatible— in both hardware and software—with every other computer in the field. The screen, disk drive, and CPU board were all bundled together, unlike the modular design of the IBM PC and the Apple II series. The Macintosh had no internal bus and was difficult to expand. The mouse controlled a user interface that was unfamiliar to everyone but Lisa owners.

The new computer should have failed, and would have if Apple had not made an epochal machine. But it made the Mac, which was unique in three ways:

- The **interface**: The graphic user interface was effective. People learned to use computers faster. The dictum "powerful = hard to use" was no longer valid.

- The **Toolbox**: Comprehensive routines were defined in the Macintosh ROM that drove the interface and allowed software designers to write powerful, easy-to-use applications.

- The use of **resources**: The building blocks for all software on the Macintosh, resources store program information in a series of templates in the program file, simplifying the creation and modification of Macintosh programs.

These three ingredients combined to make the Macintosh the basis for one of the best selling microcomputer lines in history. Half a decade later, the vision holds strong. The Macintosh environment remains unique. The careful planning that went into the original Mac has paid off handsomely, as the Mac line continues to evolve and improve.

To write successful applications for the Macintosh, the would-be Macintosh programmer must understand how those three Macintosh ingredients—interface, Toolbox, and resources—work. First, let's look at the most visible of the three: the Macintosh user interface.

The Macintosh Interface

The Macintosh makes its first impression on users with its graphic interface. Figure 1.1 shows some of the distinctive elements of the Mac "look." Because new users understand and use the windows and menus of Mac applications intuitively, the Macintosh interface represents an impressive improvement over the command-based interfaces common on other systems. Each element of the interface—windows, menus, dialog boxes, icons—has a specific function associated with it, and extensive guidelines exist for the use of each element.

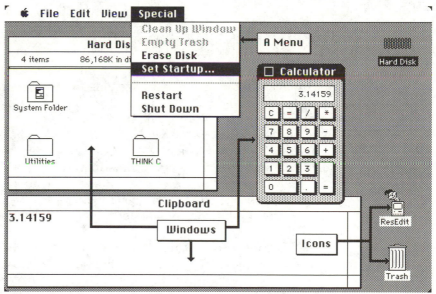

Figure 1.1 Some elements of the Macintosh interface.

The Macintosh interface was appropriated from the Lisa, which lifted it from the Xerox Alto machine. Each successive rendition of the interface improved. In addition, every new version of the interface on the Mac gets sleeker. To look at the Macintosh running Version 1 or 2 of the Finder, or to see the Lisa in operation (while not running under Mac emulation) is rather like examining a '67 Mustang. The new system software reflects Apple's ability to build on the old system without modifying it beyond recognition. Most computer manufacturers have noted Apple's success. It's very uncommon for a new computer to show up without some version of the Macintosh icon/folder/window interface.

Of course, pretty pictures aren't enough. The beauty of the Macintosh interface lies in how it is created. Each part of the interface is manipulated by a series of routines in the Macintosh ROM. For example, you can create an application's window with one call to the Macintosh ROM.

The routines that underlie the interface—that build windows, control printing, and draw menus—are collectively known as the Macintosh Toolbox.

The Macintosh Toolbox

The Toolbox can be thought of as a series of libraries that make it easy for you to create those features indigenous to Macintosh applications. For example, the Macintosh Toolbox call `GetNewWindow()` creates a new window for use in your application.

Using the Toolbox calls to create your applications gives the results a distinctive Macintosh look and feel. Operations common to most applications, such as cutting, copying, and pasting, are always handled in the same way, which makes it easier to learn a new application.

The Toolbox routines are grouped functionally into **Managers**, each of which is responsible for one part of the Macintosh environment (Figure 1.2).

The Macintosh Toolbox undergoes constant updating and modification; each new system revision gives you some shiny new tools as well as the old standbys to work with. As new routines are added to the Toolbox, Apple cleans up problems with older routines.

The Macintosh graphic interface and the Toolbox are two of the features that make the Mac unique. A third is the successfully introduced concept of resources on the Macintosh.

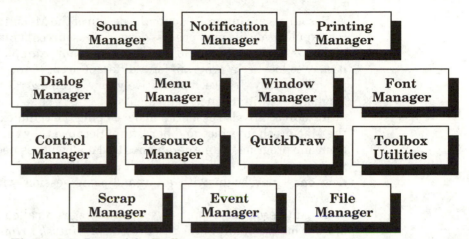

Figure 1.2 Parts of the Toolbox.

Although the Macintosh line has expanded greatly, the basic compatibility of the different Macintosh models has been maintained. Yet, more powerful machines always provide more choices—and more decisions. When the only available Macintosh workstations were the Macintosh and the Macintosh Plus, software developers thought they had a certain flexibility about how they followed the Mac programming guidelines provided by Apple. Now, in the midst of machines that support color, MultiFinder, math co-processor chips, and new peripherals, the successful developer hews closely to the Macintosh standards.

Resources

If the Toolbox is the library of routines that make up the Macintosh interface, resources are the data that your program uses to execute the library calls. `GetNewWindow()`, the Toolbox call that creates a new window, requires you to specify window parameters such as size, location, and window type. To do this, you can supply a resource containing that information, so the new window can be used in your application. Resources come in various types, each serving as a "holder" for a particular kind of data relating to windows, menus, and other parts of the Macintosh interface. For example, a resource of type `WIND` contains information for one specific window in an application. There may be a number of resources of type `WIND`, but there is only one `WIND` type, which is identical for all Mac applications.

Resources are integrated into the design of the Macintosh. Each Macintosh application file may possess dozens of resources. This simplifies many of the tasks of the applications programmer. For example, resources make it easy to localize a program for a different area. If you want to sell your program in, say, France, it is relatively easy to replace resources containing English text with French equivalents.

Resources are also essential in developing the complex code that drives the Macintosh interface and hardware. Because they can be easily copied from one program to another, menus and dialog boxes need not be created more than once. Once you have built up a collection of programs, creating new ones may begin with a cut-and-paste session with your existing programs.

To edit resources, Apple developed a program called **ResEdit**, which allows you to edit any of the resources in *Macintosh Primer* programs. You can also use them to explore other Macintosh applications—even system files! Since these resources exist as part of the completed application, they can be edited without recompilation.

We make extensive use of ResEdit throughout the *Mac Primer*. If you've never worked with ResEdit before, Chapter 8 contains a ResEdit tutorial to get you up to speed.

The Macintosh **interface**, the **Toolbox**, and **resources** are the three intertwined subjects that we'll cover using THINK C and ResEdit to create standalone Macintosh applications. The next sections discuss our approach to learning about these issues.

About the Book

Most Macintosh reference books, such as *Inside Macintosh* and *Macintosh Revealed*, are excellent texts for those who already understand the Macintosh programming paradigm. They can be frustrating, however, if you're outside the Macintosh programming world, looking in. The *Mac Primer* bridges the gap for those of you who are just learning the basics of Mac programming.

Our aim is to help you write properly structured Mac applications. If you're used to programming on a UNIX machine or on an IBM PC, the *Mac Primer* is the perfect place to start your Mac programming education. Our formative years were spent programming under UNIX, on machines like the PDP-11 and the VAX-11/780; we've also spent a lot of time with IBM PCs and compatibles. We wrote the *Macintosh Programming Primer* with you in mind.

What You Need to Know

There are only two prerequisites for reading this book. Before starting the *Macintosh Primer*, you should already have basic Mac experience: You should be able to run Macintosh applications and should have a good feel for the Mac user interface. In addition, you should have some experience with a programming language like C or Pascal. If you've never used C before, we suggest a companion text, such as *The C Programming Language* by Brian W. Kernighan and Dennis M. Ritchie (Englewood Cliffs, N.J.: Prentice-Hall, 1988), to supplement your instruction.

The *Macintosh Programming Primer* examples are all written in C, using the THINK C development environment. Our general approach, however, emphasizes the techniques involved in programming with the Mac Toolbox. The skills you learn will serve you no matter what programming language you intend to use in the future.

Why We Chose THINK C

There are many development environments available to the Mac programmer. The **Macintosh Programmer's Workshop (MPW)** is a complex and powerful development system written and marketed by Apple. Most of Apple's internal development is done with MPW, and many of the large Macintosh software development houses have made MPW their first choice. MPW uses an "everything but the kitchen sink" approach to software development. The basic system consists of an editor shell that allows you to edit your source code as well as build and execute complex command scripts. You can do just about anything in MPW, but it is definitely not a system for beginners. In addition to learning the editor and shell, you have to install, configure, and (oh, yes) pay for your choice of compilers. You can buy C and Pascal compilers for MPW, as well as Fortran, MacApp, and a few others. MPW is ideal for complex, multilanguage development efforts, but not for learning to program the Macintosh.

We did our first Mac programming using the Aztec C development system from Manx. Aztec C offers a UNIX-like shell and a very fast compiler. Again, this is not a compiler for first-time Mac programmers. The documentation is thorough but overwhelming. The shell is very much like UNIX or DOS; too much up-front knowledge is required to build and run your own applications.

When we decided to write the *Macintosh Primer,* we investigated other Mac development environments. We settled on THINK C (also known as LightspeedC). THINK C is a development environment that is powerful and friendly. It has concise, accurate documentation. For those inevitable bugs, it has a source-level debugger.

Finally, THINK C is reasonably priced (see Figure 1.3).

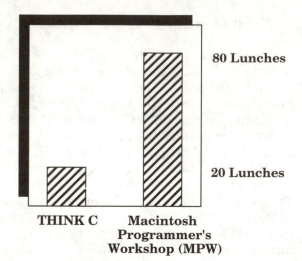

80 Lunches

20 Lunches

THINK C   **Macintosh Programmer's Workshop (MPW)**

Figure 1.3
Lunch economics.

Using THINK C

THINK C is an integrated development environment. The source code editor follows all the standard Macintosh conventions and is very easy to use. The compiler is smart: It keeps track of the files you're currently working with, noting which have been changed since they were last compiled. THINK C recompiles only what it needs to.

THINK C has a well-thought-out Macintosh interface. For example, to build a standalone application, pull down the Project menu and select **Build Application**. Installation is simple: Just pull the floppies out of the box, copy the files onto your hard drive,* and go!

THINK C's documentation consists of two clearly written manuals. The *User's Manual* explains everything you need to know about developing software using THINK C. THINK C also comes with a source-level debugger, a program that allows you to test-drive your program while you monitor its progress in a window. The debugger is well designed and also works with other Macintosh debugging tools like MacsBug and TMON. We discuss the THINK C debugger in detail in Appendix D.

Inside THINK C

The `Project` file is unique to THINK C. It contains the names of all your source code files, as well as the name you'll eventually give to your

---

*For those of you without a hard drive, there are complete instructions for running THINK C on a floppy-based system in the THINK C User's Manual.

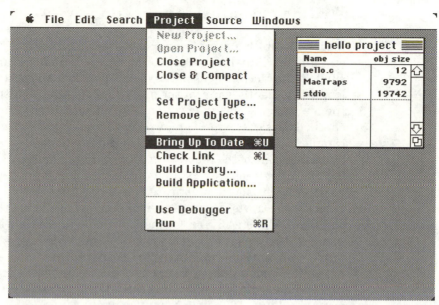

Figure 1.4 THINK C's Project window.

application. It also contains compilation information about each source file, such as which files have been modified since their last compilation (see Figure 1.4).

One of the best features of THINK C is its library of #include files, which allow THINK C to support the latest editions of the Macintosh system software, as well as the latest ROMs. This means that you can use THINK C to write programs that will run under MultiFinder, take full advantage of the Macintosh II's color capabilities, and use AppleTalk. All of these features are supported in the way Apple intended them to be. THINK C also provides routines to support extensions to Apple's **Hyper-Card**.

THINK C also comes with a full complement of utilities, including ResEdit, the resource editor we mentioned earlier, and with the full source code to a sample text editor that you can use as the basis for your own text editor.

For your convenience, we present a summary of the THINK C commands in Appendix C, a summary of the commands for the source-level debugger in Appendix D, and a description of THINK C's HyperTalk extensions with a sample XCMD in Appendix F.

Writing Macintosh Applications

Most Macintosh applications share a basic structure (Figure 1.5). They start off by initializing the Toolbox data structures and routines that support the Macintosh user interface. Then the application enters an event loop and patiently waits for the user to do something—hitting keys, moving the mouse, or some other action. Events outside the application are also checked: Desk accessories may be used, or disks inserted. No matter how complex the Macintosh program, this simple structure is maintained.

At the heart of the *Macintosh Programming Primer* is a set of fourteen sample applications. Each builds on the basic program structure to provide a successively more sophisticated use of the Macintosh Toolbox. Each new chapter constructs a more powerful implementation of the basic program structure. Chapter 3's programs show how to create windows and draw inside them, Chapter 4 demonstrates how to handle events, Chapter 5 implements menus, and Chapter 6 makes use of dialogs. Chapter 7 presents WindowMaker, a complete example of how a Macintosh application should work, from handling the interface and events to taking care of error checking and memory management.

We present each *Mac Primer* example program as completely as possible, and discuss each program listing extensively. Nothing is left as an "exercise for the reader." Each chapter contains complete instructions and figures for entering, compiling, and running the programs using THINK C.

Chapter Synopsis

The *Macintosh Primer* is made up of nine chapters and seven appendices. This introductory chapter provides an overview and starts you on your way. Chapter 2 starts by going through the installation of THINK C and

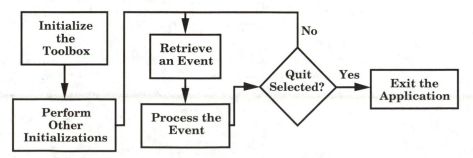

Figure 1.5 How a Macintosh application works.

ResEdit, step by step. Then, THINK C basics are introduced. We present the THINK C manual's version of the classic Hello, World program (Figure 1.6), and discuss its drawbacks. After discussing C and Pascal differences, we go on to illustrate the Macintosh and C programming conventions that we will use in the *Primer*.

Chapter 3 starts with an introduction to the fundamentals of drawing on the Macintosh using QuickDraw. The Window Manager and windows are discussed. Then, we introduce resources and the Resource Manager.

> QuickDraw, the Window Manager, and resources are very closely related. Windows are drawn using QuickDraw commands from information stored in resource files.

Four programs are introduced in Chapter 3. The Hello2 program introduces some of the QuickDraw drawing routines related to text; the Mondrian program (Figure 1.7) demonstrates QuickDraw shape-drawing routines. ShowPICT (Figure 1.8) demonstrates how easy it is to copy a picture from a program like MacDraw or MacPaint into a resource file, then draw the picture in a window of our own. Finally, as a bonus for completing the first three programs, we have included The Flying Line (Figure 1.9), an intriguing program that can be used as a screen saver.

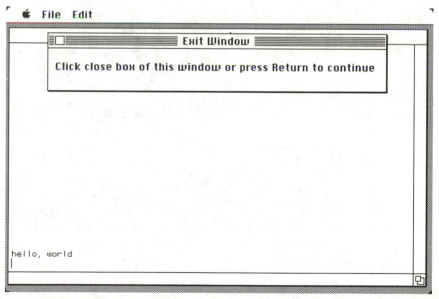

Figure 1.6 THINK C's Hello, World.

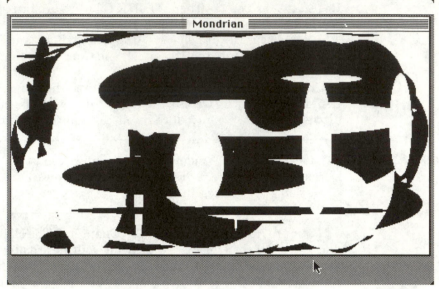

Figure 1.7   Mondrian.

Figure 1.8   ShowPICT.

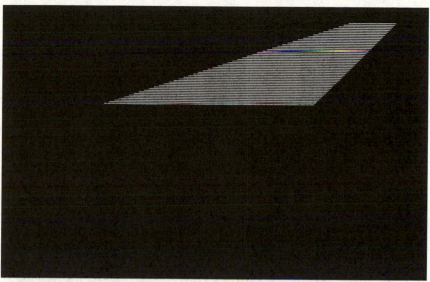

Figure 1.9 The Flying Line.

Chapter 4 introduces one of the most important concepts in Macintosh programming: events. Events are the Macintosh's mechanism for describing the user's actions to your application. When the mouse button is clicked, a key is pressed, or a disk is inserted in the floppy drive, the operating system lets your program know by queueing an event. The event architecture can be found in almost every Macintosh application written. Here we'll present the architecture of the main event loop and show how events should be handled. EventTutor, Chapter 4's sole program (Figure 1.10), provides a working model of the event architecture.

The Macintosh popularized pull-down menus (Figure 1.11). Chapter 5 shows you how to add the classic pull-down, hierarchical, and pop-up menus to your own programs. Chapter 5's first program, Timer (Figure 1.12), uses both classic pull-down and hierarchical menus. We'll also show you how to create and implement pop-up menus with a little program called Zinger (Figure 1.13).

Chapter 6 introduces dialogs and alerts (Figure 1.14). Dialog boxes are another intrinsic part of the Macintosh user interface. They provide a vehicle for customizing your applications while they are running. Alerts are simplified dialogs, used to report errors and give warnings to the user.

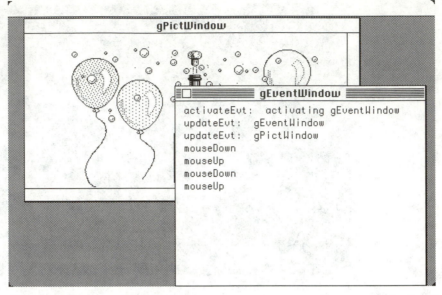

Figure 1.10 EventTutor.

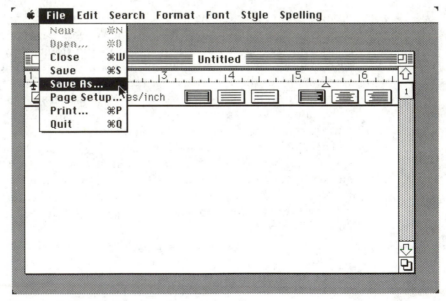

Figure 1.11 The classic pull down menu.

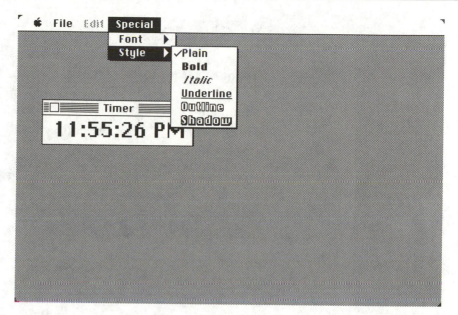

Figure 1.12 Timer with hierarchical menus.

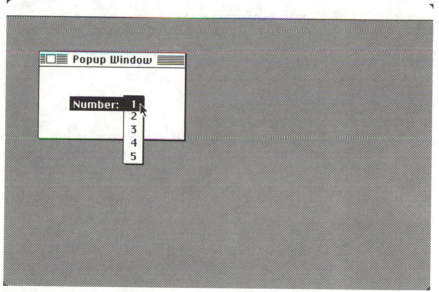

Figure 1.13 Zinger with pop-up menu.

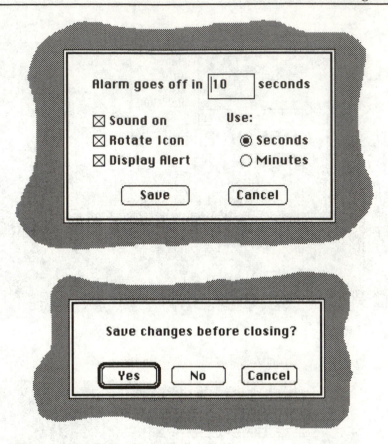

Figure 1.14   Dialog box and alert box.

The Reminder program in Chapter 6 (Figure 1.15) uses dialogs, alerts, and the Notification Manager to allow you to set an alarm. The application then starts a countdown and notifies you when it goes off—even if you are running another application.

Chapter 7, our final programming chapter, contains a potpourri of programs demonstrating concepts such as error checking, memory management, printing, generating sound, adding scroll bars to windows, and file management. Each program explores a single topic and provides a working example of reusable code. The WindowMaker program (Figure 1.16) at the beginning of the chapter, which shows how to keep track of multiple windows, represents the most mature implementation of the Macintosh interface of all the programs in the book.

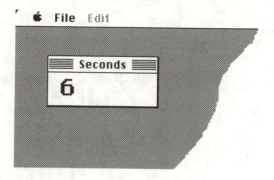

Figure 1.15 Reminder.

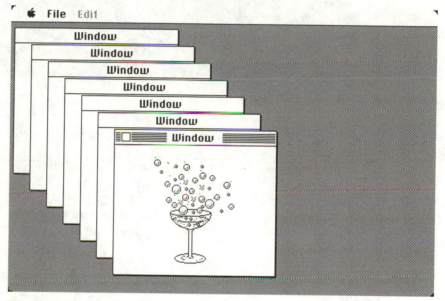

Figure 1.16 WindowMaker.

Chapter 8 discusses the creation, modification, and use of resources. It starts with a ResEdit tutorial that covers ResEdit operation and demonstrates the creation of Finder resources (Figure 1.17).

Now that you've got a handle on the essentials of Macintosh programming, what's next? In Chapter 9, we'll talk about some of the tools available to help you with your development efforts. We'll look at *Inside Macintosh* and some of the other Mac technical documentation. We'll look at software tools, from compilers to debuggers. We'll also look at Apple's Certified Developer Program and other Macintosh technical resources.

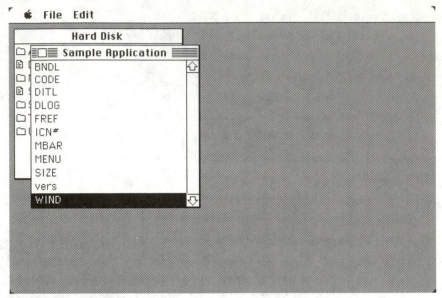

Figure 1.17 ResEdit.

Appendix A is a glossary of the technical terms used in the *Macintosh Primer*.

Appendix B contains a complete commented listing of each of the *Mac Primer* applications, presented in the same order as they appear in the book.

Appendix C contains a THINK C command summary. Each THINK C menu item is introduced, along with any accompanying dialog boxes and alerts.

Appendix D contains a summary of the THINK C debugger. The operation of the debugger is discussed, and each menu item and window is detailed.

Appendix E covers some debugging techniques that will be particularly helpful in the THINK C environment.

Appendix F contains a discussion of HyperCard XCMDs, along with an example written in THINK C, and a complete source code listing of the THINK C XCMD source code.

For those of you who are not HyperCard aficionados, XCMDs are procedures written in C or Pascal that can be called from within HyperCard. XCMDs allow you to go beyond the limits of HyperCard, performing functions not normally available within HyperCard.

Appendix G is a bibliography of Macintosh programming references.

How to Use This Book

Each *Macintosh Primer* chapter is made up of the main text and **tech blocks**. The main text is the narrative portion of this text. Read this first. It contains the information you need to input and run the example programs. Because we've placed a premium on getting you going immediately, we have you run the program before discussing how the code works. Impatient programmers are invited to go directly to Appendix B, which contains commented listings of all the programs discussed in the book. If you have questions after typing in the programs, refer to the chapter in which the program is discussed. If you prefer a more sedate pace, read a chapter at a time, type in the programs and test them as you go. Try the variants to the program if they sound interesting.

At some points, we expand on the narrative with a tech block, indicated by a distinctive gray background. It's OK to ignore them during your first read-through.

There are several important terms and conventions we make use of

> Tech blocks will have this appearance in the main text. If you feel comfortable with the subject discussed in the main text, read the tech blocks for more detail. Otherwise, come back to them later.

throughout the *Macintosh Primer*. Whenever you see a notation like this:

(III:256-272)

we are referring to a volume of *Inside Macintosh* and a set of pages within that volume. The example here refers to Volume III, pages 256 to 272. References to *Tech Notes,* documentation from Apple's Macintosh Developers Technical Support Group, are annotated like this: (TN:78) (referring to *Tech Note* 78). (See Chapter 9 to find out how to get *Tech Notes.)* These references to *Inside Macintosh* and *Tech Notes* are intended to help readers who are interested in a further discussion of a topic.

All of our source code is presented in a special font. For example:

```
while ( i < 20 )
    PassTheParameters();
```

Toolbox routines and C functions are also in the code font when they are described in the text.

Whenever we refer to a function or procedure call, we place a pair of parentheses at the end of the procedure or function name. `GetNewWindow()` is an example of a function call.

Finally, we'll use **boldface** to point out the first occurrence of important new terms.

What You Need to Get Started

First, you need THINK C from Symantec. The examples from the book use Version 3.0, which is the first version to have a source-level debugger. You'll also need a Toolbox reference. Apple's *Inside Macintosh* series is the authoritative reference on Macintosh software development. We suggest that you purchase Volume I and Volume V of *Inside Mac*. Volume I contains a description of a majority of the Toolbox routines used in this book. Volume V contains the latest changes to the Toolbox. Volumes II, III, and IV contain helpful, but not indispensable, information about less commonly used routines.

Buy Volumes I and V with your lunch money. Buy Volumes II through IV with somebody else's lunch money.

You'll also need access to a Macintosh Plus, SE, or II. You can use this book with anything from a Macintosh Plus with 1 megabyte of RAM and an external drive to a fully loaded Macintosh IIx. We strongly recommend a hard drive. The screen shots that accompany the text assume that you have a hard disk.

Finally, use the latest system files with *Mac Primer* programs. Don't use any system software older than Version 6.0 (preferably 6.0.2 or newer) in this book.

The compiled, standalone programs that will be developed in this book may or may not work in the 512K and the 128K Macintosh. In general, if we use a ROM call that is not supported by these Macintoshes, we will mention it in a tech block and suggest alternatives (if there are any) for programmers who wish to support the older machines.

Ready, Set . . .

When you finish this book, you'll be able to create your own Macintosh applications.

Get all your equipment together, take the phone off the hook, and fire up your Mac.

Go!

2

Setting Up

This chapter will introduce you to the software tools that we use in this book. We also examine some issues that are specific to the implementation of C on the Macintosh.

THINK C Is the programming environment we'll use throughout the *Macintosh Primer*. First, we'll show you how to install it; then, we'll look at how to type in and run a sample program. We'll talk about the standards that we'll be using in this book, and some of the rules you need to follow when you use the Mac and THINK C together.

Installing THINK C

Let's start by installing THINK C.

Create a folder called THINK C at the top level of your hard disk. Then, drag the contents of the two THINK C disks into the folder. The THINK C folder should look something like Figure 2.1.

Source Code Files

Set up a place for your source code by creating a folder called my source code, or something equally inspiring, inside the THINK C folder. We called our source code folder src, in memory of our good old UNIX days. We'll create a separate folder inside the src folder for each *Mac Primer* application (see Figure 2.2).

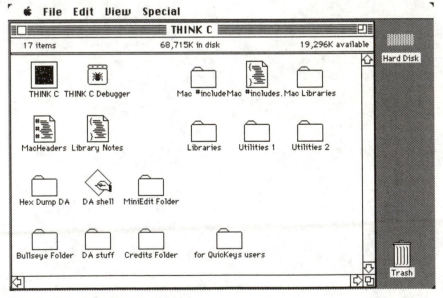

Figure 2.1 The THINK C folder.

24

ResEdit

THINK C comes with a version of **ResEdit** on one of its disks. Check the version of your copy of ResEdit. If you can, use version 1.2 or later for the projects in this book (see Figure 2.3). There is no charge for this utility, which is written and maintained by Apple. It's available on many BBSs, so download it if you wish. You can get it from the Apple Programmer's and Developer's Association (APDA), which also includes some documentation. See Chapter 9 for more information about APDA. ResEdit versions consistently improve, which is a polite way of saying that some of the older versions were rather exasperating. In this book, we use Version 1.2.

If you are unfamiliar with ResEdit, we strongly recommend that you read Chapter 8, which discusses ResEdit operations on resources. It demonstrates how to install the resources you need to complete a standalone program. (This includes the techniques you'll need to add an icon to your own applications.)

Once you have THINK C and ResEdit together on your Macintosh, you're one step away from starting to program. The next section discusses the ground rules for running THINK C code: accessing the Toolbox, Macintosh/C topics, data types, parameter passing, and coding conventions.

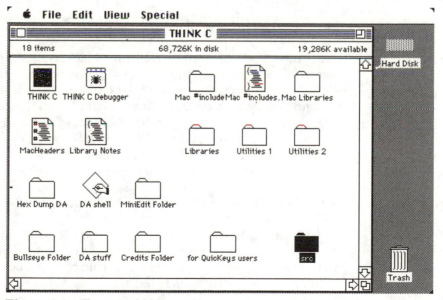

Figure 2.2 The src folder.

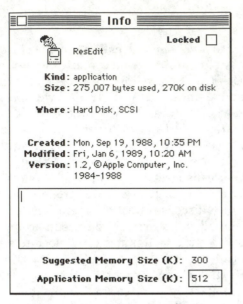

Figure 2.3
Get Info window from ResEdit 1.2.

Macintosh Programming Issues

Accessing the Toolbox with C

Built into every Macintosh Plus, SE, and Mac II is a set of over 700 routines, collectively known as the Mac Toolbox. These include routines for drawing windows on the screen, routines for handling menus, even routines for changing the date on the real-time clock built into the Mac. The existence of these routines helps explain the consistency of the Mac user interface. Everyone uses these routines. When MacDraw pulls down a menu, it's calling a Toolbox routine. When MacPaint pulls down a menu, it's calling the same routine. That's why the menus look alike from application to application, which has a rather soothing effect on users. This same principle applies to scroll bars, windows, lists, dialog boxes, alerts, and so on.

If you look at Toolbox calls in the pages of *Inside Macintosh*, you'll notice that the calling sequences and example code presented in each chapter are written in Pascal. For example, the calling sequence for the function GetNewWindow() (I:283) is listed as:

```
FUNCTION GetNewWindow (windowID: INTEGER; wStorage:Ptr;
            behind:    WindowPtr)  :  WindowPtr;
```

Each calling sequence starts with either the word FUNCTION or the word PROCEDURE. FUNCTIONs return values; PROCEDURES don't. Here's an example of a call to `GetNewWindow()` written in C:

```
#define NIL          OL

WindowPtr            myNewWindow, myOldWindow;
Ptr                  myStorage = NIL;
int                  myWindowID = 400;
myNewWindow = GetNewWindow( myWindowID, myStorage,
                myOldWindow );
```

In the Pascal calling sequence, the function `GetNewWindow()` returns a value of type `WindowPtr`. In our code, we receive this value in the variable `myNewWindow`, which is declared as a `WindowPtr`. Most of the data types found in *Inside Macintosh* are automatically available to you in THINK C. The exceptions are summarized in the following table:

Pascal Data Type	*C Equivalent*
BOOLEAN	Boolean
CHAR	int
INTEGER	int
LONGINT	long
PACKED ARRAY [1..4] OF CHAR	long

For example, the Pascal `BOOLEAN` data type corresponds to the THINK C data type `Boolean`. The Pascal calling sequence for the `Button()` function can be found on page 259 of Volume I:

```
FUNCTION Button : BOOLEAN;
```

Here's an example of a call to `Button()` in C:

```
Boolean    isButton;

isButton = Button();
if ( isButton == TRUE ) SysBeep( 20 );
```

Although Pascal is not case-sensitive, C is: `Boolean` and `BOOLEAN` are different. THINK C provides this Pascal type as a convenience to the programmer. Even though `Button()` has no parameters, you must use the parentheses. If you forget them, you'll get the compiler error message "illegal use of in-line Macintosh function."

You can also pass literals directly as parameters. For example, our call to `GetNewWindow()` can be rewritten as:

```
#define          NIL     0L
WindowPtr        myNewWindow, myOldWindow;
myNewWindow = GetNewWindow(  400, NIL, myOldWindow );
```

This code will work just fine. Passing literals as parameters, however, doesn't necessarily make for readable code. At the very least, we suggest limiting your literal parameters to `#defined` constants (as we did with `NIL`). This brings up the next topic.

#include, #define, and extern statements

The `#include` statement tells the C compiler to substitute the source code in the specified file in place of the `#include` statement. Here's an example:

```
#include "MyFile.h"
```

The `#define` statement tells the C compiler to substitute the second argument for the first argument throughout the rest of the source code file. For example:

```
#define MAXFILES 20
```

Most C compilers use two passes to compile source code. During the first pass through a source code file, the compiler pulls in `#include` files and performs all the `#define` substitutions. The actual compilation occurs during the second pass through the source code.

`extern` is a C key word used in variable and procedure declarations. Here's an example of an `extern` variable declaration:

```
extern Boolean done;
```

This `extern` declaration doesn't cause any space to be allocated for the variable `done`. Instead, references to `done` inside the `extern` declaration's file are replaced with pointers to the "real" declaration of `done`:

```
Boolean done;
```

The absence of the `extern` keyword tells the compiler to allocate space for the variable and tie all the `extern` references to the variable to this allocated space. In the code of this book, every program is only one file, so `extern` is not used. It makes sense to break down programs into modules after they reach a certain size (for example, the Reminder program in Chapter 6 could easily be broken down into three or four files). If you'd like to see how they're used in a program, examine the MiniEdit application on the THINK C disks.

C and Pascal Strings

C and Pascal use different techniques to implement their basic string data types. Pascal strings start out with a single byte, called the **length** byte, that determines the length of the string. For example, the string `Hello, World!` would be stored as a single byte with the value 13, followed by the 13 bytes containing the string:

13	H	e	l	l	o	,		W	o	r	l	d	!

The C version of this string starts off with the 13 bytes containing the string and is terminated with a single byte with the value 0:

H	e	l	l	o	,		W	o	r	l	d	!	0

The Macintosh Toolbox uses Pascal strings, embodied by the `Str255` data type. Since a single byte can hold values from 0 to 255, Pascal strings can be at most 255 bytes (not including the length byte).

Using Pascal strings in THINK C is easy. The THINK C compiler will automatically convert C strings that start with the characters "`\p`" to Pascal format. Consider the calling sequence for the Toolbox routine `DrawString()` (I:172):

```
PROCEDURE  DrawString  (s:  Str255);
```

You can call `DrawString()` in C like this:

```
DrawString( "\pHello, World!" );
```

You can also use the two routines `CtoPstr()` and `PtoCstr()` to translate between C and Pascal string formats. These routines are provided as part of THINK C. They are not part of the Macintosh Toolbox.

Passing Parameters: When to Use the &

Here are three rules to guide your use of the & operator in Toolbox calls:

1. If the parameter is declared as a VAR parameter in the Pascal calling sequence, precede it by an &. Here's the Pascal calling sequence for GetFNum() (I:223):

```
PROCEDURE  GetFNum  (fontName:  Str255;  VAR  theNum:
INTEGER);
```

Here's a C code fragment that calls GetFNum():

```
int        myFontNumber;

GetFNum( "\pGeneva", &myFontNumber );
```

2. If the parameter is bigger than 4 bytes (as is the case with most Pascal and C data structures), precede it by an & whether or not it is declared as a VAR parameter. Here's the Pascal calling sequence for UnionRect() (I:175):

```
PROCEDURE  UnionRect  (src1,src2:  Rect;  VAR  dstRect:
Rect);
```

Here's a C code fragment that calls UnionRect():

```
Rect      src1, src2, dstRect;
UnionRect( &src1, &src2, &dstRect );
```

> If you're wondering where Rect came from, it's one of the data structures defined in *Inside Macintosh* (I:141). A Rect holds the upper left and lower right points of a rectangle. We'll see more of these "predefined" Mac data structures later on.

3. If the parameter is 4 bytes or smaller and is not declared as a VAR parameter, pass it without the &. This rule applies even if the parameter is a struct. This is the Pascal declaration of the routine PtToAngle (I:175):

```
PROCEDURE      PtToAngle( r: Rect;  pt: Point;  VAR angle:
INTEGER );
```

Here's a C code fragment that calls PtToAngle():

```
Rect          r;
Point         pt;
int           angle;

PtToAngle( &r, pt, &angle );
```

Notice that `pt` was passed without a leading `&`. This is because `Point`s are only 4 bytes in size. Most of the predefined Mac types are larger than 4 bytes in size. `Point` is one of the few exceptions.

Conventions

The purpose of any standard is to ensure consistency and quality. With that in mind, we present our standard for writing C code. We use this standard and feel comfortable with it. Feel free to use your own standard or adapt ours to your own personal style. The important thing is to pick a standard and stick with it.

When discussing (i.e., arguing over) C standards, people fight most of all over indentation style. Here's an example of our indentation standard:

```
main()
{
    int i;

    for ( i=0; i<10; i++ )
    {
            DoNastyStuff();
    }
    WrapItUp();
}

DoNastyStuff()
{
    DoOneNastyThing();
}
```

Notice that all our curly brace pairs (`{` with its corresponding `}`) line up in the same column. Some people like to put the open curly brace at the end of the previous line, like this:

```
main() {
    int i;

    for ( i=0; i<10; i++ ) {
            DoNastyStuff();
    }
    WrapItUp();
}

DoNastyStuff() {
    DoOneNastyThing();
}
```

Hmmmm.
Well, do what you like, but be consistent.

Generally, we name our variables and routines according to the standards in *Inside Macintosh*. This means that the names look like Pascal names. The advantage of this is that you can use the same variable names used by *Inside Mac*. This makes your code much easier to debug and compare with *Inside Mac*. Our general rules for variable and routine naming are as follows:

- If you're naming a variable, start with a lower-case letter and capitalize the first letter of every subsequent word. This yields variables named `i`, `myWindow`, and `bigDataStructure`.

- If you're naming a routine (function, procedure, subroutine, etc.), start with a capital letter and capitalize the first letter of every subsequent word. This yields routines named `MainLoop()`, `DeleteEverything()`, and `PutThatDown()`.

Most of the Toolbox routines are built right into the Macintosh, in read-only memory, or ROM. The original Macintosh came with 64K ROMs, the Mac Plus comes with 128K ROMs, and the Mac SE, II, IIcx, and IIx each come with 256K ROMs. Many of the routines built into the Mac II, IIcx, and Mac IIx ROMs are not found in the original Mac, Mac Plus, or SE. Likewise, many routines found in the Mac Plus were not found in the original Macintosh. The point is, things change. If you're not careful, the programs you write on one machine might not work on another. In the same vein, if you don't follow Apple's programming guidelines, the program you write on today's machine may break on tomorrow's.

Resources

As we mentioned in Chapter 1, much of a program's descriptive information is stored in resources. Resources may be defined by their **type** and either their **resource ID number** or their **name**.

Each resource has a certain type, and each type has a specific function. For example, the resource type `WIND` contains the descriptive information necessary to create a window; `MENU` resources describe the menus at the top of the screen. Figure 2.4 gives a short list of some of the resource types you'll see in this book.

Each resource type is composed of four characters. Case is not ignored: `WIND` and `wind` are considered different resource types. Occasionally, resource types may include a space—for example, `'snd '`, where the fourth character is a space.

Actually, resource types are just long integers (4 bytes) represented in ASCII format. Usually, the types are selected so the ASCII version is readable (like `WIND`, `MENU`, and so on).

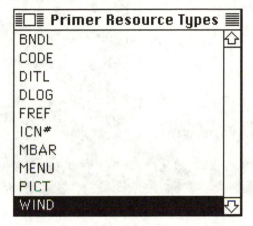

Figure 2.4
Some resource types used in the *Mac Primer*.

Resource ID numbers are unique within their resource type and file. An application can have several resources of type `DLOG`, each of which normally has a unique resource ID within the application file. For example, the program shown in Figure 2.5 has two `DLOG`s with ID = `400` and ID = `401`. The application also has a `WIND` type resource with ID = `400`. Thus, each resource is uniquely identified by ID number and type.

If you prefer, you may also **name** your resources. All the examples we present in the *Mac Primer* use the resource type and resource ID to specify resources. When you create your resources, however, you might want to specify resource names as well as resource IDs. This will make your resource files easier to read in ResEdit.

ID numbers follow these conventions:

Range	*Use*
-32,768 to -16,385	Reserved by Apple
-16,384 to 127	Used for system resources
128 to 32,767	Free for use

Certain kinds of resources may have additional restrictions; check *Inside Macintosh* for further information.

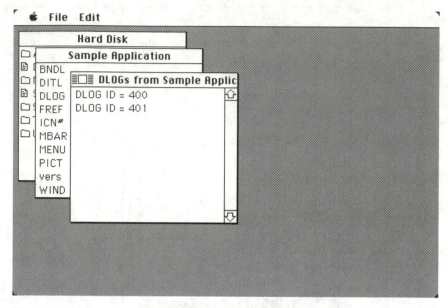

Figure 2.5   Resources in a sample application.

We'll be creating CODE resources in THINK C; most of the other resources will be created using ResEdit.

> CODE resources contain the actual code that is to be executed. You may be used to an operating environment that allows you to segment your executable code. The Mac supports segmentation as well. Each segment is stored in a separate CODE resource and is loaded and unloaded as necessary. If you are interested in learning more about code segmentation, an informative discussion begins on page 70 of the THINK C *User's Manual.*

Data Forks and Resource Forks

Macintosh files, unlike files on most other operating systems, each contain two parts: a data fork and a resource fork. The resource fork stores the resources, and the data fork contains everything else. Many word processors store a document's text in the document's data fork and use the resource fork for storing the document's formatting information. HyperCard stacks, interestingly enough, have most of their information on the data fork side. The THINK C projects in this book will use the resource fork exclusively.

Now that we've covered these weighty and important topics, let's make THINK C do something, right away!

The Hello, World Program

Now you will key in your first THINK C program. It's the classic C program listed in the THINK C *User's Manual*. **Hello, World** draws its name in a window.

Just to make things neat, put a new folder inside the src folder you created earlier. Call the new folder Hello, World. Keep all the files associated with the Hello, World project in this folder.

Create a New Project

To create your first program, double-click on the THINK C application in the THINK C folder (Figure 2.6). The first thing you'll see is the Open Project dialog box. Click on the **New** button, and you should see the Name

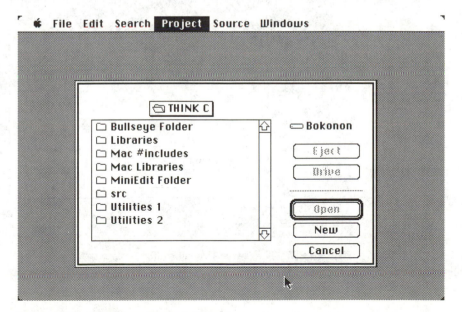

Figure 2.6 The Open Project dialog box.

Project dialog box (Figure 2.7). Open up the `src` folder by double-clicking on it. Then open up the `Hello, World` folder that you just created. Type in `Hello Proj` in the project dialog box and click the OK button (or hit a carriage return). The project window (titled `Hello Proj`) is empty (Figure 2.8), because you haven't added any files to the project yet. As you add files to your project, they will be added to the project window, with the object code size displayed in bytes.

Now, you're ready to type in your first program. First, open a new document. Then, you can type in your program and save the file. Finally, you can add any libraries that are needed to run the code.

The Project file acts as an information center for all the files involved in building an application. It contains the names of all the source code and resource files necessary to run the application. In addition, the Project file contains information about the THINK C environment like the preferred font and font size for printing source code. Projects are a THINK C concept, not a Macintosh concept.

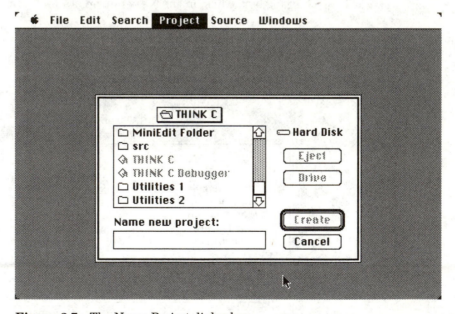

Figure 2.7   The Name Project dialog box.

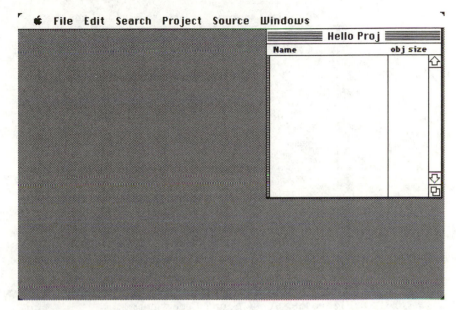

Figure 2.8 The Project window.

The Code

Enter the source code for the file Hello.c. Pull down the File menu and select New. Figure 2.9 should show the result. Now that you have a blank window, type in the following program:

```
/*******   Hello.c****************/

#include <stdio.h>

main()
{
    printf("hello, world\n");
}
```

The THINK C compiler doesn't care how you use white space, such as tabs, blanks, and spaces. Be generous with your white space—don't be afraid to throw in a blank line or two if it will improve the readability of your code.

Check the code for typing errors. If everything looks all right, then select Save from the File menu. Call the file Hello.c. Then select the Add menu item from the Source menu.

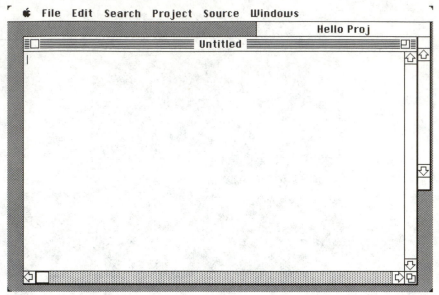

Figure 2.9   A new Source Code window.

Note that the Hello.c file is displayed in the project window (Figure 2.10). Now try running the program by choosing Run from the Project menu, or by keying ⌘R (pronounced "command-R"). Respond to the Update Project dialog box by clicking Yes.

As you can tell, the program isn't quite ready to go. The message Link Failed (Figure 2.11) should have appeared in a window at the top of the screen, and another window with the words undefined printf appeared below it. Don't worry—this is a simple problem to fix. We're missing the special link libraries that contain the definition of the printf routine.

Get rid of the bug window, either by clicking on it or by pressing the Return key. Next, close the Link Errors window by clicking in its close box. To corrrect your problem, you need to add the two libraries MacTraps and stdio to the project.

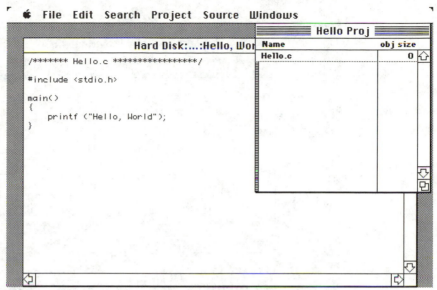

Figure 2.10 `hello.c` added to the Project window.

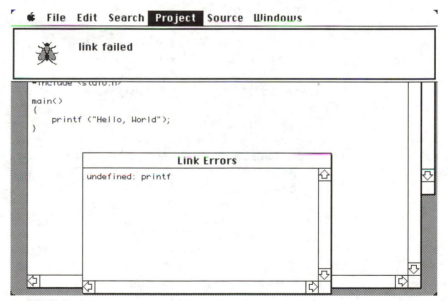

Figure 2.11 The link failed window.

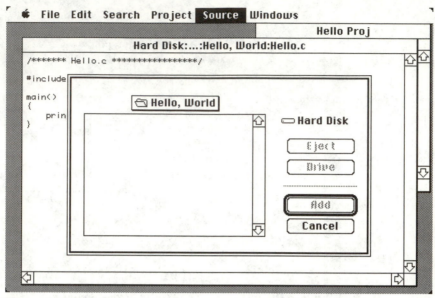

Figure 2.12   Looking for `stdio`.

Adding Libraries

Before you run Hello, World, you have to load two library files so that the `printf` command will be recognized by the compiler. The first, `stdio`, contains information about the standard input/output commands of the C language. To load `stdio`, pull down the Source menu and select Add . . . (Figure 2.12).

When the Add File dialog box appears, open up the `libraries` folder inside the `THINK C` folder and add the `stdio` file. While you're here, add the second library, `MacTraps`. `MacTraps` is necessary if you want to use any Toolbox calls (which `printf()` does). `MacTraps` is in the `Mac Libraries` folder inside the `THINK C` folder. Add `MacTraps` by clicking on the Add button. Since you don't want to add any more files to the project, click on the Cancel button. `stdio` and `MacTraps` should be displayed under `Hello.c` in the project window (Figure 2.13).

> The difference between Add... and Add in the source menu is that Add... has you select the file that you desire, whereas Add automatically adds the file that you are currently working on to the project.

The `MacTraps` library file is necessary for all the programs in the *Primer.* If you are having difficulty with these operations, go back to the THINK C *User's Manual,* or take a look at the THINK C Command Summary in Appendix E.

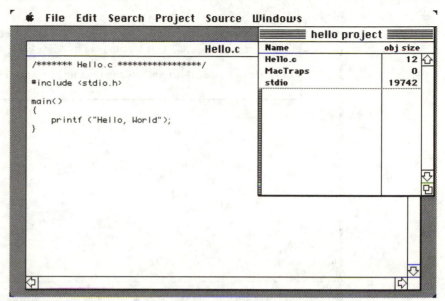

Figure 2.13 `stdio` and `MacTraps` added to Project.

Running Hello, World

Select Run from the Project menu. Respond to the Update Project dialog box by clicking Yes. If you followed the instructions properly, you should get something like Figure 2.14. The application will exit when you click the mouse in the Exit window's close box (it's in the upper left-hand corner of the window).

The Problem with Hello, World

We don't want to get you too excited about this version of Hello, World. Although it does demonstrate how to use THINK C, it does not make use of the Macintosh Toolbox. The first program in Chapter 3 is a Macintized version of Hello, World called Hello2.

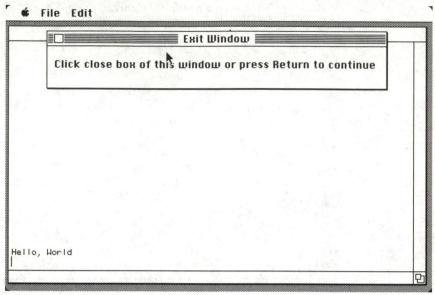

Figure 2.14   Think's Hello, World.

In Review

In Chapter 2, you installed THINK C and created your first project. In Chapter 3, we'll look at the basics of Mac programming: QuickDraw, windows, and resources. We'll also present four Macintosh applications that demonstrate the versatility of the Macintosh.

It's almost too late to turn back. To all those who have come from other environments: Beware! QuickDraw is addictive!

Drawing on the Macintosh

On the Macintosh, the Toolbox routines that are responsible for all drawing are collectively known as QuickDraw. Now that you have installed THINK C, you can start programming. A good starting point is with the unique routines that define the Macintosh graphic interface.

Introduction

QuickDraw is the Macintosh drawing environment. With it, you can draw rectangles and other shapes and fill them with different patterns. You can draw text in different fonts and sizes. The windows, menus, and dialogs that are displayed on the Macintosh screen are all created using Quick-Draw routines.

In this chapter, we'll show you how to create your own windows and draw in them with QuickDraw. Let's start by examining the QuickDraw coordinate system, the mathematical basis for QuickDraw.

The QuickDraw Coordinate System

QuickDraw drawing operations are all based on a two-dimensional grid coordinate system. The grid is finite, running from (-32,767, -32,767) to (32,767, 32,767), as shown in Figure 3.1. Every Macintosh screen is actually an array of pixels aligned to the grid. The lines of the grid surround the pixels. The grid point labeled (0,0) is just above, and to the left of, the upper left-hand corner of the Mac screen (Figure 3.2).

A screen measuring 32,768 pixels x 32,768 pixels with a screen resolution of 1 pixel = 1/72 inch would be 38 feet wide and 38 feet tall. The Mac Plus and SE monitors are 512 x 342 pixels. Apple's Mac II 13" color monitor is 640 x 480 pixels.

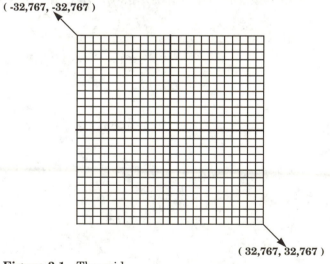

(-32,767, -32,767)

(32,767, 32,767)

Figure 3.1 The grid.

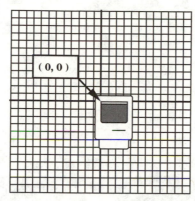

Figure 3.2
The Macintosh screen on the grid.

The grid is also referred to as the **global coordinate system**. Each window defines a rectangle in global coordinates. Every rectangle has a top, left, bottom, and right. For example, the window depicted in Figure 3.3 defines a rectangle whose top is 80, left is 50, bottom is 220, and right is 300.

> Interestingly, the window does not have to be set up within the boundaries of the screen. You can set up a window whose left is -50, top is 100, bottom is 200, and right is 800. On a Mac Plus, this window would extend past the left and right sides of the screen (Figure 3.4)! This is known as the big long window technique. Use of the big long window technique is discouraged.

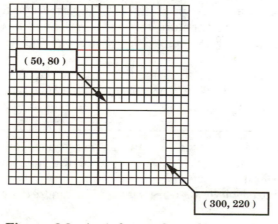

Figure 3.3 A window on the grid.

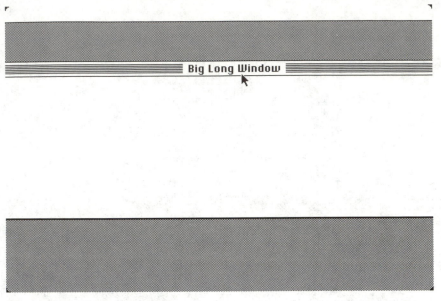

Figure 3.4   A big long window.

When drawing inside a window, you'll always draw with respect to the window's **local coordinate system**. The upper left-hand corner of a window lies at coordinate (0,0) in that window's local coordinate system (Figure 3.5). To draw a rectangle inside your window, specify the top, left, bottom, and right in your window's local coordinates (Figure 3.6). Even if you move your window to a different position on the screen, the rectangle coordinates stay the same. That's because the rectangle was specified in local coordinates.

Local coordinates are great. Suppose you write an application that puts up a window, then draws a circle in the window (Figure 3.7).

Then, the user of your application drags the window to a new position (Figure 3.8).

You still know exactly where that circle is, even though its window has been moved. That's because you specified your circle in the window's local coordinates.

On the Macintosh, text and graphics created by your programs will be displayed in windows. Windows are the device that Macintosh programs use to present information to a user.

Since we need windows to draw in, let's look more closely at windows and the Window Manager.

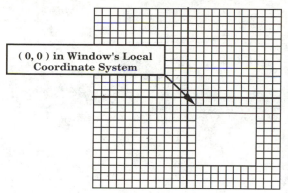

Figure 3.5   Local coordinates.

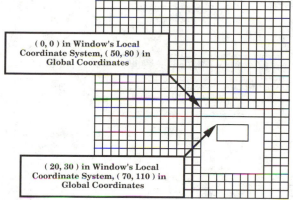

Figure 3.6   Rectangle drawn in window's local coordinates.

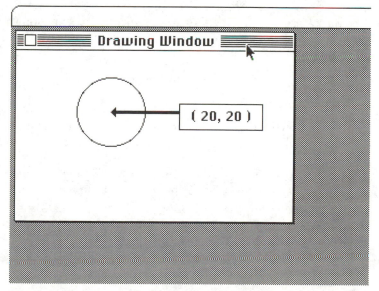

Figure 3.7   Circle drawn in window's local coordinates.

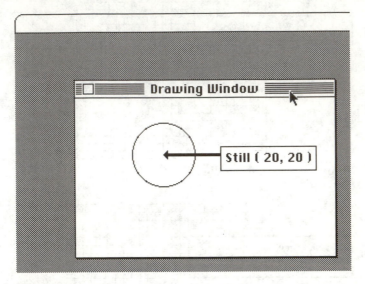

Figure 3.8   When window moves, local coordinates
stay the same.

Window Management

When you draw graphics and text on the Macintosh, you draw them inside
a window. The **Window Manager** is the collective name of all the routines
that allow you to display and maintain the windows on your screen.
Window Manager routines are called whenever a window is moved, resized,
or closed.

Window Parts

Although windows can be defined to be any shape you choose, the standard
Macintosh window is rectangular. Figure 3.9 shows the parts of a typical
window.

The **close box** is used when you wish to close the window. The **drag
region** is where you grab the window to move it around the screen; this
region also contains the window's title. **Scroll bars** are used to examine
parts of the window content not currently in view. The **grow box** (also
known as the **size box**) lets you resize the window. The **zoom box** toggles
the window between its standard size and a predefined size, normally about
the size of the full screen.

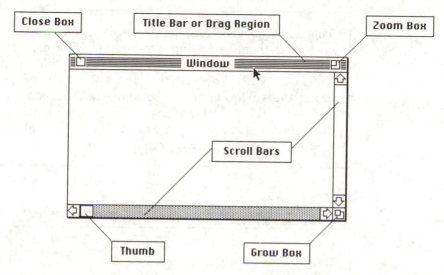

Figure 3.9 Window components.

There are several types of windows. The window in Figure 3.9 is known as a **document window**. When you use desk accessories or print documents, you will notice other kinds of windows. These windows may not have all the same components as the standard window, but they operate in the same fashion.

Window Types

Six standard types of windows are defined by the Window Manager. Each type has a specific use. In this section, each type is described and its use is discussed.

This documentProc window, shown in Figure 3.10, is the standard window used in applications. This one has a grow box, so it is resizable; it has a close box in the upper left-hand corner that closes the window.

The noGrowDocProc window (shown in Figure 3.11), is the standard window without scroll bars or a grow box. Use this window for information that has a fixed size. The rDocProc window (shown in Figure 3.12), has a black title bar; it has no scroll bars or grow box. This window is most often used with desk accessories.

The remaining three types of windows are all dialog box windows: dBoxProc, plainDBox, and altDBoxProc (Figure 3.13). Dialog boxes will be discussed in Chapter 6.

The windows described here are the standard models. You can customize them by adding a few options. For example, most of the window types supported by the Mac can come either with or without the close box (also known as the go-away box). You can specify whether or not the window has a size box (grow box). A zoom box can be added to `documentProc` and `noGrowDocProc` windows (see Chapter 4). We'll show you everything you need to know to create exactly the type of window you want for your application.

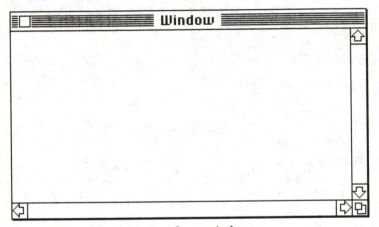

Figure 3.10 The `documentProc` window.

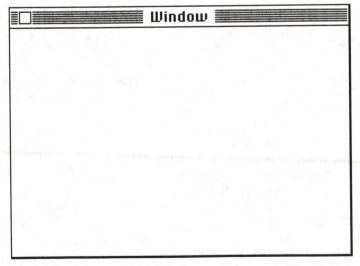

Figure 3.11 The `noGrowDocProc` window.

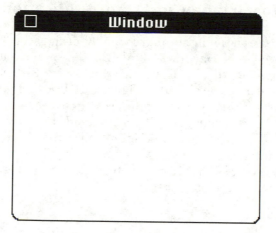

Figure 3.12 The rDocProc window.

Figure 3.13 The dBoxProc, plainDBox, and altDBoxProc.

Setting Up a Window for Your Application

If you plan to use one of the standard window designs for your applications, creating a window is easy. First, build a `WIND` resource using ResEdit (if you're not familiar with ResEdit, turn to Chapter 8). The `WIND` resource requires the information shown in Figure 3.14. Use this resource ID within your application to refer to your `WIND` resource.

Once your `WIND` resource is built, you're ready to start coding. One of the first things your program will do is initialize the Toolbox. The Window Manager is initialized at this point.

Next, load your `WIND` resource from the resource file, using the `GetNewWindow()` Toolbox routine:

```
pictureWindow = GetNewWindow( windowID, wStorage, behind);
```

`GetNewWindow()` loads the `WIND` resource that has a resource ID of `WindowID`. The `WIND` information is stored in memory at the space pointed to by `wStorage`. The Window Manager will automatically allocate its own memory if you pass `NIL` (or `0L`) as your `wStorage` parameter. For now, this technique is fine. As your applications get larger, you'll want to consider developing your own memory management scheme. The parameter `behind` determines whether your window is placed in front of or behind any other windows. If the value is `0L`, it goes to the back, `-1L` puts it in front. For example:

```
theWindow = GetNewWindow( 400, 0L, -1L );
```

loads a window with a resource ID of `400`, asks the Window Manager to allocate storage for the window record, and puts the window in front of all other windows. A pointer to the window data is returned in the variable `theWindow`.

When you create the `WIND` resource with ResEdit, you are given a choice of making the window visible or not. Visible windows appear as soon as they are loaded from the resource file with `GetNewWindow()`. If the visible flag is not set, you can use `ShowWindow()` to make the window visible:

```
ShowWindow( theWindow );
```

where `theWindow` is the pointer you got from `GetNewWindow()`. Most applications start with invisible windows and use `ShowWindow()` when they want the window to appear. The Window Manager routine `HideWindow()` makes the window invisible again. In general, you'll use `ShowWindow()` and `HideWindow()` to control the visibility of your windows.

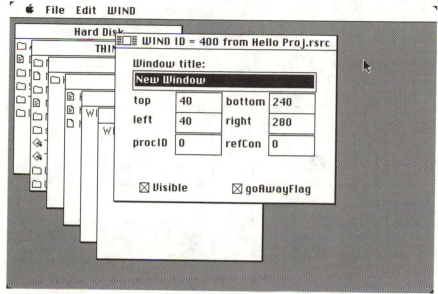

Figure 3.14 WIND resource fields.

At this point, you've learned the basics of the Window Manager. You can create a window resource using ResEdit, load the resource using GetNewWindow(), and make the window appear and disappear using ShowWindow() and HideWindow(). We'll demonstrate this technique shortly. After you have put up the kind of window you want, you can start drawing in it. The next section shows you how to use QuickDraw routines in your window.

Drawing in Your Window: The QuickDraw Toolbox Routines

There are many QuickDraw drawing routines. They can be conveniently divided into four groups: routines that draw lines, shapes, text, and pictures. These routines do all their drawing using a graphics "pen." The pen's characteristics affect all drawing, whether the drawing involves lines, shapes, or text.

Before starting to draw, you have to put the pen somewhere (MoveTo()), define the size of the line it will draw (PenSize()), choose the pattern used to fill thick lines (PenPat()), and decide how the line you are drawing changes what's already on the screen (PenMode()). Figure 3.15 shows how changing the graphics pen changes the drawing effect.

Every window you create has its own pen. The location of a window's pen is defined in the window's local coordinate system. Once a window's pen characteristics have been defined, they will stay defined until you change them.

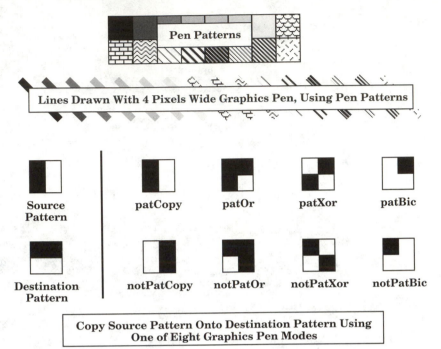

Figure 3.15   Graphics pen characteristics.

Setting the Current Window

Because your application can have more than one window open at the same time, you must first tell QuickDraw which window to draw in. This is done with a call to SetPort():

```
theWindow = GetNewWindow( 400, 0L, -1L );
SetPort( theWindow );
```

In this example, SetPort() made theWindow the current window. Until the next call to SetPort(), all QuickDraw drawing operations will occur in theWindow, using theWindow's pen. Once you've called SetPort() and set the window's pen attributes, you're ready to start drawing.

> The basic data structure behind all QuickDraw operations is the GrafPort. When you call SetPort(), you are actually setting the current GrafPort (I:271). Since every window has a GrafPort data structure associated with it, in effect you are setting the current window. The GrafPort data structure contains fields like pnSize and pnLoc, which define the GrafPort pen's current size and location. QuickDraw routines like PenSize() modify the appropriate field in the current GrafPort data structure.

Drawing Lines

The `LineTo()` routine allows you to draw lines from the current pen position (which you have set with `MoveTo()`) to any point in the current window. For example, a call to:

```
theWindow = GetNewWindow( 400, 0L, -1L );
SetPort( theWindow );
MoveTo( 39, 47 );
LineTo( 407, 231 );
```

would draw a line from (37, 47) to (407, 231) in `theWindow`'s local coordinate system (Figure 3.16).

> It is perfectly legal to draw a line outside the current boundary of a window. QuickDraw will automatically clip it so that only the portion of the line within the window is drawn. QuickDraw will keep you from scribbling outside the window boundaries. This is true for all the QuickDraw drawing routines.

The last program in this chapter is The Flying Line, an extensive example of what you can do using the QuickDraw line-drawing routines.

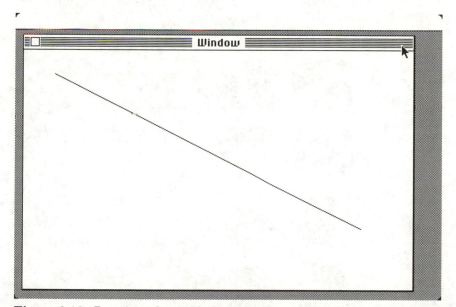

Figure 3.16 Drawing a line with QuickDraw.

Drawing Shapes

QuickDraw has a set of drawing routines for each of the following shapes: rectangles, ovals, rounded-corner rectangles, and arcs. Each shape can be drawn filled, inverted, or as an outline (Figure 3.17).

The current pen's characteristics are used to draw each shape, where appropriate. For example, the current fill pattern will have no effect on a framed rectangle. The current `PenMode()` setting, however, will affect all drawing. The second program in this chapter, Mondrian, shows you how to create different shapes with QuickDraw (Figure 3.18). It also demonstrates the different pen modes.

Drawing Text

QuickDraw allows you to draw different text formats easily on the screen. QuickDraw can vary text by font, style, , size, spacing, and mode. Let's examine each one of the text characteristics.

Font refers to the typeface of the text you are using. `Courier`, Helvetica, and `Geneva` are some of the typefaces available on the Macintosh. **Style** refers to the appearance of the typeface, (**bold**, *italic*, <u>underline</u>, etc). The **size** of text on the Macintosh is measured in points, where a point is equal to 1/72 inch. **Spacing** defines the average number of pixels in the space between letters on a line of text. Figure 3.19 shows some of these characteristics of QuickDraw text.

Figure 3.17
Some QuickDraw shapes.

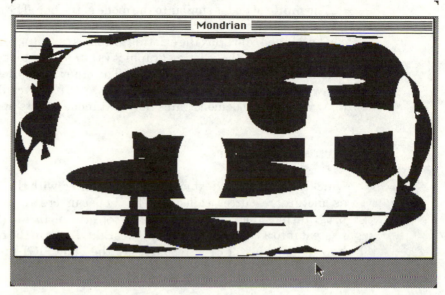

Figure 3.18   Mondrian.

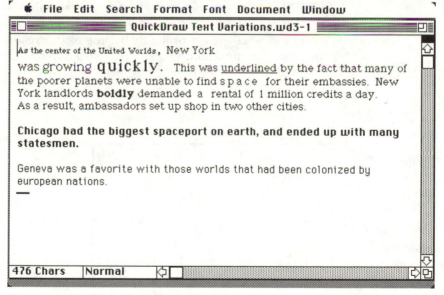

Figure 3.19   Examples of QuickDraw text.

The **mode** of text is similar to the mode of the pen. The text mode defines the way drawn text interacts with text and graphics already drawn. Text can be defined to overlay the existing graphics (`srcOr`); text can be inverted as it is placed on the existing graphics (`srcXor`); or text can simply paint over the exising graphics (`srcCopy`). The other modes described in Quick-Draw shapes (`srcBic`, `notSrcCopy`, `notSrcOr`, etc.) can also be used with text. Figure 3.20 demonstrates how text mode affects appearance.

Drawing Pictures

QuickDraw can save text and graphics created with the drawing routines as picture resources called `PICT`s. You can create a picture (using a program like MacPaint or MacDraw), copy the picture to the clipboard, and paste it into a `PICT` resource using ResEdit. Later in the chapter, you'll see how to make use of `PICT` resources in the ShowPICT program.

About Regions

QuickDraw allows you to define a collection of lines and shapes as a **region**. You can then perform operations on the entire region, as shown in Figure 3.21. Chapter 4 demonstrates some basic region-handling techniques.

By now most of you are probably itching to start coding. First, let's look at the basic Mac programming structure used in this chapter's programs. Then, we'll hit the keyboards!

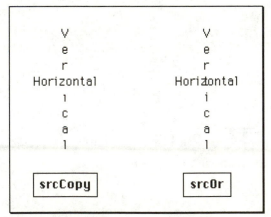

Figure 3.20   The two most popular QuickDraw text modes.

Basic Mac Program Structure

We've looked at a general outline of the QuickDraw and Window routines necessary to make a Macintosh application go. The basic algorithm we'll use in each of the Chapter 3 programs goes something like this:

```
main()
{
        ToolBoxInit();
        OtherInits();
        DoPrimeDirective();

        while( !Button() );
}
```

Like most C programs, our program starts with the routine `main()`. `main()` first initializes the Toolbox. Then, it takes care of any program-specific initialization, like loading windows or pictures from the resource file. Next, it performs the prime directive. In the case of the Hello, World program, the prime directive is drawing a text string in a window. Finally, `main()` waits for the mouse button to be pressed. This format is very basic: Except for clicking the button, there is no interaction between the user and the program. We'll add this in the next chapter.

> Danger! Normal Macintosh applications do not exit with a click of the mouse button. Mac programs are interactive. They use menus, dialogs, and events. We'll add these features later. For the purpose of demonstrating QuickDraw, we'll bend the rules a bit.

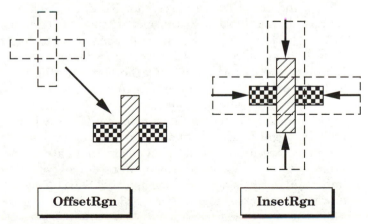

Figure 3.21 Two QuickDraw region operations.

The QuickDraw Programs

The following programs each demonstrate different parts of the Toolbox. The **Hello2** program demonstrates some of the QuickDraw routines related to text; **Mondrian** demonstrates QuickDraw shapes and modes; **ShowPICT** loads a `PICT` resource and draws the picture in a window. Finally, we present **The Flying Line**, an intriguing program that can be used as a screen saver.

Let's look at another version of the Hello, World program presented in Chapter 2.

Hello2

The new **Hello2** program will do the following:

- Initialize the Toolbox.
- Load a resource window, show it, and make it the current port.
- Draw the string `Hello, World` in the window.
- Quit when the mouse button is pressed.

To get started, create a folder in the `src` folder and call it `Hello2`. This is where you'll build your first Macintosh application.

Create a resource of type `WIND`. The `WIND` resource allows you to define a window with the appearance and size that you desire. Use the tutorial in Chapter 8 if you feel hesitant about using ResEdit.

To build the `WIND` resource, run ResEdit. Click on the window that represents your hard disk, and open up the `Hello2` folder you just created in the `src` folder. (You will have to open some folders to get to the `src` folder.) Once you've opened the `Hello2` folder window, select New from the File menu to create a new resource file. Name the file `Hello2 Proj.Rsrc.`, as in Figure 3.22. Make sure to include the space between `Hello2` and `Proj.Rsrc`.

Once you've named the new resource file, a window listing all of its resources will appear automatically. Since you just created the file, no resources are listed. Select New again to create a new resource. When prompted, enter `WIND` as the new resource type. Remember, case is important: `WIND` is not the same as `wind`. Select New yet again to create a new `WIND` resource, as in Figure 3.23.

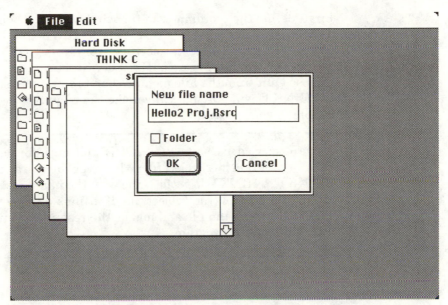

Figure 3.22 ResEdit, naming the new resource file.

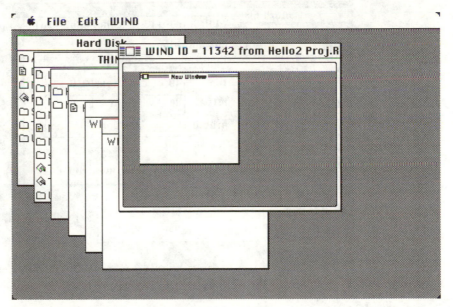

Figure 3.23 The newly created WIND resource.

First, define the coordinates of the window. Pull down the WIND menu and choose the only selection: Display as Text. Then, fill out the fields as shown in Figure 3.24. Next, select Get Info from the File menu (Figure 3.25). Set the window resource ID to 400.

Choose Quit from the File menu. When prompted to save the file, click Yes. THINK C will automatically make the resource file you just created available to your program.

As we discussed in Chapter 2, THINK C collects information about the current program in a Project file. Whenever you run a program within THINK C, THINK C looks for a file with the name xxx.Rsrc, where xxx is the name of the Project file. If it finds a file with that name, THINK C opens the file and makes the resources found in that file available to your program.

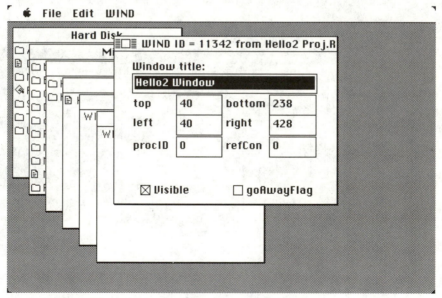

Figure 3.24   The WIND type and size parameters.

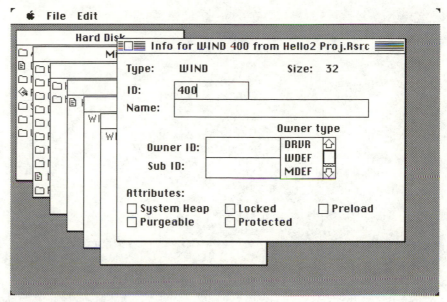

Figure 3.25 The `WIND` Get Info window.

The Hello2 Code

Get into THINK C and create a new project in the `Hello2` folder. If you need help creating a new project, refer back to Chapter 2 or just review the THINK C documentation. Call the project `Hello2 Proj`. Next, select New from the File menu and type the following source code into the window that appears.

```
#define BASE_RES_ID         400
#define NIL_POINTER         0L
#define MOVE_TO_FRONT        -1L
#define REMOVE_ALL_EVENTS    0

#define HORIZONTAL_PIXEL    30
#define VERTICAL_PIXEL      50

WindowPtr    gHelloWindow;

/********************** Main *************/
main()
{
    ToolBoxInit();
    WindowInit();
    while ( !Button() ) ;
}
```

```
/******************************** ToolBoxInit */
ToolBoxInit()

{
        InitGraf( &thePort );
        InitFonts();
        FlushEvents( everyEvent, REMOVE_ALL_EVENTS );
        InitWindows();
        InitMenus();
        TEInit();
        InitDialogs( NIL_POINTER );
        InitCursor();
}

/********************WindowInit**************/
WindowInit()
{
        gHelloWindow= GetNewWindow( BASE_RES_ID ,
                NIL_POINTER, MOVE_TO_FRONT );
        ShowWindow( gHelloWindow);
        SetPort( gHelloWindow);
        MoveTo( HORIZONTAL_PIXEL, VERTICAL_PIXEL );
        DrawString("\pHello, World");
}
```

Select Save from the File menu and save your source code as `Hello2.c`.
Select Add from the Source menu to add `Hello2.c` to the project. Finally,
add MacTraps to the project. To do this, select Add. . . (not Add) from the
Source menu. When the Add File dialog box appears, find the `MacTraps`
file in the Mac Libraries folder.When you're done, the Project window
should look like Figure 3.26.

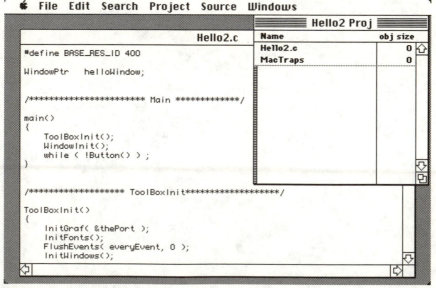

Figure 3.26   Hello2's Project window.

Running Hello2

Now that your source code is typed in, you're ready to run Hello2. Select Run from the Project menu. When asked to `Bring the project up to date?`, click Yes.

You may get a complaint about a syntax error or two. If so, just retype the line on which the cursor has been placed. If it still won't run, refer to Appendix E on debugging techniques.

If you make any changes to `Hello2.c`, you'll be asked whether you'd like to `Save changes before running?`. Click Yes.

Once you've gotten Hello2 to compile without a hitch, it will automatically start running, as shown in Figure 3.27. Voila! The new Hello, World should display a window with the text `Hello, World` in it. Quit the program by clicking the mouse button. Let's look at how the code works.

If Hello2 compiles, yet the Hello2 window fails to appear, it often indicates a problem with the resource file. If the `WIND` resource has been entered correctly, make sure that the resource file name matches up with the project name (e.g. `Hello2Proj.Rsrc` for the resource file, and `Hello2Proj` for the project file. Also make sure that both files are in the `Hello2` folder.

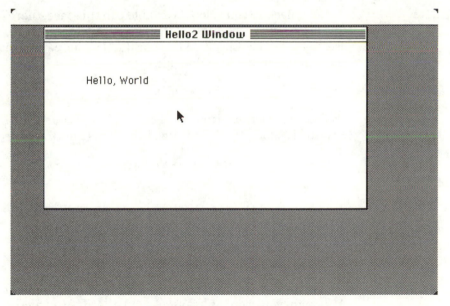

Figure 3.27   The new Hello, World.

Walking through the Hello2 Code

The first few lines of `Hello2.c` are `#defines`. THINK C `#defines` are the same as those found in other C programming environments. During compilation, THINK C takes the first argument of the `#define`, finds each occurrence in the source code, and substitutes the second argument. For example in the first `#define`, the number 400 will be substituted for each occurrence of `BASE_RES_ID`:

```
#define BASE_RES_ID        400
#define NIL_POINTER        0L
#define MOVE_TO_FRONT       -1L
#define REMOVE_ALL_EVENTS  0

#define HORIZONTAL_PIXEL   30
#define VERTICAL_PIXEL     50
```

> `#defines` don't actually modify your copy of the source code. THINK C creates its own copy of the source code and makes the substitution on its copy.

Next, declare your global variables. In this case, there is only one global, `gHelloWindow`, which is declared as a pointer to a window. `GetNewWindow()` creates a window specified by your `WIND` resource and returns a pointer to the window in the variable `gHelloWindow`.

```
WindowPtr         ghelloWindow;
```

The `main()` routine is next. `main()` calls `ToolBoxInit()` and `WindowInit()`, then loops until the mouse button is pressed.

```
/*********************** Main *************/

 main()
{
  ToolBoxInit();
  WindowInit();
  while ( !Button() ) ;
}
```

`ToolBoxInit()` will remain unchanged throughout the entire book. Although you won't always use all the data structures and variables initialized by `ToolBoxInit()`, you are perfectly safe in doing so. It is much easier and safer to initialize each of the Macintosh Toolbox managers than to try to figure out which ones you'll need and which you won't.

```
/********************************* ToolBoxInit */

ToolBoxInit()
{
    InitGraf( &thePort );
    InitFonts();
    FlushEvents( everyEvent, REMOVE_ALL_EVENTS );
    InitWindows();
    InitMenus();
    TEInit();
    InitDialogs( NIL_POINTER );
    InitCursor();
}
```

Each call initializes a different part of the Macintosh interface. The call to `InitGraf()` initializes QuickDraw.

The following global variables are initialized by InitGraf() and can be used in your routines:

- `thePort` always points to the current GrafPort. Because it is the first QuickDraw global, passing its address to `InitGraf()` tells QuickDraw where in memory all the QuickDraw globals are located.

- `white` is a pattern variable set to a white fill; `black`, `gray`, `ltGray`, and `dkGray` are initialized as different shades between black and white.

- `arrow` is set as the standard cursor shape, an arrow. You can pass arrow as an argument to QuickDraw's cursor-handling routines.

- `screenBits` is a data structure that describes the main Mac screen. The field `screenBits.bounds` is declared as a Rect and contains a rectangle that encloses the main Mac screen.

- `randSeed` is used as a seed by the Macintosh random number generator (we'll show you how to use the seed in this chapter).

`InitFonts()` initializes the Font Manager and loads the system font into memory. Since the Window Manager uses the Font Manager (to draw the window's title, for example), you must initialize fonts first. `FlushEvents()` gets rid of all the events that are currently in the event queue, such as mouse movement or keyboard actions. We'll talk about events in Chapter 4. `InitWindows()` initializes the Window Manager and draws the desktop and the empty menu bar. `InitMenus()` initializes the Menu Manager so you can use menus. (Chapter 5 shows how to use the Menu Manager.) `InitMenus()` also draws the empty menu bar.

> `InitWindows()` and `InitMenus()` both draw the empty menu bar. This is done intentionally by the ROM programmers for a reason that is such a dark secret, they didn't even document it in *Inside Macintosh*.

`TEInit()` initializes TextEdit, the Text-Editing Manager that MiniEdit uses (discussed in the THINK C *User's Manual* and in *Inside Macintosh*). `InitDialogs()` initializes the Dialog Manager (demonstrated in Chapter 6). `InitCursor()` sets the cursor to the arrow cursor and makes the cursor visible.

As we said, it's not necessary to call each of these routines in every program you'll ever write. Why, then, should you call `InitMenus()`, for example, if you don't use menus? Well, suppose you decide to add menus later. Calling `InitMenus()` now means you won't spend time later on wondering why your program is crashing when all you did was add a new menu-handling routine.

An additional reason to initialize all managers is more subtle. Routines in one manager may employ routines in another manager. So, if one manager is not initialized—even if you don't use its routines—your program may bomb. Use the `ToolboxInit()` routine in your programs.

Window Initialization Routine

`WindowInit()` calls `GetNewWindow()` to load the `WIND` with resource ID = `BASE_RES_ID` from your resource file. `GetNewWindow()` returns a pointer to the new window data structure. Then, `WindowInit()` calls `ShowWindow()` to make the window visible. It is at this point that the window actually appears on the screen. The call to `SetPort()` makes `gHelloWindow` the current window. All subsequent QuickDraw drawing operations will take place in `gHelloWindow`. Next, `gHelloWindow`'s pen is moved to the local coordinates 50 down and 30 across from the upper left-hand corner of `gHelloWindow`, and the Pascal string `Hello, World` is drawn.

```
/*********************WindowInit**************/

WindowInit()
{
    gHelloWindow= GetNewWindow( BASE_RES_ID , NIL_POINTER,
                                    MOVE_TO_FRONT );
    ShowWindow( gHelloWindow);
    SetPort( gHelloWindow);
    MoveTo( HORIZONTAL_PIXEL, VERTICAL_PIXEL );
    DrawString("\pHello, World");
}
```

The new Hello, World can easily be turned into a standalone application. Pull down the Project menu and select Build Application. When the Build Application dialog box appears, type in the name of your application and press return. THINK C will build a standalone application out of Hello2. If you'd like to add a custom icon to Hello2, take a quick tour through Chapter 8.

Variants

We'd like to present some variants to the Hello2 program. We'll start by changing the font used to draw `Hello, World`. Next, we'll modify the style of the text, using **boldface**, *italics*, and so on. We'll also show you how to change the size of your text. Finally, we'll experiment with different window types.

Changing the Font

Every window has an associated font. You can change the current window's font by calling `TextFont()`, and passing an integer that represents the font you'd like to use:

```
int         myFontNumber;
TextFont( myFontNumber );
```

If text is already drawn in the window, `TextFont()` won't affect it—only text drawn after the routine is called is affected. Macintosh font numbers stat at zero and count up from there. THINK C has predefined a number of font names for you to experiment with. For example, `monaco` is defined as `4`, `times` as `20`. If you want to check out the whole list, open the file `FontMgr.h` in the `Mac #includes` folder.

Did someone in the back ask, "How can you tell which fonts have been installed in the system?" An excellent question! Not every Mac has the same set of fonts installed. Some folks have the LaserWriter font set, others a set of fonts for their ImageWriter. Some people might even have a complete set of foreign language fonts. For the most part, your applications shouldn't care which fonts are installed. There are, however, two exceptions to this rule. Dialog boxes and menus are drawn in the **system font**, which defaults to font number 0. The default font for applications is called the **application font**, usually font number 1. In the United States, the system font is Chicago, and the applications font is Geneva.

For now, put the `TextFont()` call before your call to `DrawString()` and after your call to `SetPort()`, and try different font numbers.

```
/*********************WindowInit**************/

WindowInit()
{
    gHelloWindow= GetNewWindow( BASE_RES_ID , NIL_POINTER,
                                        MOVE_TO_FRONT );
    ShowWindow( gHelloWindow);
    SetPort( gHelloWindow);
    MoveTo( HORIZONTAL_PIXEL, VERTICAL_PIXEL );
    TextFont( monaco );
    /*  Try other predefined constants (such as times,
            if you have it installed)  */
    DrawString("\pHello, World");
}
```

Changing Text Style

The Macintosh supports seven font styles: **bold**, *italic*, underline, outline, shadow, condensed and extended, or any combination of these. In Chapter 5, we'll show you how to set text styles using menus. For now, try inserting the call `TextFace( style )` before the call to `DrawString()`. Here's one example:

```
/*********************WindowInit**************/

WindowInit()
{
    gHelloWindow= GetNewWindow( BASE_RES_ID , NIL_POINTER,
                                        MOVE_TO_FRONT );
    ShowWindow( gHelloWindow);
    SetPort( gHelloWindow);
    MoveTo( HORIZONTAL_PIXEL, VERTICAL_PIXEL );
    TextFace( bold );
    /*  Try the other styles  */
    DrawString("\pHello, World");
}
```

Here's a list of predefined styles taken from the #include file `QuickDraw.h`:

- bold
- italic
- underline
- outline
- shadow
- condense
- extend

You can also combine styles; try `TextFace( bold + italic )` or some other combination.

Changing Text Size

It's also easy to change the size of the fonts, using the `TextSize()` Toolbox routine:

```
int        myFontSize;
TextSize( myFontSize );
```

The number you supply as an argument to `TextSize()` is the font size that will be used the next time text is drawn in the current window. The Font Manager will scale a font up to the size requested; this may result in a jaggy character, as shown in Figure 3.28. The default size is 0, which specifies that the system font size (normally 12 point) be used. Try this variation.

```
/********************WindowInit**************/

WindowInit()
{
        gHelloWindow= GetNewWindow( BASE_RES_ID ,
        NIL_POINTER, MOVE_TO_FRONT );
        ShowWindow( gHelloWindow);
        SetPort( gHelloWindow);
        MoveTo( HORIZONTAL_PIXEL, VERTICAL_PIXEL );
        TextSize( 24 );
        /*  Try other sizes like 1 or 255 (you may have to
        change the VERTICAL_PIXEL #define to something
        bigger) */
        DrawString("\pHello, World");
}
```

Changing the Hello2 Window

Another modification you can try involves changing the window type from 0 to something else. Use ResEdit to change the `WIND` resource's `procID` from 0 to 1, as in Figure 3.29. (See the section on window types earlier in this chapter for other possibilities.)

Now that you have mastered QuickDraw's text-handling routines, let's exercise the shape-drawing capabilities of QuickDraw with our next program: Mondrian.

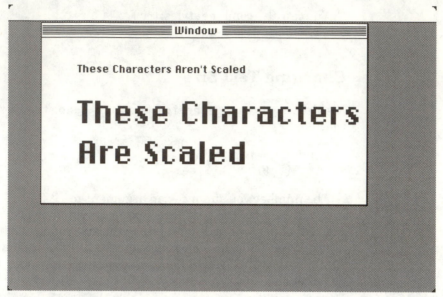

Figure 3.28   The result of font scaling.

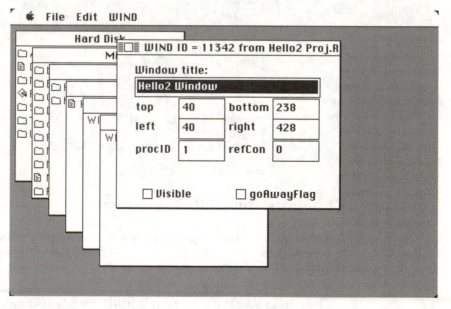

Figure 3.29   Changing the window type.

Mondrian

The **Mondrian** program opens a window and draws randomly generated ovals, alternately filled with white or black. Like Hello2, Mondrian waits for a mouse click to exit. The program, with its variants, demonstrates most of QuickDraw's shape-drawing functionality.

Mondrian is made up of three steps:

- Initialize the Toolbox.
- Initialize the window.
- Draw random QuickDraw shapes in a loop until the mouse button is clicked.

First, create a new folder called `Mondrian` in the `src` folder. Next, create the resources you need for the program, and then enter the code.

Resources

The Mondrian program needs a `WIND` resource, just as Hello2 did. In this case, create a new resource file called `Mondrian Proj.Rsrc` (don't forget the space) in the `Mondrian` folder you just made. Then create a `WIND` with size and title as shown in Figure 3.30. Before you close and save

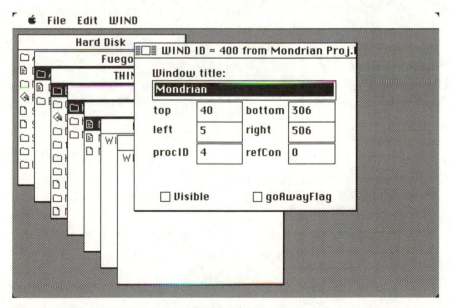

Figure 3.30   `WIND` parameters for Mondrian.

MondrianProj.rsrc, go to Get Info and change the resource ID of the new
WIND to 400. Next, go into THINK C and create a new project called
Mondrian Proj inside the Mondrian folder. Add MacTraps to your
project. Then open up a new source code window and enter the program:

```c
#define BASE_RES_ID         400
#define NIL_POINTER         0L
#define MOVE_TO_FRONT       -1L
#define REMOVE_ALL_EVENTS   0

WindowPtr       gDrawWindow;
long            gFillColor = blackColor;

/***************************** main ********/

main()
{
        ToolBoxInit();
        WindowInit();
        MainLoop();
}


/******************************** ToolBoxInit */

ToolBoxInit()
{
        InitGraf( &thePort );
        InitFonts();
        FlushEvents( everyEvent, REMOVE_ALL_EVENTS );
        InitWindows();
        InitMenus();
        TEInit();
        InitDialogs( NIL_POINTER );
        InitCursor();
}

/***************************** WindowInit ********/

WindowInit()
{
        gDrawWindow = GetNewWindow( BASE_RES_ID, NIL_POINTER,
                                        MOVE_TO_FRONT );
        ShowWindow( gDrawWindow );
        SetPort( gDrawWindow );
}

/***************************** MainLoop ********/

MainLoop()
{
        GetDateTime( &randSeed );
        while ( ! Button() )
        {
                DrawRandomRect();
                if ( gFillColor == blackColor )
                        gFillColor = whiteColor;
```

```
            else
                gFillColor = blackColor;
      }
}

/****************************** DrawRandomRect *********/

DrawRandomRect()
{
      Rect    myRect;

      RandomRect( &myRect, gDrawWindow );
      ForeColor( gFillColor );
      PaintOval( &myRect );
}

/****************************** RandomRect *********/

RandomRect( myRectPtr, boundingWindow )
Rect           *myRectPtr;
WindowPtr       boundingWindow;
{
      myRectPtr->left = Randomize( boundingWindow->portRect.right
            - boundingWindow->portRect.left );
      myRectPtr->right = Randomize( boundingWindow->portRect.right
            - boundingWindow->portRect.left );
      myRectPtr->top = Randomize( boundingWindow->portRect.bottom
            - boundingWindow->portRect.top );
      myRectPtr->bottom = Randomize( boundingWindow->portRect.bottom
            - boundingWindow->portRect.top );
}

/****************************** Randomize *********/

Randomize( range )
int    range;
{
      long   rawResult;
      rawResult = Random();
      if ( rawResult < 0 ) rawResult *= -1;
            return( (rawResult * range) / 32768 );
}
```

Running Mondrian

Once you've finished typing in the code, save it as `Mondrian.c` and add it to the project. Next, select Run from the Project menu. Click Yes to bring the project up to date. If everything went correctly, you should see something like Figure 3.31. The window should fill with overlapping black and white ovals until you click the mouse button. If you got a different result, then check out your resource file; make sure the `WIND` resource has the correct resource ID. If your resource file is all right, go through the code carefully.

Now let's walk through the Mondrian code.

Figure 3.31   Running Mondrian.

Walking through the Mondrian Code

The Mac Primer uses the convention of starting resource ID numbers at
400, adding one each time a new resource ID is needed. (In your own
programs you can use any number between 128 and 32,767.) The #defines
used in Mondrian are identical to those used in Hello2. The global variable
gDrawWindow is Mondrian's main window. Each shape you draw will be
filled with the color in gfillColor, which is initialized as blackColor.

```
#define BASE_RES_ID          400
#define NIL_POINTER          0L
#define MOVE_TO_FRONT        -1L
#define REMOVE_ALL_EVENTS    0

WindowPtr      gDrawWindow;
long           gFillColor=blackColor;
```

The main routine is exactly the same as it was in Hello2:

```
/***************************** main *********/

main()
{
   ToolBoxInit();
   WindowInit();
   MainLoop();
}
```

The Toolbox initialization routine is also the same as in Hello2.

```
/******************************** ToolBoxInit */
ToolBoxInit()
{
    InitGraf( &thePort );
    InitFonts();
    FlushEvents( everyEvent, REMOVE_ALL_EVENTS );
    InitWindows();
    InitMenus();
    TEInit();
    InitDialogs( NIL_POINTER );
    InitCursor();
}
```

WindowInit() loads WIND number 400 from the resource file, storing a pointer to it in gDrawWindow. Next, ShowWindow() is called to make the window visible, and SetPort() is called to make gDrawWindow the current window.

```
/****************************** WindowInit ********/
WindowInit()
{
    gDrawWindow = GetNewWindow( BASE_RES_ID, NIL_POINTER,
                                MOVE_TO_FRONT );
    ShowWindow( gDrawWindow );
    SetPort( gDrawWindow );
}
```

MainLoop() starts by using the current time (in seconds since January 1, 1904) to seed the Mac random number generator. The QuickDraw global randSeed is used as a seed by the random number generator. If you didn't modify randSeed, you'd generate the same patterns every time you ran Mondrian.

MainLoop() then sets up a loop that falls through when the mouse button is pressed. In the loop, DrawRandomRect() is called, which generates a random rectangular area in the window and then draws an oval in the rectangle. Then, gFillColor is flipped from black to white or from white to black.

```
/****************************** MainLoop ********/
MainLoop()
{
    GetDateTime( &randSeed );
    while ( ! Button() )
    {
        DrawRandomRect();
        if ( gFillColor == blackColor )
            gFillColor = whiteColor;
        else
            gFillColor = blackColor;
    }
}
```

DrawRandomRect() controls the actual drawing of the ovals in the window. RandomRect() generates a random rectangle inside gDrawWindow, ForeColor() sets the current drawing color to gFillColor, and PaintOval() paints the oval.

```
/*************************** DrawRandomRect ********/

DrawRandomRect()
{
    Rect    myRect;

    RandomRect( &myRect, gDrawWindow );
    ForeColor( gFillColor );
    PaintOval( &myRect );
}
```

RandomRect() sets up the rectangle to be used in drawing the oval. Each of the four sides of the rectangle is generated as a random number between the right and left (or top and bottom, as appropriate) sides of the input parameter, boundingWindow.

The notation myStructPtr->myField refers to the field myField in the struct pointed to by myStructPtr.

Every window data structure has a field named portRect that defines the boundary of the content region of the window. Since boundingWindow is a pointer to a window data structure, you use boundingWindow->portRect to access this rectangle.

```
/***************************** RandomRect ********/

RandomRect( myRectPtr, boundingWindow )
Rect          *myRectPtr;
WindowPtr     boundingWindow;
{
    myRectPtr->left = Randomize( boundingWindow->portRect.right
            - boundingWindow->portRect.left );
    myRectPtr->right = Randomize( boundingWindow->portRect.right
            - boundingWindow->portRect.left );
    myRectPtr->top = Randomize( boundingWindow->portRect.bottom
        - boundingWindow->portRect.top );
    myRectPtr->bottom = Randomize( boundingWindow->portRect.bottom
            - boundingWindow->portRect.top );
{
```

Randomize( ) takes an integer argument and returns a positive integer greater than or equal to 0, and less than the argument. This is accomplished via a call to the Random( ) Toolbox utility, which returns a random number in the range -32,767 through 32,767. You may find Randomize( ) helpful in your own applications.

```
/****************************** Randomize *********/

Randomize( range )
int      range;
{
  long   rawResult;
  rawResult = Random();
        if ( rawResult < 0 ) rawResult *= -1;
  return( (rawResult * range) / 32768 );
}
```

Variants

Here are some variants of Mondrian. The first few change the shape of the repeated figure in the window from ovals to some other shapes.

Your first new shape will be a rectangle. This one's easy: Just change the PaintOval( ) call to PaintRect( ). When you run this, you should see rectangles instead of ovals.

Your next new shape is the rounded rectangle. You'll need two new parameters for PaintRoundRect( ): ovalWidth and ovalHeight. These two parameters affect the curvature of the corners of the rectangle (I:179). Try the following values for ovalWidth and ovalHeight:

```
#define OVAL_WIDTH    20
#define OVAL_HEIGHT   20
```

Now, change the DrawRandomRect( ) routine, as follows:

```
/*************************** DrawRandomRect *******/

DrawRandomRect()
{
  Rect   myRect;

  RandomRect( &myRect, gDrawWindow );
  ForeColor( gFillColor );
  PaintRoundRect( &myRect, OVAL_WIDTH, OVAL_HEIGHT );
}
```

You should see something like Figure 3.32 if you run this variation.

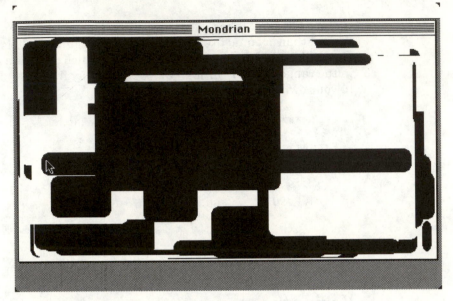

Figure 3.32   Mondrian with rounded rectangles.

Instead of filling the rectangles, try using `FrameRoundRect()` to draw just the outline of your rectangles:

```
/*************************** DrawRandomRect *********/

DrawRandomRect()
{
  Rect    myRect;

  RandomRect( &myRect, gDrawWindow );
  ForeColor( gFillColor );
  FrameRoundRect( &myRect, OVAL_WIDTH, OVAL_HEIGHT );
}
```

The framing function is more interesting if you change the state of your pen: The default setting for your pen is a size of 1 pixel wide by 1 pixel tall, and the pattern is black. Change it by modifying `WindowInit()` as shown in Figure 3.33.

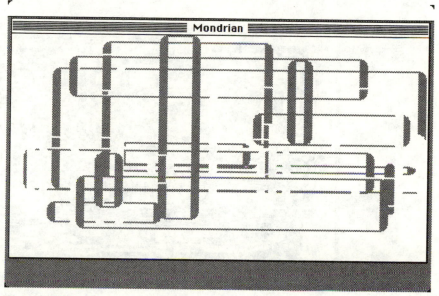

Figure 3.33 Mondrian with framed rounded rectangles.

```
/****************************** WindowInit ********/

WindowInit()
{
   gDrawWindow = GetNewWindow( BASE_RES_ID, NIL_POINTER,
                               MOVE_TO_FRONT );
   ShowWindow( gDrawWindow );
   SetPort( gDrawWindow );
   PenSize( PEN_WIDTH, PEN_HEIGHT );
   PenPat( gray );
}
```

Here, you changed the pen pattern to gray. Don't forget to #define
PEN_WIDTH and PEN_HEIGHT. We used values of 10 and 2, respectively, for
Figure 3.33.

While you're at it, try using InvertRoundRect() instead of
FrameRoundRect(). InvertRoundRect() will invert the pixels in its
rectangle. The arguments are handled in the same way (Figure 3.34).

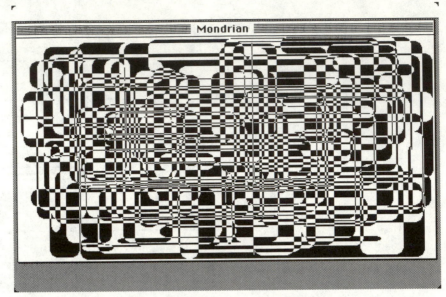

Figure 3.34   Mondrian with inverted rounded rectangles.

Next, try using `FrameArc()` in place of `InvertRoundRect()`.
`FrameArc()` requires two new parameters. The first defines the arc's
starting angle, and the second defines the size of the arc. Both are expressed
in degrees (Figure 3.35). Change `DrawRandomRect()` as follows:

```
/************************* DrawRandomRect *********/

DrawRandomRect()
{
Rect      myRect;

  RandomRect( &myRect, gDrawWindow );
  ForeColor( gFillColor );
  FrameArc( &myRect, START_DEGREES, ARC_DEGREES );
}
```

Don't forget to #define START_DEGREES and ARC_DEGREES. Try using
values of 0 and 270. Experiment with `PaintArc()` and `InvertArc()`
also, if you wish.

The final Mondrian variation is more interesting with a color monitor.
If you change the `ForeColor()` arguments in `Main()`, you can see colored
filled ovals (or whatever your program is currently producing). Modify your
`MainLoop()` routine as follows:

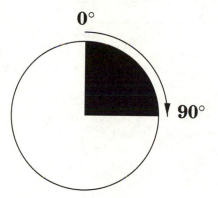

Figure 3.35 Figuring your arc.

```
/ * * * * * * * * * * * * * * * * * * * * * * * * * * * * * * *        MainLoop
* * * * * * * * * /

MainLoop()
{
   GetDateTime( &randSeed );
   while ( !Button() )
   {
        DrawRandomRect();
        if ( gFillColor == redColor )
               gFillColor = yellowColor;
        else
               gFillColor = redColor;
   }
}
```

The following colors have already been defined for you: blackColor, whiteColor, redColor, yellowColor, greenColor, blueColor, cyanColor, and magentaColor. These colors are part of Classic Quick-Draw—the original, eight-color QuickDraw model that was part of the original Macintosh. The Mac II supports a new version of QuickDraw called Color QuickDraw, which supports millions of different colors. (We'll tackle Color QuickDraw in our next volume.) The programs you write using the eight colors of Classic QuickDraw will run on any Macintosh (even the Mac Plus).

There are a million more possible variations to Mondran, but these should get you familiarized with the richness of the QuickDraw environment. The next program demonstrates how to load QuickDraw picture resources and draw them in a window.

ShowPICT

ShowPICT will take your favorite artwork (in the form of a PICT resource) and display it in a window. You can create a PICT resource by copying any graphic to the Mac Clipboard, then pasting it into a PICT resource with ResEdit. We copied our artwork from the Scrapbook that comes with the Macintosh System disks. If you're not familiar with the way that the Scrapbook works, see your Macintosh user's manuals for more information.

ShowPICT is made up of five distinct steps:

- Initialize the Toolbox.
- Load a resource window, show it, and make it the current port.
- Load a resource picture.
- Center the picture, then draw it in the window.
- Wait for the mouse button to be pressed.

Resources

Start by creating a new folder, called ShowPICT, in the src folder. Next, using ResEdit, create a new resource file called ShowPICT Proj.Rsrc in the ShowPICT folder. Create a window as shown in Figure 3.36. Select Get Info from the File menu and set the resource ID of your new WIND to 400.

Next, create your PICT resource. Close the WIND list, so you get back to the main ShowPICT Proj.Rsrc window (Figure 3.37). Create a new resource type by selecting New from the File menu. When prompted for a resource type, select PICT. Pull down the menu and select the Scrapbook. Find a picture you like, pull down the Edit menu, and select Copy. Close the Scrapbook, pull down ResEdit's Edit menu, and select Paste. The picture should appear in the PICT window. Select Get Info from the File menu and set the resource ID of the PICT to 400. Then quit ResEdit, and save your changes to ShowPICT Proj.Rsrc.

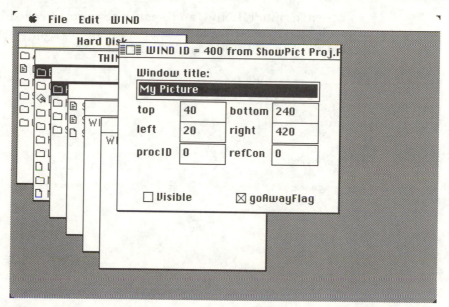

Figure 3.36 WIND parameters for ShowPict.

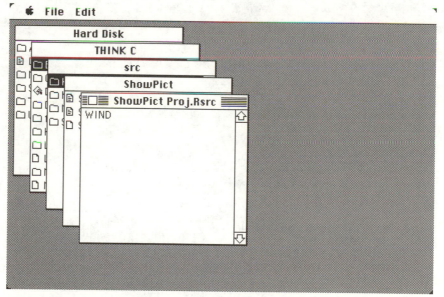

Figure 3.37 ShowPict's resource window.

Next, go into THINK C and create a new project called `ShowPICT Proj` inside the `ShowPICT` folder. Add `MacTraps` to your project. Then select New from the File Menu and enter the following code:

```
#define BASE_RES_ID        400
#define NIL_POINTER        0L
#define MOVE_TO_FRONT       -1L
#define REMOVE_ALL_EVENTS   0


PicHandle       gThePicture;
WindowPtr       gPictureWindow;

/*******************************    main    ********/

main()
{
        ToolBoxInit();
        WindowInit();
        LoadPicture();
        DrawMyPicture( gThePicture, gPictureWindow );
        while( !Button() );
}


/*********************************    ToolBoxInit    */

ToolBoxInit()
{
        InitGraf( &thePort );
        InitFonts();
        FlushEvents( everyEvent, REMOVE_ALL_EVENTS );
        InitWindows();
        InitMenus();
        TEInit();
        InitDialogs( NIL_POINTER );
        InitCursor();
}

/*******************************    WindowInit    ********/

WindowInit()
{
        gPictureWindow = GetNewWindow( BASE_RES_ID, NIL_POINTER,
                                        MOVE_TO_FRONT );
        ShowWindow( gPictureWindow );
        SetPort( gPictureWindow );
}
/****************************** LoadPicture ********/

LoadPicture()
{
        gThePicture = GetPicture( BASE_RES_ID );
}
```

```
/******************************* DrawMyPicture *********/

DrawMyPicture( thePicture, pictureWindow )
PicHandle     thePicture;
WindowPtr     pictureWindow;
{
      Rect    myRect;

      myRect = pictureWindow->portRect;
      CenterPict( thePicture, &myRect );
      DrawPicture( thePicture, &myRect );
}


/******************************* CenterPict *********/

CenterPict( thePicture, myRectPtr )
PicHandle     thePicture;
Rect          *myRectPtr;
{
      Rect    windRect, pictureRect;

      windRect = *myRectPtr;
      pictureRect = (**( thePicture )).picFrame;
      myRectPtr->top = (windRect.bottom - windRect.top -
            (pictureRect.bottom - pictureRect.top))/ 2 +
            windRect.top;
      myRectPtr->bottom = myRectPtr->top +
            (pictureRect.bottom - pictureRect.top);
      myRectPtr->left = (windRect.right - windRect.left -
            (pictureRect.right - pictureRect.left))/ 2 +
            windRect.left;
      myRectPtr->right = myRectPtr->left + (pictureRect.right -
            pictureRect.left);
}
```

Running ShowPICT

After you've finished typing in the code, save the file as ShowPICT.c and add it to your project. Next, select Run from the Project menu. If everything went well, you should get something like Figure 3.38. Your PICT should appear in your window. If it does not, check the resource ID of your PICT. Did your PICT make it into ShowPICT Proj.Rsrc? Check your WIND resource and your code for typos.

Figure 3.38   Running `ShowPict`.

Walking through the ShowPICT Code

Take a look at your global variables. The global `gThePicture` is a pointer to a pointer (also known as a handle) to a picture. `gPictureWindow` acts as a pointer to the `PICT` window.

```
#define  BASE_RES_ID          400
#define  NIL_POINTER          0L
#define  MOVE_TO_FRONT        -1L
#define  REMOVE_ALL_EVENTS    0

PicHandle       gThePicture;
WindowPtr       gPictureWindow;
```

Handles are pointers to pointers. For example, if you wanted to declare a handle to an `int`, you'd do something like this:

```
int    **myHandle;
```

Handles are a necessary part of the Mac's memory management scheme. They allow the Macintosh Memory Manager to relocate blocks of memory as it needs to, without disturbing your program. If you depend on a pointer to an object, then, when the Mac moves the object in memory, your pointer becomes invalid. If, however, you use a handle (pointer to a pointer) to an object, then, when the Mac moves the object, as long as it updates the pointer, your handle remains valid.

We'll show you some of the basics of using handles, but we won't spend a lot of time on them. You should read up on handles and the Mac memory management scheme because eventually you'll want to write code that takes advantage of handles.

In the case of gThePicture, we declared a handle to a picture (pointer to a pointer to a picture). We then set the handle to the value returned by GetPicture():

```
PicHandle      pHandle;
pHandle = GetPicture( BASE_RES_ID );
```

Like most of the Toolbox functions that return handles, GetPicture() actually allocates the memory for the picture itself, as well as the memory for the pointer to the picture. The great thing about handles is that you hardly know they're there.

If you'd like to know more about handles (and Mac memory management in general), read Chapter 3 of Volume I of *Inside Mac*. As you get into more advanced programming techniques, you'll want to have a thorough grasp of this topic.

In main(), initialize the Toolbox and window as usual. Then load your PICT from the resource file and draw it in the window. Finally, wait for a press on the mouse button to exit the program.

```
/ * * * * * * * * * * * * * * * * * * * * * * * * * * *      main
* * * * * * * * * /

main()
{
   ToolBoxInit();
   WindowInit();
   LoadPicture();
   DrawMyPicture( gThePicture, gPictureWindow );

   while ( !Button() ) ;
}
```

The Toolbox initialization routine remains the same:

```
/********************************        ToolBoxInit     */
ToolBoxInit()

{
   InitGraf( &thePort );
   InitFonts();
   FlushEvents( everyEvent, REMOVE_ALL_EVENTS );
   InitWindows();
   InitMenus();
   TEInit();
   InitDialogs( NIL_POINTER );
   InitCursor();
}
```

The window initialization code is the same as Hello2. (If you are cutting and pasting, note that the variable name has changed to gPictureWindow.)

```
/********************************        WindowInit
*********/

WindowInit()
{
   gPictureWindow = GetNewWindow( BASE_RES_ID, NIL_POINTER,
                                  MOVE_TO_FRONT  );
   ShowWindow( gPictureWindow );
   SetPort( gPictureWindow );
}
```

The LoadPicture() routine gets the handle for the PICT resource that you pasted into your resource file:

```
/***************************** LoadPicture *********/
LoadPicture()
{
   gThePicture = GetPicture( BASE_RES_ID );
}
```

DrawMyPicture() sets up a Rect the size of pictureWindow (the window passed in as a parameter). Then, it passes the Rect and thePicture (another input parameter) to CenterPict(). Finally, DrawMyPicture() draws thePicture in the newly centered Rect.

```
/***************************** DrawMyPicture *********/

DrawMyPicture( thePicture, pictureWindow )
PicHandle      thePicture;
WindowPtr      pictureWindow;
{
  Rect    myRect;

  myRect = pictureWindow->portRect;
  CenterPict( thePicture, &myRect );
  DrawPicture( thePicture, &myRect );
}
```

CenterPict() takes a PicHandle (thePicture) and a pointer to a Rect (myRectPtr) as input parameters. thePicture is a handle to a picture to be centered in the Rect pointed to by myRectPtr. CenterPict() constructs a new Rect the size of thePicture, centering it in the original Rect.

CenterPict() is used to center a picture in a window. The original Rect is copied into the local variable windRect. Then, the picture's frame Rect is copied to the local variable pictureRect. Finally, each field in the original Rect is modified, based on the corresponding fields in windRect and pictureRect. For example, myRectPtr->top is adjusted to become the new top of the picture.

CenterPict() is a good utility routine. You'll be seeing it again in other chapters.

```
/***************************** CenterPict *********/

CenterPict( thePicture, myRectPtr )
PicHandle      thePicture;
Rect           *myRectPtr;
{
  Rect    windRect, pictureRect;

  windRect = *myRectPtr;
  pictureRect = (**( thePicture )).picFrame;
  myRectPtr->top = (windRect.bottom - windRect.top -
        (pictureRect.bottom - pictureRect.top))/ 2 +
        windRect.top;
  myRectPtr->bottom = myRectPtr->top +
        (pictureRect.bottom - pictureRect.top);
  myRectPtr->left = (windRect.right - windRect.left -
        (pictureRect.right - pictureRect.left))/ 2
        + windRect.left;
  myRectPtr->right = myRectPtr->left + (pictureRect.right-
        pictureRect.left);
}
```

Variants

Try using different pictures, either from the Scrapbook or from MacPaint or MacDraw files. With a little experimentation, you should be able to copy and paste these files into your resource file. In Chapter 4, you'll see an enhanced `ShowPICT` program.

Screen Saver: The Flying Line Program

The Flying Line is the last program in the QuickDraw chapter. Although it does demonstrate the use of line drawing in QuickDraw, we included it mostly because it's fun. The Flying Line draws a set of lines that move across the screen with varying speeds, directions, and orientations. The program can be used as a screen saver (we even show you how to hide the menu bar).

The Flying Line program consists of four steps:

- Initialize the Toolbox.
- Set up the Flying Line window.
- Initialize the Flying Line data structure, drawing it once.
- Redraw the Flying Line inside a loop until a mouse click occurs.

Flying Line needs no resources. Go into THINK C and create a new project called `Flying Line Proj` inside the `Flying Line` folder. Select New from the File menu to open a new window for the Flying Line source code:

```
#define NUM_LINES              50
#define NIL_POINTER            0L
#define MOVE_TO_FRONT          -1L
#define REMOVE_ALL_EVENTS      0
#define NIL_STRING             "\p"
#define NIL_TITLE              NIL_STRING
#define VISIBLE                TRUE
#define NO_GO_AWAY             FALSE
#define NIL_REF_CON            NIL_POINTER

WindowPtr       gLineWindow;
Rect            gLines[ NUM_LINES ];
int             gDeltaTop=3, gDeltaBottom=3;
int             gDeltaLeft=2, gDeltaRight=6;
int             gOldMBarHeight;
```

```
/****************************        main      *********/

main()
{
        ToolBoxInit();
        WindowInit();
        LinesInit();
        MainLoop();
}

/********************************        ToolBoxInit      */

ToolBoxInit()
{
        InitGraf( &thePort );
        InitFonts();
        FlushEvents( everyEvent, REMOVE_ALL_EVENTS );
        InitWindows();
        InitMenus();
        TEInit();
        InitDialogs( NIL_POINTER );
        InitCursor();
}

/*****************************        WindowInit      *********/

WindowInit()
{
        Rect            totalRect, mBarRect;
        RgnHandle       mBarRgn;

        gOldMBarHeight = MBarHeight;
        MBarHeight = 0;
        gLineWindow = NewWindow( NIL_POINTER, &(screenBits.bounds),
                NIL_TITLE, VISIBLE, plainDBox, MOVE_TO_FRONT, NO_GO_AWAY,
                NIL_REF_CON );

        SetRect( &mBarRect, screenBits.bounds.left, screenBits.bounds.top,
                screenBits.bounds.right, screenBits.bounds.top+gOldMBarHeight);
        mBarRgn = NewRgn();
        RectRgn( mBarRgn, &mBarRect );
        UnionRgn( gLineWindow->visRgn, mBarRgn, gLineWindow->visRgn );
        DisposeRgn( mBarRgn );

        SetPort( gLineWindow );
        FillRect( &(gLineWindow->portRect), black ); /* Change black to
                                        ltGray, */
        PenMode( patXor );      /* <- and comment out this line */
}
```

```
/****************************** LinesInit *********/

LinesInit()
{
      int i;

      HideCursor();
      GetDateTime( &randSeed );
      RandomRect( &(gLines[ 0 ]), gLineWindow );
      DrawLine( 0 );
      for ( i=1; i<NUM_LINES; i++ )
      {
            gLines[ i ] = gLines[ i-1 ];
            RecalcLine( i );
            DrawLine( i );
      }
}

/****************************** MainLoop *********/

MainLoop()
{
      int i;

      while ( ! Button() )
      {
            DrawLine( NUM_LINES - 1 );
            for ( i=NUM_LINES-1; i>0; i--)
                  gLines[ i ] = gLines[ i-1 ];
            RecalcLine( 0 );
            DrawLine( 0 );
      }
      MBarHeight = gOldMBarHeight;
}

/****************************** RandomRect *********/

RandomRect( myRectPtr, boundingWindow )
Rect          *myRectPtr;
WindowPtr     boundingWindow;
{
      myRectPtr->left = Randomize( boundingWindow->portRect.right
            - boundingWindow->portRect.left );
      myRectPtr->right = Randomize( boundingWindow->portRect.right
            - boundingWindow->portRect.left );
      myRectPtr->top = Randomize( boundingWindow->portRect.bottom
            - boundingWindow->portRect.top );
      myRectPtr->bottom = Randomize( boundingWindow->portRect.bottom
            - boundingWindow->portRect.top );
}
```

```
/****************************** Randomize *********/
Randomize( range )
int    range;
{
      long   rawResult;

      rawResult = Random();
      if ( rawResult < 0 ) rawResult *= -1;
      return( (rawResult * range) / 32768 );
}

/***************************** RecalcLine *********/
RecalcLine( i )
int i;
{
      gLines[ i ].top += gDeltaTop;
      if ( ( gLines[ i ].top < gLineWindow->portRect.top ) ||
           ( gLines[ i ].top > gLineWindow->portRect.bottom ) )
      {
            gDeltaTop *= -1;
            gLines[ i ].top += 2*gDeltaTop;
      }

      gLines[ i ].bottom += gDeltaBottom;
      if ( ( gLines[ i ].bottom < gLineWindow->portRect.top ) ||
           ( gLines[ i ].bottom > gLineWindow->portRect.bottom ) )
      {
            gDeltaBottom *= -1;
            gLines[ i ].bottom += 2*gDeltaBottom;
      }

      gLines[ i ].left += gDeltaLeft;
      if ( ( gLines[ i ].left < gLineWindow->portRect.left ) ||
           ( gLines[ i ].left > gLineWindow->portRect.right ) )
      {
            gDeltaLeft *= -1;
            gLines[ i ].left += 2*gDeltaLeft;
      }

      gLines[ i ].right += gDeltaRight;
      if ( ( gLines[ i ].right < gLineWindow->portRect.left ) ||
           ( gLines[ i ].right > gLineWindow->portRect.right ) )
      {
            gDeltaRight *= -1;
            gLines[ i ].right += 2*gDeltaRight;
      }
}

/***************************** DrawLine *********/
DrawLine( i )
int    i;
{
      MoveTo( gLines[ i ].left, gLines[ i ].top );
      LineTo( gLines[ i ].right, gLines[ i ].bottom );
}
```

Running Flying Line

After you've finished typing in the code, save it as `Flying Line.c`. Add MacTraps to the project, and select Run from the Project menu. If everything went well, you should see something like Figure 3.39. The window will be completely black except for the flying line; the menu bar should be hidden. Now, let's take a look at the code.

Walking through the Flying Line Code

Most of Flying Line should be familiar to you. The biggest change is in `WindowInit()`, where you create a window from scratch and hide the menu bar. We won't go into exhaustive detail on the Flying Line algorithm, because it has little to do with the Toolbox. This one's just for fun!

`NUM_LINES` defines the number of lines in the Flying Line. `gDeltaBottom`, `gDeltaTop`, `gDeltaLeft`, and `gDeltaRight` are all tuning parameters. Play around with them until you get just the right Flying Line.

Draw the Flying Line in the `gLineWindow`. The array `gLines` holds all of the individual lines in the Flying Line. Finally, `gOldMBarHeight` saves the menu bar height when you start, so you can restore it when the application quits.

Figure 3.39 Running Flying Line.

```
#define NUM_LINES                      50
#define NIL_POINTER                    OL
#define MOVE_TO_FRONT                  -1L
#define REMOVE_ALL_EVENTS              0
#define NIL_STRING                     "\p"
#define NIL_TITLE                      NIL_STRING
#define VISIBLE                        TRUE
#define NO_GO_AWAY                     FALSE
#define NIL_REF_CON                    NIL_POINTER

WindowPtr       gLineWindow;
Rect            gLines[ NUM_LINES ];
int             gDeltaTop=3, gDeltaBottom=3;
int             gDeltaLeft=2, gDeltaRight=6;
int             gOldMBarHeight;
```

main( ) is unchanged from the earlier programs, except that LinesInit( ) is called before the MainLoop( ).

```
/****************************** main ********/

main()
{
   ToolBoxInit();
   WindowInit();
   LinesInit();
   MainLoop();
}
```

The Toolbox initialization for Flying Line is the same as for the previous program:

```
/********************************* ToolBoxInit */

ToolBoxInit()
{
   InitGraf( &thePort );
   InitFonts();
   FlushEvents( everyEvent, REMOVE_ALL_EVENTS );
   InitWindows();
   InitMenus();
   TEInit();
   InitDialogs( NIL_POINTER );
   InitCursor();
}
```

The window initialization code for Flying Line is unusual because the window itself is unusual. Normally, Mac programs display a menu bar. Flying Line, however, will not. Flying Line hides the menu bar (by making it 0 pixels tall) and creates a window that covers the entire screen.

The call to NewWindow() is an alternative to GetNewWindow(). GetNewWindow() creates a window using the information specified in a WIND resource. NewWindow() also creates a window, but gets the window specifications from its parameter list:

```
FUNCTION NewWindow( wStorage : Ptr; boundsRect : Rect;
    title : Str255; visible : BOOLEAN; procID : INTEGER;
    behind : WindowPtr; goAwayFlag : BOOLEAN;
    refCon : LONGINT ) : WindowPtr;
```

Specify the size of the window as a Rect, using the QuickDraw global screenBits.bounds to create a window the size of the current screen.

```
/***************************** WindowInit *********/

WindowInit()
{
    Rect            totalRect,mBarRect;
    RgnHandle       mBarRgn;

    gOldMBarHeight = MBarHeight;
    MBarHeight = 0;
    gLineWindow = NewWindow( NIL_POINTER,
            &(screenBits.bounds),
            NIL_TITLE, VISIBLE, plainDBox, MOVE_TO_FRONT,
            NO_GO_AWAY, NIL_REF_CON );
```

The next bit of code is tricky. Call SetRect() to create a rectangle surrounding the normal menu bar. Use this Rect to create a new region, and then add this region to the visible region of your window. As a result of this hocus-pocus, your window can overlap the menu bar, taking up the entire screen. If this makes you uncomfortable, don't panic. The call to NewWindow() is normally all you'll need in your applications. This extra code is just here to allow your window to obscure the menu bar.

```
SetRect( &mBarRect, screenBits.bounds.left,
    screenBits.bounds.top,
    screenBits.bounds.right,
    screenBits.bounds.top+gOldMBarHeight );
mBarRgn = NewRgn();
RectRgn( mBarRgn, &mBarRect );
UnionRgn( gLineWindow->visRgn, mBarRgn,gLineWindow->
visRgn );
DisposeRgn( mBarRgn );
```

Next, call `SetPort()` so all your drawing will occur in `lineWindow()`. Then, fill the window with the black pattern. Set the `PenMode()` to `patXor`. Try some other pen modes, too. We suggest changing the second `FillRect()` parameter to `ltGray`, and commenting out the call to `PenMode()`.

```
SetPort( gLineWindow );
FillRect( &(gLineWindow->portRect), black ); /*  Try this:
                            Change black to ltGray and  */
PenMode( patXor );     /*   <- comment out this line  */
}
```

> Don't be fooled by imitations. The second parameter to `FillRect()` is a pattern, not a color. These are the fill patterns you normally associate with the paint bucket in MacPaint, not the eight colors of Classic QuickDraw. You can experiment with colors by using a call to `PaintRect()`.

`LinesInit()` starts off by hiding the cursor. Next, seed the random number generator with the current date (*à la* Mondrian). Finally, generate the first line of the Flying Line, draw it, then generate the rest of the lines and draw them.

```
/******************************** LinesInit ********/

LinesInit()
{
  int i;

  HideCursor();
  GetDateTime( &randSeed );
  RandomRect( &(gLines[ 0 ]), gLineWindow );
  DrawLine( 0 );
  for ( i=1; i<NUM_LINES; i++ )
  {
        gLines[ i ] = gLines[ i-1 ];
        RecalcLine( i );
        DrawLine( i );
  }
}
```

`MainLoop()` sets up a loop that falls through when the mouse button is pressed. At the end of the loop, the menu bar height is restored. If you don't do this, you won't be able to pick from the menu bar when you exit the program. (If this does happen, just reboot the machine to reset `MBarHeight`.)

Inside the loop, erase and redraw each line in the Flying Line. Erase lines by redrawing them in exactly the same position. Since the pen mode is set to `patXor`, this has the effect of erasing the line. Thus, the first call to `DrawLine()` in `MainLoop()` erases the last line in the `gLines` array. This simulates the line moving across the screen.

```
/***************************** MainLoop *********/

MainLoop()
{
   int   i;

   while ( !Button() )
   {
        DrawLine( NUM_LINES - 1 );
        for ( i=NUM_LINES-1; i>0; i-- )
            gLines[ i ]=gLines[ i-1 ];
        RecalcLine( 0 );
        DrawLine( 0 );
   }
   MBarHeight = gOldMBarHeight;
}
```

You've seen this routine in Mondrian:

```
/****************************** RandomRect *********/
RandomRect( myRectPtr, boundingWindow )
Rect          *myRectPtr;
WindowPtr     boundingWindow;
{
    myRectPtr->left = Randomize( boundingWindow->portRect.right
         - boundingWindow->portRect.left );
    myRectPtr->right = Randomize( boundingWindow->portRect.right
         - boundingWindow->portRect.left );
    myRectPtr->top = Randomize( boundingWindow->portRect.bottom
         - boundingWindow->portRect.top );
    myRect Ptr->bottom = Randomize( boundingWindow->portRect.bottom
         - boundingWindow->portRect.top );
}
```

You've also seen `Randomize()` in Mondrian:

```
/***************************** Randomize *********/
Randomize( range )
int        range;
{
   long    rawResult;

   rawResult = Random();
   if ( rawResult < 0 ) rawResult *= -1;
   return( (rawResult * range) / 32768 );
}
```

The `ReCalc()` routine determines where to draw the next line:

```
/***************************** RecalcLine *********/

RecalcLine( i )
int i;
{
        gLines[ i ].top += gDeltaTop;
        if ( ( gLines[ i ].top < gLineWindow->portRect.top ) ||
               ( gLines[ i ].top > gLineWindow->portRect.bottom ))
        {
                gDeltaTop *= -1;
                gLines[ i ].top += 2*gDeltaTop;
        }

        gLines[ i ].bottom += gDeltaBottom;
        if ( ( gLines[ i ].bottom < gLineWindow->portRect.top ) ||
               ( gLines[ i ].bottom > gLineWindow->portRect.bottom ) )
        {
                gDeltaBottom *= -1;
                gLines[ i ].bottom += 2*gDeltaBottom;
        }

        gLines[ i ].left += gDeltaLeft;
        if ( ( gLines[ i ].left < gLineWindow->portRect.left ) ||
               ( gLines[ i ].left > gLineWindow->portRect.right ) )
        {
                gDeltaLeft *= -1;
                gLines[ i ].left += 2*gDeltaLeft;
        }

        gLines[ i ].right += gDeltaRight;
        if ( ( gLines[ i ].right < gLineWindow->portRect.left ) ||
               ( gLines[ i ].right > gLineWindow->portRect.right ) )
        {
                gDeltaRight *= -1;
                gLines[ i ].right += 2*gDeltaRight;
        }
}
```

`DrawLine()` draws line number *i*, using the coordinates stored in `gLines[ i ]`. Since the pen mode is set to `patXor`, this may actually have the effect of erasing the line.

```
/***************************** DrawLine *********/

DrawLine( i )
int      i;
{
  MoveTo( gLines[ i ].left, gLines[ i ].top );
  LineTo( gLines[ i ].right, gLines[ i ].bottom );
}
```

In Review

Whew! We've covered a lot in this chapter. We examined the basic Macintosh drawing model, QuickDraw, and showed you how to use many of the QuickDraw Toolbox routines. We also looked at the Window Manager and the routines that allow you to create and draw in windows. Experiment with the programs presented here, and try using some of the other QuickDraw routines.

We've also shown you different ways of using resources in your programs. If you haven't already, you may want to skip ahead to Chapter 8, to read up on ResEdit. Build a standalone application; then add an icon to your application. Chapter 8 will show you how.

Now that you understand how the Mac draws to the screen, you're ready to learn how the Mac interacts with users. In Chapter 4, we'll look at the Event Manager—the Manager that stage directs operations.

4

The Event Mechanism

In this chapter, we'll tell you about events, the Mac's mechanism for describing the user's actions to your application. When the mouse button is clicked, a key is pressed, or a disk is inserted in the floppy drive, the operating system lets your program know by queueing an event.

ONE OF THE basic differences between programming on the Mac and programming on other machines lies in the use of events. **Events** are descriptions of actions taken by the user of your application. For example, when a key is pressed on the keyboard, a piece of the Mac operating system (known as the **Event Manager**) captures some important information about the keystroke in an `EventRecord`. As more keys are pressed, more `EventRecords` are created and joined to the first, forming the **event queue** (Figure 4.1).

> The event queue is a FIFO (First In, First Out) queue: The event at the front of the queue is the oldest event in the queue. As you can see in Figure 4.1, different types of events live together in the same event queue. All events, no matter what their type, pass under the watchful eye of the Event Manager.
>
> The Event Manager gets events from many different sources, queues them up, and passes them to your application, one at a time.

Your application can get at this information by retrieving `EventRecords` from the event queue, one at a time. If the retrieved `EventRecord` describes a keystroke, your application can jump to some code that handles keystrokes. If it describes the pressing of the mouse button, it can jump to some code that deals with the mouse button. Let's look at the mouse button case.

When the mouse button is pressed, what does it mean to the application? Maybe the user wants to select from a menu. Maybe the user is clicking on a window to bring it to the front, or has clicked in a scroll bar to move up or down in the document. One way to tell what the user is trying to accomplish is to compare the location of the mouse when its button was pressed with the locations of the menu bar, the windows on the screen, scroll bars, and so on.

If the user clicked in the menu bar, you can jump to some code that handles menu selection. If the user clicked on a scroll bar, you can jump to the scroll bar handling routine.

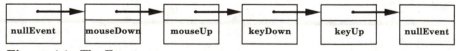

Figure 4.1   The Event queue.

The Event Manager handles 15 distinct events (V:249).

- **nullEvent** : This event is queued when the Event Manager has no other events to report.
- **mouseDown**: `mouseDown` events are queued whenever the mouse button is pressed. Note that the button doesn't have to be released for the event to qualify as a `mouseDown`.
- **mouseUp** : `mouseUps` are queued whenever the mouse button is released.
- **keyDown**: `keyDown` events are queued every time a key is pressed. Like `mouseDowns`, `keyDowns` are queued even if the key has not yet been released.
- **keyUp**: `keyUps` are queued whenever a key is released.
- **autoKey**: `autoKey` events are queued when a key is held down for a certain length of time (beyond the `autoKey` threshhold). Usually, an `autoKey` event is treated just like a `keyDown`.

> The `autoKey` threshhold represents the time from the first `keyDown` until the `autoKey` event is generated. The default value is 16 ticks (sixtieths of a second). The `autoKey` rate is the interval between `autoKeys`. The default `autoKey` rate is 4 ticks. The user can change both of these from the control panel desk accessory. Their values are stored in the system global variables `KeyThresh` and `KeyRepThresh`.

- `updateEvt`: `updateEvts` are queued whenever a window needs redrawing. They are always associated with a specific window. This usually happens when a window is partially obscured and the obstruction is moved, revealing more of the window, as shown in Figure 4.2.
- `diskEvt`: `diskEvts` are queued whenever a disk is inserted into a disk drive, or when an action is taken that requires that a volume be mounted. Don't worry too much about these right now. We'll tell you how to deal with disks and files in Chapter 7.
- `activateEvt`: `activateEvts` are also associated with windows. An `activateEvt` is queued whenever a window is activated (made to come to the front) or deactivated (replaced as the frontmost window by another

window). As you might guess, `activateEvt`s always occur in pairs (Figures 4.3 and 4.4).

- `networkEvt`: `networkEvt`s are no longer used.

- `driverEvt`: `driverEvt`s are used by device drivers to signal special conditions. They (and device drivers in general) are beyond the scope of this book.

- `app1Evt, app2Evt, app3Evt`: These events are defined by your application and can be used for just about anything. With the advent of MultiFinder, the use of application-defined events is discouraged.

- `app4Evt` **(Suspend/Resume/mouseMoved events)**: The `app4Evt` has been reserved by Apple for use with MultiFinder. MultiFinder will post an `app4Evt` just before it moves your application into the background (suspends it) and just after it brings your application back to the foreground (resumes it). You can also set your application up to receive `mouseMoved` events. `mouseMoved` events are posted when the user moves the cursor outside a predefined region (like a text-editing window) or back in again. When your application receives a `mouseMoved` event, it can change the cursor to one appropriate to that region. We'll discuss `app4Evt`s in more detail later in the chapter.

The next section discusses a new Macintosh application model based on event handling. After that, we'll present `EventTutor`, our first event-based application.

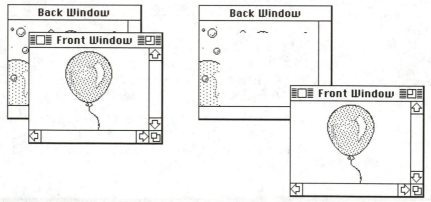

Figure 4.2   FrontWindow is moved down and to the right, generating an `updateEvt` for BackWindow.

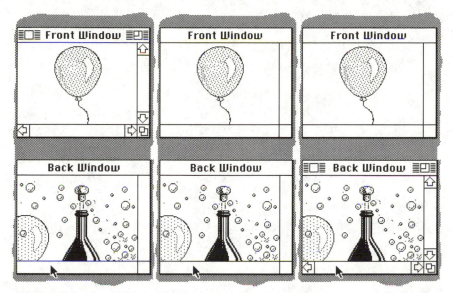

Figure 4.3   BackWindow is selected, an `activateEvt` is generated to deactivate FrontWindow, and an `activateEvt` is generated to activate BackWindow.

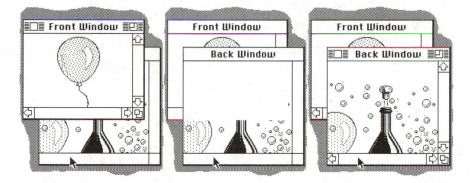

Figure 4.4   BackWindow is selected, an `activateEvt` is generated to deactivate FrontWindow, an `activateEvt` is generated to activate BackWindow, and an `updateEvt` is generated to redraw BackWindow.

The Structure of a Mac Program: New and Improved

In Chapter 3, we presented a very primitive Macintosh application model that looked like this:

```
main()
{
    ToolBoxInit();
    OtherInits();
    DoPrimeDirective();
    while ( !Button() ) ;
}
```

First, we initialized the Toolbox. Then, we took care of any program-specific initialization like loading windows or pictures from the resource file. Next, we performed our "prime directive." In the case of ShowPict, our prime directive was drawing a PICT in the main application. Finally, we waited for the mouse button to be pressed.

There is one basic problem with this model: It does not reflect reality. Macintosh applications do not exit when the mouse button is pressed. Clearly, we need a better model.

Our new model does things a little differently:

```
EventRecord    gTheEvent;
Boolean        gDone;

main()
{
    ToolBoxInit();
    OtherInits();
    MainLoop();
}

MainLoop()
{
    gDone = FALSE;
    while ( gDone == FALSE )
    {
        HandleEvent();
    }
}

HandleEvent()
{
    if ( waitNextEventIsInstalled )
        WaitNextEvent( everyEvent, &gTheEvent, sleepValue,
                               mouseRgn );
    else
    {
        SystemTask();
        GetNextEvent( everyEvent, &gTheEvent );
    }
    switch( gTheEvent.what )
    {
        case mouseDown:
            •
            •
            •
            if( .... ) gDone = TRUE;
    }
}
```

This model starts off the same way as the basic model, with calls to our initialization routines. The difference lies in our call of `MainLoop()`. `MainLoop()` contains the **main event loop**. The main event loop is part of the basic structure of any Mac program. Each time through the loop, your program retrieves an event from the event queue, and processes the event.

> As we'll explain in the next section, events are retrieved in one of two ways. If the Toolbox routine `WaitNextEvent()` is available (it isn't on older systems), it gets called. If `WaitNextEvent()` isn't available, the older Toolbox routine, `GetNextEvent()`, is used.

Eventually, some event will cause `HandleEvent()` to set `gDone` to `TRUE`, and the program will end. This might be the result of a `mouseDown` in the menu bar (selecting Quit from the File menu) or a `keyDown` (typing the key sequence ⌘ Q). You can design your ending conditions any way you like.

> We should warn you that Apple has a little-known squad of mercenaries who seek out and eradicate application writers who don't meet the user interface guidelines. Beware!

Retrieving Events from the Event Queue

In the early days of Mac programming, the Toolbox routine `GetNextEvent()` was used to retrieve events from the event queue. `GetNextEvent()` worked just fine until MultiFinder was introduced. MultiFinder is a set of operating system functions that extend the capabilities of the Macintosh. Most notably, MultiFinder allows the Macintosh to run several applications at the same time.

Figure 4.5 shows MultiFinder in action. Notice that only one application at a time can be "in front." Notice also that the Finder is one of the applications under MultiFinder. To bring an application to the front, you click on one of its windows.

One of the nicest features of MultiFinder is its ability to run applications in the background. Figure 4.5 shows the alarm clock desk accessory running in the background. Even though the alarm clock window is not the

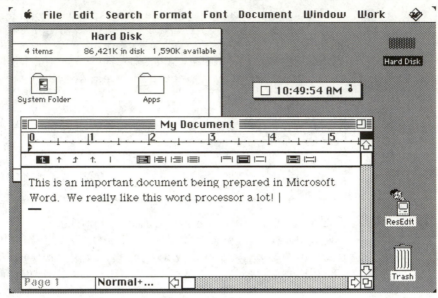

Figure 4.5   MultiFinder in action.

frontmost window, the time is updated because the alarm clock is running in the background.

GetNextEvent() was written with the Finder in mind. When MultiFinder was introduced, Apple added a new routine to the Toolbox to handle things like background processing more efficiently. The new routine is called WaitNextEvent().

As you'll see when you get to the EventTutor application, you should always check to see if WaitNextEvent() is installed before you call it. If it isn't installed, call GetNextEvent() instead.

You may have noticed a call to the Toolbox routine SystemTask() just before the call to GetNextEvent() in our new application model. SystemTask() gives the Mac operating system a slice of time to do things like update desk accessories (like the alarm clock), process AppleTalk messages, and so on. WaitNextEvent() has this functionality built right in, so an accompanying call to SystemTask() isn't necessary.

Calling GetNextEvent() and WaitNextEvent()

The first parameter to both `GetNextEvent()` and `WaitNextEvent()` is an event mask, used to limit the types of events your program will handle. Figure 4.6 contains a list of predefined event mask constants. If your program needs only `mouseDown`s and `keyDown`s, for example, you might use the following call:

```
EventRecord      gTheEvent;
GetNextEvent( (mDownMask | keyDownMask), &gTheEvent )
```

In this case, `GetNextEvent()` will return only `mouseDown`, `keyDown`, or `nullEvent` information. `nullEvent`s are never masked out. To handle all possible events, pass the predefined constant `everyEvent` as the `eventMask` parameter. *Inside Mac* recommends that you use `everyEvent` as your event mask in all your applications unless there's a specific reason not to.

The second parameter to both `GetNextEvent()` and `WaitNextEvent()` is `gTheEvent`, declared as an `EventRecord`. Here's the type definition of an `EventRecord`:

```
typedef struct EventRecord
{
  int        what;
  long       message;
  long       when;
  Point      where;
  int        modifiers;
} EventRecord;
```

```
#define mDownMask      0x2
#define mUpMask        0x4
#define keyDownMask    0x8
#define keyUpMask      0x10
#define autoKeyMask    0x20
#define updateMask     0x40
#define diskMask       0x80
#define activMask      0x100
#define networkMask    0x400
#define driverMask     0x800
#define app1Mask       0x1000
#define app2Mask       0x2000
#define app3Mask       0x4000
#define app4Mask       0x8000
#define everyEvent     0xFFFF
```

Figure 4.6 Event masks predefined in THINK C.

Here's a description of each of the fields:

- **what**: What type of event just occurred? Was it a nullEvent, keyDown, mouseDown, or updateEvt?
- **message**: This part of the EventRecord is specific to the event. For keyDown events, the message field contains information about the actual key that was pressed (the key code) and the character that key represents (the character code). For activateEvts and updateEvts, the message field contains a pointer to the affected window.
- **when**: When did the event occur? The Event Manager tells us, in ticks since the system was last started up (or booted).
- **where**: Where was the mouse when the event occurred? This information is specified in global coordinates (see Chapter 3).
- **modifiers**: This part of the EventRecord describes the state of the mouse button and the modifier keys (the shift, option, control, command, and caps lock keys) when the event occurred.

The third parameter to WaitNextEvent() is the sleep parameter. sleep is a long integer specifying the amount of time (in clock ticks) your application is willing to not perform any background processing while waiting for an event. By passing a sleep value of OL, you tell WaitNextEvent() to regain control of the processor as soon as possible.

The fourth parameter to WaitNextEvent() is the mouseRgn parameter, used to simplify cursor tracking. If your application requires different cursors, depending on which part of the screen the cursor is in, the mouseRgn parameter is essential. With it, you can specify the screen region appropriate to the current cursor. Whenever the mouse is outside that region, the Event Manager queues up a mouseMoved event. When your program receives the mouseMoved event, the region is changed to reflect the new mouse position and is passed as a parameter to the next WaitNextEvent() call.

Calling WaitNextEvent() with a sleep value of OL and a mouseRgn of OL is exactly equivalent to calling SystemTask() and GetNextEvent(). The programs presented throughout the rest of the book will do just that. The *Programmer's Guide to MultiFinder* includes a program that uses the sleep and mouseRgn parameters of WaitNextEvent(). The program was written by Apple's Macintosh Technical Support Group. The *Programmer's Guide to MultiFinder,* published by Apple, is essential reading for writing truly MultiFinder-friendly applications.

Handling Events

Once you've retrieved an event via GetNextEvent() or WaitNextEvent(), your next step is to process it. If the event is a mouseDown event, figure out where the mouse was clicked. If the mouse was clicked in a window's drag region, as shown in Figure 4.7, you can call a Toolbox routine that handles window dragging. If the event is an `updateEvt`, you might want to redraw the window pointed to by `theEvent.message`.

If this sounds vague, don't worry. The concept of events may be unfamiliar to you, but it will be easier to understand once you see it in operation. This chapter's program, EventTutor, will show you how all types of events are handled.

EventTutor: The Return of ShowPICT

Back in Chapter 3, we wrote a program called ShowPICT, which works like this:

- It initializes the Toolbox.
- It loads a resource window, shows it, and makes it the current port.
- It loads a resource picture.
- It centers the picture, then draws it in the window.
- It waits for the mouse button to be pressed.

Our new program, EventTutor, adds a main event loop to this model. EventTutor also adds a new window, `gEventWindow`. `gEventWindow` keeps a scrolling list of events, updated as the events occur. You can also drag both windows around the screen, as well as zoom and grow the picture window. EventTutor works like this:

- It initializes the Toolbox.
- It loads the picture and event windows from the resource file, shows them, and makes `gEventWindow` the current port.

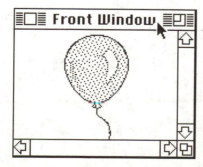

Figure 4.7 Arrow cursor in window's drag region.

- It loads a picture from the resource file.
- `While ( gDone == FALSE )`, EventTutor handles events.
- As events occur, it displays their names in `gEventWindow`, then calls the appropriate routines to process them.

Setting Up the EventTutor Project

Start by creating a new project folder, called `EventTutor`. Use ResEdit to create a new file inside this folder called `EventTutor Proj.Rsrc`.

Resources

Create three new resources. The first two are `WIND`s with resource IDs `400` and `401`. Figure 4.8 shows the specifications for these `WIND`s.

The third resource is a `PICT`. In our example, we use the champagne picture from the standard Scrapbook, but feel free to use any `PICT` you'd like. Make sure you change the resource ID to `400`.

Next, start up THINK C. When prompted, create a new project inside the `EventTutor` folder. Call it `EventTutor Proj`. Select New from the File menu to create a new source code file. Type the code listing in and save the file inside the `EventTutor` folder as `EventTutor.c`. Select Add from the Source menu to add `EventTutor.c` to the project. Finally, add `MacTraps` to your project. The Project window should now look like Figure 4.9.

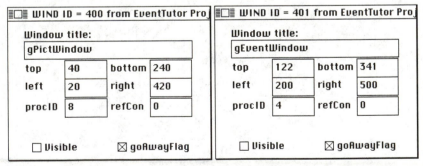

Figure 4.8 EventTutor WIND specifications.

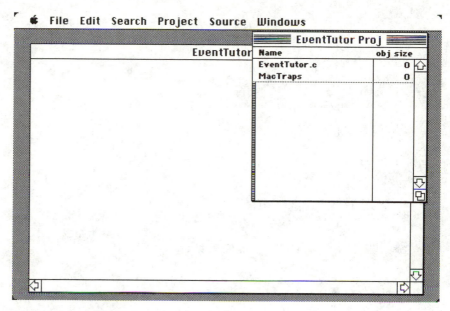

Figure 4.9   EventTutor Project.

Here's the source code for EventTutor.c:

```
#define BASE_RES_ID          400
#define NIL_POINTER          0L
#define MOVE_TO_FRONT        -1L
#define REMOVE_ALL_EVENTS    0

#define LEAVE_WHERE_IT_IS    FALSE
#define NORMAL_UPDATES       TRUE

#define SLEEP                0L
#define NIL_MOUSE_REGION     0L
#define WNE_TRAP_NUM         0x60
#define UNIMPL_TRAP_NUM      0x9F
#define SUSPEND_RESUME_BIT   0x0001
#define ACTIVATING           1
#define RESUMING             1

#define TEXT_FONT_SIZE       12

#define DRAG_THRESHOLD       30
#define MIN_WINDOW_HEIGHT    50
#define MIN_WINDOW_WIDTH     50
#define SCROLL_BAR_PIXELS    16

#define ROWHEIGHT            15
#define LEFTMARGIN           10
#define STARTROW             0
#define HORIZONTAL_OFFSET    0
```

```
PicHandle          gPictureHandle;
WindowPtr          gPictWindow, gEventWindow;
Boolean            gDone, gWNEImplemented;
EventRecord        gTheEvent;
int                gCurRow, gMaxRow;
Rect               gDragRect, gSizeRect;

/****************************** main ********/

main()
{
      ToolBoxInit();
      WindowInit();
      LoadPicture();
      SetUpDragRect();
      SetUpSizeRect();

      MainLoop();
}

/*********************************** ToolBoxInit */

ToolBoxInit()
{
      InitGraf( &thePort );
      InitFonts();
      FlushEvents( everyEvent, REMOVE_ALL_EVENTS );
      InitWindows();
      InitMenus();
      TEInit();
      InitDialogs( NIL_POINTER );
      InitCursor();
}

/****************************** WindowInit ********/

WindowInit()
{
      gPictWindow = GetNewWindow( BASE_RES_ID, NIL_POINTER, MOVE_TO_FRONT);
      gEventWindow = GetNewWindow( BASE_RES_ID+1, NIL_POINTER,
                              MOVE_TO_FRONT );

      SetPort( gEventWindow );
      SetupEventWindow();

      ShowWindow( gEventWindow );
      ShowWindow( gPictWindow );

      SelectWindow( gEventWindow );
}
```

```
/****************************** SetupEventWindow ********/

SetupEventWindow()
{
      Rect    eventRect;

      eventRect = gEventWindow->portRect;
      gMaxRow = eventRect.bottom - eventRect.top - ROWHEIGHT;
      gCurRow = STARTROW;

      TextFont( monaco );
      TextSize( TEXT_FONT_SIZE );
}

/****************************** LoadPicture ********/

LoadPicture()
{
      gPictureHandle = GetPicture( BASE_RES_ID );
}

/****************************** SetUpDragRect ********/

SetUpDragRect()
{
      gDragRect = screenBits.bounds;
      gDragRect.left += DRAG_THRESHOLD;
      gDragRect.right -= DRAG_THRESHOLD;
      gDragRect.bottom -= DRAG_THRESHOLD;
}

/****************************** SetUpSizeRect ********/

SetUpSizeRect()
{
      gSizeRect.top = MIN_WINDOW_HEIGHT;
      gSizeRect.left = MIN_WINDOW_WIDTH;

      gSizeRect.bottom = screenBits.bounds.bottom - screenBits.bounds.top;
      gSizeRect.right = screenBits.bounds.right - screenBits.bounds.left;
}

/****************************** MainLoop ********/

MainLoop()
{
      gDone = FALSE;
      gWNEImplemented = ( NGetTrapAddress( WNE_TRAP_NUM, ToolTrap ) !=
                  NGetTrapAddress( UNIMPL_TRAP_NUM, ToolTrap ) );
      while ( gDone == FALSE )
      {
            HandleEvent();
      }
}
```

```
/************************************ HandleEvent    */

HandleEvent()
{
      if ( gWNEImplemented )
            WaitNextEvent( everyEvent, &gTheEvent, SLEEP,
             NIL_MOUSE_REGION );
      else
      {
            SystemTask();
            GetNextEvent( everyEvent, &gTheEvent );
      }

      switch ( gTheEvent.what )
      {
            case nullEvent:
                  /*DrawEventString( "\pnullEvent" );*/
                  /*    Uncomment the previous line for a burst of
                  flavor! */
                  break;
            case mouseDown:
                  DrawEventString( "\pmouseDown" );
                  HandleMouseDown();
                  break;
            case mouseUp:
                  DrawEventString( "\pmouseUp" );
                  break;
            case keyDown:
                  DrawEventString( "\pkeyDown" );
                  break;
            case keyUp:
                  DrawEventString( "\pkeyUp" );
                  break;
            case autoKey:
                  DrawEventString( "\pautoKey" );
                  break;
            case updateEvt:
                  if ( (WindowPtr)gTheEvent.message == gPictWindow )
                  {
                        DrawEventString( "\pupdateEvt: gPictWindow" );
                        BeginUpdate( gTheEvent.message );
                        DrawMyPicture( gTheEvent.message,
                         gPictureHandle );
                        EndUpdate( gTheEvent.message );
                  } else
                  {
                        DrawEventString( "\pupdateEvt: gEventWindow" );
                        BeginUpdate( gTheEvent.message );
                        /*
                        *     We won't handle updates to gEventWindow,
                        * but we still need to empty the gEventWindow
                        * Update Region so the Window Manager will stop
```

```
                    * queueing UpdateEvts.
                    *       We do this with calls to
                            BeginUpdate()
                    * and EndUpdate().
                    */
                    EndUpdate( gTheEvent.message );
             }
         break;
    case diskEvt:
         DrawEventString( "\pdiskEvt" );
         break;
    case activateEvt:
         if ( (WindowPtr)gTheEvent.message == gPictWindow )
         {
                 DrawGrowIcon( gTheEvent.message );
                 if ( ( gTheEvent.modifiers & activeFlag ) ==
                 ACTIVATING )
                 {
                         DrawEventString(
                         "\pactivateEvt: activating gPictWindow" );
                 }
         else
                         DrawEventString(
                 "\pactivateEvt: deactivating gPictWindow" );
         } else
         {
                 if ( ( gTheEvent.modifiers & activeFlag ) ==
                 ACTIVATING )
                         DrawEventString(
                         "\pactivateEvt: activating gEventWindow" );
                 else
                         DrawEventString(
                         "\pactivateEvt: deactivatinggEventWindow");
         }
         break;
    case networkEvt:
         DrawEventString( "\pnetworkEvt" );
         break;
    case driverEvt:
         DrawEventString( "\pdriverEvt" );
         break;
    case app1Evt:
         DrawEventString( "\papp1Evt" );
         break;
    case app2Evt:
         DrawEventString( "\papp2Evt" );
         break;
    case app3Evt:
         DrawEventString( "\papp3Evt" );
         break;
```

```
                    case app4Evt:
                            if ( (gTheEvent.message & SUSPEND_RESUME_BIT) ==
                            RESUMING )
                                    DrawEventString( "\pResume event" );
                            else
                                    DrawEventString( "\pSuspend event" );
                            break;
            }
}

/*******************************          DrawEventString      *******/

DrawEventString( s )
Str255 s;
{
        if ( gCurRow > gMaxRow )
        {
                ScrollWindow();
        }
        else
        {
                gCurRow += ROWHEIGHT;
        }
        MoveTo( LEFTMARGIN, gCurRow );
        DrawString( s );
}

/********************************          ScrollWindow *******/

ScrollWindow()
{
        RgnHandle       tempRgn;

        tempRgn = NewRgn();
        ScrollRect( &gEventWindow->portRect, HORIZONTAL_OFFSET,
                    -ROWHEIGHT, tempRgn );
        DisposeRgn( tempRgn );
}

/********************************** HandleMouseDown */
HandleMouseDown()

{
        WindowPtr           whichWindow;
        short int           thePart;
        long                windSize;
        GrafPtr             oldPort;

        thePart = FindWindow( gTheEvent.where, &whichWindow );
        switch ( thePart )
        {
                case inSysWindow :
                        SystemClick( &gTheEvent, whichWindow );
                        break;
```

```
                case inDrag :
                        DragWindow( whichWindow, gTheEvent.where, &gDragRect );
                        break;
                case inContent:
                        SelectWindow( whichWindow );
                        break;
                case inGrow:
                        windSize = GrowWindow( whichWindow,
                                gTheEvent.where,&gSizeRect );
                        if ( windSize != 0 )
                        {
                                GetPort( &oldPort );
                                SetPort( whichWindow );
                                EraseRect( &whichWindow->portRect );
                                SizeWindow( whichWindow, LoWord( windSize ),
                                        HiWord( windSize ), NORMAL_UPDATES );
                                InvalRect( &whichWindow->portRect );
                                SetPort( oldPort );
                        }
                        break;
                case inGoAway :
                        gDone = TRUE;
                        break;
                case inZoomIn:
                case inZoomOut:
                        if ( TrackBox( whichWindow, gTheEvent.where, thePart ) )
                        {
                                GetPort( &oldPort );
                                SetPort( whichWindow );
                                EraseRect( &whichWindow->portRect );
                                ZoomWindow( whichWindow, thePart,
                                LEAVE_WHERE_IT_IS );
                                InvalRect( &whichWindow->portRect );
                                SetPort( oldPort );
                        }
                        break;
        }
}


/****************************** DrawMyPicture ********/

DrawMyPicture( drawingWindow, thePicture )
WindowPtr       drawingWindow;
PicHandle       thePicture;
{
        Rect    drawingClipRect, myRect;
        GrafPtr         oldPort;
        RgnHandle       tempRgn;

        GetPort( &oldPort );
        SetPort( drawingWindow );
        tempRgn = NewRgn();
        GetClip( tempRgn );
        EraseRect( &drawingWindow->portRect );
        DrawGrowIcon( drawingWindow );
```

```
        drawingClipRect = drawingWindow->portRect;
        drawingClipRect.right -= SCROLL_BAR_PIXELS;
        drawingClipRect.bottom -= SCROLL_BAR_PIXELS;

        myRect = drawingWindow->portRect;
        CenterPict( thePicture, &myRect );
        ClipRect( &drawingClipRect );
        DrawPicture( thePicture, &myRect );

        SetClip( tempRgn );
        DisposeRgn( tempRgn );
        SetPort( oldPort );
}

/******************************** CenterPict *********/

CenterPict( thePicture, myRectPtr )
PicHandle     thePicture;
Rect          *myRectPtr;
{
        Rect    windRect, pictureRect;

        windRect = *myRectPtr;
        pictureRect = (**( thePicture )).picFrame;
        myRectPtr->top = (windRect.bottom - windRect.top -
                (pictureRect.bottom -
                pictureRect.top)) / 2 + windRect.top;
        myRectPtr->bottom = myRectPtr->top + (pictureRect.bottom -
                pictureRect.top);
        myRectPtr->left = (windRect.right - windRect.left -
                (pictureRect.right - pictureRect.left))
                / 2 + windRect.left;
        myRectPtr->right = myRectPtr->left + (pictureRect.right -
                pictureRect.left);
}
```

Running EventTutor

Now that your source code is entered, you're ready to run EventTutor. Select Run from the Project menu. When asked to "Bring the project up to date," click Yes. If you run into any compilation problems, try the debugging tips discussed in Appendix E.

Once the code compiles, you'll be asked whether you'd like to "Save changes before running." Click Yes, and EventTutor will execute. Figure 4.10 shows EventTutor running under the Finder.

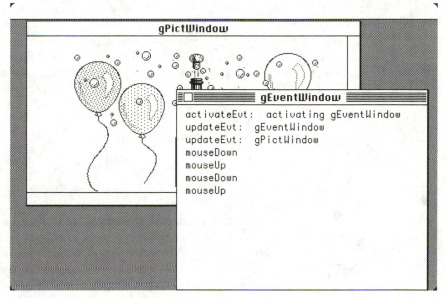

Figure 4.10 EventTutor running under Finder.

EventTutor puts two windows up on the screen. The background window, gPictWindow, should display your centered picture. The foreground window, gEventWindow, should already list three events:

- activateEvt:activating gEventWindow: This event was caused by your code. You called SelectWindow(), requesting that gEventWindow be made the frontmost window.
- updateEvt: gEventWindow, and
- updateEvt:gPictWindow: The Window Manager automatically generates an updateEvt for each of its windows as soon as they are drawn for the first time.

> When the Window Manager draws a window, it first draws the window frame. The window frame includes the border, as well as a drag region, zoom box, and a go-away box, if appropriate. Next, it generates an updateEvt for the window, so the application will draw the window contents.

Press the mouse button in the middle of gEventWindow. Now release the mouse button. You should see first a mouseDown and then a mouseUp event. Press the mouse button in the gEventWindow drag region (you'll see a `mouseDown`)and drag `gEventWindow` down and to the right. You should see an `updateEvt` for `gPictWindow`. This is because you just revealed a piece of `gPictWindow` that was covered before. The reason you didn't get a `mouseUp` when you released the mouse button is that the `mouseUp` was swallowed by the system routine that handles window dragging. This is also true when you zoom or resize a window.

> In Chapter 3 we established a standard of starting our program global variable names with the letter g. This led to `WindowPtrs` named `gEventWindow` and `gPictWindow`. For clarity, we used these variable names as titles for their respective windows, but we could have used any titles we wanted.

Click the mouse button in the center of `gPictWindow`. You should see a `mouseDown`, a deactivate event for `gEventWindow`, an activate event for `gPictWindow`, an update event for `gPictWindow` (assuming you clicked on it while it was still at least partially covered by `gEventWindow`), and a `mouseUp` (Figure 4.11).

> There is no such thing as a `deactivateEvt`. We use the term **deactivate event** to indicate an `activateEvt` with the `activeFlag` cleared There's an example of this in the code.

Figure 4.11   After `gPictWindow` is activated.

Try clicking in gPictWindow's zoom box. The picture should remain centered in gPictWindow. Click in the zoom box again. gPictWindow should return to its original size. Resize gPictWindow by clicking and dragging the grow box. Keep an eye on gEventWindow. As you create events, review the list of event types presented earlier in the chapter. All these features were made possible by the use of events. Now, let's take a look at the code.

Writing MultiFinder-friendly applications is not extremely difficult. We will try to get the basics across in our code, but we again recommend that you read the *Programmer's Guide to MultiFinder* from Apple for a thorough background (oops!) in MultiFinder programming.

For starters, you can get your program to handle suspend and resume events by selecting Set Project Type... from the Project menu. When the Set Project Type... dialog box appears, use the MF Attrs pop-up menu to turn all three MultiFinder attributes on. Basically, you've just set some bits in a resource of type SIZE with ID = -1. Now, when you run EventTutor, you get suspend and resume events when you send EventTutor to the background and bring it back again under MultiFinder.

In Chapter 5, you'll build a clock that runs in the background under MultiFinder, and in Chapter 6, you'll build a countdown timer that also runs in the background under MultiFinder.

Walking through the EventTutor Code

EventTutor starts with a slew of #defines, some of which should be familiar from Chapter 3. We'll discuss each #define as it appears in the code:

```
#define BASE_RES_ID          400
#define NIL_POINTER          0L

#define MOVE_TO_FRONT        -1L
#define REMOVE_ALL_EVENTS    0

#define LEAVE_WHERE_IT_IS    FALSE
#define NORMAL_UPDATES       TRUE
#define SLEEP                0L
#define NIL_MOUSE_REGION     0L
#define WNE_TRAP_NUM         0x60
#define UNIMPL_TRAP_NUM      0x9F
#define SUSPEND_RESUME_BIT   0x0001
#define ACTIVATING           1
#define RESUMING             1
```

```
#define TEXT_FONT_SIZE          12

#define DRAG_THRESHOLD          30
#define MIN_WINDOW_HEIGHT       50
#define MIN_WINDOW_WIDTH        50
#define SCROLL_BAR_PIXELS       16

#define ROWHEIGHT               15
#define LEFTMARGIN              10
#define STARTROW                0
#define HORIZONTAL_OFFSET       0
```

gPictureHandle is the handle to your gPictWindow picture.
gPictWindow and gEventWindow are pointers to the two program windows.
gDone is initialized to FALSE and checked each time through the main
event loop. If anyone sets gDone to TRUE, the program exits.
gWNEImplemented is a Boolean you'll set to TRUE if WaitNextEvent() is
implemented in the current version of the system. gTheEvent is your
EventRecord. Whenever you retrieve an event from the event queue, use
gTheEvent to hold the event information. gCurRow holds the vertical pixel
coordinate (in gEventWindow's local coordinate system) for drawing the
next event string in gEventWindow. gMaxRow is the maximum value
allowed for gCurRow. If gCurRow gets bigger than gMaxRow, you'll scroll
the text in gEventWindow. gDragRect limits the dragging area of a
window, and gSizeRect controls the size of a window.

```
PicHandle           gPictureHandle;
WindowPtr           gPictWindow, gEventWindow;
Boolean             gDone, gWNEImplemented;
EventRecord         gTheEvent;
int                 gCurRow, gMaxRow;
Rect                gDragRect, gSizeRect;
```

main() starts by calling the Toolbox and window initialization routines.
Then, main() calls LoadPicture() to load the picture from the resource
file. Next, main() calls SetUpDragRect() and SetUpSizeRect() to set
up Rects for dragging and resizing our windows (see HandleMouseDown()).
Finally, main() enters the main event loop by calling MainLoop().

```
/******************************* main *********/

main()
{
   ToolBoxInit();
   WindowInit();
   LoadPicture();
   SetUpDragRect();
   SetUpSizeRect();

   MainLoop();
}
```

ToolBoxInit() is the same as it was in Chapter 3. In fact, you'll use the same Toolbox initialization routine throughout the book.

```
/********************************* ToolBoxInit */

ToolBoxInit()
{
    InitGraf( &thePort );
    InitFonts();
    FlushEvents( everyEvent, REMOVE_ALL_EVENTS );
    InitWindows();
    InitMenus();
    TEInit();
    InitDialogs( NIL_POINTER );
    InitCursor();
}
```

WindowInit() starts by loading the two windows from the resource file. Next, gEventWindow is made the current window, and its attributes are set via the call to SetupEventWindow(). Both windows are made visible with ShowWindow(), and SelectWindow() is called to ensure that gEventWindow is the frontmost window.

```
/******************************* WindowInit *********/

WindowInit()
{
    gPictWindow = GetNewWindow( BASE_RES_ID, NIL_POINTER,
            MOVE_TO_FRONT );
    gEventWindow = GetNewWindow( BASE_RES_ID+1, NIL_POINTER,
                                MOVE_TO_FRONT );

    SetPort( gEventWindow );
    SetupEventWindow();

    ShowWindow( gEventWindow );
    ShowWindow( gPictWindow );

    SelectWindow( gEventWindow );
}
```

SetupEventWindow() sets some of the gEventWindow global variables. eventRect is a placeholder for gEventWindow's boundary rectangle. gMaxRow is set to the maximum row you'll draw into (in gEventWindow's local coordinates). gCurRow holds the current row number (also in local coordinates). gEventWindow's font is set to 12-point Monaco.

```
/************************* SetupEventWindow *********/

SetupEventWindow()
{
    Rect    eventRect;

    eventRect = gEventWindow->portRect;
    gMaxRow = eventRect.bottom - eventRect.top - ROWHEIGHT;
    gCurRow = STARTROW;

    TextFont( monaco );
    TextSize( TEXT_FONT_SIZE );
}
```

LoadPicture( ) loads your picture from the resource file into memory,
and gPictureHandle is set to be a handle to the picture. For a refresher
on handles, check out the tech block on handles in Chapter 3.

```
/****************************** LoadPicture *********/

LoadPicture()
{
    gPictureHandle = GetPicture( BASE_RES_ID );
}
```

SetUpDragRect( ) sets up a bounding rectangle to pass to DragWindow( )
(see HandleMouseDown( )). Start off with a rectangle the size of the main
screen by using the system global variable, screenBits.bounds. When
you click on the title bar of a window and drag it around the screen, the
bounding rectangle forces you to leave DRAG_THRESHOLD pixels of the
window on the screen. This will prevent the user from dragging all but a few
pixels of a window off the screen (making that window tough to find later
on). The reason you don't have to worry about the top of the drag rectangle
is that the drag region is on the top of the window.

```
/****************************** SetUpDragRect *********/

SetUpDragRect()
{
    gDragRect = screenBits.bounds;
    gDragRect.left += DRAG_THRESHOLD;
    gDragRect.right -= DRAG_THRESHOLD;
    gDragRect.bottom -= DRAG_THRESHOLD;
}
```

SetUpSizeRect( ) sets up a resizing rectangle for your call to
GrowWindow( ) (see HandleMouseDown( )). gSizeRect.top defines the
minimum number of pixels allowed for window height. gSizeRect.left
defines the minimum number of pixels allowed for window width.

`gSizeRect.bottom` defines the maximum number of pixels allowed for window height, and `gSizeRect.right` defines the maximum number for width. Use the size of the main screen (from your old friend `screenBits.bounds`) for these two.

```
/****************************** SetUpSizeRect ********/

SetUpSizeRect()
{
   gSizeRect.top = MIN_WINDOW_HEIGHT;
   gSizeRect.left = MIN_WINDOW_WIDTH;

   gSizeRect.bottom = screenBits.bounds.bottom -
         screenBits.bounds.top;
   gSizeRect.right = screenBits.bounds.right -
         screenBits.bounds.left;
}
```

`MainLoop()` starts by initializing `gDone`. Your application will exit when `gDone` is set to `TRUE`. Next, check to see if `WaitNextEvent()` is installed. Essentially, you're checking to see if `WaitNextEvent()` and an unimplemented Toolbox routine have the same address in memory. If so, you know that `WaitNextEvent()` is not implemented in the currently booted system.

> This piece of code has changed several times since `WaitNextEvent()` was first made available. To be on the safe side, get the very latest copy of the *Programmer's Guide to MultiFinder* from APDA. In the back, you'll see an example program that reflects Apple's current thinking on `WaitNextEvent()`. By following this example, you'll minimize the chances of your program breaking under future releases of the Mac operating system.

Finally, `MainLoop()` loops on `HandleEvent()` until `gDone` is set to `TRUE`.

```
/****************************** MainLoop ********/

MainLoop()
{
   gDone = FALSE;
   gWNEImplemented = ( NGetTrapAddress( WNE_TRAP_NUM,
               ToolTrap ) !=
               NGetTrapAddress( UNIMPL_TRAP_NUM,
               ToolTrap ) );
   while ( gDone == FALSE )
   {
         HandleEvent();
   }
}
```

HandleEvent() starts with a call to either WaitNextEvent() (if it's implemented), or SystemTask() and GetNextEvent(). Either way, gTheEvent gets filled with the latest event info. Each event is handled by drawing the name of the event in gEventWindow using Draw-EventString(). If you uncomment the code in the nullEvent case, you'll get a feel for the number of nullEvents the system generates.

---

nullEvents offer an excellent opportunity to do things like cursor tracking and internal housekeeping. For example, Chapter 5's Timer program updates a clock window when it gets a nullEvent.

```
/*************************************** HandleEvent      */
HandleEvent()
{
    if ( gWNEImplemented )
        WaitNextEvent( everyEvent, &gTheEvent, SLEEP,
                NIL_MOUSE_REGION );
    else
    {
        SystemTask();
        GetNextEvent( everyEvent, &gTheEvent );
    }

    switch ( gTheEvent.what )
    {
        case nullEvent:
            /*DrawEventString( "\pnullEvent" );*/
            /*      Uncomment the previous line for a
                    burst of flavor! */
            break;
        case mouseDown:
            DrawEventString( "\pmouseDown" );
            HandleMouseDown();
            break;
        case mouseUp:
            DrawEventString( "\pmouseUp" );
            break;
        case keyDown:
            DrawEventString( "\pkeyDown" );
            break;
        case keyUp:
            DrawEventString( "\pkeyUp" );
            break;
        case autoKey:
            DrawEventString( "\pautoKey" );
            break;
```

updateEvts are handled in a special way. First, figure out which window the updateEvt is for. The Event Manager stores a pointer to the window requiring updating in gTheEvent.message. By comparing this pointer to gEventWindow and gPictWindow, you can tell which window the `updateEvt` is for. If the `updateEvt` is for `gPictWindow`, draw the appropriate event string into `gEventWindow`, and then call `BeginUpdate()`.

`BeginUpdate()` tells the Event Manager that you're about to take care of the condition that caused the update. In this case, you'll redraw the picture in `gPictWindow` using `DrawMyPicture()`. Finally, call `EndUpdate()` to let the Event Manager know you're done .

If you commented out the calls to `BeginUpdate()` and `EndUpdate()`, you'd get an unending stream of `updateEvts` for `gPictWindow`. The Event Manager, thinking you were ignoring the ones you'd already retrieved, would just keep generating them. Try it for yourself.

Every window has an update region associated with it. When a previously covered section of a window is uncovered, the uncovered area is added to the window's update region. The Window Manager is constantly on the lookout for windows with nonempty update regions. When it finds one, it generates an `updateEvt` for that window. `BeginUpdate()`, as part of its processing, replaces the update region of the specified window with the empty region. Therefore, if you don't call `BeginUpdate()`, you'll never empty the window's update region, and the Window Manager will never stop generating `updateEvts` for the window.

If you have not done so already, you should absolutely read the Window Manager chapter of *Inside Macintosh* (Volume I, Chapter 9) The information presented in the Window Manager chapter is crucial to writing proper Macintosh applications.

You won't redraw the contents of `gEventWindow` in response to `updateEvts`. If you want to add this capability, add a data structure to the program that keeps track of all the strings currently in the window, and redraw them whenever an `updateEvt` occurs for `gEventWindow`. In this version, you'll just call `DrawEventString()` to add the `updateEvt` to your list of events, and `BeginUpdate()` and `EndUpdate()` to let the Window Manager know that you've responded to the `updateEvt`.

Before `BeginUpdate()` empties the update region, it first replaces the visible region of the window (called the `visRgn`) with the intersection of the `visRgn` and the update region (see Figure 4.12). The application then redraws the contents of the window. If it wants to, it can use this newly cropped `visRgn` to help reduce the amount of drawing necessary. For now, you'll just redraw the entire contents of the window. Finally, `EndUpdate()` is called. `EndUpdate()` replaces the original version of the `visRgn`. A call to `BeginUpdate()` without a corresponding call to `EndUpdate()` will leave your window in a very unpredictable state.

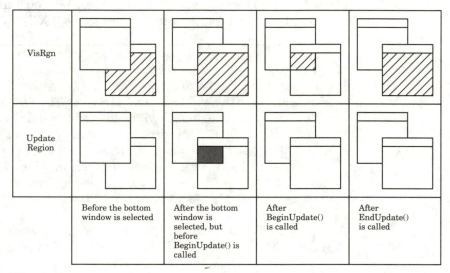

VisRgn				
Update Region				
	Before the bottom window is selected	After the bottom window is selected, but before BeginUpdate() is called	After BeginUpdate() is called	After EndUpdate() is called

Figure 4.12   `BeginUpdate()` in action.

```
case updateEvt:
    if ( (WindowPtr)gTheEvent.message == gPictWindow )
    {
        DrawEventString(
        "\pupdateEvt: gPictWindow" );
        BeginUpdate( gTheEvent.message );
        DrawMyPicture( gTheEvent.message,
            gPictureHandle );
        EndUpdate( gTheEvent.message );
    } else
    {
        DrawEventString(
        "\pupdateEvt: gEventWindow" );
        BeginUpdate( gTheEvent.message );
        /*
         *      We won't handle updates to
                    gEventWindow,
         * but we still need to empty the
                    gEventWindow
         * Update Region so the Window Manager
                will stop
         * queing UpdateEvts.
```

```
          *        We do this with calls to
                             BeginUpdate()
          * and EndUpdate().
          */
          EndUpdate( gTheEvent.message );
        }
      break;
  case diskEvt:
          DrawEventString( "\pdiskEvt" );
          break;
```

Another special case is the activateEvt. As you did with updateEvt, first check to see which window the activateEvt was intended for. If the activateEvt was for gPictWindow, call DrawGrowIcon() to redraw the grow box and the empty scroll bar areas. The grow box looks different depending on whether the window was activated or deactivated (see Figure 4.13). DrawGrowIcon() is smart enough to draw the grow box correctly.

Next, check a bit in the modifiers field to see if the event was an activate or a deactivate event. Remember, activateEvts usually occur in pairs: The frontmost window is first deactivated, and then the new front window is activated. Also draw the appropriate strings for networkEvts, driverEvts, and appl through app3Evts, although you probably won't get any of these.

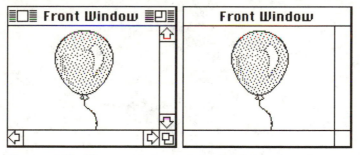

Figure 4.13   The grow box—activated and deactivated.

```
        case activateEvt:
                if ( (WindowPtr)gTheEvent.message ==
                    gPictWindow )
                {
                        DrawGrowIcon( gTheEvent.message );
                        if ( ( gTheEvent.modifiers &
                                activeFlag ) == ACTIVATING )
                        {
                                DrawEventString(
                "\pactivateEvt:activatinggPictWindow"   );
                        }
                        else
                                DrawEventString(
                "\pactivateEvt: deactivating gPictWindow);
                } else
                {
                        if ( ( gTheEvent.modifiers &
                                activeFlag ) == ACTIVATING )
                                DrawEventString(
                "\pactivateEvt: activating gEventWindow" );
                        else
                                DrawEventString(
                "\pactivateEvt:deactivatinggEventWindow");
                }
                break;
        case networkEvt:
                DrawEventString( "\pnetworkEvt" );
                break;
        case driverEvt:
                DrawEventString( "\pdriverEvt" );
                break;
        case app1Evt:
                DrawEventString( "\papp1Evt" );
                break;
        case app2Evt:
                DrawEventString( "\papp2Evt" );
                break;
        case app3Evt:
                DrawEventString( "\papp3Evt" );
                break;
```

If you handle resume and suspend events, you'll get them in the form of an app4Evt. The SUSPEND_RESUME_BIT is set if the event is a resume event and cleared if the event is a suspend event.

```
case app4Evt:
        if ( (gTheEvent.message & SUSPEND_RESUME_BIT) ==
                        RESUMING )
                DrawEventString( "\pResume event" );
        else
                DrawEventString( "\pSuspend event" );
        break;
    }
}
```

DrawEventString() handles the text positioning in gEventWindow. If the QuickDraw pen is near the bottom of the window, ScrollWindow() is called. The string is drawn with DrawString(). ROWHEIGHT is the height in pixels of a single row of text. LEFTMARGIN is the pixel coordinate (in gEventWindow's local coordinate system) of the left margin of the text in gEventWindow.

```
/*************************** DrawEventString *******/

DrawEventString( s )
Str255   s;
{
  if ( gCurRow > gMaxRow )
  {
        ScrollWindow();
  }
  else
  {
        gCurRow += ROWHEIGHT;
  }
  MoveTo( LEFTMARGIN, gCurRow );
  DrawString( s );
}
```

ScrollWindow() calls ScrollRect() to scroll the pixels in gEventWindow up one row. ScrollRect() scrolls the contents of the current GrafPort (in this case, gEventWindow) within the rectangle specified in the first parameter. The rectangle is scrolled to the right by the number of pixels specified in the second parameter and down by the number of pixels specified in the third parameter. Since you specified a negative third parameter, the contents of gEventWindow will be scrolled up.

The last parameter to `ScrollRect()` is a `RgnHandle`, or a handle to a region. **Regions** are collections of drawn lines, shapes, and curves, as shown in Figure 4.14. After the pixels in the rectangle are scrolled, `ScrollRect()` will fill the vacated area of the rectangle with the `GrafPort`'s background pattern. Then, these new areas are collected into the region handled by `RgnHandle` (Figure 4.15).

Many programs use this region as a guide to redrawing the window so that they don't have to redraw the entire window. This is especially useful if your window is extremely complex and takes a long time to redraw. In that case, a handle to the window's `UpdateRgn` is passed to `ScrollRect()`. Whenever the Window Manager detects that a window's `updateRgn` is nonempty, the Window Manager generates an `updateEvt` for the window. As part of its processing, `BeginUpdate()` sets the specified window's `updateRgn` to the empty region.

Figure 4.14 A region.

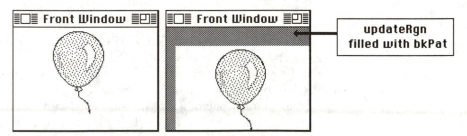

Figure 4.15 FrontWindow's `updateRgn` after `ScrollRect` (`r`, 10, 20, `updateRgn`).

Since you're not redrawing gEventWindow in response to updateEvts, you'll use a temporary region (tempRgn) as a parameter to ScrollRect(). Deallocate the tempRgn's memory by calling DisposeRgn().

```
/***************************        ScrollWindow *******/

ScrollWindow()
{
  RgnHandle     tempRgn;

  tempRgn = NewRgn();
  ScrollRect( &gEventWindow->portRect, HORIZONTAL_OFFSET,
              -ROWHEIGHT, tempRgn );
  DisposeRgn( tempRgn );
}
```

Handling mouseDown Events

When you receive a mouseDown event, the first thing to do is find out which window the mouse was clicked in, by calling the Toolbox routine FindWindow(). FindWindow() takes, as input, a point on the screen and returns, in the parameter whichWindow, a WindowPtr to the window containing the point. In addition, FindWindow() returns an integer part code, describing the part of the window the point was in.

Once you have your part code, compare it to the predefined Toolbox part codes (you can find a list of legal part codes in I:287). The part code inSysWindow means that the mouse was clicked in a system window, very likely, a desk accessory. (Since EventTutor doesn't support desk accessories, you probably won't see any inSysWindow mouseDowns, but you will see them in Chapter 5.) The appropriate thing to do in this case is to pass the event and the WindowPtr to the system so it can handle the event. Do this with the Toolbox routine SystemClick().

The part code inDrag indicates a mouse click in whichWindow's drag region. Handle this with a call to the Toolbox routine DragWindow(). DragWindow() wants a WindowPtr, the point on the screen where the mouse was clicked, and a boundary rectangle. DragWindow() will allow the user to drag the window anywhere on the screen as long as it's within the boundary rectangle. Use gDragRect, which you initialized with the routine SetUpDragRect().

The inContent part code represents the part of the window in which you draw. When you detect a mouse click inContent, call SelectWindow(). If the mouse click was not in the frontmost window, SelectWindow() deactivates the frontmost window and activates the clicked-in window. A call to SelectWindow() usually results in a pair of activateEvts.

```
/***************************************** HandleMouseDown */

HandleMouseDown()
{
   WindowPtr              whichWindow;
   short int              thePart;
   long                   windSize;
   GrafPtr                oldPort;

   thePart = FindWindow( gTheEvent.where, &whichWindow );
   switch ( thePart )
   {
        case inSysWindow :
               SystemClick( &gTheEvent, whichWindow );
               break;
        case inDrag :
               DragWindow( whichWindow, gTheEvent.where,
                   &gDragRect );
               break;
        case inContent:
               SelectWindow( whichWindow );
               break;
```

A click in the grow box is handled by a call to `GrowWindow()`, which takes the same arguments as `DragWindow()` but allows the window to grow and shrink instead of move. `GrowWindow()` returns a long integer composed of two words (four bytes) that define the number of pixels the window will grow or shrink in each direction. These words are passed to `SizeWindow()`, causing the window to be resized accordingly. The last parameter to `SizeWindow()` tells the Window Manager to accumulate any newly created content region into the update region. This means that the Window Manager will generate an update event whenever the window is made either taller or wider.

The update event strategy is fairly simple. Use the routine `InvalRect()` to add the entire contents of the window to the window's `updateRgn`, guaranteeing that an `updateEvt` will be generated whether or not the window was grown. When you plan your applications, spend some time working out an appropriate update strategy. If redrawing the contents of your windows will be fairly easy and won't take too long, you may want to use the `InvalRect()` approach. But if the contents of your window are potentially complex (as is true of many drawing and CAD packages), you'll probably want to avoid the call to `InvalRect()` and, instead, use the shape of the update region to aid you in updating your window efficiently.

```
   case inGrow:
          windSize = GrowWindow( whichWindow,
                      gTheEvent.where,&gSizeRect );
          if ( windSize != 0 )
          {
                  GetPort( &oldPort );
                  SetPort( whichWindow );
```

```
                        EraseRect( &whichWindow->portRect );
                        SizeWindow( whichWindow, LoWord( windSize),
                                HiWord( windSize ),
                                NORMAL_UPDATES );
                        InvalRect( &whichWindow->portRect );
                        SetPort( oldPort );
                }
                break;
```

A click in the go-away box of either window will result in gdone being set
to TRUE. This will cause the program to exit.

```
case inGoAway :
        gDone = TRUE;
        break;
```

A note from the thought police: A proper Macintosh application would
never think of exiting just because someone clicked in the close box of
a window! When we get to menu handling in Chapter 5, we'll show you
the correct way to Quit.

If the mouse is clicked in the zoom box, respond by calling TrackBox(),
which will return TRUE if the mouse button is released while the mouse is
still in the zoom box. ZoomWindow() zooms the window in or out, depending on the part code passed as a parameter. The constant
LEAVE_WHERE_IT_IS tells ZoomWindow() to leave the window in front if
it was in front when the zoom box was pressed or in back if the window was
in back when the zoom box was pressed. Just as you did with SizeWindow(),
call InvalRect() to guarantee that an updateEvt is generated when the
window is zoomed in or out.

```
                case inZoomIn:
                case inZoomOut:
                        if ( TrackBox( whichWindow,
                                gTheEvent.where, thePart ) )
                        {
                                GetPort( &oldPort );
                                SetPort( whichWindow );
                                EraseRect( &whichWindow->portRect );
                                ZoomWindow( whichWindow, thePart,
                                        LEAVE_WHERE_IT_IS );
                                InvalRect( &whichWindow->portRect );
                                SetPort( oldPort );
                        }
                        break;
        }
}
```

DrawMyPicture() will draw the picture handled by thePicture in the window pointed to by drawingWindow, clipping the drawing so that the scroll bar and grow areas aren't overwritten. Copy drawingWindow's portRect to drawingClipRect, and adjust the left and bottom to clip the two scroll bar areas. Use this new Rect as a parameter to ClipRect() so that when you draw your picture, it gets clipped properly.

Start by saving a pointer to the current GrafPort in oldPort so you can restore it at the end of DrawMyPicture(). Next, make drawingWindow the current GrafPort so the picture will be drawn in the correct window:

```
/****************************** DrawMyPicture *********/

DrawMyPicture( drawingWindow, thePicture )
WindowPtr        drawingWindow;
PicHandle        thePicture;
{
   Rect          drawingClipRect, myRect;
   GrafPtr       oldPort;
   RgnHandle     tempRgn;

   GetPort( &oldPort );
   SetPort( drawingWindow );
```

Then, allocate memory for a region to save a copy of the current clip region. Call GetClip() to copy the current clip region into tempRgn. NewRgn() allocates enough memory for the minimum-sized region. GetClip() resizes the region to accommodate the current clip region.

```
   tempRgn = NewRgn();
   GetClip( tempRgn );
```

> If you created a region in the shape of a star, and used SetClip() to set the clip region to your star region, all drawing in that window would be clipped in the shape of a star. You can read more about regions in *Inside Macintosh* (I:141-142 and I:166-167).

Next, erase the whole window with a call to EraseRect(). You've just erased the GrowIcon, so call DrawGrowIcon() to redraw it. Next, set up your clipping Rect, drawingClipRect, so that it excludes the right and bottom scroll bar areas (and, as a result, the grow area). Then, set myRect to the drawingWindow portRect. You'll use myRect as a parameter to CenterPict(), where it will be adjusted to reflect the size of the picture, centered in the input Rect.

At this point, you have not changed the clip region of `drawingWindow`. You are about to. Call `ClipRect()` to set the clipping region to the rectangle defined by `drawingClipRect`. Now, draw the picture with `DrawPicture()`.

```
EraseRect( &drawingWindow->portRect );
DrawGrowIcon( drawingWindow );

drawingClipRect = drawingWindow->portRect;
drawingClipRect.right -= SCROLL_BAR_PIXELS;
drawingClipRect.bottom -= SCROLL_BAR_PIXELS;

myRect = drawingWindow->portRect;
CenterPict( thePicture, &myRect );
ClipRect( &drawingClipRect );
DrawPicture( thePicture, &myRect );
```

Finally, reset the `ClipRect` to the setting saved in `tempRgn`, release the memory allocated to `tempRgn`, and set the current `GrafPort` back to the original setting.

```
SetClip( tempRgn );
DisposeRgn( tempRgn );
SetPort( oldPort );
}
```

`CenterRect()` is the same as in Chapter 3's ShowPict program:

```
/********************************* CenterPict *********/

CenterPict( thePicture, myRectPtr )
PicHandle       thePicture;
Rect            *myRectPtr;
{
  Rect   windRect, pictureRect;

  windRect = *myRectPtr;
  pictureRect = (**( thePicture )).picFrame;
  myRectPtr->top = (windRect.bottom - windRect.top -
        (pictureRect.bottom -
        pictureRect.top)) / 2 + windRect.top;
  myRectPtr->bottom = myRectPtr->top + (pictureRect.bottom
        - pictureRect.top);
  myRectPtr->left = (windRect.right - windRect.left -
        (pictureRect.right - pictureRect.left))
        / 2 + windRect.left;
  myRectPtr->right = myRectPtr->left + (pictureRect.right
        - pictureRect.left);
}
```

If you'd like to learn more about event handling, read the Toolbox Event Manager chapter of *Inside Macintosh* (I:241–266).

In Review

At the heart of every Macintosh application is the main event loop. Mac applications are built around this loop. Each pass through the main event loop consists of the retrieval of an event from the event queue and the processing of the event.

The Window Manager plays an important role in the handling of events by generating `updateEvts` as a means of getting the application to draw (or update) the contents of a window. In addition, Window Manager routines like `FindWindow()` offer a mechanism for linking an event to a window.

An underlying theme of this chapter is a concern for good user interface design. When you set out to build an application, concentrate on the user's view of your application. Use the main event loop in this chapter as your basic skeleton. Then, determine how you will handle each of the different events your user might initiate.

In Chapter 5, you'll learn all about menus. You'll learn how to design and implement regular menus, hierarchical menus, and pop-up menus!

5

Menu Management

This chapter explains the use of menus in your programs. We'll show you how to install menus via MBAR and MENU resources, and describe the routines available from the Menu Manager. We'll also discuss the best way to support desk accessories and do event handling with menus.

MACINTOSH MENUS HAVEN'T been the same since the advent of the Mac SE and the Mac II. The classic Mac menu was the pull-down menu—the strip at the top of the screen with options that, when clicked on, displayed the possibilities available to each program (Figure 5.1). The situation has changed for the better with two additional menu types: the **hierarchical** menu and the **pop-up** menu. We'll discuss and demonstrate both. But first, let's look at the standard parts of all menu systems.

Menu Components

Before we discuss the structure of menus, let's examine the parts of a menu and their functions. Figure 5.2 shows the main parts of Macintosh menus. We'll discuss the parts of the classic menu first, then discuss differences in the new menu types in the section devoted to each type.

The menu bar displayed at the top of the Mac screen is normally 20 pixels high. The font type and size are always the same as the system font. The menu bar height may be changed, using the global variable MBarHeight, as we saw in Chapter 3's screen saver program, The Flying Line.

On the menu bar, each list of choices is known as a **menu**. The ⌘, File, and Edit menus are found in most Macintosh applications. Menus are dimmed, or disabled, when none of their options is available.

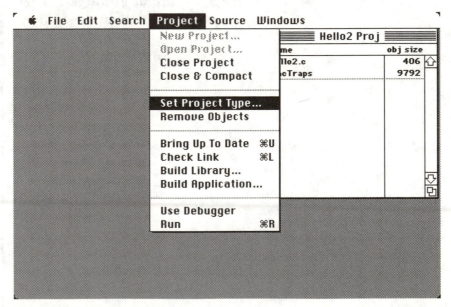

Figure 5.1 Classic pull down menu.

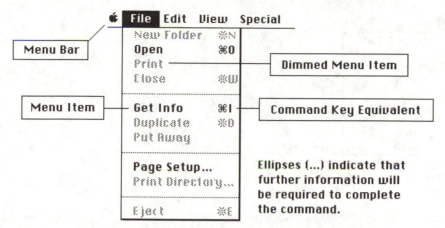

Figure 5.2 Components of Macintosh menus.

Menu items are the choices that are available in a given menu. For example, the File menu items in MacWrite are as shown in Figure 5.3.

A menu item is selected if the mouse button is released while the item is still highlighted. Individual items may also be disabled (dimmed). An icon or a check mark can be placed to the left of an item's text. The font and size of the item may be varied; command key equivalents may be placed to the right of a menu item. If a menu item list becomes too long for the screen, not uncommon on a Mac Plus or SE, the last item that would normally be seen is replaced with a downward-pointing arrow [▼]. If the user pulls the mouse pointer down further, more menu items will scroll into view.

The ⌘ menu is different in several respects from the other menus in the menu bar. By convention, the first item in the ⌘ menu is used by your program to display information about your program. The remaining menu items make up a list of available desk accessories (Figure 5.4).

Let's take a look at the classic pull down menu and how it works.

File

New	⌘N
Open...	⌘O
Close	⌘W
Save	⌘S
Save As...	
Page Setup...	
Print...	⌘P
Quit	⌘Q

Figure 5.3 MacWrite File menu.

Figure 5.4   The ♦ menu.

The Pull Down Menu

The **pull down menu**, displayed at the top of the screen, is standard for most Macintosh applications. Pull-down menus are created by the Menu Manager, which also takes care of drawing the menu items; handling menu selection (as well as command key equivalents); and, finally, restoring the screen when the menu is released. All you have to do is provide the menu information in the form of two resources, MBAR and MENU, and call them with Menu Manager routines. The MBAR resource contains a list of the menus that will be displayed on the menu bar. Each MENU resource contains information about the individual menu items.

On the Mac II, menus and menu items can also be displayed in different colors (V:235).

The Hierarchical Menu

The **hierarchical menu** came on board in 1987, when it was added to the Toolbox. It was needed for the new, complex programs that had become available for the Mac. As more bells and whistles were added to Mac applications, it became harder to find a place for them on the menu bar. Hierarchical menus made it possible to put a whole menu into one item without inconveniencing the user (Figure 5.5).

Menu items that have a hierarchical submenu associated with them have a small right-pointing triangle (▶) on their right side. When the menu item is selected, the hierarchical submenu is displayed. The user then moves the arrow over to the item desired on the hierarchical menu.

The Pop-Up Menu

The pop-up menu is the only menu that can be placed anywhere on the screen. This menu is similar to a hierarchical menu, except that pop-up menus can be placed in windows, dialog boxes, even on the desktop.

A pop-up menu appears when a mouseDown occurs in an area defined by an application (Figure 5.6). Once the pop-up menu appears, the user can select an item by moving the cursor up or down. When the mouse button is released, the selection is processed. Pop-up menu routines require a little more work than the other menu types, but the additional functionality is worth it. We will build a pop-up menu project at the end of this chapter.

Other Kinds of Menus

As with most other parts of the interface, you can make your own unique menus that use the same calls yet look very different from the three kinds of menus already described. Building your own menus, however, is more complicated than using the standards. And since many current applications don't even use the pop-up and hierarchical menus yet, there's no need to rush out and create something new.

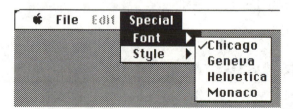

Figure 5.5 Hierarchical menu.

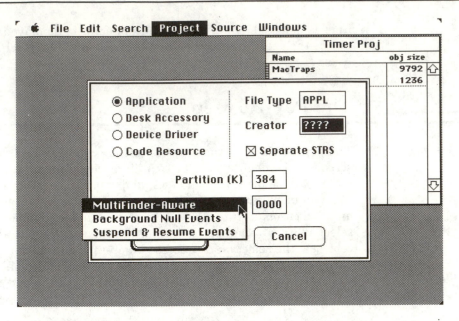

Figure 5.6   Dialog box with pop-up menu.

A fourth type of Macintosh menu that has become quite popular recently is the **tear-off menu**, which can be torn off the menu bar and moved around the screen like a window. Its use in HyperCard and MacPaint 2.0 have probably guaranteed its eventual enshrinement in the Toolbox. We suggest that you wait until it is available in the Toolbox before trying to make one on your own.

Menu formats from MS-DOS programs or other non-Macintosh systems are sometimes ported over to the Macintosh. A result of this might be something like Figure 5.7. These MS-DOS style menus do not follow the Macintosh user interface guidelines. Don't use them or associate with developers that do.

Putting Menus into Your Programs

There are a number of ways to add menus to the applications you create: You can insert menus at the end of the current menu bar (e.g., desk accessories like QuickDex or DiskTop), you can build a new set of menus from scratch right inside your program, or you can create your menus in ResEdit and load them into your program. We're going to do it the last way, which makes for clean programming and easy changes without recompiling.

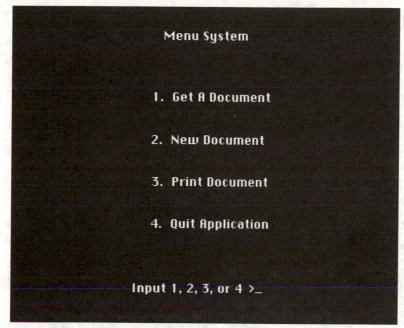

Figure 5.7 MS-DOS menu.

We'll use two menu resources: MENU and MBAR. The MBAR resource contains a list of all of the MENU resources that will be used to draw the menu bar. The MBAR resource also controls the order in which the menus are drawn on the menu bar. Each MENU resource contains a menu title, a list of the menu items, and detailed information about the display of each item.

Now, let's look at **Timer**, our first program with menus.

Timer

Timer displays the current time in a window and refreshes the time once per second. The standard ⬤, File, and Edit menus are supported as well as an additional menu, Special. The Special menu has two hierarchical submenus, which allow you to change the display's font and style.

Timer's menu supports desk accessories. The File menu has a single item, Quit. The Edit menu is disabled but is provided as a service to desk accessories. Every Macintosh application you write should support the standard Edit menu, as it is part of the Macintosh interface standards.

Timer works like this:

- It initializes the Toolbox.
- It loads the MBAR and MENU resources.

- It initializes the Timer window.
- It displays the time in the window.
- It handles events for the menus and the window, refreshing the Timer window once per second.

Setting Up the Project

Create a folder called `Timer`; keep your project and resource files inside the folder.

Resources

Now, add the resources you'll need for your Timer program. Create a file in your new `Timer` folder using ResEdit. Call it `Timer Proj.Rsrc`. Then build a `WIND` with ID = `400`, with the specifications as shown in Figure 5.8.

Next, you need an `MBAR` resource, that lists the resource IDs of the four `MENU`s that will be part of Timer's menu bar. Create a new `MBAR` resource inside `Timer Proj.Rsrc`. You should see something like Figure 5.9. Click on the row of asterisks and select New from the File menu. A field for the first menu should appear, as well as a new row of asterisks. Create three more menu fields and fill all four as shown in Figure 5.10. Finally, change

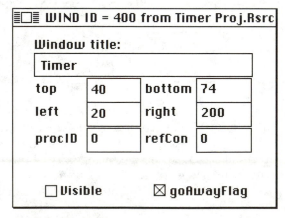

Figure 5.8   Timer `WIND` specifications.

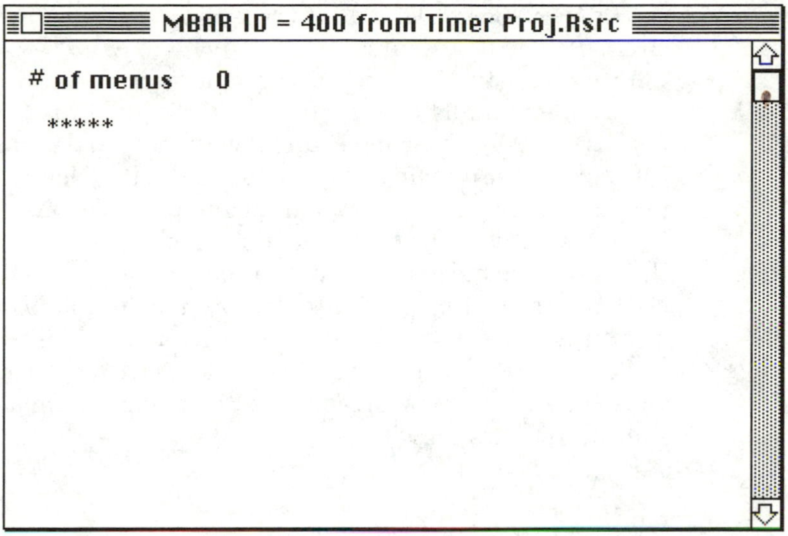

```
┌─────────────────────────────────────────────────────────┐
│ ▤□▦▦▦▦═ MBAR ID = 400 from Timer Proj.Rsrc ▦▦▦ │ ⬆
│                                                          │ ▣
│   # of menus    0                                        │ │
│     *****                                                │ │
│                                                          │ │
│                                                          │ │
│                                                          │ │
│                                                          │ │
│                                                          │ │
│                                                          │ ⬇
└─────────────────────────────────────────────────────────┘
```

Figure 5.9   A new MBAR resource.

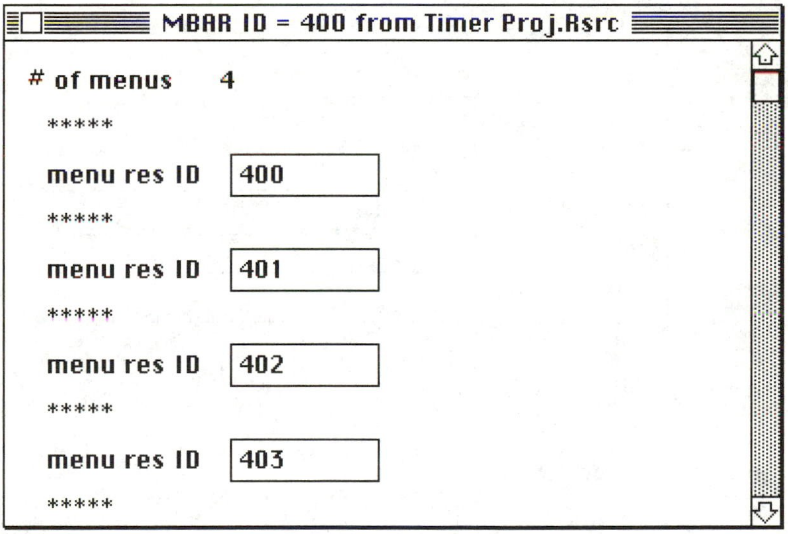

```
┌─────────────────────────────────────────────────────────┐
│ ▤□▦▦▦▦═ MBAR ID = 400 from Timer Proj.Rsrc ▦▦ │ ⬆
│                                                          │ │
│   # of menus    4                                        │ │
│     *****                                                │ │
│                                                          │ │
│     menu res ID   │ 400 │                                │ │
│     *****                                                │ │
│                                                          │ │
│     menu res ID   │ 401 │                                │ │
│     *****                                                │ │
│                                                          │ │
│     menu res ID   │ 402 │                                │ │
│     *****                                                │ │
│     menu res ID   │ 403 │                                │ │
│     *****                                                │ ⬇
└─────────────────────────────────────────────────────────┘
```

Figure 5.10   A complete MBAR resource.

the MBAR resource ID to 400. Close the MBAR window. Now, you need to create four MENU resources.

First, build the MENU resource as shown in Figure 5.11. When the MENU resource is initially displayed by ResEdit, only the first seven fields are displayed. When you have completed these fields, click on the row of asterisks at the bottom of the window and select New from the menu to add information for each subsequent menu item. You may encounter difficulties in generating the ⌘ character for this menu. The simplest way to get the ⌘ is to go into another application with an ⌘ MENU resource, copy the ⌘ character and paste it into Timer's resources. Using the ⌘ is just a convention; the program will run fine, if amateurishly, with any character.

Close the ⌘ MENU resource window and give it a resource number of 400. Open a new MENU resource for the File menu information, and fill it in as shown in Figure 5.12.

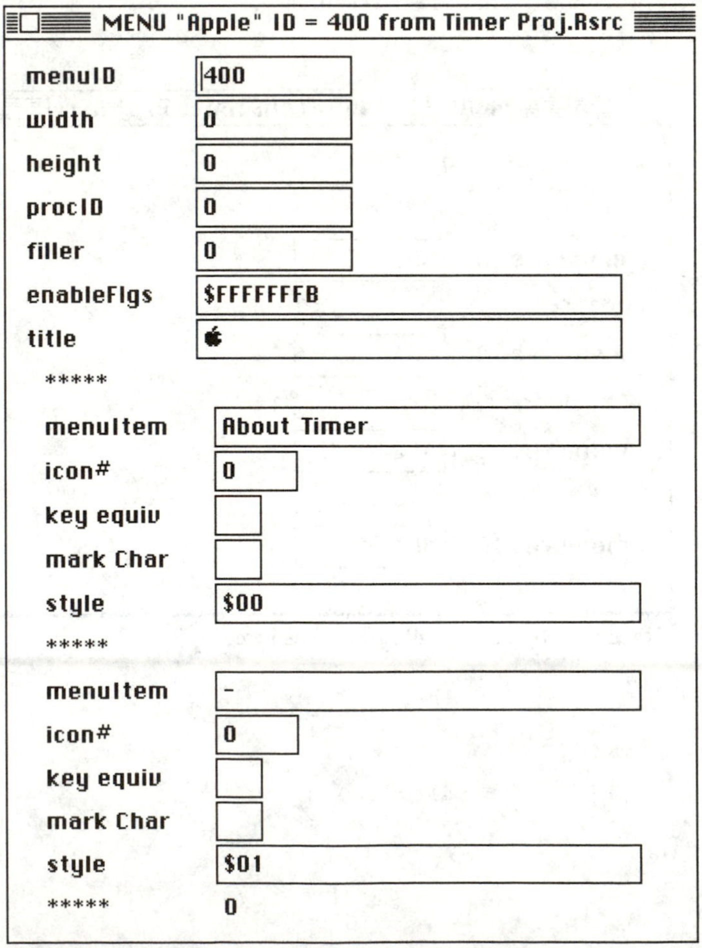

MENU "Apple" ID = 400 from Timer Proj.Rsrc	
menuID	400
width	0
height	0
procID	0
filler	0
enableFlgs	$FFFFFFFB
title	⌘
*****	
menuItem	About Timer
icon#	0
key equiv	
mark Char	
style	$00
*****	
menuItem	–
icon#	0
key equiv	
mark Char	
style	$01
*****	0

Figure 5.11 Apple MENU specifications.

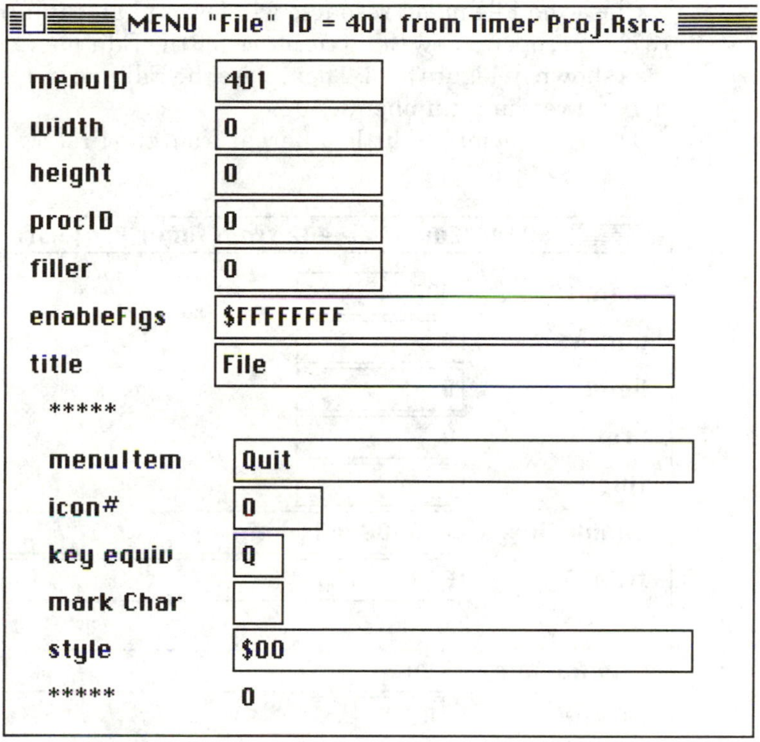

Figure 5.12 File MENU specifications.

The MENU resource allows you to specify the appearance of the displayed menu in your program. The first seven items of the MENU resource relate to the entire menu. The MenuID field is the resource ID of the MENU, the enableFlgs field allows you to specify which menu items are initially disabled (dimmed) so that the user cannot select them. The title field contains the menu's title that is displayed on the menu bar. The other fields will be filled in for you by ResEdit.

The enableFlgs field contains a set of flags for the Menu Manager. These flags tell the Manager which menu items are selectable and which should be displayed in a dimmed state. In the menu, $FFFFFFFB has been entered.

In binary, this becomes:

1111-1111-1111-1111-1111-1111-1111-1011

The rightmost bit corresponds to the MENU title, the second rightmost to the first MENU item the third from the right corresponds to the second MENU item,, and so on. $FFFFFFFB tells the Menu Manager to make the second MENU item (the line under About Timer) unselectable.

Close the File menu resource window and give it a resource number of 401. Now, open a new MENU resource for the Edit menu information. Fill it in as shown in Figure 5.13. Then, close the Edit menu resource window and give it a resource number of 402.

The Edit menu is a little different from the first two, in that the menu

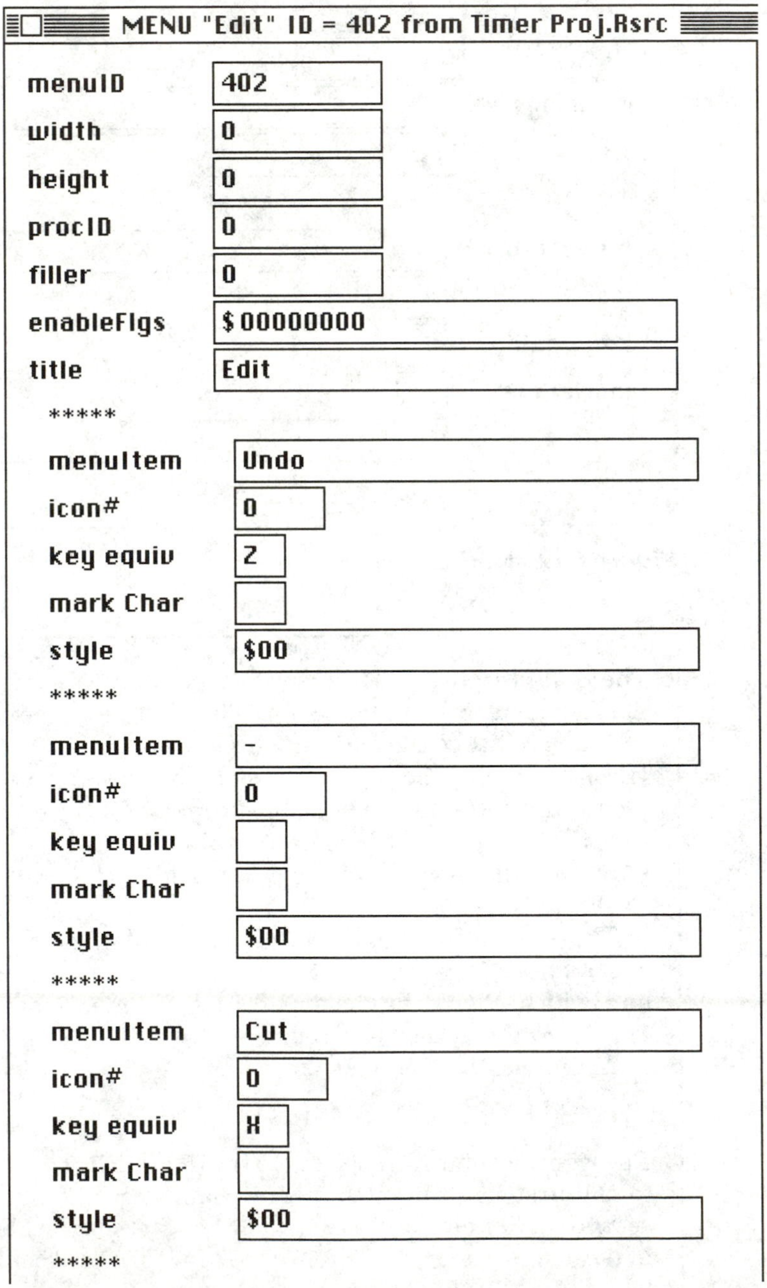

```
┌──────────────────────────────────────────────────┐
│ ≣□≣══ MENU "Edit" ID = 402 from Timer Proj.Rsrc ══≣│
├──────────────────────────────────────────────────┤
│  menuID         │ 402       │                      │
│  width          │ 0         │                      │
│  height         │ 0         │                      │
│  procID         │ 0         │                      │
│  filler         │ 0         │                      │
│  enableFlgs     │ $ 00000000         │             │
│  title          │ Edit               │             │
│       *****                                         │
│    menuItem     │ Undo                 │            │
│    icon#        │ 0         │                       │
│    key equiv    │ Z │                               │
│    mark Char    │   │                               │
│    style        │ $00                │              │
│       *****                                         │
│    menuItem     │ -                    │            │
│    icon#        │ 0         │                       │
│    key equiv    │   │                               │
│    mark Char    │   │                               │
│    style        │ $00                │              │
│       *****                                         │
│    menuItem     │ Cut                  │            │
│    icon#        │ 0         │                       │
│    key equiv    │ X │                               │
│    mark Char    │   │                               │
│    style        │ $00                │              │
│       *****                                         │
└──────────────────────────────────────────────────┘
```

Figure 5.13 Edit MENU specifications.

menuItem	Copy
icon#	0
key equiv	C
mark Char	
style	$00
*****	
menuItem	Paste
icon#	0
key equiv	V
mark Char	
style	$00
*****	
menuItem	Clear
icon#	0
key equiv	
mark Char	
style	$00
*****	0

Figure 5.13   Edit MENU specifications (*continued*).

items in it have all been disabled. In fact, this application does not use the Edit menu at all. So why add it? The reason is that although your application may not use the Edit menu, the desk accesories that you support may. Many desk accessories expect an Edit menu on Mac applications. If you don't put one there, the accessory may not be able to function properly.

Now, add the Special menu. Open up a new MENU resource and fill it as shown in Figure 5.14. Close the Special menu and give it a resource ID of 403.

The next step is a little tricky. You may have wondered why the Font and Style items each used a * in the key equiv field. In order to mark a menu item as a hierarchical menu item, the key equiv field is filled with a special

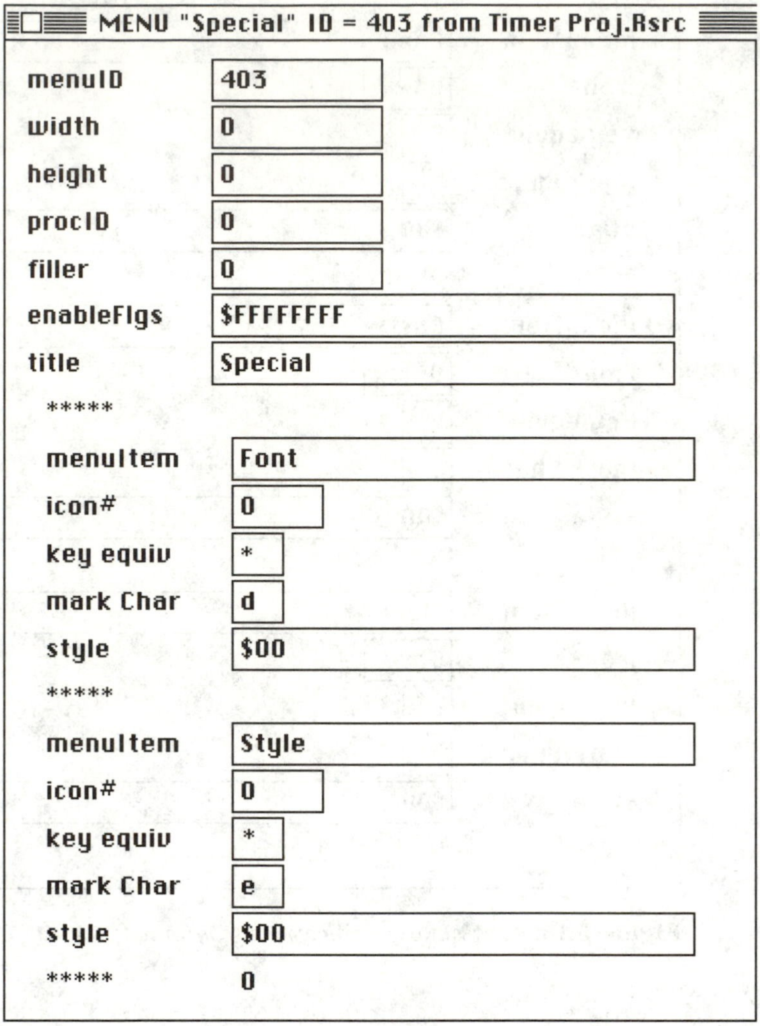

```
▇□▇  MENU "Special" ID = 403 from Timer Proj.Rsrc ▇▇

      menuID        403
      width         0
      height        0
      procID        0
      filler        0
      enableFlgs    $FFFFFFFF
      title         Special
        *****
        menuItem    Font
        icon#       0
        key equiv   *
        mark Char   d
        style       $00
        *****
        menuItem    Style
        icon#       0
        key equiv   *
        mark Char   e
        style       $00
        *****       0
```

Figure 5.14 Special MENU specifications.

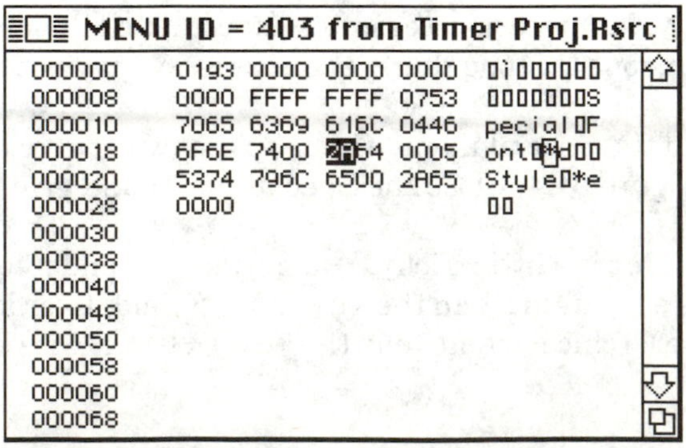

```
▇□▇  MENU ID = 403 from Timer Proj.Rsrc
 000000    0193 0000 0000 0000    □ì□□□□□□  ⇧
 000008    0000 FFFF FFFF 0753    □□□□□□□S
 000010    7065 6369 616C 0446    pecial□F
 000018    6F6E 7400 2A64 0005    ont□*d□□
 000020    5374 796C 6500 2A65    Style□*e
 000028    0000                   □□
 000030
 000038
 000040
 000048
 000050
 000058                                     ⇩
 000060
 000068                                     ▣
```

Figure 5.15 The Special menu, using
Open General.

hex character, which, unfortunately, cannot be typed from the keyboard. The * acts as a placeholder for this special character. Now, replace the * with the hex character 1B. To do this, highlight the Special MENU (ID = 403) and select Open General from the File menu (Figure 5.15)

Find the first * on the right side of the window and the corresponding hex code for * (2A) on the left side. Select the 2A. Notice that a rectangle appeared around the * on the right. Key in the characters 1B. Repeat this procedure for the second * on the right side of the window, and compare your result with Figure 5.16. Finally, close the Special MENU window, reopen it normally, and compare it with Figure 5.17.

Notice that the * placeholders have been replaced by the ASCII version of hex 1B. That's because a hex 1B in a MENU item's key equiv field tells the Menu Manager to look for a hierarchical submenu. The Menu Manager uses the value in the item's mark Char field to indicate the resource ID of a MENU to use as a hierarchical submenu. The Font item has an ASCII d in the mark Char field. ASCII d is equivalent to hex 64, or 100 decimal. Therefore, the Menu Manager will look for a MENU with resource ID = 100 to use as the Font hierarchical submenu. In the same way, the Style item has ASCII e (101 decimal) in its mark Char field, so the Menu Manager will look for a MENU with resource ID = 101 for the Style hierarchical submenu. Now let's build these submenus.

Here's why you don't use 404 and 405 instead of 100 and 101 for hierarchical submenu resource IDs. The hierarchical menu structure was defined in Volume 5 of *Inside Macintosh*. Only one byte is used to designate hierarchical menus in the menu structure. Since the biggest one byte hexadecimal number is FF, or 255 decimal, that's the biggest hierarchical menu number that you can use.

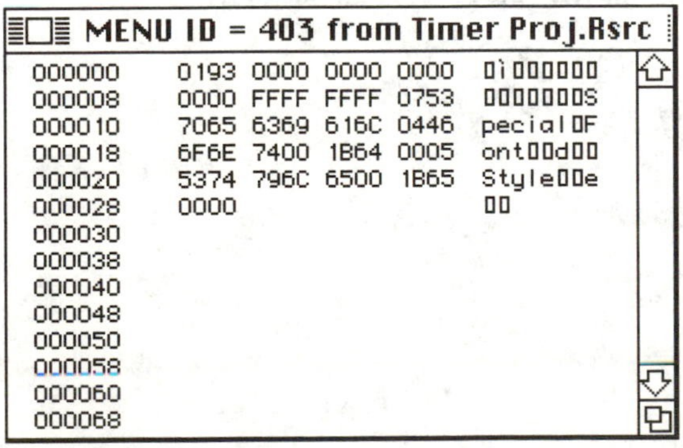

```
▤▢▤ MENU ID = 403 from Timer Proj.Rsrc
000000    0193 0000 0000 0000    0·□000000   ⇧
000008    0000 FFFF FFFF 0753    0000000S
000010    7065 6369 616C 0446    pecial□F
000018    6F6E 7400 1B64 0005    ont□□d□□
000020    5374 796C 6500 1B65    Style□□e
000028    0000                   □□
000030
000038
000040
000048
000050
000058
000060                                       ⇩
000068                                       ▱
```

Figure 5.16 The completed Special menu, using Open General.

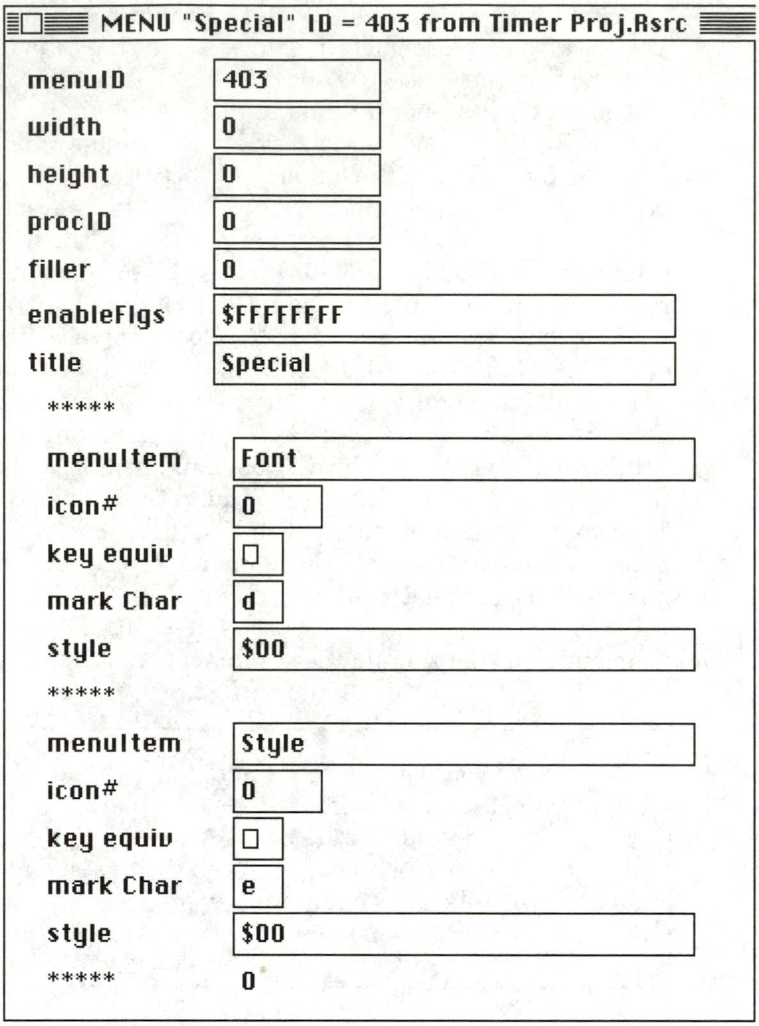

MENU "Special" ID = 403 from Timer Proj.Rsrc

menuID	403
width	0
height	0
procID	0
filler	0
enableFlgs	$FFFFFFFF
title	Special

*****

menuItem	Font
icon#	0
key equiv	☐
mark Char	d
style	$00

*****

menuItem	Style
icon#	0
key equiv	☐
mark Char	e
style	$00

*****   0

Figure 5.17   Special menu, opened normally.

Close the Special MENU window. Create a new MENU resource and fill it as shown in Figure 5.18. Note that the Font MENU has no menu items. As with the menu, the items will be inserted from system resources. Change the Font MENU resource ID to 100. Create another new MENU resource and fill it as shown in Figure 5.19. Change its resource ID to 101. When you're finished with the Font MENU, close and save your work.

You've completed the resources necessary for the window and menus of Timer. Now, you'll create an Alert that is displayed when About Timer is selected from the menu. For the moment, don't worry too much about the alert mechanism (the ALRT and DITL resources). We'll cover alerts in Chapter 6.

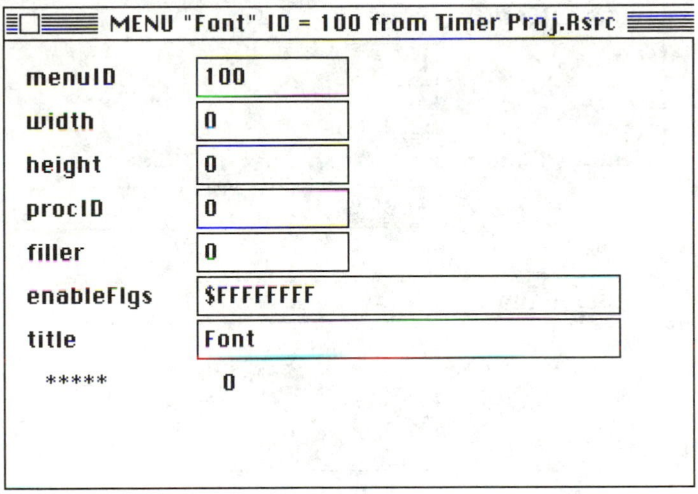

Figure 5.18 Font MENU specifications.

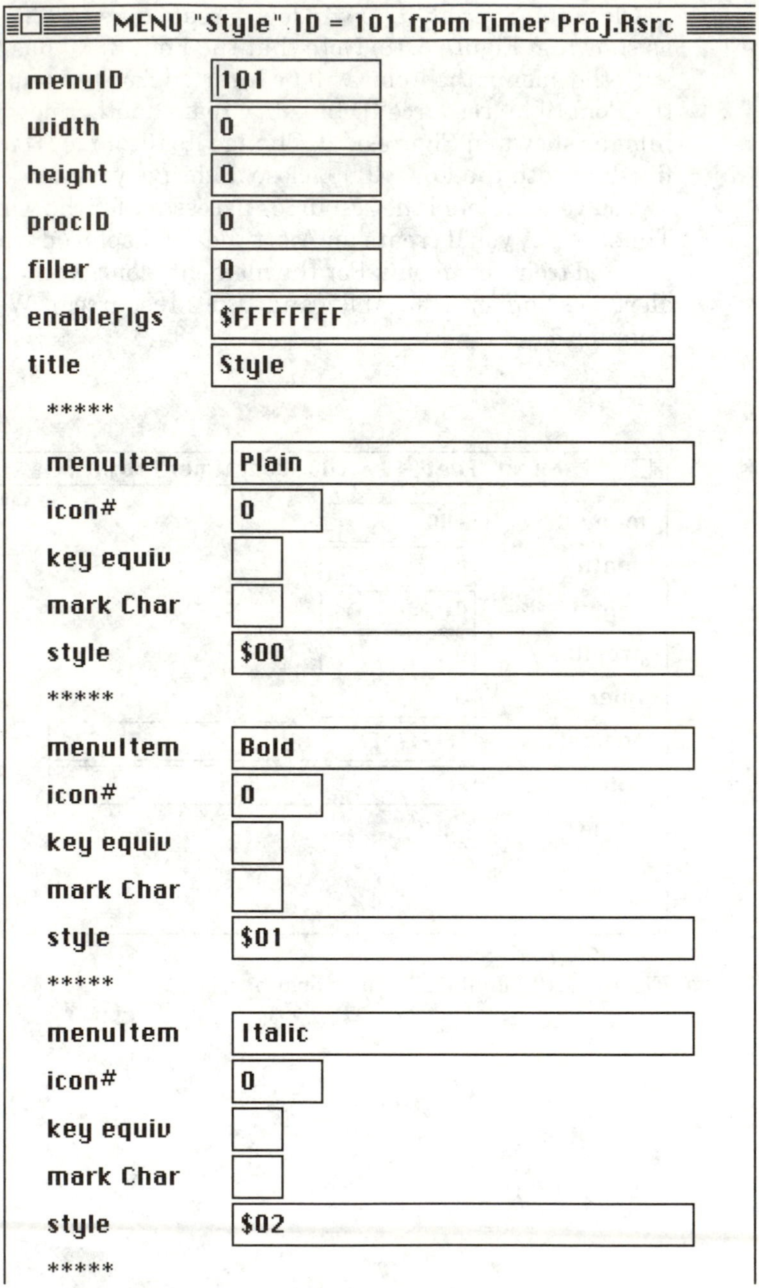

☰▢▦ MENU "Style" ID = 101 from Timer Proj.Rsrc ▦

menuID	101
width	0
height	0
procID	0
filler	0
enableFlgs	$FFFFFFFF
title	Style

*****

menuItem	Plain
icon#	0
key equiv	
mark Char	
style	$00

*****

menuItem	Bold
icon#	0
key equiv	
mark Char	
style	$01

*****

menuItem	Italic
icon#	0
key equiv	
mark Char	
style	$02

*****

Figure 5.19 Style MENU specifications.

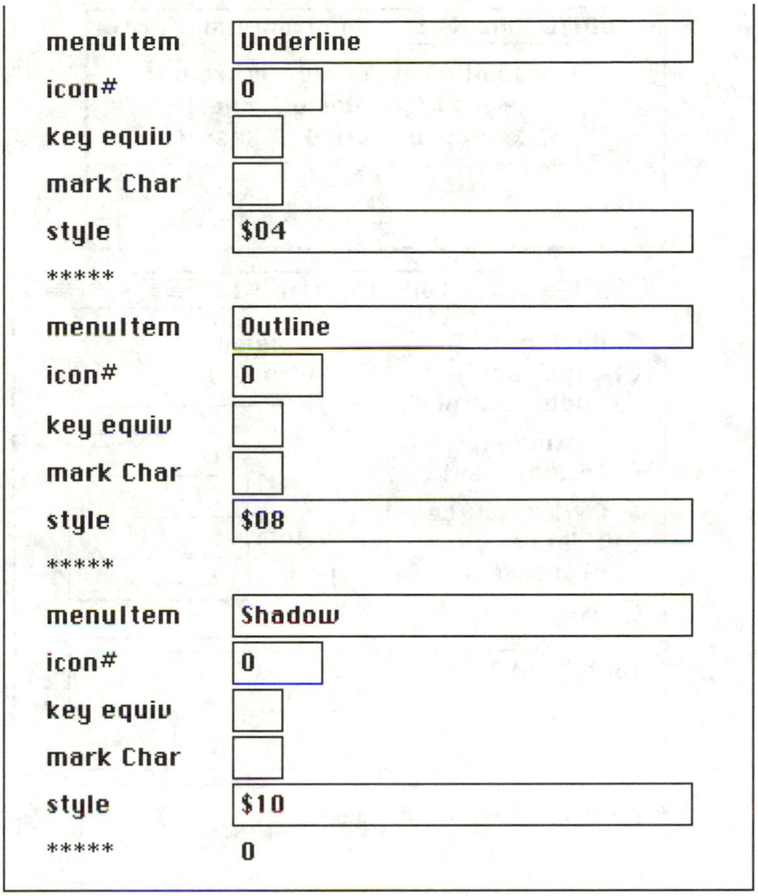

menuItem	Underline
icon#	0
key equiv	
mark Char	
style	$04

*****

menuItem	Outline
icon#	0
key equiv	
mark Char	
style	$08

*****

menuItem	Shadow
icon#	0
key equiv	
mark Char	
style	$10

*****   0

Figure 5.19 Style MENU specifications (*continued*).

Create a DITL resource (select New, enter DITL, and select New again). The DITL (for Dialog Item List) contains the list of items you want to appear in your alert. By convention, the first item is always the OK button that the user clicks to make the alert disappear. Create a new item by selecting New from the File menu, making it look like Figure 5.20. Close the Item #1 window and create a second item, making it look like Figure 5.21.

Close the Item #2 window. Now, choose Get Info from the File menu and change the DITL resource ID to 400.

Next, you'll create an alert template to display the DITL items. From the Timer Proj.Rsrc's main window, create a new ALRT resource. A new ALRT menu should appear in ResEdit's menu bar. Select Display as Text from the ALRT menu. Change the alert fields so they look like those in Figure 5.22. Finally, change the ALRT resource ID to 400. All the resources are now done. Select Quit from the File menu and save your changes. You're ready to code!

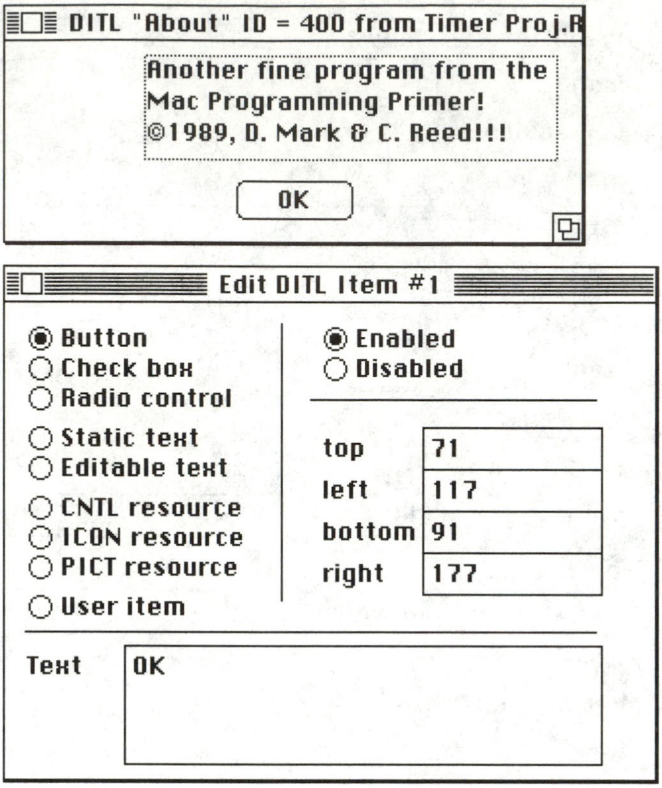

DITL "About" ID = 400 from Timer Proj.R

Another fine program from the
Mac Programming Primer!
©1989, D. Mark & C. Reed!!!

OK

Edit DITL Item #1

- ● Button
- ○ Check box
- ○ Radio control

- ○ Static text
- ○ Editable text

- ○ CNTL resource
- ○ ICON resource
- ○ PICT resource

- ○ User item

- ● Enabled
- ○ Disabled

top	71
left	117
bottom	91
right	177

Text   OK

Figure 5.20   The OK button.

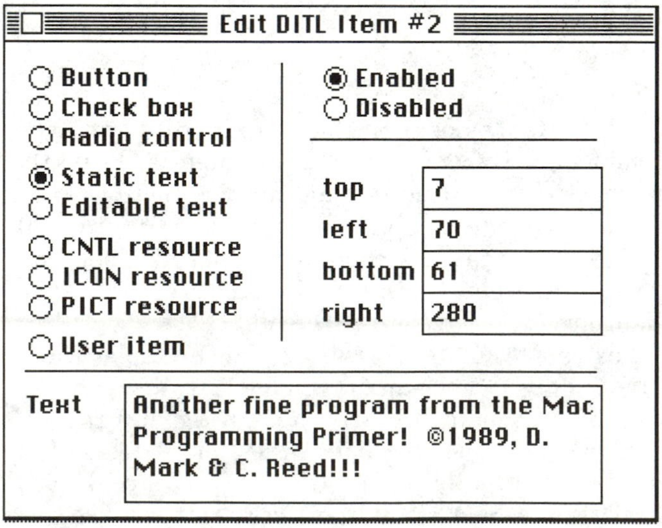

Edit DITL Item #2

- ○ Button
- ○ Check box
- ○ Radio control

- ● Static text
- ○ Editable text

- ○ CNTL resource
- ○ ICON resource
- ○ PICT resource

- ○ User item

- ● Enabled
- ○ Disabled

top	7
left	70
bottom	61
right	280

Text   Another fine program from the Mac
Programming Primer! ©1989, D.
Mark & C. Reed!!!

Figure 5.21   The About Box text.

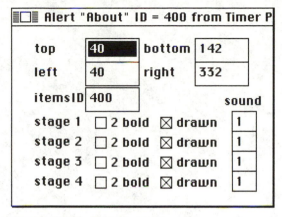

Figure 5.22 The About Alert, displayed as text.

Timer Code

Some of this code can be cannibalized from EventTutor. Just be careful with variable names and the like.

Get into THINK C, and start a new project in the Timer folder. Call the project Timer Proj. Add `MacTraps` to your project. Now, add the code.

```
#define BASE_RES_ID              400
#define NIL_POINTER              0L
#define MOVE_TO_FRONT            -1
#define REMOVE_ALL_EVENTS        0

#define PLAIN                    0
#define PLAIN_ITEM               1
#define BOLD_ITEM                2
#define ITALIC_ITEM              3
#define UNDERLINE_ITEM           4
#define OUTLINE_ITEM             5
#define SHADOW_ITEM              6

#define INCLUDE_SECONDS          TRUE

#define ADD_CHECK_MARK           TRUE
#define REMOVE_CHECK_MARK        FALSE

#define DRAG_THRESHOLD           30

#define MIN_SLEEP                0L
#define NIL_MOUSE_REGION         0L
```

```
#define WNE_TRAP_NUM              0x60
#define UNIMPL_TRAP_NUM           0x9F

#define QUIT_ITEM                 1
#define ABOUT_ITEM                1

#define NOT_A_NORMAL_MENU         -1
#define APPLE_MENU_ID             BASE_RES_ID
#define FILE_MENU_ID              BASE_RES_ID+1
#define FONT_MENU_ID              100
#define STYLE_MENU_ID             101

#define CLOCK_LEFT                12
#define CLOCK_TOP                 25
#define CLOCK_SIZE                24

#define ABOUT_ALERT               400


WindowPtr       gClockWindow;
Boolean         gDone, gWNEImplemented;
long            gCurrentTime, gOldTime;
EventRecord     gTheEvent;
MenuHandle      gAppleMenu, gFontMenu, gStyleMenu;
int             gLastFont;
Rect            gDragRect;
Style           gCurrentStyle = PLAIN;


/****************************** main ********/

main()
{
    ToolBoxInit();
    WindowInit();
    SetUpDragRect();
    MenuBarInit();
    MainLoop();
}


/******************************** ToolBoxInit */

ToolBoxInit()
{
    InitGraf( &thePort );
    InitFonts();
    FlushEvents( everyEvent, REMOVE_ALL_EVENTS );
    InitWindows();
    InitMenus();
    TEInit();
    InitDialogs( NIL_POINTER );
    InitCursor();
}
```

```
/****************************** WindowInit   */

WindowInit()
{
        gClockWindow = GetNewWindow( BASE_RES_ID, NIL_POINTER,
                                                MOVE_TO_FRONT );
        SetPort( gClockWindow );
        ShowWindow( gClockWindow );

        TextSize( CLOCK_SIZE );
}



/****************************** SetUpDragRect ********/

SetUpDragRect()
{
        gDragRect = screenBits.bounds;
        gDragRect.left += DRAG_THRESHOLD;
        gDragRect.right -= DRAG_THRESHOLD;
        gDragRect.bottom -= DRAG_THRESHOLD;
}



/****************************** MenuBarInit   */

MenuBarInit()
{
        Handle          myMenuBar;

        myMenuBar = GetNewMBar( BASE_RES_ID );
        SetMenuBar( myMenuBar );
        gAppleMenu = GetMHandle( APPLE_MENU_ID );
        gFontMenu = GetMenu( FONT_MENU_ID );
        gStyleMenu = GetMenu( STYLE_MENU_ID );

        InsertMenu( gFontMenu, NOT_A_NORMAL_MENU );
        AddResMenu( gFontMenu, 'FONT' );
        InsertMenu( gStyleMenu, NOT_A_NORMAL_MENU );

        CheckItem( gStyleMenu, PLAIN_ITEM, TRUE );
        AddResMenu( gAppleMenu, 'DRVR' );
        DrawMenuBar();

        gLastFont = 1;
        HandleFontChoice( gLastFont );
}
```

```
/****************************** MainLoop ********/

MainLoop()
{
      gDone = FALSE;
      gWNEImplemented = ( NGetTrapAddress( WNE_TRAP_NUM, ToolTrap ) !=
                          NGetTrapAddress( UNIMPL_TRAP_NUM, ToolTrap ) );
      while ( gDone == FALSE )
      {
            HandleEvent();
      }
}


/************************************ HandleEvent   */

HandleEvent()
{
      char    theChar;

      if ( gWNEImplemented )
            WaitNextEvent( everyEvent, &gTheEvent, MIN_SLEEP,
                                               NIL_MOUSE_REGION );
      else
      {
            SystemTask();
            GetNextEvent( everyEvent, &gTheEvent );
      }


      switch ( gTheEvent.what )
      {
            case nullEvent:
                  HandleNull();
                  break;
            case mouseDown:
                  HandleMouseDown();
                  break;
            case keyDown:
            case autoKey:
                  theChar = gTheEvent.message & charCodeMask;
                  if (( gTheEvent.modifiers & cmdKey ) != 0)
                        HandleMenuChoice( MenuKey( theChar ) );
                  break;
            case updateEvt:
                  BeginUpdate( gTheEvent.message );
                  EndUpdate( gTheEvent.message );
                  break;
      }
}
```

```
/****************************** HandleNull *********/

HandleNull()
{
      GetDateTime( &gCurrentTime );
      if ( gCurrentTime != gOldTime )
      {
            DrawClock( gClockWindow );
      }
}


/****************************** DrawClock *********/

DrawClock( theWindow )
WindowPtr     theWindow;
{
      Str255          myTimeString;

      IUTimeString( gCurrentTime, INCLUDE_SECONDS, myTimeString );
      EraseRect( &( theWindow->portRect ) );
      MoveTo( CLOCK_LEFT, CLOCK_TOP );
      DrawString( myTimeString );
      gOldTime = gCurrentTime;
}


/******************************** HandleMouseDown */

HandleMouseDown()
{
      WindowPtr     whichWindow;
      short int     thePart;
      long int      menuChoice, windSize;

      thePart = FindWindow( gTheEvent.where, &whichWindow );
      switch ( thePart )
      {
            case inMenuBar:
                  menuChoice = MenuSelect( gTheEvent.where );
                  HandleMenuChoice( menuChoice );
                  break;
            case inSysWindow :
                  SystemClick( &gTheEvent, whichWindow );
                  break;
            case inDrag :
                  DragWindow( whichWindow, gTheEvent.where, &gDragRect);
                  break;
            case inGoAway :
                  gDone = TRUE;
                  break;
      }
}
```

```
/************************************* HandleMenuChoice */

HandleMenuChoice( menuChoice )
long int     menuChoice;
{
     int     theMenu;
     int     theItem;

     if ( menuChoice != 0 )
     {
             theMenu = HiWord( menuChoice );
             theItem = LoWord( menuChoice );
             switch ( theMenu )
             {
                     case APPLE_MENU_ID :
                             HandleAppleChoice( theItem );
                             break;
                     case FILE_MENU_ID :
                             HandleFileChoice( theItem );
                             break;
                     case FONT_MENU_ID :
                             HandleFontChoice( theItem );
                             break;
                     case STYLE_MENU_ID:
                             HandleStyleChoice( theItem );
                             break;
             }
             HiliteMenu( 0 );
     }
}


/******************************        HandleAppleChoice   ******/

HandleAppleChoice( theItem )
int     theItem;
{
     Str255        accName;
     int           accNumber;
     short int     itemNumber;
     DialogPtr     AboutDialog;

     switch ( theItem )
     {
             case ABOUT_ITEM :
                     NoteAlert( ABOUT_ALERT, NIL_POINTER );
                     break;
             default :
                     GetItem( gAppleMenu, theItem, accName );
                     accNumber = OpenDeskAcc( accName );
                     break;
     }
}
```

```
/*****************************          HandleFileChoice    *******/

HandleFileChoice( theItem )
int    theItem;
{
        switch ( theItem )
        {
                case QUIT_ITEM :
                        gDone = TRUE;
                        break;
        }
}


/*******************************          HandleFontChoice    *******/

HandleFontChoice( theItem )
int    theItem;
{
        int     fontNumber;
        Str255 fontName;

        CheckItem( gFontMenu, gLastFont, REMOVE_CHECK_MARK );
        CheckItem( gFontMenu, theItem, ADD_CHECK_MARK );
        gLastFont = theItem;
        GetItem( gFontMenu , theItem , fontName );
        GetFNum( fontName , &fontNumber );
        TextFont( fontNumber );
}


/*******************************          HandleStyleChoice   *******/

HandleStyleChoice( theItem )
int    theItem;
{
        switch( theItem )
        {
                case PLAIN_ITEM:
                        gCurrentStyle = PLAIN;
                        break;
                case BOLD_ITEM:
                        if ( gCurrentStyle & bold )
                                gCurrentStyle -= bold;
                        else
                                gCurrentStyle |= bold;
                        break;
                case ITALIC_ITEM:
                        if ( gCurrentStyle & italic )
                                gCurrentStyle -= italic;
                        else
                                gCurrentStyle |= italic;
                        break;
```

```
                if ( gCurrentStyle & underline )
                        gCurrentStyle -= underline;
                else
                        gCurrentStyle |= underline;
                break;
        case OUTLINE_ITEM:
                if ( gCurrentStyle & outline )
                        gCurrentStyle -= outline;
                else
                        gCurrentStyle |= outline;
                break;
        case SHADOW_ITEM:
                if ( gCurrentStyle & shadow )
                        gCurrentStyle -= shadow;
                else
                        gCurrentStyle |= shadow;
                break;
        }
    CheckStyles();
    TextFace( gCurrentStyle );
}


/*******************************        CheckStyles   *******/

CheckStyles()
{
        CheckItem( gStyleMenu, PLAIN_ITEM, gCurrentStyle == PLAIN );
        CheckItem( gStyleMenu, BOLD_ITEM, gCurrentStyle & bold );
        CheckItem( gStyleMenu, ITALIC_ITEM, gCurrentStyle & italic );
        CheckItem( gStyleMenu, UNDERLINE_ITEM, gCurrentStyle & underline);
        CheckItem( gStyleMenu, OUTLINE_ITEM, gCurrentStyle & outline );
        CheckItem( gStyleMenu, SHADOW_ITEM, gCurrentStyle & shadow );
}
```

Running Timer

Now that your source code is in, you're ready to run Timer. Select Run from the Project menu. When asked to "Bring the project up to date," click Yes. If you run into any compilation problems, consult the debugging tips found in the appendix. When asked to "Save changes before running," click Yes. Timer should now be up and running (see Figure 5.23).

Figure 5.23   Running Timer.

Timer should display the time in a window in the upper left-hand corner. The menu bar should display the 🍎, File, Edit, and Special menus. Desk accessories should work. The File Menu has just one option, Quit, which should be operational. The Edit menu contains the standard menu items but is dimmed. The Special menu contains two hierarchical menu items: Font and Style. If you select Font, the hierarchical Font submenu should be displayed (Figure 5.24a). If you select Style, the hierarchical Style sub-menu should be displayed (Figure 5.24b). Both hierarchical menus should show a check mark next to the currently used font and style. If you change the style or font with the menus, the appearance of the timer window should change appropriately. Selecting About Timer from the menu should bring up the alert that you just created. Click on the OK button (or hit return) to make the alert disappear.

Choose Quit from the File menu. Let's look at the code.

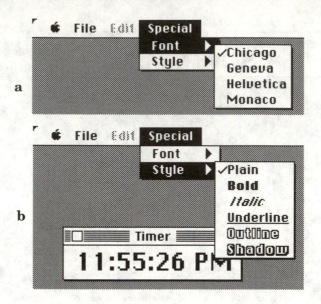

Figure 5.24   Timer hierarchical menus.

Walking through the Timer Code

Timer starts off with a set of #defines. The first global, gClockWindow, is the pointer to Timer's clock window. gDone and gWNEImplemented are the same as in Chapter 4's EventTutor. gCurrentTime and gOldTime are used to determine when to change the clock display. You'll use gAppleMenu when you add desk accessories to the   menu. You'll use gFontMenu and gStyleMenu when you add and remove check marks from the Font and Style menus. gLastFont is used to determine the current font number in use, gDragRect is the Rect used to limit the dragging area of the clock window, and gCurrentStyle contains the current style used by Timer.

```
#define BASE_RES_ID             400
#define NIL_POINTER             0L
#define MOVE_TO_FRONT           -1L
#define REMOVE_ALL_EVENTS       0

#define PLAIN                   0
#define PLAIN_ITEM              1
#define BOLD_ITEM               2
#define ITALIC_ITEM             3
#define UNDERLINE_ITEM          4
#define OUTLINE_ITEM            5
#define SHADOW_ITEM             6
```

```
#define INCLUDE_SECONDS            TRUE

#define ADD_CHECK_MARK             TRUE
#define REMOVE_CHECK_MARK          FALSE

#define DRAG_THRESHOLD             30

#define MIN_SLEEP                  0L
#define NIL_MOUSE_REGION           0L

#define WNE_TRAP_NUM               0x60
#define UNIMPL_TRAP_NUM            0x9F

#define QUIT_ITEM                  1
#define ABOUT_ITEM                 1

#define NOT_A_NORMAL_MENU          -1
#define APPLE_MENU_ID              BASE_RES_ID
#define FILE_MENU_ID               BASE_RES_ID+1
#define FONT_MENU_ID               100
#define STYLE_MENU_ID              101

#define CLOCK_LEFT                 12
#define CLOCK_TOP                  25
#define CLOCK_SIZE                 24

#define ABOUT_ALERT                400


WindowPtr       gClockWindow;
Boolean         gDone, gWNEImplemented;
long            gCurrentTime, gOldTime;
EventRecord     gTheEvent;
MenuHandle      gAppleMenu, gFontMenu, gStyleMenu;
int             gLastFont;
Rect            gDragRect;
Style           gCurrentStyle = PLAIN;
```

main() should be familiar. It calls ToolBoxInit(), WindowInit(), and SetUpDragRect(). The menu bar is then initialized in MenuBarInit(), and then MainLoop() is run:

```
/*********************************** main *********/
main()
{
  ToolBoxInit();
  WindowInit();
  SetUpDragRect();
  MenuBarInit();
  MainLoop();
}
```

`ToolBoxInit()` is unchanged:

```
/******************************** ToolBoxInit */

ToolBoxInit()
{
   InitGraf( &thePort );
   InitFonts();
   FlushEvents( everyEvent, REMOVE_ALL_EVENTS );
   InitWindows();
   InitMenus();
   TEInit();
   InitDialogs( NIL_POINTER );
   InitCursor();
}
```

`WindowInit()` has a few new lines in it. `gClockWindow` is created from the `WIND` resource, made visible, and set as the current port. Then, the standard text size is set to `CLOCK_SIZE`.

```
/******************************** WindowInit  */

WindowInit()
{
   gClockWindow = GetNewWindow( BASE_RES_ID, NIL_POINTER,
                                          MOVE_TO_FRONT );
   SetPort( gClockWindow );
   ShowWindow( gClockWindow );

   TextSize( CLOCK_SIZE );
}
```

`SetUpDragRect()` is the same as in Chapter 4.

```
/****************************** SetUpDragRect ********/

SetUpDragRect()
{
   gDragRect = screenBits.bounds;
   gDragRect.left += DRAG_THRESHOLD;
   gDragRect.right -= DRAG_THRESHOLD;
   gDragRect.bottom -= DRAG_THRESHOLD;
}
```

You now have an initialization routine called `MenuBarInit()`. `MenuBarInit()` starts off by calling `GetNewMBar()` to load the `MBAR` resource you created into memory. `GetNewMBar()` automatically loads the individual MENUs pointed to by the `MBAR`.

Then `SetMenuBar()` tells the system to use the `MBAR` handled by `myMenuBar` as the current menu bar. (The phrase, "xxx is handled by `myMenuBar`" really means that `myMenuBar` is a handle to xxx.)

```
/********************************         MenuBarInit    */
MenuBarInit()
{
  Handle         myMenuBar;

  myMenuBar = GetNewMBar( BASE_RES_ID );
  SetMenuBar( myMenuBar );
  gAppleMenu = GetMHandle( APPLE_MENU_ID );
  gFontMenu = GetMenu( FONT_MENU_ID );
  gStyleMenu = GetMenu( STYLE_MENU_ID );

  InsertMenu( gFontMenu, NOT_A_NORMAL_MENU );
  AddResMenu( gFontMenu, 'FONT' );
  InsertMenu( gStyleMenu, NOT_A_NORMAL_MENU );
  CheckItem( gStyleMenu, PLAIN_ITEM, TRUE );
  AddResMenu( gAppleMenu, 'DRVR' );
  DrawMenuBar();

  gLastFont = 1;
  HandleFontChoice( gLastFont );
}
```

After that, the globals gAppleMenu, gFontMenu, and gStyleMenu are
set to handle their respective MENU data structures. InsertMenu() is
called to add the Font hierarchical submenu to the Menu Manager's list of
available menus. The NOT_A_NORMAL_MENU parameter tells the Menu
Manager not to place the Font menu directly on the menu bar. AddResMenu()
adds the name of all resources of type FONT to the Font menu. Next,
InsertMenu() is called for the Style hierarchical submenu. A check mark
is placed next to the PLAIN item on the Style menu with the call to
CheckItem().You use the handle to the ⌘ menu so you can add desk
accessories to it via the call to AddResMenu(). All desk accessories are
resources of type DRVR. AddResMenu() looks for all resources of the
specified type (we specified DRVR) and adds the resource names found to the
specified menu.

Next, DrawMenuBar() draws the menu bar, and HandleFontChoice()
sets the current font to the first font on the Font menu.

MainLoop() is the same as in Chapter 4:

```
/******************************* MainLoop ********/
MainLoop()
{
  gDone = FALSE;
  gWNEImplemented = ( NGetTrapAddress( WNE_TRAP_NUM,
ToolTrap ) !=
                      NGetTrapAddress( UNIMPL_TRAP_NUM,
ToolTrap ) );
  while ( gDone == FALSE )
  {
        HandleEvent();
  }
}
```

HandleEvent() is very similar to the version in Chapter 4. Start by checking for the existence of WaitNextEvent() and then make the appropriate call. Then, switch on gTheEvent.what. nullEvents are handled by the routine HandleNull(). As usual, mouseDowns are handled by HandleMouseDown(). keyDown and autoKey events are handled by the same code. In either case, check to see if the command ⌘ key was depressed when the event occurred. If it was, convert the keystroke to a menu selection via MenuKey() and pass that result to HandleMenuChoice(). Finally, handle updateEvts by calling BeginUpdate() and EndUpdate().

Since updateEvts have a higher priority than nullEvt, it is imperative that you respond to every updateEvt by calling BeginUpdate() and EndUpdate(). If you didn't, the Window Manager would keep queueing updateEvts, thinking you hadn't received them, and no nullEvts would ever make it into the event queue. One type of event can prevent another from making it into the event queue because the queue is finite. If the queue is big enough for 20 events, and 20 updateEvts are pending, there's no room for even one nullEvt.

```
/************************************* HandleEvent     */

HandleEvent()
{
    char    theChar;

    if ( gWNEImplemented )
        WaitNextEvent( everyEvent, &gTheEvent, MIN_SLEEP,
                                        NIL_MOUSE_REGION );
    else
    {
        SystemTask();
        GetNextEvent( everyEvent, &gTheEvent );
    }


    switch ( gTheEvent.what )
    {
        case nullEvent:
            HandleNull();
            break;
        case mouseDown:
            HandleMouseDown();
            break;
        case keyDown:
```

```
case autoKey:
        theChar = gTheEvent.message & charCodeMask;
        if (( gTheEvent.modifiers & cmdKey ) != 0)
                HandleMenuChoice( MenuKey( theChar ) );
        break;
case updateEvt:
        BeginUpdate( gTheEvent.message );
        EndUpdate( gTheEvent.message );
        break;
    }
}
```

HandleNull( ) is called whenever a nullEvent is retrieved from the event queue. HandleNull( ) checks the current time (in seconds) and compares it to the last check performed. If the time has changed, the clock window is refreshed.

```
/****************************** HandleNull ********/

HandleNull()
{
    GetDateTime( &gCurrentTime );
    if ( gCurrentTime != gOldTime )
    {
            DrawClock( gClockWindow );
    }
}
```

DrawClock( ) calls the International Utility IUTimeString( ) to get the current time in a format suitable for display. Next, the window is erased, the pen is positioned, and the new time string is drawn. Finally, gOldTime is updated.

```
/****************************** DrawClock ********/

DrawClock( theWindow )
WindowPtr        theWindow;
{
    Str255          myTimeString;

    IUTimeString( gCurrentTime, INCLUDE_SECONDS,
  myTimeString );
    EraseRect( &( theWindow->portRect ) );
    MoveTo( CLOCK_LEFT, CLOCK_TOP );
    DrawString( myTimeString );
    gOldTime = gCurrentTime;
}
```

HandleMouseDown( ) is similar to its Chapter 4 counterpart. FindWindow( ) is called, returning a part code that indicates the part of the window in which the mouseDown event occurred. In addition, FindWindow( ) sets whichWindow to the window in which the mouseDown occurred.

If the `mouseDown` occurred in the menu bar, `MenuSelect()` is called, allowing the user to make a selection from the menu bar. The user's selection is passed on to `HandleMenuChoice()`.

The rest of the part codes are handled as they were in Chapter 4.

```
/********************************* HandleMouseDown */

HandleMouseDown()
{
   WindowPtr    whichWindow;
   short int    thePart;
   long int     menuChoice, windSize;

   thePart = FindWindow( gTheEvent.where, &whichWindow );
   switch ( thePart )
   {
        case inMenuBar:
                menuChoice = MenuSelect( gTheEvent.where );
                HandleMenuChoice( menuChoice );
                break;
        case inSysWindow :
                SystemClick( &gTheEvent, whichWindow );
                break;
        case inDrag :
                DragWindow( whichWindow, gTheEvent.where,
                        &gDragRect);
                break;
        case inGoAway :
                gDone = TRUE;
                break;
   }
}
```

`HandleMenuChoice()` takes a four-byte argument. The first two bytes contain the menu selected, and the last two bytes contain the item selected from that menu. First, `theMenu` is set to the first two bytes and `theItem` to the last two bytes. After that, `theMenu` is compared against the four `MENU` resource IDs to find which one was selected. A different routine exists for each of the four menus. When `MenuSelect()` was called, the selected menu title was left inverted. When you finish processing the menu selection, the menu title is uninverted with a call to `HiliteMenu( 0 )` (I:357).

```
/********************************* HandleMenuChoice */

HandleMenuChoice( menuChoice )
long int menuChoice;
{
   int    theMenu;
   int    theItem;
```

```
        if ( menuChoice != 0 )
        {
                theMenu = HiWord( menuChoice );
                theItem = LoWord( menuChoice );
                switch ( theMenu )
                {
                        case APPLE_MENU_ID :
                                HandleAppleChoice( theItem );
                                break;
                        case FILE_MENU_ID :
                                HandleFileChoice( theItem );
                                break;
                        case FONT_MENU_ID :
                                HandleFontChoice( theItem );
                                break;
                        case STYLE_MENU_ID:
                                HandleStyleChoice( theItem );
                                break;
                }
                HiliteMenu( 0 );
        }
}
```

HandleAppleChoice() handles all ⌘ menu selections. If the About Timer menu item is selected, the alert with resource ID = ABOUT_ALERT is drawn with NoteAlert(). Alerts are discussed in more detail in Chapter 6. Any other item selected is assumed to be a desk accessory. The name of the desk accessory is retrieved with GetItem(), and the desk accessory is opened with OpenDeskAcc().

```
/*************************** HandleAppleChoice  *******/

HandleAppleChoice( theItem )
int       theItem;
{
   Str255       accName;
   int          accNumber;
   short int    itemNumber;
   DialogPtr    AboutDialog;

   switch ( theItem )
   {
        case ABOUT_ITEM :
                NoteAlert( ABOUT_ALERT, NIL_POINTER );
                break;
        default :
                GetItem( gAppleMenu, theItem, accName );
                accNumber = OpenDeskAcc( accName );
                break;
   }
}
```

Because there's only one item under the File menu, the code for
HandleFileChoice() is pretty simple. The global variable done is set to
TRUE if Quit is selected. The value of gDone is checked every time through
the main loop. When gDone = TRUE, the program knows that it's time to
exit.

```
/************************    HandleFileChoice    *******/

HandleFileChoice( theItem )
int        theItem;
{
   switch ( theItem )
   {
        case QUIT_ITEM :
                gDone = TRUE;
                break;
   }
}
```

The Edit menu is in this application only to support desk accessories. All
items were dimmed when you created the MENU resource. Since you don't
care what happens as far as your application is concerned, you need not do
anything.

> Actually, we've only done half the job so far; although Timer allows
> the use of desk accessories, the cut, copy, paste commands are not yet
> supported. We'll add this in Chapter 7's WindowMaker program.

The Font menu is displayed when the Font item in the Special menu is
selected. The first CheckItem() call removes the check mark from whatever had been the last font selected. Then, the same call is used to place a
check mark on the newly selected font. Then, gLastFont is set to the
selected item number. Next, the GetItem() call returns the fontName for
the menu selection that you picked. GetFNum() provides the font number
given the fontName, and finally the ont of the text is changed with the
TextFont() call, given the font ID number.

```
/************************** HandleFontChoice    *******/

HandleFontChoice( theItem )
int        theItem;
{
   int    fontNumber;
   Str255 fontName;
```

```
        CheckItem( gFontMenu, gLastFont, REMOVE_CHECK_MARK );
        CheckItem( gFontMenu, theItem, ADD_CHECK_MARK );
        gLastFont = theItem;
        GetItem( gFontMenu, theItem , fontName );
        GetFNum( fontName, &fontNumber );
        TextFont( fontNumber );
}
```

The Style hierarchical submenu controls gCurrentStyle. When a style is selected, it must be checked against gCurrentStyle. If the style is currently in use, it must be removed, and vice versa. CheckStyles() is then called to update the check marks on the Style menu. Finally, TextFace() is called to implement the styles in gCurrentStyle.

```
/************************* HandleStyleChoice   ***/

HandleStyleChoice( theItem )
int        theItem;
{
   switch( theItem )
   {
           case PLAIN_ITEM:
                gCurrentStyle = PLAIN;
                break;
           case BOLD_ITEM:
                if ( gCurrentStyle & bold )
                     gCurrentStyle -= bold;
                else
                     gCurrentStyle |= bold;
                break;
           case ITALIC_ITEM:
                if ( gCurrentStyle & italic )
                     gCurrentStyle -= italic;
                else
                     gCurrentStyle |= italic;
                break;
           case UNDERLINE_ITEM:
                if ( gCurrentStyle & underline )
                     gCurrentStyle -= underline;
                else
                     gCurrentStyle |= underline;
                break;
           case OUTLINE_ITEM:
                if ( gCurrentStyle & outline )
                     gCurrentStyle -= outline;
                else
                     gCurrentStyle |= outline;
                break;
           case SHADOW_ITEM:
                if ( gCurrentStyle & shadow )
                     gCurrentStyle -= shadow;
                else
                     gCurrentStyle |= shadow;
                break;
```

```
        case SHADOW_ITEM:
                if ( gCurrentStyle & shadow )
                    gCurrentStyle -= shadow;
                else
                    gCurrentStyle |= shadow;
                break;
    }
    CheckStyles();
    TextFace( gCurrentStyle );
}
```

`CheckStyles()` steps through each item in the Style menu, placing a check mark next to those styles set in `gCurrentStyle`:

```
/******************************  CheckStyles   *******/

CheckStyles()
{
  CheckItem( gStyleMenu, PLAIN_ITEM, gCurrentStyle ==
        PLAIN );
  CheckItem( gStyleMenu, BOLD_ITEM, gCurrentStyle & bold);
  CheckItem( gStyleMenu, ITALIC_ITEM, gCurrentStyle &
        italic );
  CheckItem( gStyleMenu, UNDERLINE_ITEM, gCurrentStyle &
        underline);
  CheckItem( gStyleMenu, OUTLINE_ITEM, gCurrentStyle &
        outline );
  CheckItem( gStyleMenu, SHADOW_ITEM, gCurrentStyle &
        shadow );
}
```

That's it for our discussion of Timer. With this code, you should be able to add pull down and hierarchical menus to your programs. The last menu type, pop-up menus, are explored in the next program.

Zinger

Zinger opens a window on the desktop and implements a pop-up menu of numbers inside the window. When a number is selected from the pop-up, Zinger beeps that number of times and resets the value on the face of the pop-up to reflect this selection.

Zinger works like this:

- It initializes the Toolbox, window, and drag `Rect`.

- It initializes the pop-up menus, drawing the pop-up for the first time.

- It activates the pop-up menu when a `mouseDown` occurs in the menu rectangle, and redraws the pop-up when an `updateEvt` occurs.

- Finally, Zinger quits when the window's close box is clicked.

Since you've seen much of Zinger's code in previous chapters, we'll concentrate on the code that makes the pop-up menu work. Start by building a folder called `Zinger` for the project files.

Next, create a resource file called `Zinger Proj.Rsrc`. Then, build a resource of type `MENU` with ID = `400` and with the specifications in Figure 5.25 (see page 188). Build a `WIND` with the specifications of Figure 5.26 (see page 189). Now, start a new project called `Zinger Proj`, add `MacTraps` to it, and type in the following code:

```
#define BASE_RES_ID          400
#define NIL_POINTER          0L
#define MOVE_TO_FRONT        -1L
#define REMOVE_ALL_EVENTS    0

#define MIN_SLEEP            0L
#define NIL_MOUSE_REGION     0L

#define DRAG_THRESHOLD       30

#define WNE_TRAP_NUM         0x60
#define UNIMPL_TRAP_NUM      0x9F

#define POPUP_MENU_ID        BASE_RES_ID
#define NOT_A_NORMAL_MENU    -1

#define POPUP_LEFT           100
#define POPUP_TOP            35
#define POPUP_RIGHT          125
#define POPUP_BOTTOM         52
#define SHADOW_PIXELS        1
#define RIGHT_MARGIN         5
#define BOTTOM_MARGIN        4
#define LEFT_MARGIN          5
#define PIXEL_FOR_TOP_LINE1


Boolean       gDone, gWNEImplemented;
int           gPopUpItem = 1, gPopUpLabelWidth;
MenuHandle    gPopUpMenu;
EventRecord   gTheEvent;
Rect          gPopUpRect, gLabelRect, gDragRect;


/*********************** Main *************/

main()
{
      ToolBoxInit();
      WindowInit();
      SetUpDragRect();
      MenuBarInit();
      DrawPopUp();
      MainLoop();
}
```

```
/******************************* ToolBoxInit */

ToolBoxInit()
{
      InitGraf( &thePort );
      InitFonts();
      FlushEvents( everyEvent, REMOVE_ALL_EVENTS );
      InitWindows();
      InitMenus();
      TEInit();
      InitDialogs( NIL_POINTER );
      InitCursor();
}


/*********************WindowInit**************/

WindowInit()
{
      WindowPtr      popUpWindow;

      popUpWindow = GetNewWindow( BASE_RES_ID , NIL_POINTER,
                                              MOVE_TO_FRONT );
      ShowWindow( popUpWindow );
      SetPort( popUpWindow );
      TextFont( systemFont );
      TextMode( srcCopy );
}


/***************************** SetUpDragRect *********/

SetUpDragRect()
{
      gDragRect = screenBits.bounds;
      gDragRect.left += DRAG_THRESHOLD;
      gDragRect.right -= DRAG_THRESHOLD;
      gDragRect.bottom -= DRAG_THRESHOLD;
}


/*********************MenuBarInit**************/

MenuBarInit()
{
      gPopUpMenu = GetMenu( POPUP_MENU_ID );
      InsertMenu( gPopUpMenu, NOT_A_NORMAL_MENU );
      HLock( gPopUpMenu );
      gPopUpLabelWidth = StringWidth( (**gPopUpMenu).menuData );
      HUnlock( gPopUpMenu );
}
```

```
/******************** DrawPopUp **************/

DrawPopUp()
{
        SetRect( &gPopUpRect, POPUP_LEFT, POPUP_TOP,
                                POPUP_RIGHT, POPUP_BOTTOM );
        FrameRect( &gPopUpRect );

        MoveTo( gPopUpRect.left+SHADOW_PIXELS, gPopUpRect.bottom );
        LineTo( gPopUpRect.right, gPopUpRect.bottom );
        LineTo( gPopUpRect.right, gPopUpRect.top+SHADOW_PIXELS );

        MoveTo( gPopUpRect.left - gPopUpLabelWidth - RIGHT_MARGIN,
                    gPopUpRect.bottom - BOTTOM_MARGIN );
        HLock( gPopUpMenu );
        DrawString( (**gPopUpMenu).menuData );
        HUnlock( gPopUpMenu );

        gLabelRect.top = gPopUpRect.top + PIXEL_FOR_TOP_LINE;
        gLabelRect.left = gPopUpRect.left - gPopUpLabelWidth
                                - LEFT_MARGIN - RIGHT_MARGIN;
        gLabelRect.right = gPopUpRect.left;
        gLabelRect.bottom = gPopUpRect.bottom;

        DrawPopUpNumber();
}


/******************** DrawPopUpNumber **************/

DrawPopUpNumber()
{
        Str255 menuItem;
        int    itemLeftMargin;

        GetItem( gPopUpMenu, gPopUpItem, &menuItem );
        itemLeftMargin = ( gPopUpRect.right - gPopUpRect.left -
                                StringWidth( menuItem ) ) / 2;
        MoveTo( gPopUpRect.left + itemLeftMargin,
                            gPopUpRect.bottom - BOTTOM_MARGIN );
        DrawString( menuItem );
}


/**************************** MainLoop *********/

MainLoop()
{
        gDone = FALSE;
        gWNEImplemented = ( NGetTrapAddress( WNE_TRAP_NUM, ToolTrap ) !=
                            NGetTrapAddress( UNIMPL_TRAP_NUM, ToolTrap ) );
        while ( gDone == FALSE )
        {
                HandleEvent();
        }
}
```

```
/*********************************** HandleEvent    */

HandleEvent()
{
    if ( gWNEImplemented )
        WaitNextEvent( everyEvent, &gTheEvent, MIN_SLEEP,
                                NIL_MOUSE_REGION );
    else
    {
        SystemTask();
        GetNextEvent( everyEvent, &gTheEvent );
    }

    switch ( gTheEvent.what )
    {
        case mouseDown:
            HandleMouseDown();
            break;
        case updateEvt:
            BeginUpdate( gTheEvent.message );
            DrawPopUp();
            EndUpdate( gTheEvent.message );
            break;
    }
}


/*********************************** HandleMouseDown */

HandleMouseDown()
{
    WindowPtr       whichWindow;
    short int       thePart, i;
    long int        theChoice;
    Point           myPoint, popUpUpperLeft;

    thePart = FindWindow( gTheEvent.where, &whichWindow );
    switch ( thePart )
    {
```

```
                    case inContent:
                            myPoint = gTheEvent.where;
                            GlobalToLocal( &myPoint );
                            if ( PtInRect( myPoint, &gPopUpRect ) )
                            {
                                    InvertRect( &gLabelRect );
                                    popUpUpperLeft.v = gPopUpRect.top +
                                                    PIXEL_FOR_TOP_LINE;
                                    popUpUpperLeft.h = gPopUpRect.left;
                                    LocalToGlobal( &popUpUpperLeft );
                                    theChoice = PopUpMenuSelect( gPopUpMenu,
                                            popUpUpperLeft.v, popUpUpperLeft.h,
                                            gPopUpItem );
                                    InvertRect( &gLabelRect );
                                    if ( LoWord( theChoice ) > 0 )
                                    {
                                            gPopUpItem = LoWord( theChoice );
                                            DrawPopUpNumber();
                                            for ( i=0; i<gPopUpItem; i++ )
                                                    SysBeep( 20 );
                                    }
                            }
                            break;
                case inSysWindow:
                            SystemClick( &gTheEvent, whichWindow );
                            break;
                case inDrag:
                            DragWindow( whichWindow, gTheEvent.where, &gDragRect);
                            break;
                case inGoAway :
                            gDone = TRUE;
                            break;
        }
}
```

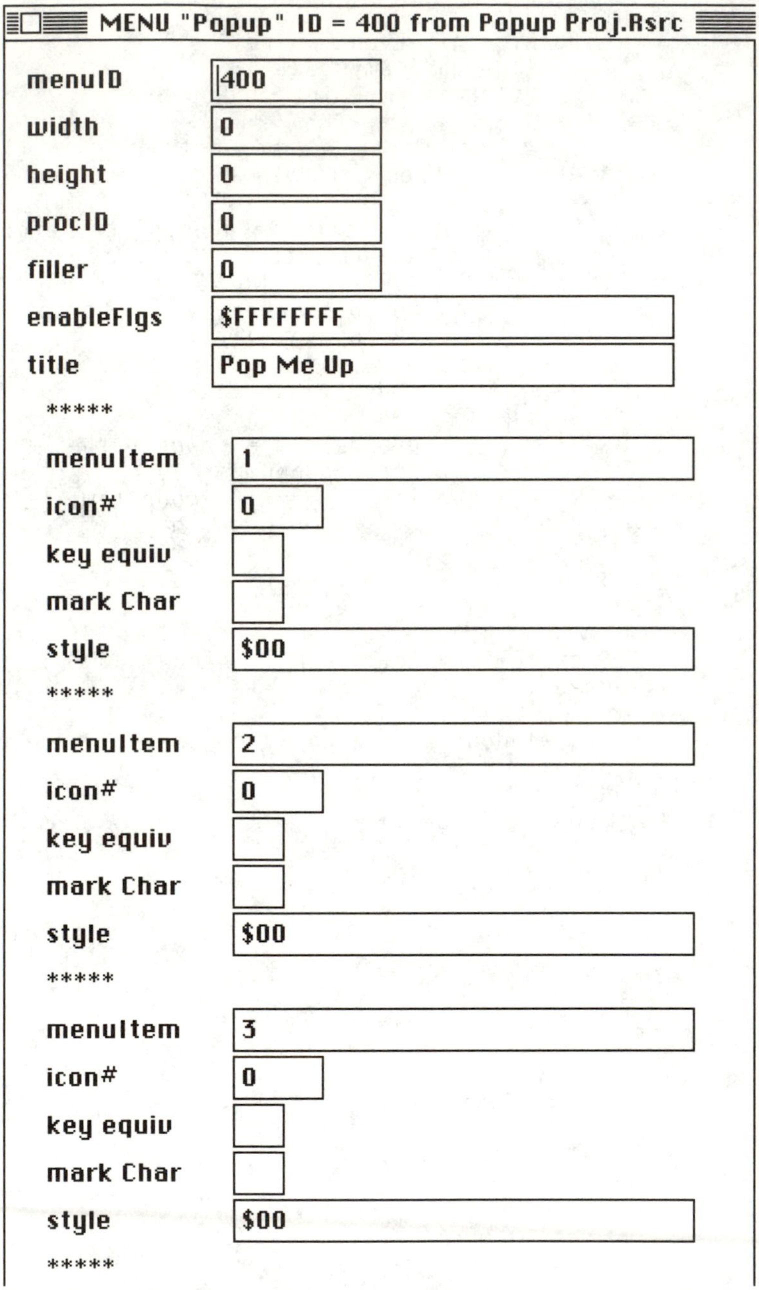

▣ ▤▤ MENU "Popup" ID = 400 from Popup Proj.Rsrc ▤▤

menuID	400
width	0
height	0
procID	0
filler	0
enableFlgs	$FFFFFFFF
title	Pop Me Up

*****

menuItem	1
icon#	0
key equiv	
mark Char	
style	$00

*****

menuItem	2
icon#	0
key equiv	
mark Char	
style	$00

*****

menuItem	3
icon#	0
key equiv	
mark Char	
style	$00

*****

Figure 5.25 Zinger MENU specifications.

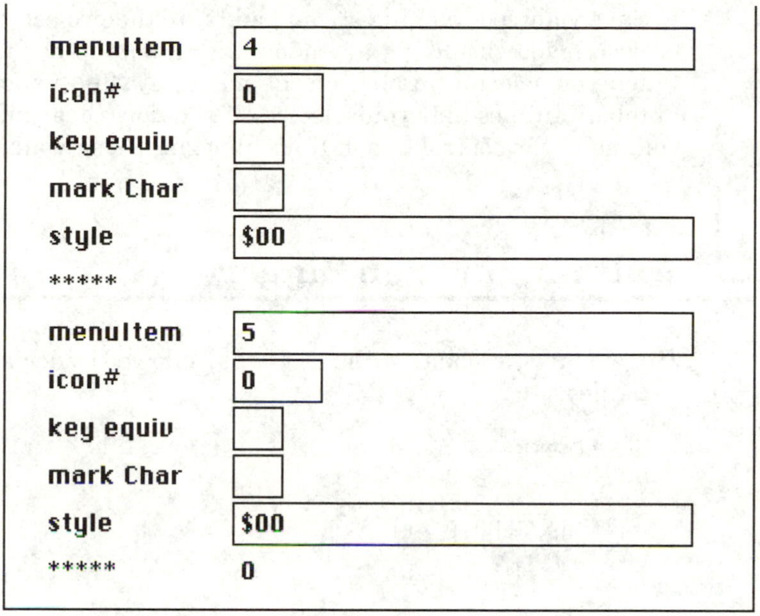

menuItem	4
icon#	0
key equiv	
mark Char	
style	$00

*****

menuItem	5
icon#	0
key equiv	
mark Char	
style	$00

***** 0

Figure 5.25 Zinger MENU specifications (*continued*).

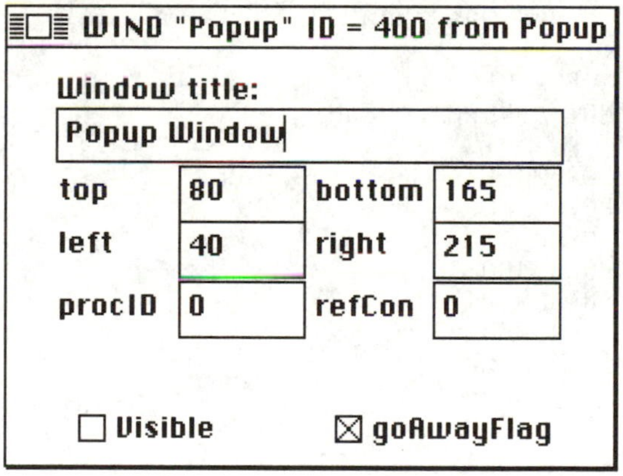

WIND "Popup" ID = 400 from Popup

Window title:

Popup Window

top	80	bottom	165
left	40	right	215
procID	0	refCon	0

☐ Visible   ☒ goAwayFlag

Figure 5.26 WIND resource.

Save your code as Zinger.c and add it to the project. When you run the program, you should get a window with a pop-up box in it (Figure 5.27). When you select a number on the menu, SysBeep should sound for the number of times that you selected. If you don't hear anything, check the volume in the control panel. If it's all right, check your code.

Walking through Zinger

Zinger starts, as usual, with #defines, followed by declaration of its global variables:

```
#define BASE_RES_ID            400
#define NIL_POINTER            0L
#define MOVE_TO_FRONT -1L
#define REMOVE_ALL_EVENTS      0

#define MIN_SLEEP              0L
#define NIL_MOUSE_REGION       0L

#define DRAG_THRESHOLD         30

#define WNE_TRAP_NUM           0x60
#define UNIMPL_TRAP_NUM        0x9F

#define POPUP_MENU_ID          BASE_RES_ID
#define NOT_A_NORMAL_MENU      -1

#define POPUP_LEFT             100
#define POPUP_TOP              35
#define POPUP_RIGHT            125
#define POPUP_BOTTOM           52
#define SHADOW_PIXELS 1
#define RIGHT_MARGIN           5
#define BOTTOM_MARGIN 4
#define LEFT_MARGIN            5
#define PIXEL_FOR_TOP_LINE     1


Boolean         gDone, gWNEImplemented;
int             gPopUpItem = 1, gPopUpLabelWidth;
MenuHandle      gPopUpMenu;
EventRecord     gTheEvent;
Rect            gPopUpRect, gLabelRect, gDragRect;
```

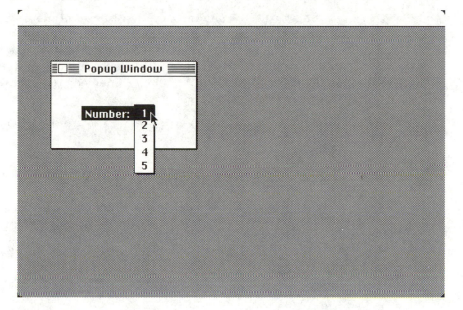

Figure 5.27 Zinger!

`main()` is much like its Timer counterpart, except that it calls `DrawPopUp()` before it enters the `MainLoop()`:

```
/*********************** Main *************/
main()
{
   ToolBoxInit();
   WindowInit();
   SetUpDragRect();
   MenuBarInit();
   DrawPopUp();
   MainLoop();
}
```

`ToolBoxInit()` remains the same as in previous incarnations:

```
/******************************** ToolBoxInit */

ToolBoxInit()
{
   InitGraf( &thePort );
   InitFonts();
   FlushEvents( everyEvent, REMOVE_ALL_EVENTS );
   InitWindows();
   InitMenus();
   TEInit();
   InitDialogs( NIL_POINTER );
   InitCursor();
}
```

`WindowInit()` may give you a sense of déjà vu, as well. The `popUpWindow()` is loaded, made visible, and made the current port. Next, the font is changed to `systemFont`, the same font used to draw the regular pull-down menus. The `srcCopy` text mode is used to simplify drawing of the pop-up menu item. With `srcCopy` enabled, text drawn in a window overlays existing graphics.

```
/**********************WindowInit**************/

WindowInit()
{
   WindowPtr      popUpWindow;

   popUpWindow = GetNewWindow( BASE_RES_ID , NIL_POINTER,
                                        MOVE_TO_FRONT );
   ShowWindow( popUpWindow );
   SetPort( popUpWindow );
   TextFont( systemFont );
   TextMode( srcCopy );
}
```

`SetUpDragRect()` is identical to the Timer version:

```
/***************************** SetUpDragRect *********/

SetUpDragRect()
{
   gDragRect = screenBits.bounds;
   gDragRect.left += DRAG_THRESHOLD;
   gDragRect.right -= DRAG_THRESHOLD;
   gDragRect.bottom -= DRAG_THRESHOLD;
}
```

In `MenuBarInit()`, just as you did with the hierarchical menus in Timer, you load the `MENU` and add it to the menu list via the call to `InsertMenu()`. Next, get the pop-up label from the menu data structure and calculate its width in pixels. You'll use this information later.

```
/**********************MenuBarInit**************/

MenuBarInit()
{
   gPopUpMenu = GetMenu( POPUP_MENU_ID );
   InsertMenu( gPopUpMenu, NOT_A_NORMAL_MENU );
   HLock( gPopUpMenu );
   gPopUpLabelWidth = StringWidth( (**gPopUpMenu).menuData
);
   HUnlock( gPopUpMenu );
}
```

DrawPopUp( ) will draw the pop-up outline, its one-pixel drop shadow, the pop-up label, and set gLabelRect, which you'll invert when the pop-up is selected. DrawPopUp( ) will also be called to handle updateEvts. After the background is drawn, call DrawPopUpNumber( ) to draw the current menu value—in this case, a number.

```
/******************** DrawPopUp **************/

DrawPopUp()
{
        SetRect( &gPopUpRect, POPUP_LEFT, POPUP_TOP,
                                POPUP_RIGHT, POPUP_BOTTOM );
        FrameRect( &gPopUpRect );

        MoveTo( gPopUpRect.left+SHADOW_PIXELS, gPopUpRect.bottom );
        LineTo( gPopUpRect.right, gPopUpRect.bottom );
        LineTo( gPopUpRect.right, gPopUpRect.top+SHADOW_PIXELS );

        MoveTo( gPopUpRect.left - gPopUpLabelWidth - RIGHT_MARGIN,
                    gPopUpRect.bottom - BOTTOM_MARGIN );
        HLock( gPopUpMenu );
        DrawString( (**gPopUpMenu).menuData );
        HUnlock( gPopUpMenu );

        gLabelRect.top = gPopUpRect.top + PIXEL_FOR_TOP_LINE;
        gLabelRect.left = gPopUpRect.left - gPopUpLabelWidth
                                - LEFT_MARGIN - RIGHT_MARGIN;
        gLabelRect.right = gPopUpRect.left;
        gLabelRect.bottom = gPopUpRect.bottom;

        DrawPopUpNumber();
}
```

DrawPopUpNumber( ) gets the menu item corresponding to gPopUp-Item, calculates the margin, and draws it:

```
/******************** DrawPopUpNumber **************/

DrawPopUpNumber()
{
        Str255 menuItem;
        int     itemLeftMargin;

        GetItem( gPopUpMenu, gPopUpItem, &menuItem );
        itemLeftMargin = ( gPopUpRect.right - gPopUpRect.left -
                                StringWidth( menuItem ) ) / 2;
        MoveTo( gPopUpRect.left + itemLeftMargin,
                            gPopUpRect.bottom - BOTTOM_MARGIN );
        DrawString( menuItem );
}
```

`MainLoop()` works as it did in Timer:

```
/***************************** MainLoop ********/

MainLoop()
{
     gDone = FALSE;
     gWNEImplemented = ( NGetTrapAddress( WNE_TRAP_NUM, ToolTrap ) !=
                         NGetTrapAddress( UNIMPL_TRAP_NUM, ToolTrap ) );
     while ( gDone == FALSE )
     {
          HandleEvent();
     }
}



/************************************ HandleEvent    */

HandleEvent()
{
     if ( gWNEImplemented )
          WaitNextEvent( everyEvent, &gTheEvent, MIN_SLEEP,
                                      NIL_MOUSE_REGION );
     else
     {
          SystemTask();
          GetNextEvent( everyEvent, &gTheEvent );
     }

     switch ( gTheEvent.what )
     {
          case mouseDown:
               HandleMouseDown();
               break;
```

When Zinger gets an `updateEvt`, it redraws the pop-up menu:

```
          case updateEvt:
               BeginUpdate( gTheEvent.message );
               DrawPopUp();
               EndUpdate( gTheEvent.message );
               break;
     }
}
```

If the mouse was clicked in the window, copy the Point, convert it to the window's local coordinate system, and check to see if it's inside `gPopUpRect`. If so . . .

```
/****************************** HandleMouseDown */

HandleMouseDown()
{
  WindowPtr     whichWindow;
  short int     thePart, i;
  long int      theChoice;
  Point         myPoint, popUpUpperLeft;

  thePart = FindWindow( gTheEvent.where, &whichWindow );
  switch ( thePart )
  {
        case inContent:
                myPoint = gTheEvent.where;
                GlobalToLocal( &myPoint );
                if ( PtInRect( myPoint, &gPopUpRect ) )
                {
```

. . . invert the label and use gPopUpRect to determine where the pop-up menu should appear. Since PopUpMenuSelect() works with global coordinates, call LocalToGlobal() to convert popUpUpperLeft. Next, call PopUpMenuSelect() to implement the pop-up menu. Then, uninvert the label. Finally, handle the selection by calling SysBeep() the selected number of times. gPopUpItem is set to the selected item number, so the next time the pop-up appears, gPopUpItem will be the default.

Some versions of Apple's system software experiences problems with the SysBeep() call. If you experience problems with Zinger, do not adjust your set. The problem may be with your system.

```
                InvertRect( &gLabelRect );
                popUpUpperLeft.v = gPopUpRect.top +
                                PIXEL_FOR_TOP_LINE;
                popUpUpperLeft.h = gPopUpRect.left;
                LocalToGlobal( &popUpUpperLeft );
                theChoice = PopUpMenuSelect( gPopUpMenu,
                        popUpUpperLeft.v, popUpUpperLeft.h,
                        gPopUpItem );
                InvertRect( &gLabelRect );
                if ( LoWord( theChoice ) > 0 )
                {
                        gPopUpItem = LoWord( theChoice );
                        DrawPopUpNumber();
                        for ( i=0; i<gPopUpItem; i++ )
                                SysBeep( 20 );
                }
        }
        break;
```

```
case inSysWindow:
     SystemClick( &gTheEvent, whichWindow );
     break;
case inDrag:
     DragWindow( whichWindow, gTheEvent.where, &gDragRect);
     break;
case inGoAway :
```

This is not the way "proper" Macintosh applications exit. You would normally use a Quit item in the File menu.

```
          gDone = TRUE;
          break;
     }
   }
```

In Review

Menus are an intrinsic part of the Macintosh interface. Designing them correctly allows the developer to take advantage of the familiarity of users with standard Mac menus. The standard pull-down menu does the job for many applications, and hierarchical and pop-up menus bring freshness to the interface.

In Chapter 6, you'll learn about another essential part of the Mac interface: creating and controlling dialog boxes. While you're there, you'll also look at one of the newest managers on the Macintosh: the Notification Manager.

Working with Dialogs

In a dialog box, the computer presents a list of alternatives for the user to choose from. Alerts are simplified dialogs, used to report errors and give warnings to the user. Chapter 6 discusses both of these, along with the Notification Manager, Apple's new background notification mechanism.

DIALOGS ARE AN important part of the Macintosh interface; they provide a friendly, standardized way of communicating and receiving feedback from the user. Some dialogs ask questions of the user, as in Figure 6.1. Others offer the user the opportunity to modify current program parameters (Figure 6.2). Some dialogs are the direct result of a user menu selection. For example, when you select **Print...** from within an application, the **Print Job dialog** appears (Figure 6.3).

Dialogs that appear as a direct result of menu commands give you a chance to change your mind (with the Cancel button), to continue on as planned (with the OK button), or to change things around a bit before continuing.

> By convention, menu items that spawn dialog boxes always end with an ellipsis (...). For example, the Print... item on the File menu brings up a print dialog box.

Another important part of the Mac Interface is the **alert mechanism**. **Alerts** (Figure 6.4) are simplified dialogs, used to report errors and give warnings to the user. From a programmer's point of view, alerts are easier to deal with than dialogs, so we'll use them when we can.

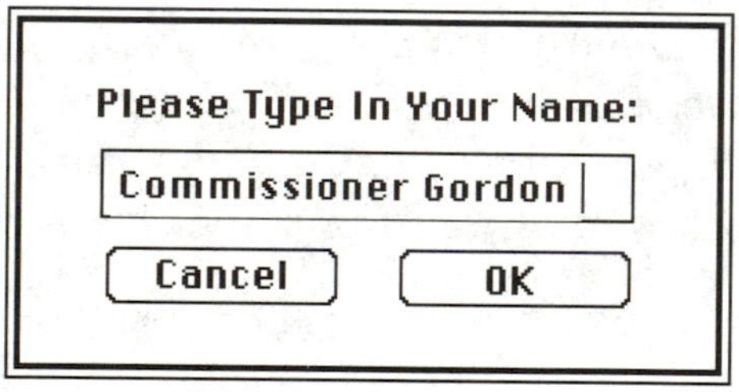

Figure 6.1 "What's Your Name?" dialog box.

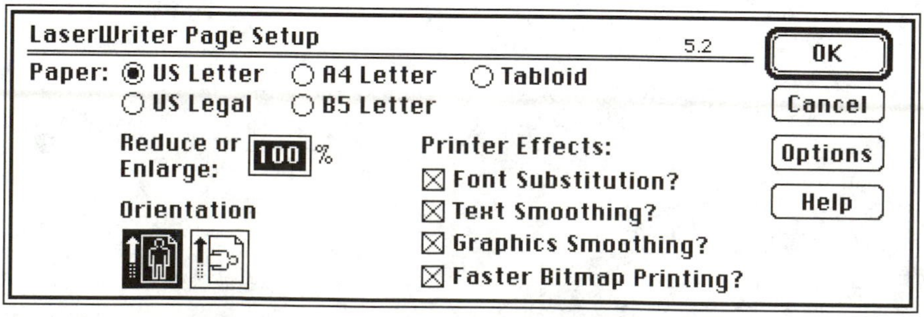

Figure 6.2 Page Setup dialog box.

LaserWriter "LaserWriter" 5.2	OK

Figure 6.3 Print Job dialog box.

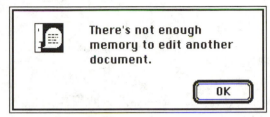

Figure 6.4 An Alert!

Chapter 6 also presents the Notification Manager, Apple's newest addition to the Toolbox. The Notification Manager is designed to work with MultiFinder, so that a program not currently in the foreground has a way of notifying the user of an important event.

How Dialogs Work

Dialog boxes consist of a window and a list of dialog items. When the dialog first appears, each item on the dialog item list is drawn. Typical dialog items include check boxes, radio buttons, and push buttons. These items are called controls. In addition, static text fields, editable text fields, PICTs, and ICONs may also be part of an item list (Figure 6.5). Every dialog box has at least one exit item (by convention, most dialog boxes offer an OK button for this purpose). There are two different kinds of dialogs: modal dialogs and modeless dialogs.

Modal Dialogs

A **modal dialog** is one to which the user must respond before the program can continue. Modal dialogs are used for decisions that must be made immediately. They represent the vast majority of dialog boxes.

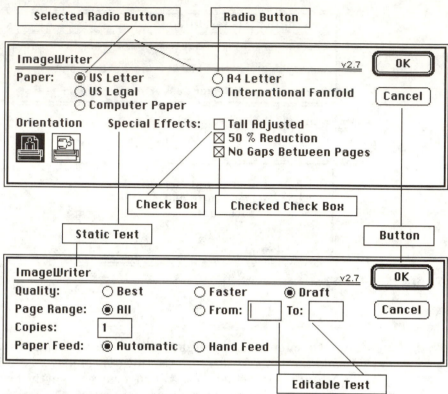

Figure 6.5 Dialog items.

The Macintosh is generally a modeless machine. This means that most of the operations performed by an application are available to the user most of the time. For example, most of the operations performed by THINK C are available via pull-down menus. Modal dialogs come into play when you must focus the user's attention on a specific task or issue. Alerts are always modal. Dialog boxes aren't always modal.

Modeless Dialogs

Modeless dialogs act more like regular windows; they appear to the user like any other window and can be brought to the front with a mouse click, or even dragged around the screen. Whereas modal dialogs require an immediate response from the user, modeless dialogs may be set aside until they are needed. The algorithms used to implement modal and modeless dialogs are quite different.

The Modal Dialog Algorithm

- First, load the dialog (including the dialog's item list) from the resource file using `GetNewDialog()`.
- Then, make the dialog window visible (just as you would a new window).
- Next, enter a loop, first calling `ModalDialog()` to find out which item the user selected, then processing that item. When an exit item (like OK or Cancel) is selected, exit the loop.

The Modeless Dialog Algorithm

- First, load the dialog and make it visible (as was done with the modal dialog).
- As an event is returned by `GetNextEvent()` or `WaitNextEvent()`, pass it on to `IsDialogEvent()`.
- If `IsDialogEvent()` returns `FALSE`, the event is not related to the dialog and should be handled normally. Otherwise, the event should be passed to `DialogSelect()`.
- `DialogSelect()` returns a pointer to the dialog box whose item was selected, as well as the number of the item selected by the user. Process the item as you would with `ModalDialog()`.

Let's look at the types of items found in dialogs.

Dialog Items: Controls

One of the most important types of dialog items is the control. **Controls** are items that exist in at least two different states. For example, the check box can be checked or unchecked (Figure 6.6). Although controls may be defined by the program designer, four controls are already defined in the Toolbox. They are: **buttons**, **check boxes**, **radio buttons**, and **dials**.

These controls fall under the jurisdiction of the **Control Manager**, which handles the creation, editing, and use of controls.

Figure 6.6 The Checkbox.

Buttons

The classic example of a button is the OK button found in most dialog boxes (Figure 6.7). When the mouse button is released with the cursor inside the button, the button's action is performed. For example, clicking an OK button might start a print job or save an application's data. Those of you who are familiar with HyperCard should note the similarity of HyperCard buttons to Toolbox buttons. Toolbox buttons are generally rounded-corner rectangles, whereas HyperCard buttons have more variation in shape and appearance.

Check Boxes

Check boxes are generally used to set options or arguments of an action. For example, you might use a check box to determine whether the user wants sound turned on or off in an application (Figure 6.8).

Radio Buttons

Radio buttons are similar to check boxes in function, in that they also are used to set options or choices in a dialog box. Figure 6.9 shows some radio buttons. The difference between radio buttons and check boxes is that the choices displayed in radio buttons are mutually exclusive. Radio buttons appear in sets, and one and only one radio button in a set may be on (or highlighted) at any given time (Figure 6.10).

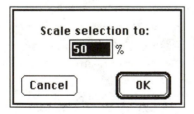

Figure 6.7   The Button.

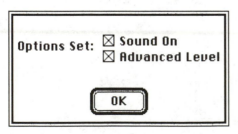

Figure 6.8   Check box example.

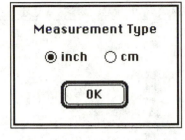

Figure 6.9 Radio button example.

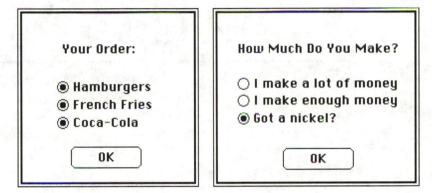

Wrong Way: radio buttons
should indicate mutually
exclusive options.

Right Way: Only one of the
options would reasonably
be picked.

Figure 6.10 Radio button pointers.

Dials

Dials are different from other controls: They display and supply qualitative instead of off/on information. The only dial controls predefined in the Toolbox are **scroll bars** (Figure 6.11), which are an integral part of many Mac application windows. In Chapter 7, we'll show you how to set up a scroll bar.

Figure 6.11 Scroll bar example (from Pager in Chapter 7).

Other Dialog Items

Controls are only one type of item used in dialogs. You can also display PICTs and ICONs in dialog boxes. You can also add static and editable text fields, as well as user items, to your dialogs (Figure 6.12). User items designate an area of the dialog box that will be drawn in by a userItem procedure. If the procedure draws outside the user item Rect, the drawing is clipped. For example, you can define a clock-drawing procedure that gets updated each time ModalDialog() is called.

ResEdit makes it easy to define dialog item lists. Figure 6.13 shows how ResEdit allows you to graphically edit the appearance of a dialog and the items within it.

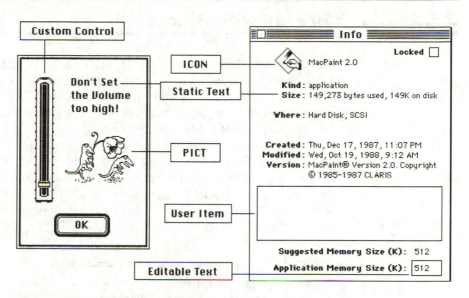

Figure 6.12 Other dialog items.

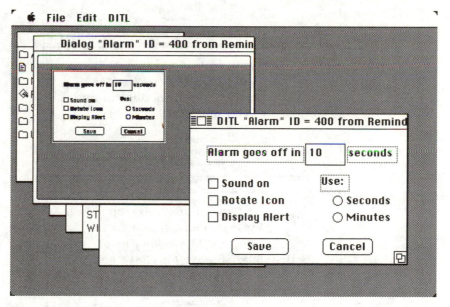

Figure 6.13 Making dialogs (in ResEdit).

Working with Alerts

Alerts are very much like dialogs: You build them using ResEdit, and they consist of a window and a dialog item list. But there are some differences. Alerts are completely self contained. While `ModalDialog()` is called repeatedly inside a loop, the alert procedures are called once. Each alert routine takes care of its own housekeeping.

There are three standard types of alerts: stop alerts, note alerts, and caution alerts (Figure 6.14). **Stop alerts** indicate a critical situation, like a fatal error, that must be brought to the user's attention. **Note alerts** have a more informative tone. **Caution alerts** tell the user that the next step taken should be considered carefully, as it may lead to unexpected results.

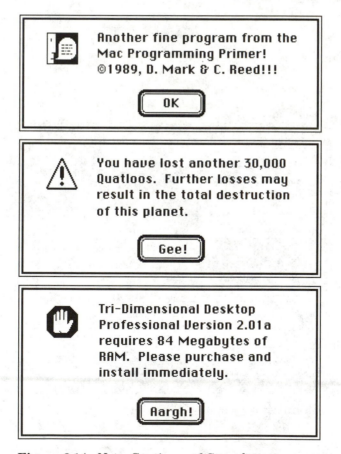

Figure 6.14 Note, Caution, and Stop alerts.

Each alert exists in stages. The first time an alert is presented, it is a stage 1 alert; the second time, a stage 2 alert; the third time, a stage 3 alert; the fourth and subsequent times, a stage 4 alert. You can design your alerts so that stage 1 alerts are silent but stage 2, 3, and 4 alerts beep when the alert is presented. You can also specify whether or not the alert is presented at different stages.

The Alert Algorithm

Working with alerts is easy. Build your alert with ResEdit by creating an `ALRT` and a `DITL`. Unlike regular dialogs, the only type of control you should put in your alert dialog item list is a button.

- Load and present the alert with a call to `StopAlert()`, `NoteAlert()`, or `CautionAlert()`.
- Use the value returned from each of these functions to determine which item was hit (i.e., which button was pressed).

Adding Dialogs to Your Programs

In this chapter, we'll show you how to build modal dialog boxes and alerts through the use of `DLOG` and `DITL` resources. Although we could create the dialog structure in THINK C instead, we choose to emphasize the resource-based approach.

As we stated in the dialog algorithm, to put a dialog box in your application, you do the following things: (1) initialize the Dialog Manager and get your dialog box resources; (2) call `ModalDialog()`; and (3) respond to the events that occur in the dialog box window.

Here's an outline of the procedure. First, initialize the Dialog Manager:

```
InitDialogs( NIL_POINTER );
```

Then, load a dialog from your resource file with the `GetNewDialog()` routine:

```
myDialog = GetNewDialog( resource ID,
  NIL_POINTER, MOVE_TO_FRONT );
```

Now, initialize each of your controls. Each control has a unique item number, defined in the DITL resource (Figure 6.15.). Use GetDItem() to get a handle to each control item in the dialog box; then use SetCtlValue() to set the buttons, radio buttons, and check boxes to their initial values. For example, the following routine will fill the first radio button and clear the second radio button in a dialog box:

```
#define FIRST_RADIO    2
#define SECOND_RADIO   3
#define ON             1
#define OFF            0

GetDItem( myDialog, FIRST_RADIO, &itemType, &itemHandle,
    &itemRect );
SetCtlValue( itemHandle, ON );
GetDItem( myDialog, SECOND_RADIO, &itemType, &itemHandle,
    &itemRect );
SetCtlValue( itemHandle, OFF );
```

FIRST_RADIO and SECOND_RADIO are the radio button item numbers defined in the DITL resource. The first radio button will be set to ON, the second to OFF (Figure 6.16).

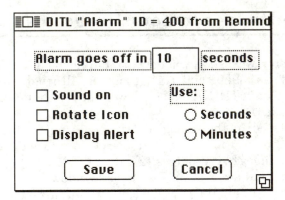

Figure 6.15   A sample DITL.

Figure 6.16   Radio buttons #1 and #2.

Here's an example of initialization of a series of check boxes. This code fragment clears the first check box and checks the second and third check boxes (Figure 6.17).

```
#define FIRST_CHECKBOX      4
#define SECOND_CHECKBOX     5
#define THIRD_CHECKBOX      6

#define ON                  1
#define OFF                 0

GetDItem( myDialog, FIRST_CHECKBOX, &itemType,
    &itemHandle, &itemRect );
SetCtlValue( itemHandle, OFF );
GetDItem( myDialog, SECOND_CHECKBOX, &itemType,
    &itemHandle, &itemRect );
SetCtlValue( itemHandle, ON );
GetDItem( myDialog, THIRD_CHECKBOX, &itemType,
    &itemHandle, &itemRect );
SetCtlValue( itemHandle, ON );
```

If you plan on drawing in the dialog box with QuickDraw (which you might want to do with a userItem procedure), make it the current port:

```
SetPort( myDialog );
```

> When you create your DLOG in ResEdit, make sure the Visible box is unchecked. That way, if you load your dialog at the beginning of your program, it won't appear until you're ready.

Figure 6.17   Three check boxes.

Make the dialog visible by calling ShowWindow(). You're now ready to call ModalDialog() to handle the events that occur in the dialog window.

```
dialogDone = FALSE;
ShowWindow( myDialog );
while ( dialogDone == FALSE )
{
  ModalDialog( NIL_POINTER, &itemHit );
  switch ( itemHit )
  {
        case OK_BUTTON:
                dialogDone = TRUE;
                break;
        case FIRST_RADIO:
                HandleRadio( SECOND_BUTTON );
                break;
        .
        .
        .
        case THIRD_CHECKBOX :
                HandleCheck( THIRD_CHECKBOX );
                break;
  }
}
HideWindow( myDialog );
```

When the user clicks the OK button, the dialog loop exits and the dialog window is made invisible again.

If you 're dealing with more than one window, make sure you are aware of routines like SelectWindow(), which brings the window specified in the parameter to the front. You may also want to consider hiding your other windows while your dialog box is visible, then showing them when you drop out of the dialog loop.

Dialog items are either **enabled** or **disabled**. If an item is disabled, ModalDialog() will not report mouse clicks in the item. In general, clicking ICONs and PICTs in a dialog box has no special significance, so disable both of these types of items.

Static text fields are usually disabled, although you may change them in response to other events. For example, a timer might display the time in minutes or seconds, depending on the value of a set of radio buttons (Figure 6.18). If the Seconds radio button is clicked, the static text field could read Seconds. If the Minutes radio button is clicked, the static text field could be changed to read Minutes. Use the routines GetIText() and SetIText() to read and set the values of static text fields.

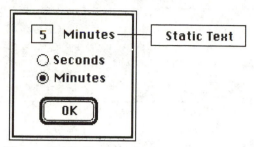

Figure 6.18 Static text.

ParamText() allows you to create a set of four default strings that can be substituted in your static text fields. To specify them, call ParamText() with four Str255s:

```
ParamText( "\pthe tiny republic of Togo", "\pporkpie
    hats", "\pbabar", "\pAltarian dog biscuits" );
```

From now on, whenever the strings "^0", "^1", "^2", or "^3" appear in a static text item, they will be replaced by the appropriate ParamText() parameter. We use ParamText() in Chapter 7's error handling routines.

You can store ParamText() strings in your resource file as resources of type 'STR ' or inside a single 'STR#' resource, read the strings in with GetResource() or GetString(), and then pass them to ParamText(). If, during the course of running your program, you decide to change the values of your strings, you can write them back out to the resource file with WriteResource(). This is a little tricky, but it gives you a great way to store program defaults. The mechanism for modifying resources is covered in *Inside Macintosh*, Volume I, pages 122-127.

GetIText() and SetIText() can also be used to modify the contents of an editable text field. Here's an example:

```
GetDItem( myDialog, TEXT_FIELD, &itemType, &itemHandle,
    &itemRect );
GetIText( itemHandle, &myString );
SetIText( itemHandle, "\pI've been replaced!!!" );
```

The last three arguments to `GetDItem()` are placeholders. That is, they won't always be used, but you always need to provide a variable to receive the values returned. In the previous example, `itemHandle` was used, but `itemType` and `itemRect` were not.

The Notification Manager

The Notification Manager contains calls that allow applications running in the background to communicate with the user. The Notification Manager was first implemented in System 6.0. Because the Notification Manager is not described in *Inside Macintosh,* we've provided the following tech block. We should warn you, though. that this is an experimental, highly classified, multipage Tech Block. Take your time. Remember, read *all* the directions before you start.

How the Notification Manager Works

The Notification Manager alerts the user that a background application requires the user's attention. The following notification techniques can be used. First, a small diamond-shaped mark (◆) may be placed on the notifying application's item in the menu.

Next, the small icon may be rotated with another icon (see Figure 6.19). Then, the user may be notified of the event by a sound designated by the background application. Finally, an alert can be displayed with a message regarding the event (see Figure 6.20). After the user clicks on the Alert button, a response procedure defined in the notifiying application can be called.

The Notification Manager will still run, even if your program is not running under MultiFinder. Since your program can't run in the background, however, the Notification Manager's functionality will be limited.

```
   ⌐  ⌘  File   Edit   View   Special
```

```
   ⌐  ♨  File   Edit   View   Special
```

```
   ⌐  ⌘  File   Edit   View   Special
```

Figure 6.19 Small icon rotation in the menu bar.

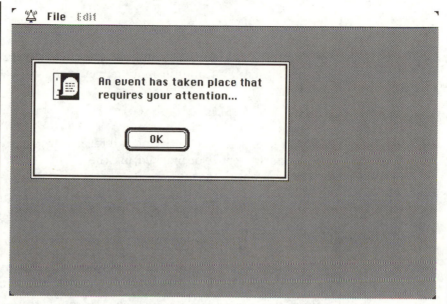

Figure 6.20   Alert message from the Notification Manager.

The Notification Manager Structure

Each call to the Notification Manager makes use of the NMRec data
structure:

```
typedef struct NMRec
{
  QElemPtr       qLink;        /* the next queue entry*/
  short          qType;        /* queue type          */
  short          nmFlags;      /* reserved            */
  long           nmPrivate;    /* reservedPoint       */
  short          nmReserved;   /* reserved            */
  short          nmMark;       /* Application ID to
                                    mark in Apple Menu */
  Handle         nmSIcon;      /* handle to small icon*/
  Handle         nmSound;      /* handle to sound
                                    record*/
  StringPtr      nmStr;        /* string to appear in
                                    alert              */
  ProcPtr        nmResp;       /* pointer to response
                                    routine            */
  long           nmRefCon;     /* for application use*/
} NMRec;
```

Here's an explanation of the `NMRec` fields:

- `qLink`, `qType`, `nmFlags`, `nmPrivate`, and `nmReserved` are either reserved or contain information about the notification queue; you won't adjust these values.

- `nmMark`: If `nmMark` is 0, the (◆) will not be displayed in the menu when the notification occurs; if `nmMark` is 1, then the application that is making the notifying call receives the mark. If you want a desk accessory to be marked, use the `refnum` of the desk accessory. Drivers should pass 0.

- `nmSIcon`: If `nmSIcon` is `NIL_POINTER`, no icon is used; otherwise, the handle to the small icon (`'SICN'` resource) to be used should be placed here.

- `nmSound`: if `nmSound` is 0, no sound is played; -1 will result in the system sound being played. To play an `'snd '` sound resource, put a handle to the resource here. The handle must be nonpurgeable.

- `nmStr` contains the pointer to the text string to be used in the Alert box. Put in `NIL_POINTER` for no Alert box.

- `nmResp` is a pointer to a response procedure that gets called once the notification is complete. We'll set `nmResp` to -1, which removes the request from the notification queue once the notification is complete.

There are only two calls in the Notification Manager. The first, `NMInstall()`, adds the notification request to the Notification Queue, which is checked periodically:

```
OSErr NMInstall( QElemPtr );
QElemPtr nmReqPtr;
```

The second, `NMRemove()`, removes the notification from the Notification Queue:

```
OSErr NMRemove( nmReqPtr: QElemPtr );
QElemPtr nmReqPtr;
```

The next section lists and describes Reminder, the biggest and most complex program in this book. Reminder will show you how to put together all the pieces we've talked about so far: windows, events, menus, fonts, dialogs, alerts, and the Notification Manager.

Reminder

Reminder sets a countdown timer and, when the time runs out, alerts the user of the event via the Notification Manager. Reminder also supports a dialog box that allows you to change some of its settings. Here's a quick look at the Reminder algorithm:

- It initializes the Toolbox.
- It checks for System 6.0 or later. If not, it puts up an alert and exits.
- It loads and initializes the settings dialog.
- It loads the , File, and Edit menus.
- It initializes the Notification Manager data structure.
- It handles events.
- If the Change Settings menu item is selected, it handles the settings dialog box.
- If the Start Countdown menu item is selected, it pulls the number of seconds from the settings dialog, loads and shows the countdown window, counts down, and sets the notification.
- If the Kill Notification menu item is selected, it removes the notification from the Notification Queue.
- If the Quit menu item is selected, it exits.

> Warning: This is the longest of all of the Primer programs. You can save a little time by using resources and code from Chapter 5, but it's still going to take a while. You may wish to take a brief recess.

Setting Up the Project

Start by creating your project files. You can save some time by copying your Timer folder from Chapter 5 and renaming it Reminder. But remember, if you do this, you'll need to change the source code file name, the project file name, and the resource file name. We'll assume you're starting from scratch.

Making the Resources for Reminder

Go into ResEdit and create a file named `Reminder Proj.rsrc`. Create a
`DITL` with the Get Info information shown in Figure 6.21. This `DITL` will
have eleven items. The table in Figure 6.22 lists the values for these items.
Next, create a `DITL` with the Get Info information shown in Figure 6.23.
You'll use this `DITL` in your About box alert. The About `DITL` has two items.
Create them from the table shown in Figure 6.24.

Finally, create a `DITL` with the Get Info information shown in Figure
6.25. This `DITL` belongs to the alert shown for a system earlier than Version
6.0. The Bad System `DITL` also has two items. Create them from the table
in Figure 6.26.

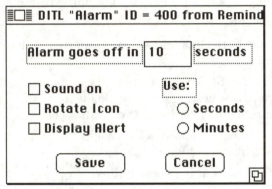

Figure 6.21 Settings `DITL` appearance.

Item#	Type	Enabled	top	left	bottom	right	Text/Resource ID
1	Button	Yes	130	50	150	120	Save
2	Button	Yes	130	160	150	220	Cancel
3	Static Text	Yes	20	20	40	138	Alarm goes off in
4	Editable Text	Yes	20	142	40	184	10
5	Static Text	Yes	20	189	40	249	seconds
6	Check Box	Yes	55	20	75	102	Sound on
7	Check Box	Yes	75	20	95	122	Rotate Icon
8	Check Box	Yes	95	20	115	130	Display Alert
9	Radio Button	Yes	54	157	74	192	Use:
10	Radio Button	Yes	75	170	95	247	Seconds
11	Static Text	Yes	95	170	115	249	Minutes

Figure 6.22 Item specifications for settings `DITL`.

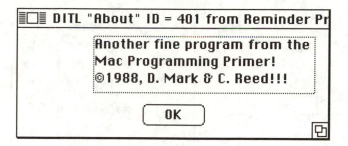

Figure 6.23 About box `DITL` Get Info window.

Item#	Type	Enabled	top	left	bottom	right	Text/Resource ID
1	Button	Yes	71	117	91	177	OK
2	Static Text	Yes	7	70	61	280	Another fine program from the Mac Programming Primer! ©1989, D. Mark & C. Reed!!!

Figure 6.24 Item specifications for About `DITL`.

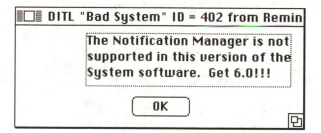

Figure 6.25 Bad system `DITL` Get Info window.

Item#	Type	Enabled	top	left	bottom	right	Text/Resource ID
1	Button	Yes	71	117	91	177	OK
2	Static Text	Yes	7	70	61	280	The Notification Manager is not supported in this version of the System software. Get 6.0!!!

Figure 6.26   Item specifications for Bad System `DITL`.

Create an `ALRT` resource with ID = `401` that matches Figure 6.27. This snapshot was made by selecting Display as Text from the `ALRT` menu that appears when the `ALRT` is opened. Don't forget to set the `itemsID` field to `401`. This links the `ALRT` to `DITL` `401`.

Next, create an `ALRT` resource with ID = `402` that matches the table in Figure 6.28.

You're now ready to create your Settings dialog box. Create a `DLOG` with ID = `400` that matches Figure 6.29. Remember to set the `procID` to 1. This tells the Dialog Manager to draw a classic modal dialog type window.

Next, we'll create two '`STR` ' resources to use in the Settings dialog. The first contains the default value to use when the time is displayed in seconds. The second contains the default value to use when the time is displayed in minutes. Figure 6.30a shows the value for '`STR`' `401`, and Figure 6.30b shows the value for '`STR`' `402`.

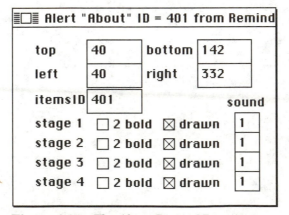

Figure 6.27   The About Box `ALRT`, displayed as text.

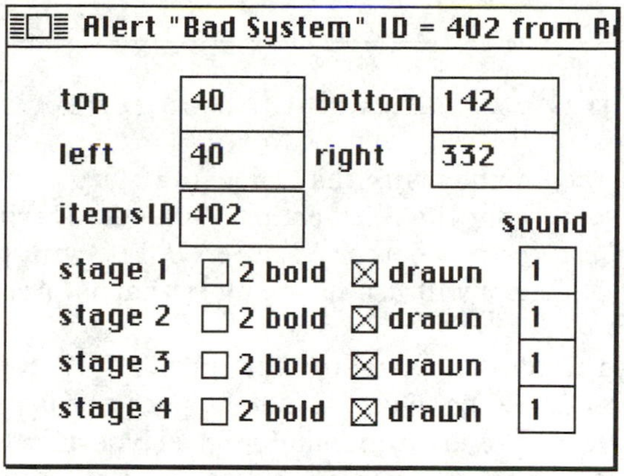

Figure 6.28 The Bad System ALRT, displayed as text.

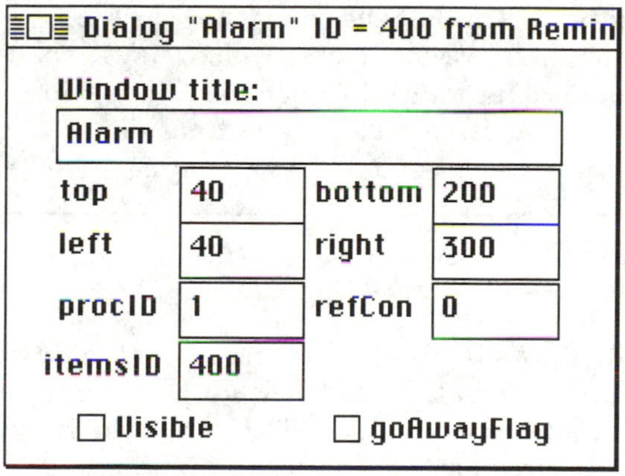

Figure 6.29 The Settings DLOG, displayed as text.

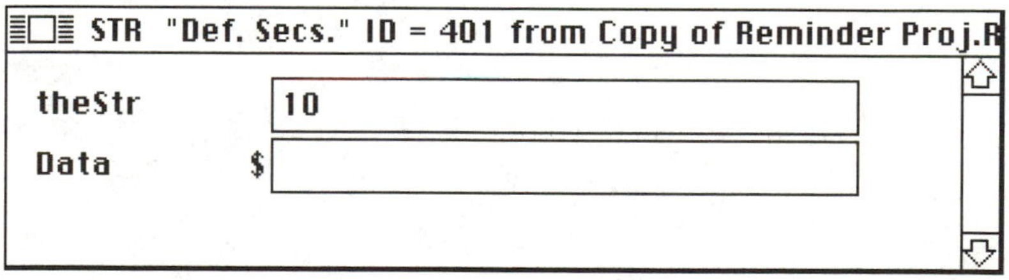

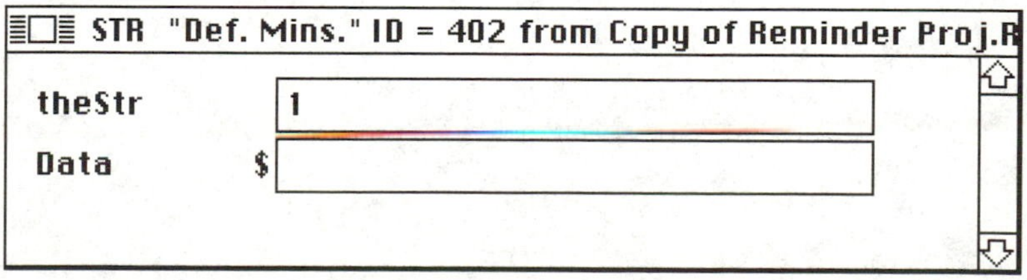

Figure 6.30 Default time 'STR' resources.

Setting Up the Notification Manager Resources

Now that you've finished with the dialog and alert resources, you need to add three resources for the Notification Manager: a string, a sound, and a small icon. First, create another 'STR' resource, with ID = 400, that the Notification Manager will use in the alert that is presented to the user (Figure 6.31).

Now, add the sound. There are a number of different sound resource types. The resource type to use is 'snd' (space at the end), with resource ID = 400. If you have a favorite sound from a HyperCard stack, you can cut it out using ResEdit and paste it into Reminder Proj.rsrc.

A good check on whether the sound will work properly is to use the play it option in the 'snd' menu, which shows when you are editing 'snd' resources. If that works, then the Notification Manager should be able to use it. If your 'snd' is a large file, you may have some problems. Start with a small 'snd' resource.

Figure 6.32 shows the 'snd' resources found in System 6.0.2. Open up the system file and copy the 'snd' of your choice into your Resource file if you don't have any other good sounds. Change the ID of the 'snd' to 400.

The final resource for the Notification Manager is the small icon that rotates with the menu icon. Ours is a little bell. Use it or create your own small icon. Create a resource of type 'SICN', with ID = 400. Figure 6.33 is a snapshot of our SICN editing session.

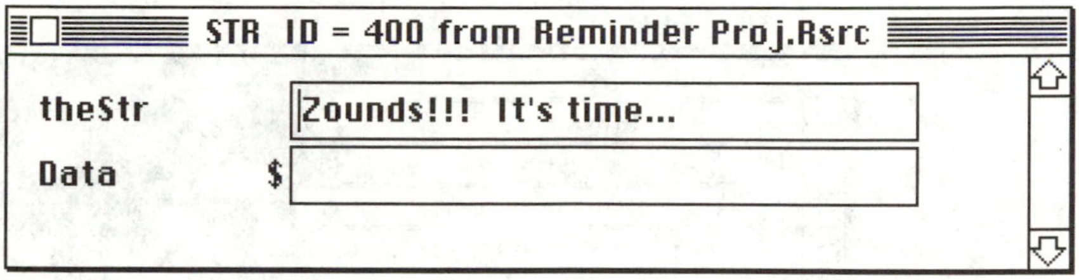

STR ID = 400 from Reminder Proj.Rsrc

theStr	Zounds!!! It's time...
Data $	

Figure 6.31 The 'STR' resource for the Notification Manager.

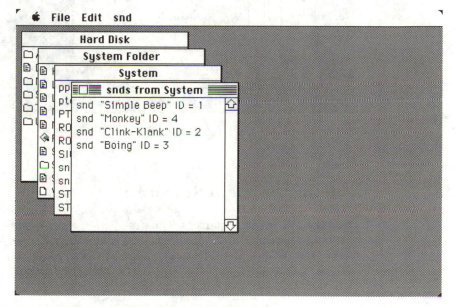

Figure 6.32 System 6.0.2 'snd' resources.

File
Edit
Hard Disk
THINK C
src
Reminder
Reminder Proj.Rsrc
SICNs from Reminder Proj.Rsrc
SICN ID = 400

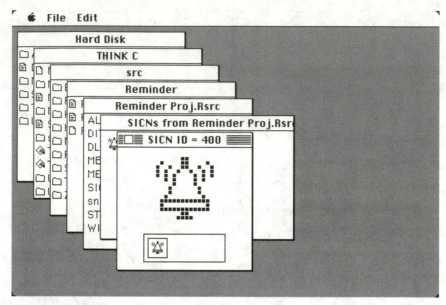

Figure 6.33 The SICN resource for the Notification Manager.

Adding the Menu Resources

Add the two menu resources. The first, MBAR, contains the three menu IDs (400, 401, and 402). Create a resource of type MBAR, with ID = 400 (Figure 6.34). Remember, to add a new menu to the list, click on the asterisks and select New from the File menu.

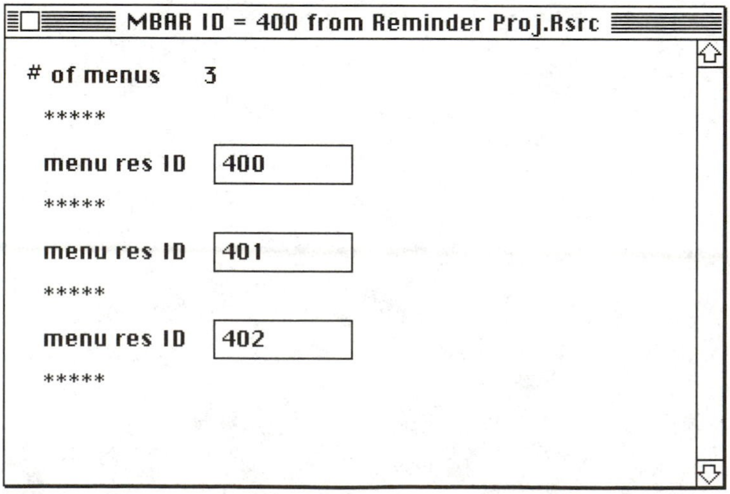

MBAR ID = 400 from Reminder Proj.Rsrc
# of menus 3
*****
menu res ID
400
*****
menu res ID
401
*****
menu res ID
402
*****

Figure 6.34 MBAR resource.

Now you need to create each menu with its items. Create the MENU, ID = 400, and make it look like the window in Figure 6.35. If you have trouble typing the symbol, open up an existing application and copy it from their MENU.

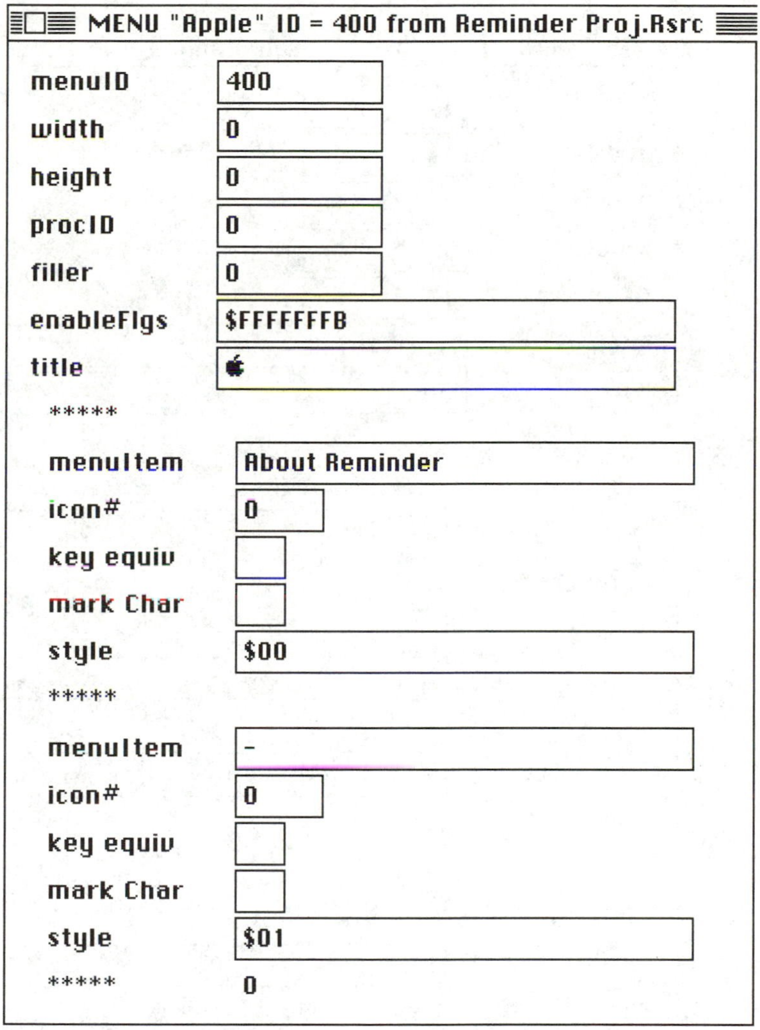

```
▤▢▤  MENU "Apple" ID = 400 from Reminder Proj.Rsrc  ▤

    menuID          400

    width           0

    height          0

    procID          0

    filler          0

    enableFlgs      $FFFFFFFB

    title           

        *****

        menuItem    About Reminder

        icon#       0

        key equiv

        mark Char

        style       $00

        *****

        menuItem    -

        icon#       0

        key equiv

        mark Char

        style       $01

        *****       0
```

Figure 6.35 MBAR resources.

Next, create the File MENU, ID = 401, and make it look like the window in Figure 6.36. Finally, create the Edit MENU, ID = 402, and make it look like the window in Figure 6.37 (see page 226). The Edit menu is disabled and is provided only as a courtesy for desk accessories.

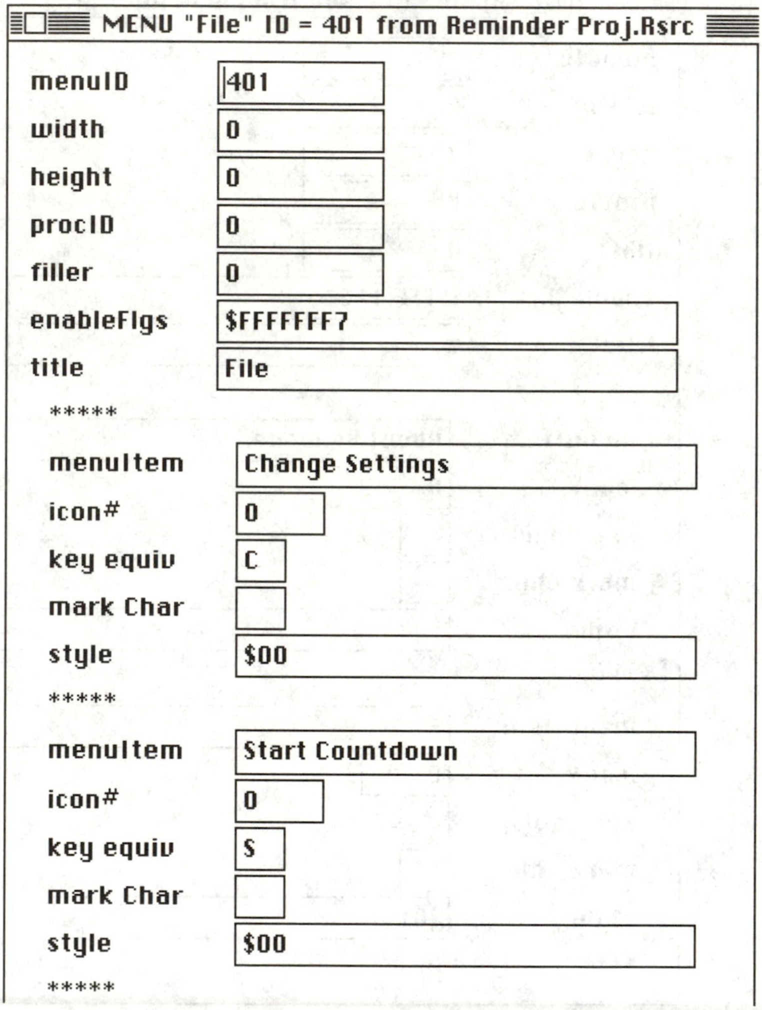

```
▓▢▤  MENU "File" ID = 401 from Reminder Proj.Rsrc  ▤

    menuID          |401
    width           0
    height          0
    procID          0
    filler          0
    enableFlgs      $FFFFFFF7
    title           File
       *****
    menuItem        Change Settings
    icon#           0
    key equiv       C
    mark Char
    style           $00
       *****
    menuItem        Start Countdown
    icon#           0
    key equiv       S
    mark Char
    style           $00
       *****
```

Figure 6.36   File MENU resource (stretched).

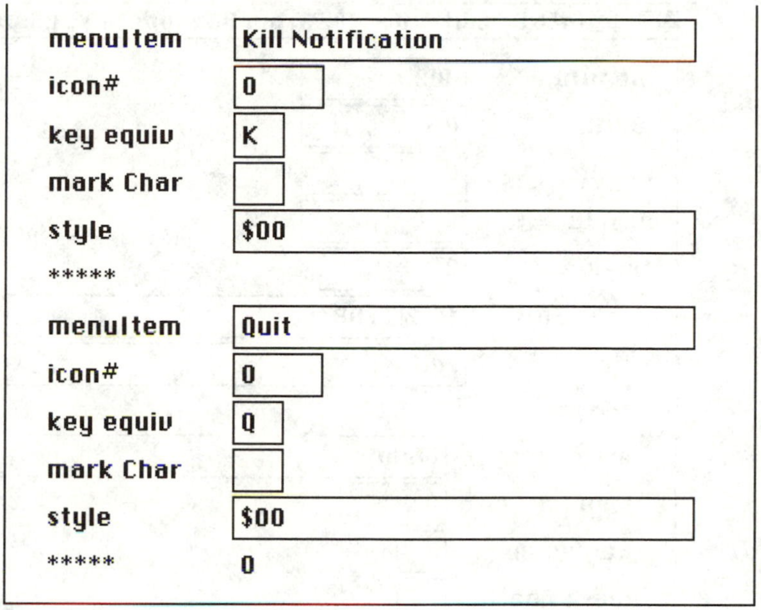

menuItem	Kill Notification
icon#	0
key equiv	K
mark Char	
style	$00

*****

menuItem	Quit
icon#	0
key equiv	Q
mark Char	
style	$00

***** 0

Figure 6.36 (*continued*)

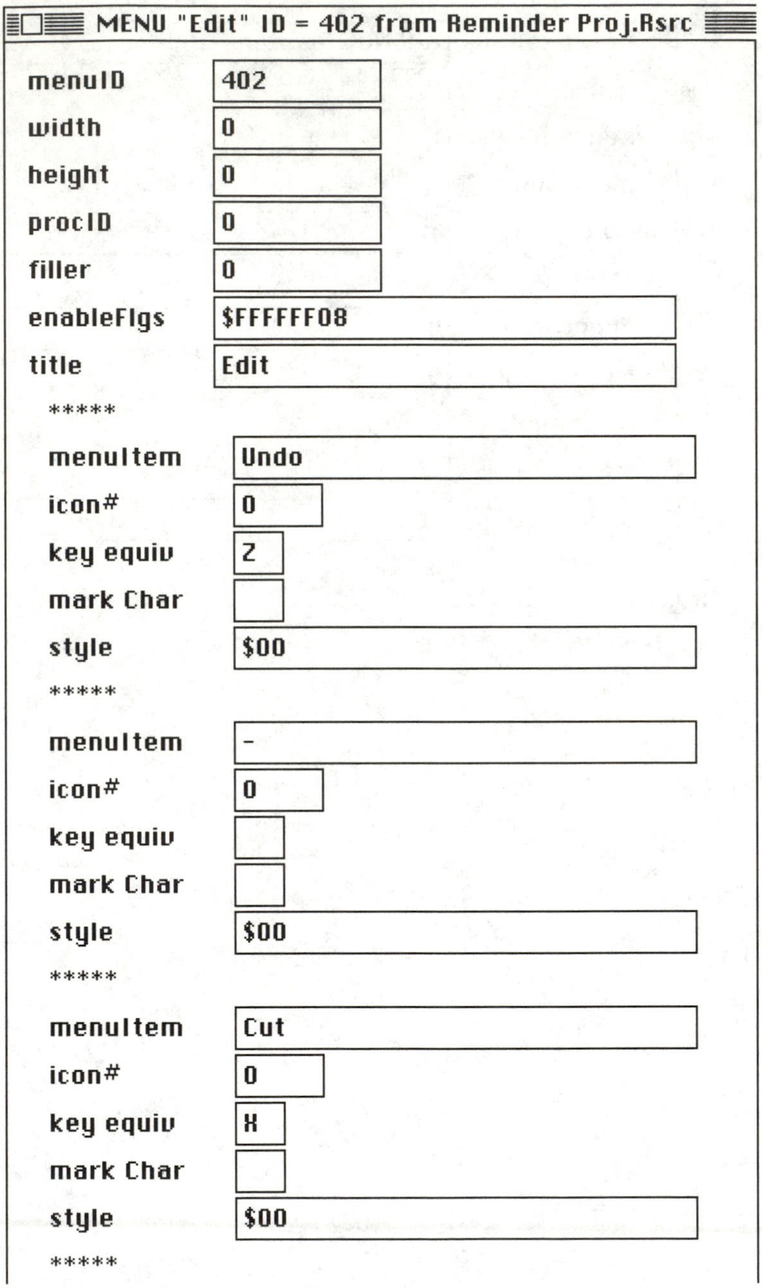

▤▯▤ MENU "Edit" ID = 402 from Reminder Proj.Rsrc ▤

menuID	402
width	0
height	0
procID	0
filler	0
enableFlgs	$FFFFFF08
title	Edit

*****

menuItem	Undo
icon#	0
key equiv	Z
mark Char	
style	$00

*****

menuItem	–
icon#	0
key equiv	
mark Char	
style	$00

*****

menuItem	Cut
icon#	0
key equiv	X
mark Char	
style	$00

*****

Figure 6.37   Edit MENU resource (stretched).

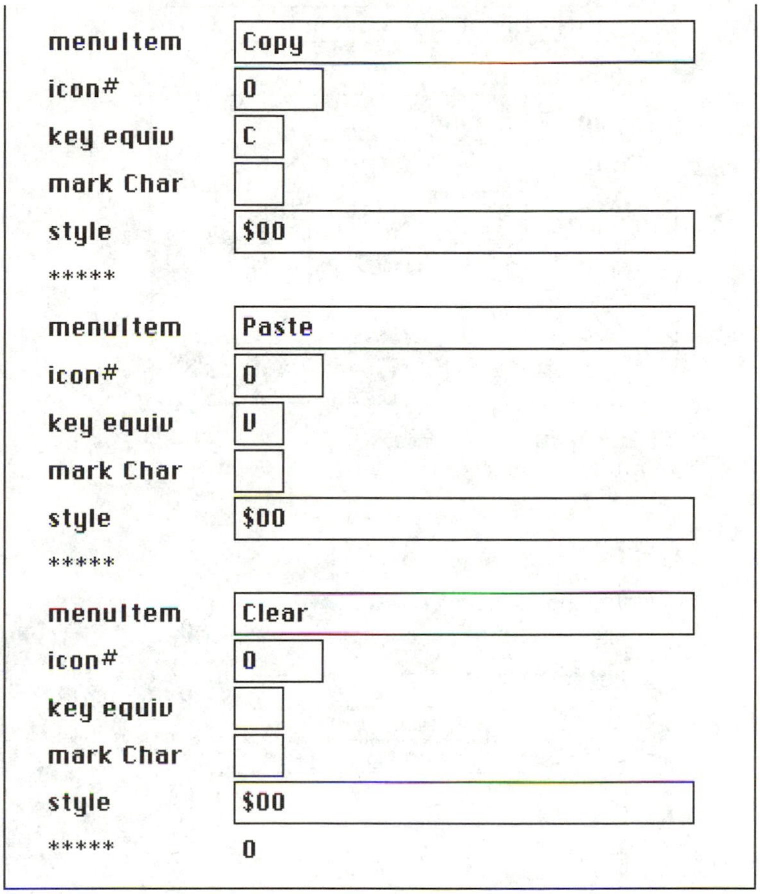

menuItem	Copy
icon#	0
key equiv	C
mark Char	
style	$00

*****

menuItem	Paste
icon#	0
key equiv	V
mark Char	
style	$00

*****

menuItem	Clear
icon#	0
key equiv	
mark Char	
style	$00

*****   0

Figure 6.37 (*continued*)

The Home Stretch

Finally, add the old `WIND` resource for your countdown window. Create a `WIND`, ID = 400, with the specifications in Figure 6.38. When you're done, save the resource file (whew!). Then, check it to see if you have all the resources listed in Figure 6.39. If you don't, go back and add them.

This is, by far, the biggest set of resources in the book. It is not uncommon at this point to start making mistakes (like mangling your motherboard and switching on the TV), so you might want to take a break before you start entering the code.

* * * * *

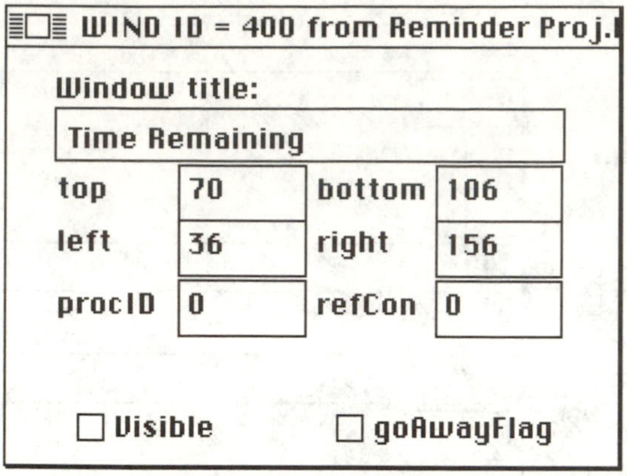

WIND ID = 400 from Reminder Proj.
Window title:
Time Remaining
top
70
bottom
106
left
36
right
156
procID
0
refCon
0
Visible
goAwayFlag

Figure 6.38 WIND resource for countdown window.

File
Edit
Hard Disk
THINK C
src
Reminder
Reminder Proj.Rsrc
ALRT
DITL
DLOG
MBAR
MENU
SICN
snd
STR
WIND

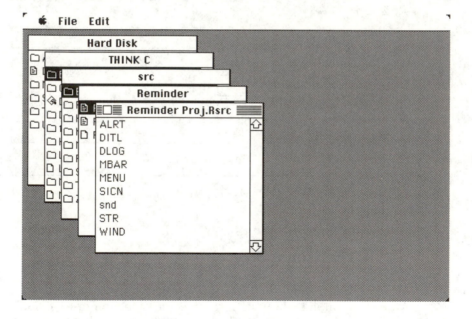

Figure 6.39 Reminder resources completed.

The Reminder Code

If you haven't done so already, go into THINK C, create a new project file named `Reminder Proj`, and add `MacTraps` to it. Next, create a new source code file named `Reminder.c`, and add it to the project as well.

Some of the Reminder code can be copied from Chapter 5's Timer. Just be careful with variable names and the like.

```
#define BASE_RES_ID          400
#define ABOUT_ALERT          401
#define BAD_SYS_ALERT        402
#define NIL_POINTER          0L
#define MOVE_TO_FRONT        -1L
#define REMOVE_ALL_EVENTS    0

#define MIN_SLEEP            0L
#define NIL_MOUSE_REGION     0L

#define DRAG_THRESHOLD       30

#define SAVE_BUTTON          1
#define CANCEL_BUTTON        2
#define TIME_FIELD           4
#define S_OR_M_FIELD         5
#define SOUND_ON_BOX         6
#define ICON_ON_BOX          7
#define ALERT_ON_BOX         8
#define SECS_RADIO           10
#define MINS_RADIO           11

#define DEFAULT_SECS_ID      401
#define DEFAULT_MINS_ID      402

#define ON                   1
#define OFF                  0

#define SECONDS              0
#define MINUTES              1
#define SECONDS_PER_MINUTE   60

#define TOP                  25
#define LEFT                 12

#define MARK_APPLICATION     1

#define APPLE_MENU_ID        BASE_RES_ID
#define FILE_MENU_ID         BASE_RES_ID+1
#define ABOUT_ITEM_ID        1

#define CHANGE_ITEM          1
#define START_STOP_ITEM      2
```

```
#define KILL_ITEM            3
#define QUIT_ITEM            4

#define SYS_VERSION          1


DialogPtr       gSettingsDialog;
Rect            gDragRect;
Boolean         gDone, gCounting, gNotify_set;
char            gSeconds_or_minutes = SECONDS;
StringHandle    gNotifyStrH, gDefaultSecsH, gDefaultMinsH;
NMRec           gMyNMRec;
MenuHandle      gAppleMenu, gFileMenu;
EventRecord     gTheEvent;

struct
{
        Str255 timeString;
        int    sound;
        int    icon;
        int    alert;
        int    secsRadio;
        int    minsRadio;
}   savedSettings;


/****************************** main ********/

main()
{
        ToolBoxInit();
        if ( Sys6OrLater() )
        {
                DialogInit();
                MenuBarInit();
                SetUpDragRect();
                NotifyInit();
                MainLoop();
        }
}


/******************************** ToolBoxInit */

ToolBoxInit()
{
        InitGraf( &thePort );
        InitFonts();
        FlushEvents( everyEvent, REMOVE_ALL_EVENTS );
        InitWindows();
        InitMenus();
        TEInit();
        InitDialogs( NIL_POINTER );
        InitCursor();
}
```

```
/****************************** Sys6OrLater ********/

int     Sys6OrLater()
{
        OSErr           status;
        SysEnvRec       SysEnvData;

        status = SysEnvirons( SYS_VERSION, &SysEnvData );
        if (( status != noErr ) || ( SysEnvData.systemVersion < 0x0600 ))
        {
                StopAlert( BAD_SYS_ALERT, NIL_POINTER );
                return( FALSE );
        }
        else
                return( TRUE );
}


/****************************** DialogInit ********/

DialogInit()
{
        int             itemType;
        Rect            itemRect;
        Handle          itemHandle;

        gDefaultSecsH = GetString( DEFAULT_SECS_ID );
        gDefaultMinsH = GetString( DEFAULT_MINS_ID );

        gSettingsDialog = GetNewDialog( BASE_RES_ID, NIL_POINTER,
                                                MOVE_TO_FRONT );
        GetDItem( gSettingsDialog, SECS_RADIO, &itemType, &itemHandle,
                                                &itemRect );
        SetCtlValue( itemHandle, ON );
        GetDItem( gSettingsDialog, SOUND_ON_BOX, &itemType, &itemHandle,
                                                &itemRect );
        SetCtlValue( itemHandle, ON );
        GetDItem( gSettingsDialog, ICON_ON_BOX, &itemType, &itemHandle,
                                                &itemRect );
        SetCtlValue( itemHandle, ON );
        GetDItem( gSettingsDialog, ALERT_ON_BOX, &itemType, &itemHandle,
                                                &itemRect );
        SetCtlValue( itemHandle, ON );
}
```

```
/********************************     MenuBarInit    */

MenuBarInit()
{
     Handle        myMenuBar;

     myMenuBar = GetNewMBar( BASE_RES_ID );
     SetMenuBar( myMenuBar );
     gAppleMenu = GetMHandle( APPLE_MENU_ID );
     AddResMenu( gAppleMenu, 'DRVR' );
     gFileMenu = GetMHandle( FILE_MENU_ID );
     DrawMenuBar();
}


/******************************** SetUpDragRect ********/

SetUpDragRect()
{
     gDragRect = screenBits.bounds;
     gDragRect.left += DRAG_THRESHOLD;
     gDragRect.right -= DRAG_THRESHOLD;
     gDragRect.bottom -= DRAG_THRESHOLD;
}


/******************************** NotifyInit ********/

NotifyInit()
{
     gNotifyStrH = GetString( BASE_RES_ID );
     gMyNMRec.qType = nmType;
     gMyNMRec.nmMark = MARK_APPLICATION;
     gMyNMRec.nmResp = NIL_POINTER;
}


/******************************** MainLoop ********/

MainLoop()
{
     gDone = FALSE;
     gCounting = FALSE;
     gNotify_set = FALSE;

     while ( gDone == FALSE )
     {
          HandleEvent();
     }
}
```

```
/********************************* HandleEvent    */

HandleEvent()
{
      char    theChar;

      WaitNextEvent( everyEvent, &gTheEvent, MIN_SLEEP,
                                     NIL_MOUSE_REGION );

      switch ( gTheEvent.what )
      {
            case mouseDown:
                  HandleMouseDown();
                  break;
            case keyDown:
            case autoKey:
                  theChar = gTheEvent.message & charCodeMask;
                  if (( gTheEvent.modifiers & cmdKey ) != 0 )
                        HandleMenuChoice( MenuKey( theChar ) );
                  break;
      }
}


/********************************* HandleMouseDown */

HandleMouseDown()
{
      WindowPtr     whichWindow;
      short int     thePart;
      long int      menuChoice, windSize;

      thePart = FindWindow( gTheEvent.where, &whichWindow );
      switch ( thePart )
      {
            case inMenuBar:
                  menuChoice = MenuSelect( gTheEvent.where );
                  HandleMenuChoice( menuChoice );
                  break;
            case inSysWindow :
                  SystemClick( &gTheEvent, whichWindow );
                  break;
            case inDrag :
                  DragWindow( whichWindow, gTheEvent.where, &gDragRect);
                  break;
            case inGoAway :
                  gDone = TRUE;
                  break;
      }
}
```

```
/********************************** HandleMenuChoice */

HandleMenuChoice( menuChoice )
long int      menuChoice;
{
      int     theMenu;
      int     theItem;

      if ( menuChoice != 0 )
      {
            theMenu = HiWord( menuChoice );
            theItem = LoWord( menuChoice );
            switch ( theMenu )
            {
                  case APPLE_MENU_ID :
                        HandleAppleChoice( theItem );
                        break;
                  case FILE_MENU_ID :
                        HandleFileChoice( theItem );
                        break;
            }
      }
      HiliteMenu( 0 );
}


/******************************       HandleAppleChoice    *******/

HandleAppleChoice( theItem )
int   theItem;
{
      Str255        accName;
      int           accNumber;
      short int     itemNumber;

      switch ( theItem )
      {
            case ABOUT_ITEM_ID :
                  NoteAlert( ABOUT_ALERT, NIL_POINTER );
                  break;
            default :
                  GetItem( gAppleMenu, theItem, accName );
                  accNumber = OpenDeskAcc( accName );
                  break;
      }
}
```

```
/*******************************          HandleFileChoice      *******/

HandleFileChoice( theItem )
int     theItem;
{
        Str255 timeString;
        long   countDownTime;
        int    itemType;
        Rect   itemRect;
        Handle itemHandle;

        switch ( theItem )
        {
                case CHANGE_ITEM :
                        HandleDialog();
                        break;
                case START_STOP_ITEM :
                        if ( gCounting )
                        {
                                SetItem( gFileMenu,theItem,"\pStart Countdown");
                                gCounting = FALSE;
                        } else
                        {
                                HiliteMenu( 0 );
                                GetDItem( gSettingsDialog, TIME_FIELD,
                                        &itemType, &itemHandle, &itemRect );
                                GetIText( itemHandle, &timeString );
                                StringToNum( timeString, &countDownTime );

                                DisableItem( gFileMenu, CHANGE_ITEM );
                                SetItem( gFileMenu, theItem,"\pStop Countdown");
                                CountDown( countDownTime );
                                EnableItem( gFileMenu, CHANGE_ITEM );
                                SetItem( gFileMenu,theItem,"\pStart Countdown");
                        }
                        break;
                case KILL_ITEM :
                        NMRemove( &gMyNMRec );
                        HUnlock( gNotifyStrH );
                        DisableItem( gFileMenu, KILL_ITEM );
                        gNotify_set = FALSE;
                        break;
                case QUIT_ITEM :
                        gCounting = FALSE;
                        gDone = TRUE;
                        break;
        }
}
```

```
/****************************** HandleDialog ********/

HandleDialog()
{
        int    itemHit, dialogDone = FALSE;
        long   alarmDelay;
        Str255 delayString;
        int    itemType;
        Rect   itemRect;
        Handle itemHandle;

        ShowWindow( gSettingsDialog );
        SaveSettings();

        while ( dialogDone == FALSE )
        {
                ModalDialog( NIL_POINTER, &itemHit );
                switch ( itemHit )
                {
                        case SAVE_BUTTON:
                                HideWindow( gSettingsDialog );
                                dialogDone = TRUE;
                                break;
                        case CANCEL_BUTTON:
                                HideWindow( gSettingsDialog );
                                RestoreSettings();
                                dialogDone = TRUE;
                                break;
                        case SOUND_ON_BOX:
                                GetDItem( gSettingsDialog, SOUND_ON_BOX,
                                        &itemType, &itemHandle, &itemRect );
                                SetCtlValue( itemHandle,
                                                ! GetCtlValue( itemHandle ) );
                                break;
                        case ICON_ON_BOX:
                                GetDItem( gSettingsDialog, ICON_ON_BOX,
                                        &itemType, &itemHandle, &itemRect );
                                SetCtlValue( itemHandle,
                                                ! GetCtlValue( itemHandle ) );
                                break;
                        case ALERT_ON_BOX:
                                GetDItem( gSettingsDialog, ALERT_ON_BOX,
                                        &itemType, &itemHandle, &itemRect );
                                SetCtlValue( itemHandle,
                                                ! GetCtlValue( itemHandle ) );
                                break;
                        case SECS_RADIO:
                                gSeconds_or_minutes = SECONDS;
                                GetDItem( gSettingsDialog, MINS_RADIO,
                                        &itemType, &itemHandle, &itemRect );
                                SetCtlValue( itemHandle, OFF );
                                GetDItem( gSettingsDialog, SECS_RADIO,
                                        &itemType, &itemHandle, &itemRect );
```

```
                                    SetCtlValue( itemHandle, ON );
                                    GetDItem( gSettingsDialog, S_OR_M_FIELD,
                                            &itemType, &itemHandle, &itemRect );
                                    SetIText( itemHandle, "\pseconds" );
                                    GetDItem( gSettingsDialog, TIME_FIELD,
                                            &itemType, &itemHandle, &itemRect );
                                    HLock( gDefaultSecsH );
                                    SetIText( itemHandle, *gDefaultSecsH );
                                    HUnlock( gDefaultSecsH );
                                    break;
                            case MINS_RADIO:
                                    gSeconds_or_minutes = MINUTES;
                                    GetDItem( gSettingsDialog, SECS_RADIO,
                                            &itemType, &itemHandle, &itemRect );
                                    SetCtlValue( itemHandle, OFF );
                                    GetDItem( gSettingsDialog, MINS_RADIO,
                                            &itemType, &itemHandle, &itemRect );
                                    SetCtlValue( itemHandle, ON );
                                    GetDItem( gSettingsDialog, S_OR_M_FIELD,
                                            &itemType, &itemHandle, &itemRect );
                                    SetIText( itemHandle, "\pminutes" );
                                    GetDItem( gSettingsDialog, TIME_FIELD,
                                            &itemType, &itemHandle, &itemRect );
                                    HLock( gDefaultMinsH );
                                    SetIText( itemHandle, *gDefaultMinsH );
                                    HUnlock( gDefaultMinsH );
                                    break;
                    }
            }
    }


/************************************** SaveSettings */

SaveSettings()
{
        int     itemType;
        Rect    itemRect;
        Handle itemHandle;

        GetDItem( gSettingsDialog, TIME_FIELD, &itemType, &itemHandle,
                                                        &itemRect );
        GetIText( itemHandle, &(savedSettings.timeString) );
        GetDItem( gSettingsDialog, SOUND_ON_BOX, &itemType, &itemHandle,
                                                        &itemRect );
        savedSettings.sound = GetCtlValue( itemHandle );
        GetDItem( gSettingsDialog, ICON_ON_BOX, &itemType, &itemHandle,
                                                        &itemRect );
        savedSettings.icon = GetCtlValue( itemHandle );
        GetDItem( gSettingsDialog, ALERT_ON_BOX, &itemType, &itemHandle,
                                                        &itemRect );
```

```
        savedSettings.alert = GetCtlValue( itemHandle );
        GetDItem( gSettingsDialog, SECS_RADIO, &itemType, &itemHandle,
                                                        &itemRect );
        savedSettings.secsRadio = GetCtlValue( itemHandle );
        GetDItem( gSettingsDialog, MINS_RADIO, &itemType, &itemHandle,
                                                        &itemRect );
        savedSettings.minsRadio = GetCtlValue( itemHandle );
}


/*************************************** RestoreSettings */

RestoreSettings()
{
        int    itemType;
        Rect   itemRect;
        Handle itemHandle;

        GetDItem( gSettingsDialog, TIME_FIELD, &itemType, &itemHandle,
                                                        &itemRect );
        SetIText( itemHandle, savedSettings.timeString );
        GetDItem( gSettingsDialog, SOUND_ON_BOX, &itemType, &itemHandle,
                                                        &itemRect );
        SetCtlValue( itemHandle, savedSettings.sound );
        GetDItem( gSettingsDialog, ICON_ON_BOX, &itemType, &itemHandle,
                                                        &itemRect );
        SetCtlValue( itemHandle, savedSettings.icon );
        GetDItem( gSettingsDialog, ALERT_ON_BOX, &itemType, &itemHandle,
                                                        &itemRect );
        SetCtlValue( itemHandle, savedSettings.alert );
        GetDItem( gSettingsDialog, SECS_RADIO, &itemType, &itemHandle,
                                                        &itemRect );
        SetCtlValue( itemHandle, savedSettings.secsRadio );
        GetDItem( gSettingsDialog, MINS_RADIO, &itemType, &itemHandle,
                                                        &itemRect );
        SetCtlValue( itemHandle, savedSettings.minsRadio );

        if ( savedSettings.secsRadio == ON )
        {
                GetDItem( gSettingsDialog, S_OR_M_FIELD, &itemType,
                                                &itemHandle, &itemRect );
                SetIText( itemHandle, "\pseconds" );
        } else
        {
                GetDItem( gSettingsDialog, S_OR_M_FIELD, &itemType,
                                                &itemHandle, &itemRect );
                SetIText( itemHandle, "\pminutes" );
        }
}
```

```
/*****************************          CountDown      *******/

CountDown( numSecs )
long numSecs;
{
        long          myTime, oldTime, difTime;
        Str255        myTimeString;
        WindowPtr     countDownWindow;

        countDownWindow = GetNewWindow( BASE_RES_ID, NIL_POINTER,
                                        MOVE_TO_FRONT );
        SetPort( countDownWindow );
        ShowWindow( countDownWindow );
        TextFace( bold );
        TextSize( 24 );

        GetDateTime( &myTime );
        oldTime = myTime;
        if ( gSeconds_or_minutes == MINUTES )
                numSecs *= SECONDS_PER_MINUTE;
        gCounting = TRUE;

        while ( ( numSecs > 0 ) && ( gCounting ) )
        {
                HandleEvent();
                if ( gCounting )
                {
                        MoveTo( LEFT, TOP );
                        GetDateTime( &myTime );
                        if ( myTime != oldTime )
                        {
                                difTime = myTime - oldTime;
                                numSecs = numSecs - difTime;
                                oldTime = myTime;
                                NumToString( numSecs , myTimeString );
                                EraseRect ( &(countDownWindow->portRect) );
                                DrawString( myTimeString );
                        }
                }
        }
        if ( gCounting )
                SetNotification();
        gCounting = FALSE;
        HideWindow( countDownWindow );
}
```

```
/*******************************          SetNotification      *******/

SetNotification()
{
        int    itemType;
        Rect   itemRect;
        Handle itemHandle;

        if ( gNotify_set )
        {
                NMRemove( &gMyNMRec );
                HUnlock( gNotifyStrH );
        }

        GetDItem( gSettingsDialog, ICON_ON_BOX, &itemType, &itemHandle,
                                                &itemRect );
        if ( GetCtlValue( itemHandle ) )
                gMyNMRec.nmSIcon = GetResource( 'SICN', BASE_RES_ID );
        else
                gMyNMRec.nmSIcon = NIL_POINTER;

        GetDItem( gSettingsDialog, SOUND_ON_BOX, &itemType, &itemHandle,
                                                &itemRect );
        if ( GetCtlValue( itemHandle ) )
                gMyNMRec.nmSound = GetResource( 'snd ', BASE_RES_ID );
        else
                gMyNMRec.nmSound = NIL_POINTER;

        GetDItem( gSettingsDialog, ALERT_ON_BOX, &itemType, &itemHandle,
                                                &itemRect );
        if ( GetCtlValue( itemHandle ) )
        {
                MoveHHi( gNotifyStrH );
                HLock( gNotifyStrH );
                gMyNMRec.nmStr = *gNotifyStrH;
        }
        else
                gMyNMRec.nmStr = NIL_POINTER;

        NMInstall( &gMyNMRec );
        EnableItem( gFileMenu, KILL_ITEM );
        gNotify_set = TRUE;
}
```

Running Reminder

Now that your source code is updated, you're almost ready to run Reminder. First, we'll show you how to set the MultiFinder attributes that will allow Reminder to continue executing, even in the background.

Pull down the Project menu and select Set Project Type. . . . The Project Type dialog box will appear (Figure 6.40). Click the mouse on the MF Attrs pop-up menu, selecting items until all three have a check mark next to them (Figure 6.41). Click the OK button. Now you're ready to run Reminder.

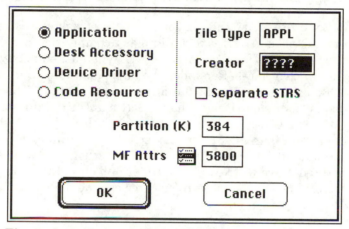

Figure 6.40   Project Type dialog box.

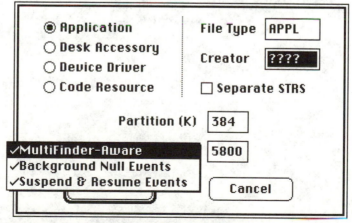

Figure 6.41   Project Type dialog with MultiFinder attributes set.

> Creating applications that are MultiFinder-friendly is very impor-
> tant. We've touched on the basics of MultiFinder friendliness by using
> `WaitNextEvent()` and handling Suspend/Resume events, but there's
> a lot more to learn. If you want to write MultiFinder-friendly applica-
> tions, read the *Programmer's Guide to MultiFinder* from Apple and
> APDA.
>
> To be truly MultiFinder-friendly, Reminder would have to worry
> about things like scrap conversion (we discuss the scrap in Chapter 7),
> mouse regions, sleep times, and much more.

Select Run from the Project menu. When asked to Bring the project up
to date, click Yes. If you run into any compilation problems, consult the
debugging tips found in Appendix E. When asked to Save changes before
running, click Yes. Reminder should be up and running (Figure 6.42).

Reminder does not display any windows initially. The File menu should
display four menu items: Change Settings, Start Countdown, Kill Notification, and Quit. If Change Settings is selected, the Settings dialog box
appears (Figure 6.43). You can select the countdown time in minutes or
seconds, and choose the method or methods by which you wish to be
notified. Save will keep the settings and close the dialog box. Cancel will
restore the last saved settings and close the dialog box.

Figure 6.42 Running Reminder.

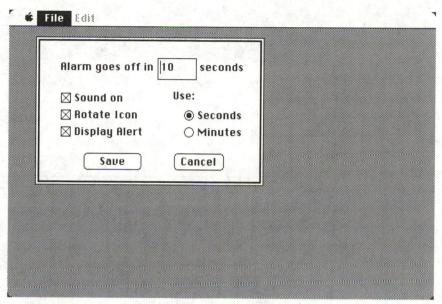

Figure 6.43   Using the Change Settings dialog box.

Start Countdown will begin the countdown: The countdown window is displayed, and the timer will count down in seconds. In the File menu, Start Countdown is changed to Stop Countdown, and may be selected to cancel the countdown and close the countdown window. During countdown, the Change Settings item is dimmed. When the countdown reaches zero, up to three methods will be used to notify you that the time has been reached (Figure 6.44).

Once the notification is set, the Kill Notification item under the File menu will become available. When it is used to cancel a notification, it will become dim again.

If you are running under MultiFinder, use Change Settings to set the countdown time to 20 seconds, then start the countdown. Before time runs out, click on another application's window (like the Finder) so that the countdown window is in the background. The countdown should continue and, when it reaches zero, you should be notified. If this doesn't work, check your MF Attrs in the Set Project Type dialog box. Make sure all three bits are turned on. Of course, Reminder works fine in the regular Finder, but is somewhat less useful there.

Choose Quit from the File menu. Let's take a look at the code.

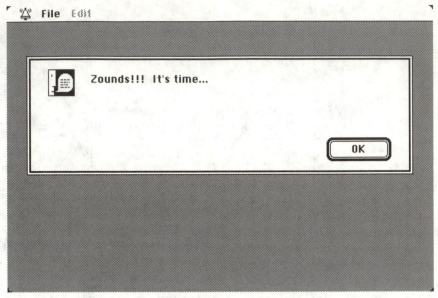

Figure 6.44   The Notification Manager comes through.

Walking Through the Reminder Code

First, set up your #defines. Most of them relate to the Settings dialog box. Each dialog item is given an appropriate name. SAVE_BUTTON is dialog item number 1, CANCEL_BUTTON is dialog item number 2, and so on. DEFAULT_SECS_ID and DEFAULT_MINS_ID are the resource IDs of the 'STR ' resources used as second and minute defaults in the Settings dialog. ON and OFF are set to 1 and 0 for ease of use in setting controls. SYS_VERSION is set to 1. You use this in the Sys6OrLater() function to indicate which version of SysEnvirons() to call.

> SysEnvirons() fills out a record that describes the Mac operating environment. Most important, we can use it to tell what version of the system is running and, therefore, whether or not Toolbox routines like WaitNextEvent() or the Notification Manager are present. SysEnvirons() is completely described in *Inside Macintosh* (V:5).

```
#define BASE_RES_ID          400
#define ABOUT_ALERT          401
#define BAD_SYS_ALERT        402
#define NIL_POINTER          0L
#define MOVE_TO_FRONT        -1L
#define REMOVE_ALL_EVENTS    0

#define MIN_SLEEP            0L
#define NIL_MOUSE_REGION     0L

#define DRAG_THRESHOLD       30

#define SAVE_BUTTON          1
#define CANCEL_BUTTON  2
#define TIME_FIELD           4
#define S_OR_M_FIELD    5
#define SOUND_ON_BOX    6
#define ICON_ON_BOX          7
#define ALERT_ON_BOX    8
#define SECS_RADIO           10
#define MINS_RADIO           11

#define DEFAULT_SECS_ID      401
#define DEFAULT_MINS_ID      402

#define ON                   1
#define OFF                  0

#define SECONDS              0
#define MINUTES              1
#define SECONDS_PER_MINUTE   60

#define TOP                  25
#define LEFT                 12

#define MARK_APPLICATION     1

#define APPLE_MENU_ID        BASE_RES_ID
#define FILE_MENU_ID         BASE_RES_ID+1
#define ABOUT_ITEM_ID        1

#define CHANGE_ITEM          1
#define START_STOP_ITEM      2
#define KILL_ITEM            3
#define QUIT_ITEM            4

#define SYS_VERSION          1
```

The variable `gSettingsDialog` will point to your Settings dialog. Remember, you can treat a `DialogPtr` just like a `WindowPtr`. For example, you could pass `gSettingsDialog` as an argument to `SetPort()`.

When gDone is set to TRUE, the program will exit. gCounting is TRUE only when the countdown window is displayed. gNotify_set is TRUE when a notification has been set. gSeconds_or_minutes is set to SECONDS or MINUTES, depending on the setting in the Settings dialog. It is reset to FALSE when Kill Notification is selected from the File menu.

gDefaultSecsH and gDefaultMinsH are handles to the default time 'STR ' resources. gNotifyStrH and gMyNMRec are used by the Notification Manager.

gAppleMenu and gFileMenu are handles to their respective menus. You need the handle to the Apple menu so you can add desk accessories. You need the handle to the File menu so you can change menu items.

The savedSettings struct is used to hold all the settings from the Settings dialog box, in case they need to be restored (if the user clicks the Cancel button).

```
DialogPtr        gSettingsDialog;
Rect             gDragRect;
Boolean          gDone, gCounting, gNotify_set;
char             gSeconds_or_minutes = SECONDS;
StringHandle     gNotifyStrH, gDefaultSecsH, gDefaultMinsH;
NMRec            gMyNMRec;
MenuHandle       gAppleMenu, gFileMenu;
EventRecord      gTheEvent;

struct
{
  Str255 timeString;
  int    sound;
  int    icon;
  int    alert;
  int    secsRadio;
  int    minsRadio;
}  savedSettings;
```

main() starts by initializing the Toolbox, using the same routine you always have. Then, test to see if System 6.0 or later is installed. If it is, you can use the Notification Manager. Initialize your dialogs, your menus, and the notification data structure.

Finally, enter your main event loop.

```
/******************************* main *********/

main()
{
  ToolBoxInit();
  if ( Sys6OrLater() )
  {
```

```
                        DialogInit();
                        MenuBarInit();
                        SetUpDragRect();
                        NotifyInit();
                        MainLoop();
                }
        }
```

This routine is the same routine you've been using all along.

```
/****************************** ToolBoxInit */

ToolBoxInit()
{
   InitGraf( &thePort );
   InitFonts();
   FlushEvents( everyEvent, REMOVE_ALL_EVENTS );
   InitWindows();
   InitMenus();
   TEInit();
   InitDialogs( NIL_POINTER );
   InitCursor();
}
```

Sys6OrLater() will return TRUE if System Version 6.0 or later is installed. Otherwise, it returns FALSE. The key to this function lies in the call to SysEnvirons(). Pass in the version number of SysEnvirons() that you'd like to use. In this case, use SYS_VERSION, which is set to 1. Apple will eventually add new features to the SysEnvirons() call, but they'll always provide compatibility with older versions via the version parameter.

SysEnvData is a data structure that gets filled by SysEnvirons(). One of the fields, systemVersion, gets filled with the current system version number. The first two bytes get the major version number, and the last two bytes get the minor version number. (In Version 5.3, the major version number is 5, and the minor version number is 3.) As long as the version number is greater than 0x0600 (hex for 6*256), you know you have a system with a major version greater than 6.0.

If there is a problem, call StopAlert() to put up your "You don't have version 6.0 or later" alert.

```
/******************************* Sys6OrLater *********/

int     Sys6OrLater()
{
        OSErr status;
        SysEnvRec       SysEnvData;

        status = SysEnvirons( SYS_VERSION, &SysEnvData );
        if (( status != noErr ) || ( SysEnvData.systemVersion < 0x0600 ))
        {
                StopAlert( BAD_SYS_ALERT, NIL_POINTER );
                return( FALSE );
        }
        else
                return( TRUE );
}
```

DialogInit() starts by loading the default second and minute settings into the StringHandles gDefaultSecsH and gDefaultMinsH. The Settings dialog is then loaded from the resource file. When you designed the dialog box in ResEdit, you set it up to be invisible. When the time is right, you can call ShowWindow() to make it visible.

Call GetDItem() and SetCtlValue() in pairs to set the SECS_RADIO, SOUND_ON_BOX, ICON_ON_BOX, and ALERT_ON_BOX items to ON.

```
/******************************* DialogInit *********/

DialogInit()
{
        int             itemType;
        Rect            itemRect;
        Handle          itemHandle;

        gDefaultSecsH = GetString( DEFAULT_SECS_ID );
        gDefaultMinsH = GetString( DEFAULT_MINS_ID );

        gSettingsDialog = GetNewDialog( BASE_RES_ID, NIL_POINTER,
                                        MOVE_TO_FRONT );
        GetDItem( gSettingsDialog, SECS_RADIO, &itemType, &itemHandle,
                                        &itemRect );
        SetCtlValue( itemHandle, ON );
        GetDItem( gSettingsDialog, SOUND_ON_BOX, &itemType, &itemHandle,
                                        &itemRect );
        SetCtlValue( itemHandle, ON );
        GetDItem( gSettingsDialog, ICON_ON_BOX, &itemType, &itemHandle,
                                        &itemRect );
        SetCtlValue( itemHandle, ON );
        GetDItem( gSettingsDialog, ALERT_ON_BOX, &itemType, &itemHandle,
                                        &itemRect );
        SetCtlValue( itemHandle, ON );
}
```

MenuBarInit() is similar to the earlier menu routines you've seen. First, you load your MBAR resource, and then you get a handle to the ⌘ menu so you can add all the desk accessories to it. Next, you get a handle to the File menu so you can change menu items later on. Finally, you draw the menu bar:

```
/***************************          MenuBarInit   */

MenuBarInit()
{
  Handle        myMenuBar;

  myMenuBar = GetNewMBar( BASE_RES_ID );
  SetMenuBar( myMenuBar );
  gAppleMenu = GetMHandle( APPLE_MENU_ID );
  AddResMenu( gAppleMenu, 'DRVR' );
  gFileMenu = GetMHandle( FILE_MENU_ID );
  DrawMenuBar();
}
```

SetUpDragRect() is the same as always:

```
/***************************** SetUpDragRect ********/

SetUpDragRect()
{
  gDragRect = screenBits.bounds;
  gDragRect.left += DRAG_THRESHOLD;
  gDragRect.right -= DRAG_THRESHOLD;
  gDragRect.bottom -= DRAG_THRESHOLD;
}
```

The Macintosh operating system, like most other operating systems, supports a set of operating system queues. You're already familiar with the Event Manager's queue. The Notification Manager maintains a queue, as well. Under MultiFinder, several applications might post notifications at the same time. Each notification request is handled by the operating system and posted on the Notification Manager's queue.

In NotifyInit(), load the 'STR' you want to appear in the notification alert with GetString(). Then, qType is set to nmType. This tells the part of the operating system that manages queues that this request is destined for the Notification Manager's queue.

Next, nmMark is set to MARK_APPLICATION, which means the (◆) will be placed next to Reminder in the ⌘ Menu (if you're in MultiFinder). NMResp is set to NIL_POINTER, which means you have no response routine after the notification has been successfully made.

```
/****************************** NotifyInit *********/

NotifyInit()
{
   gNotifyStrH = GetString( BASE_RES_ID );
   gMyNMRec.qType = nmType;
   gMyNMRec.nmMark = MARK_APPLICATION;
   gMyNMRec.nmResp = NIL_POINTER;
}
```

MainLoop() **initializes** gDone, gCounting, **and** gNotify_set **and then loops on** HandleEvent().

```
/*************************** MainLoop *********/

MainLoop()
{
   gDone = FALSE;
   gCounting = FALSE;
   gNotify_set = FALSE;

   while ( gDone == FALSE )
   {
         HandleEvent();
   }
}
```

The HandleEvent() routine is set up much like HandleEvent() in Chapter 5. Call WaitNextEvent() to see what is in the event queue. (Because you're running System 6.0 or later, you know that WaitNextEvent() is installed.) Use a switch to find out what the event was. If the mouse button is depressed, the HandleMouseDown() routine is called. If a keydown or autoKey event occurs, check to see if the command key was depressed. If so, the HandleMenuChoice() routine is called. If you don't check for a keydown event first, you won't ever see the command key sequence (for example, when you type ⌘Q to Quit).

We've left out some of the standard event handling, like updateEvts, to simplify the code. Don't worry—Reminder will work just fine without the extra code.

```
/******************************** HandleEvent          */

HandleEvent()
{
      char    theChar;

      WaitNextEvent( everyEvent, &gTheEvent, MIN_SLEEP,
                                    NIL_MOUSE_REGION );

      switch ( gTheEvent.what )
      {
```

```
                case mouseDown:
                        HandleMouseDown();
                        break;
                case keyDown:
                case autoKey:
                        theChar = gTheEvent.message & charCodeMask;
                        if (( gTheEvent.modifiers & cmdKey ) != 0 )
                                HandleMenuChoice( MenuKey( theChar ) );
                        break;
        }
}
```

HandleMouseDown( ) **is the same as its Chapter 5 counterpart:**

```
/************************************ HandleMouseDown */

HandleMouseDown()
{
        WindowPtr       whichWindow;
        short int       thePart;
        long int        menuChoice, windSize;

        thePart = FindWindow( gTheEvent.where, &whichWindow );
        switch ( thePart )
        {
                case inMenuBar:
                        menuChoice = MenuSelect( gTheEvent.where );
                        HandleMenuChoice( menuChoice );
                        break;
                case inSysWindow :
                        SystemClick( &gTheEvent, whichWindow );
                        break;
                case inDrag :
                        DragWindow( whichWindow, gTheEvent.where, &gDragRect);
                        break;
                case inGoAway :
                        gDone = TRUE;
                        break;
        }
}
```

HandleMenuChoice( ) **is also the same as its Chapter 5 counterpart:**

```
/******************************* HandleMenuChoice */

HandleMenuChoice( menuChoice )
long int        menuChoice;
{
        int     theMenu;
        int     theItem;

        if ( menuChoice != 0 )
        {
                theMenu = HiWord( menuChoice );
                theItem = LoWord( menuChoice );
                switch ( theMenu )
                {
                        case APPLE_MENU_ID :
                                HandleAppleChoice( theItem );
                                break;
                        case FILE_MENU_ID :
                                HandleFileChoice( theItem );
                                break;
                }
        }
        HiliteMenu( 0 );
}
```

Guess what?

```
/******************************         HandleAppleChoice   *******/

HandleAppleChoice( theItem )
int     theItem;
{
        Str255 accName;
        int             accNumber;
        short int       itemNumber;

        switch ( theItem )
        {
                case ABOUT_ITEM_ID :
                        NoteAlert( ABOUT_ALERT, NIL_POINTER );
                        break;
                default :
                        GetItem( gAppleMenu, theItem, accName );
                        accNumber = OpenDeskAcc( accName );
                        break;
        }
}
```

HandleFileChoice( ) takes care of the four items under the File menu.
If **Change Settings** is selected call HandleDialog( ). If **Start Countdown** (or its counterpart, **Stop Countdown**) is selected, check to see if you are currently counting down. If you are, then the menu item must have been **Stop Countdown**, so change the item back to **Start Countdown** and set gCounting to FALSE to stop the countdown.

If you were not counting down, Start Countdown was the item selected. In this case, unhighlight the File menu (try commenting this line to get a feel for why this is necessary). Then, pull the countdown time from the settings dialog and convert it to a number. Dim the Change Settings item (you don't want to change the settings while you're actually counting down), and change the Start Countdown menu item to Stop Countdown. Next, call CountDown(). When CountDown() returns, reenable the Change Settings item and change Stop Countdown to Start Countdown.

If the menu item selected was **Kill Notification**, call NMRemove() to remove the notification from the Notification Manager's queue. Then, unlock the notification string you locked in SetNotification(). (We discuss handle locking and unlocking in a tech block a little later on.) Also, dim the Kill Notification item, since the notification is no longer active. Finally, set gNotify_set to FALSE, so everyone else knows that the notification is no longer active.

If Quit is selected, set gCounting to FALSE so you'll drop out of the counting loop (if the selection was made during the countdown). In addition, set gDone to FALSE.

```
/***************************    HandleFileChoice    *******/

HandleFileChoice( theItem )
int     theItem;
{
     Str255 timeString;
     long   countDownTime;
     int    itemType;
     Rect   itemRect;
     Handle itemHandle;

     switch ( theItem )
     {
          case CHANGE_ITEM :
               HandleDialog();
               break;
          case START_STOP_ITEM :
               if ( gCounting )
               {
                    SetItem( gFileMenu,theItem,"\pStart Countdown");
                    gCounting = FALSE;
               } else
               {
                    HiliteMenu( 0 );
                    GetDItem( gSettingsDialog, TIME_FIELD,
                         &itemType, &itemHandle, &itemRect );
                    GetIText( itemHandle, &timeString );
                    StringToNum( timeString, &countDownTime );
```

```
                         DisableItem( gFileMenu, CHANGE_ITEM );
                         SetItem( gFileMenu, theItem,"\pStop Countdown");
                         CountDown( countDownTime );
                         EnableItem( gFileMenu, CHANGE_ITEM );
                         SetItem( gFileMenu,theItem,"\pStart Countdown");
                  }
               break;
        case KILL_ITEM :
               NMRemove( &gMyNMRec );
               HUnlock( gNotifyStrH );
               DisableItem( gFileMenu, KILL_ITEM );
               gNotify_set = FALSE;
               break;
        case QUIT_ITEM :
               gCounting = FALSE;
               gDone = TRUE;
               break;
     }
}
```

As with Chapter 5's Timer, we still haven't added support for copy, cut, and paste operations to desk accessories. Look at WindowMaker in Chapter 7 to see how to support desk accessories with the Edit menu.

HandleDialog() is the key to Reminder's modal dialog. As we discussed in the beginning of the chapter, modal dialogs are implemented in a loop. First ModalDialog() is called, returning the number of the selected item. The selected item is processed and, if it was an exit item, the loop ends.

HandleDialog() is a very long routine, but it is not complex. Most of it is a big switch with cases for most of the items in the dialog.

Start by making the Settings dialog visible and saving the settings you start off with (in case the user clicks on the Cancel button). You then enter the ModalDialog() loop. If the user selects an exit item (in this case, Save or Cancel), dialogDone is set to TRUE. If the user selects the Save button, make the dialog window invisible and set dialogDone to TRUE.

If the user selects the Cancel button, make the dialog window invisible and restore the old settings. (We made the window invisible first because we didn't want the user to watch as we changed the items back. It's not a pretty sight.) Again, set dialogDone to TRUE to drop out of the while loop.

```
/**************************** HandleDialog *********/

HandleDialog()
{
    int    itemHit, dialogDone = FALSE;
    long   alarmDelay;
    Str255 delayString;
    int    itemType;
    Rect   itemRect;
    Handle itemHandle;

    ShowWindow( gSettingsDialog );
    SaveSettings();

    while ( dialogDone == FALSE )
    {
        ModalDialog( NIL_POINTER, &itemHit );
        switch ( itemHit )
        {
            case SAVE_BUTTON:
                HideWindow( gSettingsDialog );
                dialogDone = TRUE;
                break;
            case CANCEL_BUTTON:
                HideWindow( gSettingsDialog );
                RestoreSettings();
                dialogDone = TRUE;
                break;
```

If the user clicks in the sound, icon, or alert check box, set them to OFF if they were ON or to ON if they were OFF. Note that (! GetCtlValue(itemHandle)) returns the setting opposite to itemHandle's current setting.

```
            case SOUND_ON_BOX:
                GetDItem( gSettingsDialog, SOUND_ON_BOX,
                    &itemType, &itemHandle, &itemRect );
                SetCtlValue( itemHandle,
                            ! GetCtlValue( itemHandle ) );
                break;
            case ICON_ON_BOX:
                GetDItem( gSettingsDialog, ICON_ON_BOX,
                    &itemType, &itemHandle, &itemRect );
                SetCtlValue( itemHandle,
                            ! GetCtlValue( itemHandle ) );
                break;
            case ALERT_ON_BOX:
                GetDItem( gSettingsDialog, ALERT_ON_BOX,
                    &itemType, &itemHandle, &itemRect );
                SetCtlValue( itemHandle,
                            ! GetCtlValue( itemHandle ) );
                break;
```

If the user clicks in the Seconds radio button, change the global gSeconds_or_minutes to SECONDS, turn off the Minutes radio button, and turn on the Seconds radio button. (It's important to turn off the old button and then turn on the new one, so the user never sees two radio buttons on at the same time.) Next, set the static text field to read seconds, and place the default value loaded into gDefaultSecsH in the editable text field (the resource was loaded in DialogInit()). Lock the string handle, since you're passing a pointer to the string and not the string's handle to SetIText().

> Remember, a handle is a pointer to a pointer, allowing the system to move the data around in memory without changing the value of the handle. In this case, we need to use a pointer to our string instead of a handle to it, so we can't afford to let the system move our data around (relocate it). We can solve this problem in one of two ways. We can lock the handle and its data with HLock() or we can make a copy of the data and dispose of the handle. Each of these techniques has its place. For simplicity, we used the HLock() method, but this method is not necessarily the best. For more information, read about the Memory Manager in *Inside Macintosh,* Volume II, pages 9-51.

If the user clicks in the Minutes radio button, you will go through a similar exercise, using a default value in gDefaultMinsH in the editable text field.

```
case SECS_RADIO:
        gSeconds_or_minutes = SECONDS;
        GetDItem( gSettingsDialog, MINS_RADIO,
            &itemType, &itemHandle, &itemRect );
        SetCtlValue( itemHandle, OFF );
        GetDItem( gSettingsDialog, SECS_RADIO,
            &itemType, &itemHandle, &itemRect );
        SetCtlValue( itemHandle, ON );
        GetDItem( gSettingsDialog, S_OR_M_FIELD,
            &itemType, &itemHandle, &itemRect );
        SetIText( itemHandle, "\pseconds" );
        GetDItem( gSettingsDialog, TIME_FIELD,
            &itemType, &itemHandle, &itemRect );
        HLock( gDefaultSecsH );
        SetIText( itemHandle, *gDefaultSecsH );
        HUnlock( gDefaultSecsH );
        break;
case MINS_RADIO:
        gSeconds_or_minutes = MINUTES;
        GetDItem( gSettingsDialog, SECS_RADIO,
            &itemType, &itemHandle, &itemRect );
        SetCtlValue( itemHandle, OFF );
```

```
                       GetDItem( gSettingsDialog, MINS_RADIO,
                               &itemType, &itemHandle, &itemRect );
                       SetCtlValue( itemHandle, ON );
                       GetDItem( gSettingsDialog, S_OR_M_FIELD,
                               &itemType, &itemHandle, &itemRect );
                       SetIText( itemHandle, "\pminutes" );
                       GetDItem( gSettingsDialog, TIME_FIELD,
                               &itemType, &itemHandle, &itemRect );
                       HLock( gDefaultMinsH );
                       SetIText( itemHandle, *gDefaultMinsH );
                       HUnlock( gDefaultMinsH );
                       break;
               }
       }
}
```

SaveSettings() uses GetDItem() and either GetIText() or GetCtlValue() to fill the savedSettings data structure with the values currently set in the settings dialog items.

```
/************************************ SaveSettings */

SaveSettings()
{
       int    itemType;
       Rect   itemRect;
       Handle itemHandle;

       GetDItem( gSettingsDialog, TIME_FIELD, &itemType, &itemHandle,
                                               &itemRect );
       GetIText( itemHandle, &(savedSettings.timeString) );
       GetDItem( gSettingsDialog, SOUND_ON_BOX, &itemType, &itemHandle,
                                               &itemRect );
       savedSettings.sound = GetCtlValue( itemHandle );
       GetDItem( gSettingsDialog, ICON_ON_BOX, &itemType, &itemHandle,
                                               &itemRect );
       savedSettings.icon = GetCtlValue( itemHandle );
       GetDItem( gSettingsDialog, ALERT_ON_BOX, &itemType, &itemHandle,
                                               &itemRect );
       savedSettings.alert = GetCtlValue( itemHandle );
       GetDItem( gSettingsDialog, SECS_RADIO, &itemType, &itemHandle,
                                               &itemRect );
       savedSettings.secsRadio = GetCtlValue( itemHandle );
       GetDItem( gSettingsDialog, MINS_RADIO, &itemType, &itemHandle,
                                               &itemRect );
       savedSettings.minsRadio = GetCtlValue( itemHandle );
}
```

RestoreSettings() uses GetDItem(), SetIText(), and SetCtlValue() to restore the settings dialog items to the values saved in the savedSettings data structure. Use the value saved in savedSettings.secsRadio to determine if the static text field should read seconds or minutes.

```
/*********************************** RestoreSettings */

RestoreSettings()
{
        int     itemType;
        Rect    itemRect;
        Handle  itemHandle;

        GetDItem( gSettingsDialog, TIME_FIELD, &itemType, &itemHandle,
                                                &itemRect );
        SetIText( itemHandle, savedSettings.timeString );
        GetDItem( gSettingsDialog, SOUND_ON_BOX, &itemType, &itemHandle,
                                                &itemRect );
        SetCtlValue( itemHandle, savedSettings.sound );
        GetDItem( gSettingsDialog, ICON_ON_BOX, &itemType, &itemHandle,
                                                &itemRect );
        SetCtlValue( itemHandle, savedSettings.icon );
        GetDItem( gSettingsDialog, ALERT_ON_BOX, &itemType, &itemHandle,
                                                &itemRect );
        SetCtlValue( itemHandle, savedSettings.alert );
        GetDItem( gSettingsDialog, SECS_RADIO, &itemType, &itemHandle,
                                                &itemRect );
        SetCtlValue( itemHandle, savedSettings.secsRadio );
        GetDItem( gSettingsDialog, MINS_RADIO, &itemType, &itemHandle,
                                                &itemRect );
        SetCtlValue( itemHandle, savedSettings.minsRadio );

        if ( savedSettings.secsRadio == ON )
        {
                GetDItem( gSettingsDialog, S_OR_M_FIELD, &itemType,
                                                &itemHandle, &itemRect );
                SetIText( itemHandle, "\pseconds" );
        } else
        {
                GetDItem( gSettingsDialog, S_OR_M_FIELD, &itemType,
                                                &itemHandle, &itemRect );
                SetIText( itemHandle, "\pminutes" );
        }
}
```

CountDown( ) takes the number of seconds (or minutes) to count down
as its only argument, puts up the countdown window, and goes to it.

Start by loading the countdown window from the resource file. Set the
current GrafPort to the countdown window, make it visible, and set the
current font's size to 24 point. Make the current font appear in **boldface**.

```
/******************************      CountDown     ******/

CountDown( numSecs )
long numSecs;
{
        long            myTime, oldTime, difTime;
        Str255          myTimeString;
        WindowPtr       countDownWindow;
```

```
countDownWindow = GetNewWindow( BASE_RES_ID, NIL_POINTER,
                                      MOVE_TO_FRONT );
SetPort( countDownWindow );
ShowWindow( countDownWindow );
TextFace( bold );
TextSize( 24 );
```

Your next step is to get the current time (in seconds since midnight, January 1, 1904), and to convert the countdown time from minutes to seconds, if necessary. Also, set the global `gCounting` to `TRUE`.

```
GetDateTime( &myTime );
oldTime = myTime;
if ( gSeconds_or_minutes == MINUTES )
        numSecs *= SECONDS_PER_MINUTE;
gCounting = TRUE;
```

While you count down, call `HandleEvent()`. This lets the user drag the countdown window around the screen or make menu selections while you count down. This is very important because it keeps your program from falling into a mode. Users won't feel as though they're in countdown mode because they'll be able to pull down desk accessories and, if they're in MultiFinder, switch to other applications.

Every time `myTime` changes, a second has passed, and you have to redraw the countdown time. Call `EraseRect()` to clear the window and redraw the time.

```
while ( ( numSecs > 0 ) && ( gCounting ) )
{
        HandleEvent();
        if ( gCounting )
        {
                MoveTo( LEFT, TOP );
                GetDateTime( &myTime );
                if ( myTime != oldTime )
                {
                        difTime = myTime - oldTime;
                        numSecs = numSecs - difTime;
                        oldTime = myTime;
                        NumToString( numSecs , myTimeString );
                        EraseRect ( &(countDownWindow->portRect) );
                        DrawString( myTimeString );
                }
        }
}
```

If gCounting is still TRUE, then no one interrupted the countdown, and you can set your notification. Finally, set gCounting to FALSE and hide the countdown window.

```
if ( gCounting )
        SetNotification();
  gCounting = FALSE;
  HideWindow( countDownWindow );
}
```

If a notification is already set, remove it so you can set a new one. If appropriate, load the small icon ('SICN') from the resource file and put its handle in the notification data structure. Do the same for the 'snd ' resource and the string you loaded earlier.

Then, call NMInstall() to set the notification. Also turn on the Kill Notification item in the File menu. Finally, set gNotify_set to TRUE.

```
/******************************  SetNotification      *******/

SetNotification()
{
      int    itemType;
      Rect   itemRect;
      Handle itemHandle;

      if ( gNotify_set )
      {
            NMRemove( &gMyNMRec );
            HUnlock( gNotifyStrH );
      }

      GetDItem( gSettingsDialog, ICON_ON_BOX, &itemType, &itemHandle,
                                                  &itemRect );
      if ( GetCtlValue( itemHandle ) )
            gMyNMRec.nmSIcon = GetResource( 'SICN', BASE_RES_ID );
      else
            gMyNMRec.nmSIcon = NIL_POINTER;

      GetDItem( gSettingsDialog, SOUND_ON_BOX, &itemType, &itemHandle,
                                                  &itemRect );
      if ( GetCtlValue( itemHandle ) )
            gMyNMRec.nmSound = GetResource( 'snd ', BASE_RES_ID );
      else
            gMyNMRec.nmSound = NIL_POINTER;

      GetDItem( gSettingsDialog, ALERT_ON_BOX, &itemType, &itemHandle,
                                                  &itemRect );
      if ( GetCtlValue( itemHandle ) )
      {
```

```
            MoveHHi( gNotifyStrH );
            HLock( gNotifyStrH );
            gMyNMRec.nmStr = *gNotifyStrH;
    }
    else
            gMyNMRec.nmStr = NIL_POINTER;

    NMInstall( &gMyNMRec );
    EnableItem( gFileMenu, KILL_ITEM );
    gNotify_set = TRUE;
}
```

Note that the routine MoveHHi() was called before gNotifyStrH was locked. Normally, before you work with a pointer to a handled object, you HLock() the handle. When you're done with the pointer, you HUnlock() the handle again. As we mentioned earlier, HLock() creates an obstruction in the middle of the application heap. If the handle will only be HLocked for a short period of time (a few lines of code), this won't be a problem. In Reminder, you keep gNotifyStrH HLocked from the time the notification is installed until the notification is removed. That's too long to keep a handle locked in the middle of the heap. MoveHHi() reduces this problem by relocating the handled memory as high in the heap as possible. Locking the handle at this point creates an obstruction at one end of the heap instead of in the middle.

The topic of memory management on the Macintosh is important, but beyond the scope of this book. *Inside Macintosh,* Volume II, Chapter 1 contains a complete description of the Memory Manager. As your programs get larger and more sophisticated, you'll make more and more use of this part of the Toolbox.

In Review

This chapter examined some of the oldest parts of the Macintosh toolbox (dialog boxes), together with some of the newest parts (SysEnvirons() and the Notification Manager). You built an application that used most of the Toolbox routines presented in the previous three chapters.

In Chapter 7, we'll address some of the programming issues that we have not touched on so far, like error handling, managing multiple windows, using the clipboard, printing, and working with scroll bars. We'll end with a brief sojourn into the Macintosh Sound Manager.

Congratulations! The toughest part of the book is behind you.

7

Toolbox
Potpourri

Congratulations! Now that you have the Macintosh interface under your belt, youll see how to implement other traits that Mac programs should possess: multiple window handling, error checking, the Clipboard, file and print management, scroll bars, and sound.

THE FIRST APPLICATION, WindowMaker, shows you how to manage a dynamic windowing environment. In addition to supporting window creation, movement, and disposal, WindowMaker introduces an error-handling mechanism that you can use in your own applications.

Next, the desk scrap, more commonly known as the Clipboard, is introduced. The Scrap Manager utilities that support cut, copy, and paste operations are discussed. The second application, ShowClip, uses these routines to display the current scrap in a window.

The third application, PrintPICT, introduces the File Manager and the Printing Manager. You'll learn how to support the standard Open, Save, and Save As... File menu options in your own code.

Next, we present a discussion on the use of scroll bars. The fourth application, Pager, uses the Control Manager, as well as the Resource Manager, to build a kinescopic display of `PICT` resources.

For the pièce de résistance, we present Sounder, an alternative to the dreary world of `SysBeep()`.

Keeping Track of Windows: WindowMaker

Most applications on the Macintosh allow you to open more than one window at a time. **WindowMaker** lets you create as many windows as you desire. After they are created, you can select, move, and close any window.

WindowMaker Specifications

Here's how WindowMaker works:

- It initializes the Toolbox.
- It initializes the menu bar.
- It loads a `PICT` resource.
- It enters the Main Event Loop and performs the following functions.
- It creates a new window whenever the New menu item is selected, centering the `PICT` in the window.
- It closes the currently selected window whenever the Close menu item is selected.
- It handles events for moving and updating windows.
- It quits when the Quit menu item is selected.

WindowMaker is the first *Primer* program that does error checking. Every time a Toolbox function is called, there is the possibility that it may not execute properly. For example, if you call GetMenu() to load a MENU resource, and the operating system can't find the resource, the call returns an error code. Your program should check for and respond to these error codes. If you ignore Toolbox error code, you do so at your own risk. Check Toolbox calls the way we do it in WindowMaker and the other programs in this chapter. WindowMaker also fully supports desk accessory editing operations.

Because WindowMaker uses the concepts of the previous chapters and also handles error checking and multiple windows, you should consider using it as the model for your own applications.

Setting up the WindowMaker Project

Create a folder called WindowMaker in your source code folder. Then use ResEdit to create a new file inside the new folder called WindowMaker Proj.Rsrc. Build a WIND with an ID of 400. Figure 7.1 shows the specifications of the WIND you need.

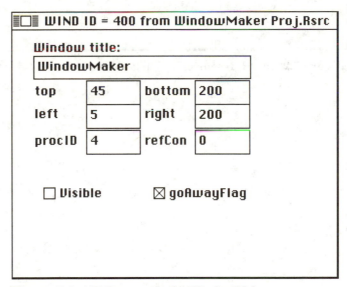

Figure 7.1 WIND resource for WindowMaker.

Now, create the menu resources. First, build the MBAR resource (Figure 7.2). Change the MBAR resource ID to 400. Now build the individual MENU items. Figure 7.3 displays the ⌘, File, and Edit menus for WindowMaker. (The Edit menu is the same as Chapter 5's Timer program and Chapter 6's Reminder program; copy resources from the older programs whenever possible.)

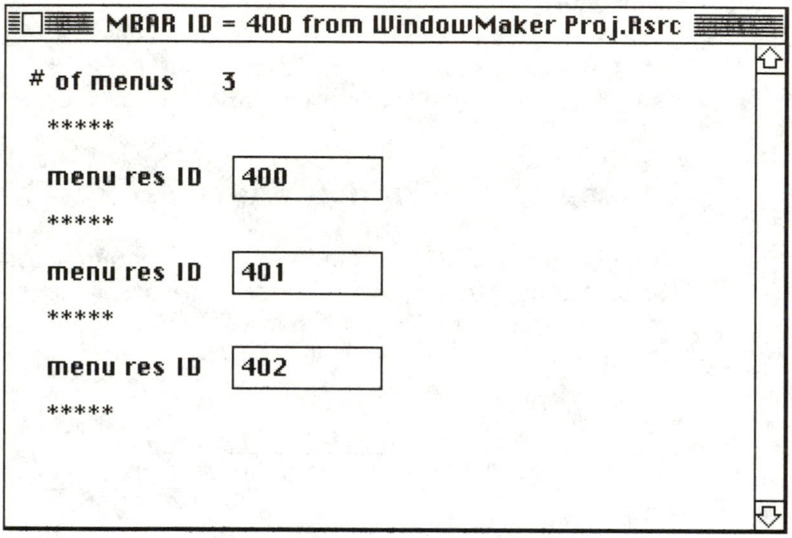

```
┌─────────────────────────────────────────────────────┐
│ ▣□▤▤ MBAR ID = 400 from WindowMaker Proj.Rsrc ▤▤▤ │ ⬆
├─────────────────────────────────────────────────────┤
│   # of menus      3                                 │
│      *****                                          │
│                                                     │
│      menu res ID    ┌─────────────┐                 │
│                     │ 400         │                 │
│                     └─────────────┘                 │
│      *****                                          │
│                                                     │
│      menu res ID    ┌─────────────┐                 │
│                     │ 401         │                 │
│                     └─────────────┘                 │
│      *****                                          │
│                                                     │
│      menu res ID    ┌─────────────┐                 │
│                     │ 402         │                 │
│                     └─────────────┘                 │
│      *****                                          │
│                                                     │
│                                                  ⬇ │
└─────────────────────────────────────────────────────┘
```

Figure 7.2   MBAR resource for WindowMaker.

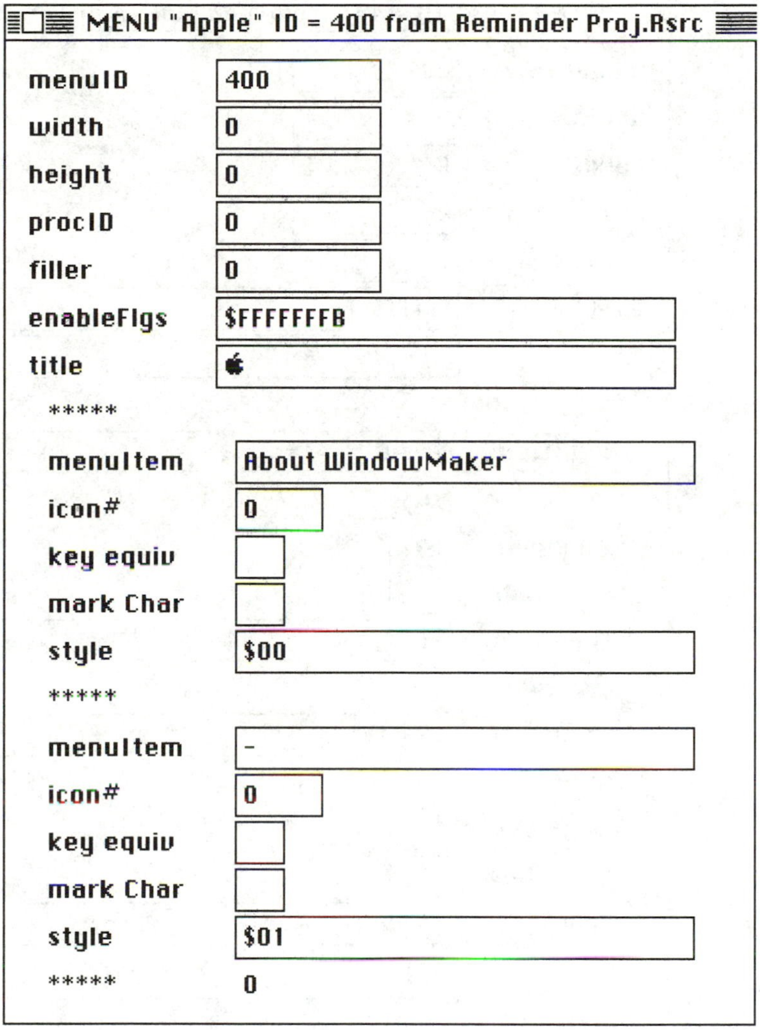

```
▣□≣  MENU "Apple" ID = 400 from Reminder Proj.Rsrc ≣

  menuID          [400        ]
  width           [0          ]
  height          [0          ]
  procID          [0          ]
  filler          [0          ]
  enableFlgs      [$FFFFFFFB              ]
  title           [  ]

     *****

   menuItem       [About WindowMaker        ]
   icon#          [0      ]
   key equiv      [   ]
   mark Char      [   ]
   style          [$00                  ]

     *****

   menuItem       [-                        ]
   icon#          [0      ]
   key equiv      [   ]
   mark Char      [   ]
   style          [$01                  ]

     *****           0
```

Figure 7.3 MENU resources for WindowMaker.

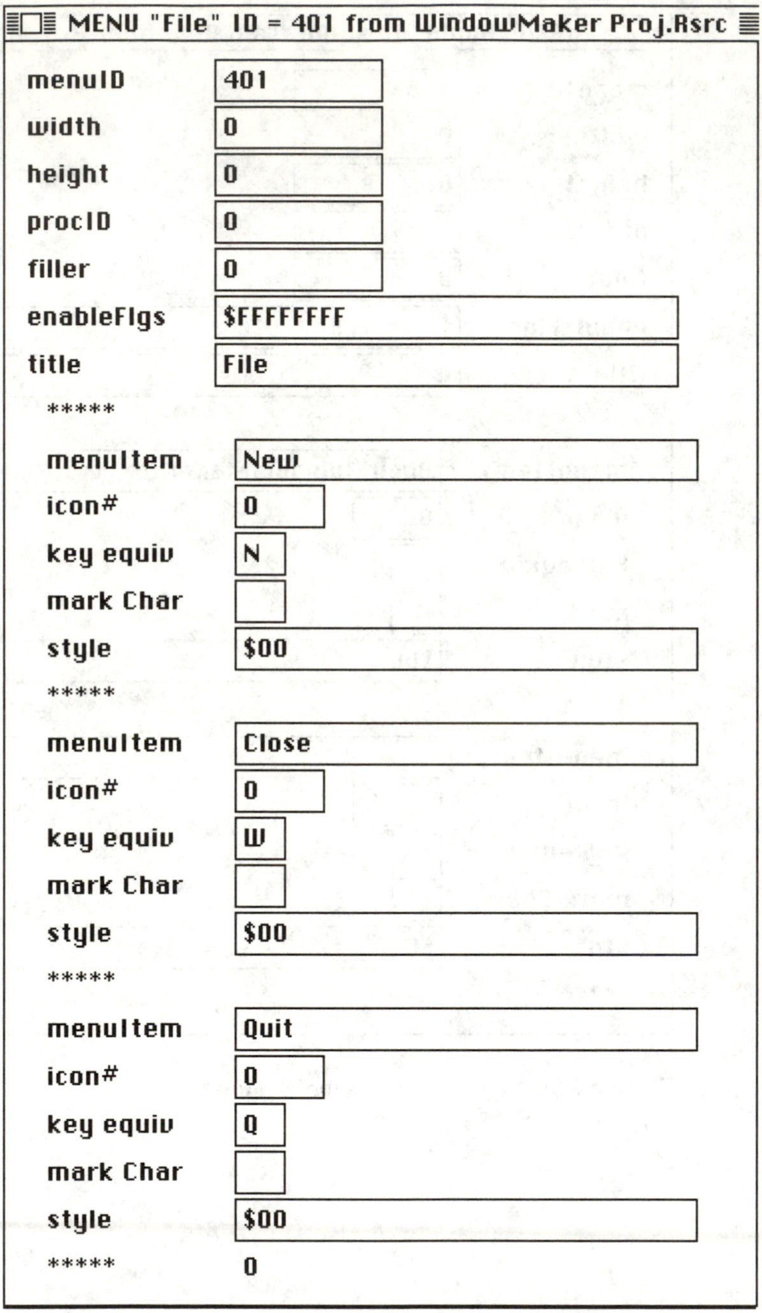

▤☐▤ MENU "File" ID = 401 from WindowMaker Proj.Rsrc ▤

menuID	401
width	0
height	0
procID	0
filler	0
enableFlgs	$FFFFFFFF
title	File

*****

menuItem	New
icon#	0
key equiv	N
mark Char	
style	$00

*****

menuItem	Close
icon#	0
key equiv	W
mark Char	
style	$00

*****

menuItem	Quit
icon#	0
key equiv	Q
mark Char	
style	$00

*****   0

Figure 7.3 (*continued*)

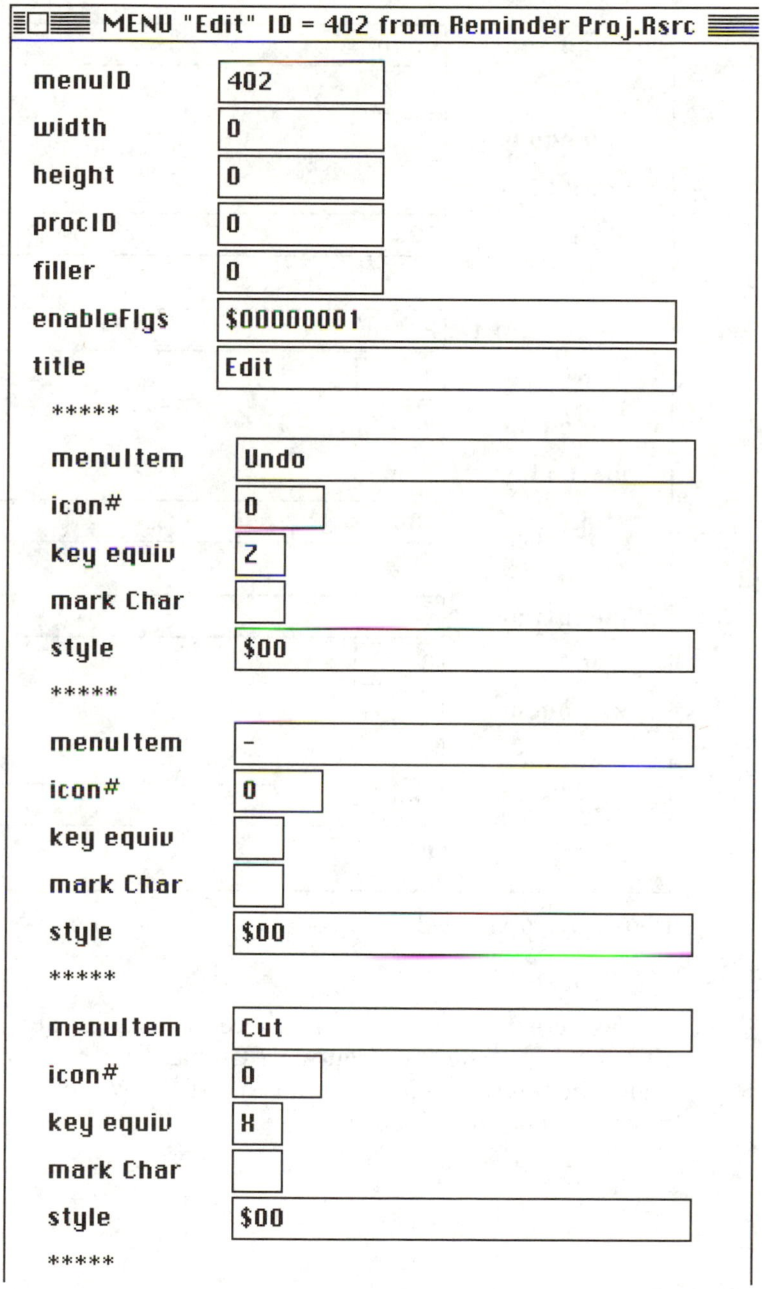

```
▤▢▤  MENU "Edit" ID = 402 from Reminder Proj.Rsrc  ▤

   menuID        402

   width         0

   height        0

   procID        0

   filler        0

   enableFlgs    $00000001

   title         Edit

       *****

     menuItem     Undo

     icon#        0

     key equiv    Z

     mark Char

     style        $00

       *****

     menuItem     –

     icon#        0

     key equiv

     mark Char

     style        $00

       *****

     menuItem     Cut

     icon#        0

     key equiv    X

     mark Char

     style        $00

       *****
```

Figure 7.3 (*continued*)

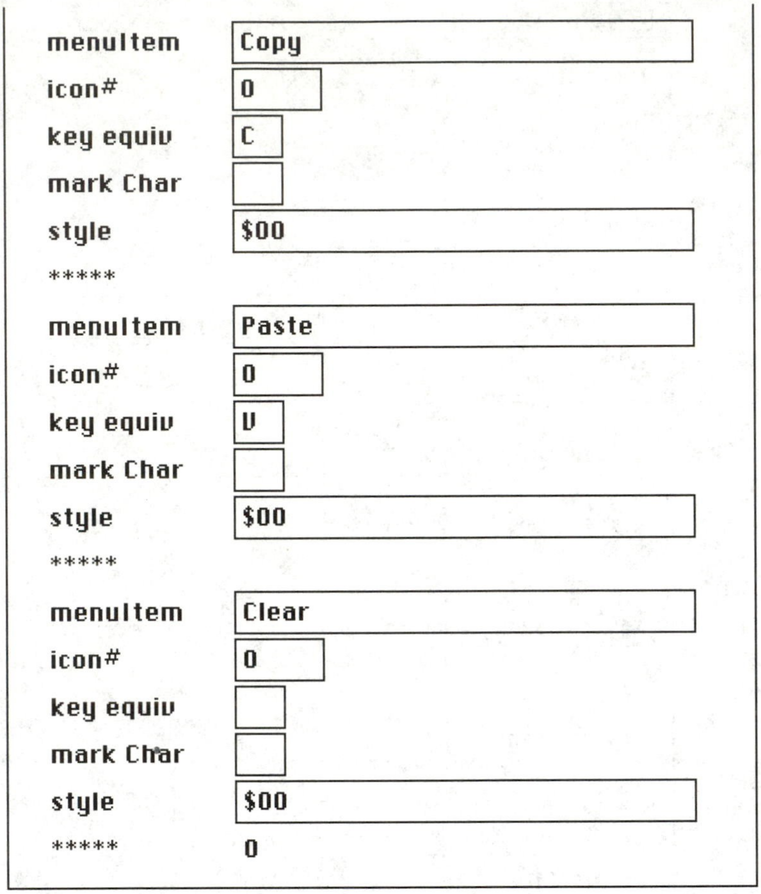

menuItem	Copy
icon#	0
key equiv	C
mark Char	
style	$00

*****

menuItem	Paste
icon#	0
key equiv	U
mark Char	
style	$00

*****

menuItem	Clear
icon#	0
key equiv	
mark Char	
style	$00

*****   0

Figure 7.3 *(continued)*

Next, create the two DITL resources, one for the about box, the other for the new error-checking routines. Change the resource IDs to the ones shown in Figure 7.4. To frame those two DITL resources, build the two ALRT resources shown in Figure 7.5.

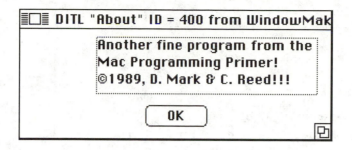

Item#	Type	Enabled	top	left	bottom	right	Text/Resource ID
1	Button	Yes	71	117	91	177	OK
2	Static Text	Yes	7	70	61	280	Another fine program from the Mac Programming Primer! ©1989, D. Mark & C. Reed!!!

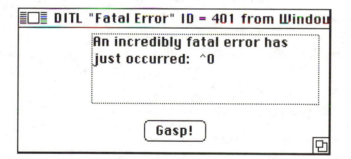

Item#	Type	Enabled	top	left	bottom	right	Text/Resource ID
1	Button	Yes	86	117	106	177	Gasp!
2	Static Text	Yes	5	67	71	283	An incredibly fatal error has just occurred: ^0

Figure 7.4 `DITL` resources for WindowMaker.

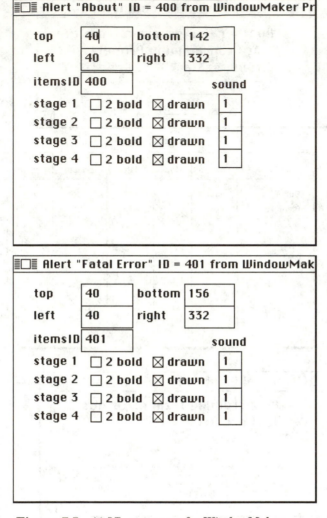

Figure 7.5 ALRT resources for WindowMaker.

All you need now are the PICT resources that you'll display in the WindowMaker windows and the STR resources that will be used in the error-checking routine. Use Chapter 3's ShowPICT PICT resource, or just cut and paste a picture from the Scrapbook. Be sure the resource ID for the PICT is 400. Finally, add the four STR resources shown in Figure 7.6 to the WindowMaker Proj.Rsrc file. Again, make sure to change the resource IDs of each resource to those shown in the figure. When you're done, the resource window of WindowMaker Proj.Rsrc should look like Figure 7.7.

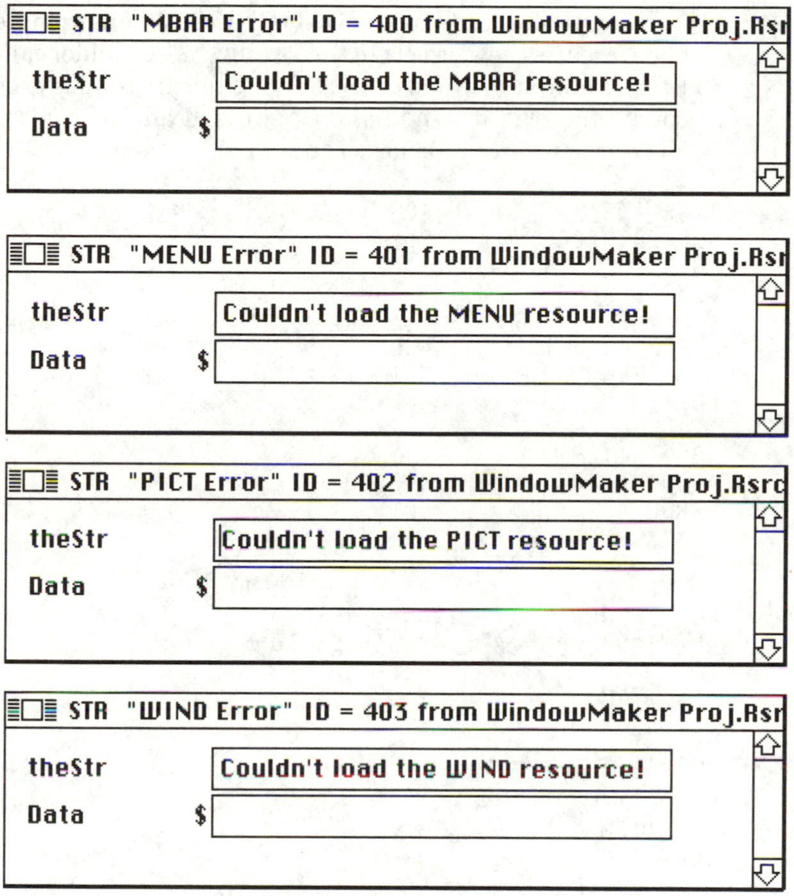

STR "MBAR Error" ID = 400 from WindowMaker Proj.Rsr

theStr   Couldn't load the MBAR resource!

Data $

STR "MENU Error" ID = 401 from WindowMaker Proj.Rsr

theStr   Couldn't load the MENU resource!

Data $

STR "PICT Error" ID = 402 from WindowMaker Proj.Rsrc

theStr   Couldn't load the PICT resource!

Data $

STR "WIND Error" ID = 403 from WindowMaker Proj.Rsr

theStr   Couldn't load the WIND resource!

Data $

Figure 7.6   STR   resources for WindowMaker.

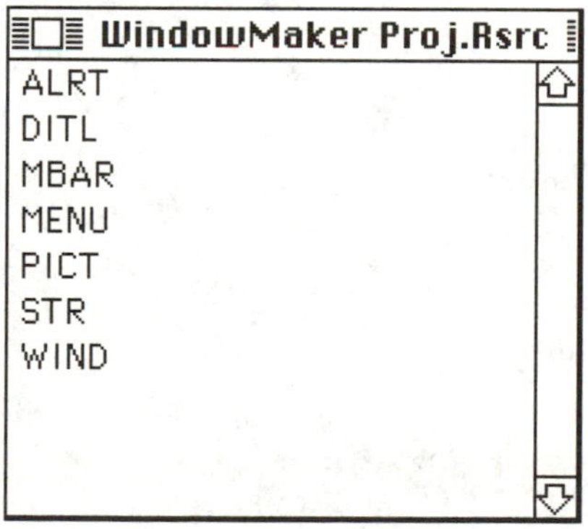

WindowMaker Proj.Rsrc

ALRT
DITL
MBAR
MENU
PICT
STR
WIND

Figure 7.7   WindowMaker resources completed.

Now, you're ready to launch THINK C. When prompted for a project to open, create a new project in the `WindowMaker` folder called `WindowMaker Proj`. Make sure to add the `MacTraps` library to your project. Create a new source file (call it `WindowMaker.c`), and add it to `WindowMaker Proj`. Here's the source code for `WindowMaker.c`:

```
#define     BASE_RES_ID             400
#define     NIL_POINTER             0L
#define     MOVE_TO_FRONT           -1L
#define     REMOVE_ALL_EVENTS       0

#define     APPLE_MENU_ID           400
#define     FILE_MENU_ID            401
#define     EDIT_MENU_ID            402

#define     ABOUT_ITEM              1
#define     ABOUT_ALERT             400
#define     ERROR_ALERT_ID          401

#define     NO_MBAR                 BASE_RES_ID
#define     NO_MENU                 BASE_RES_ID+1
#define     NO_PICTURE              BASE_RES_ID+2
#define     NO_WIND                 BASE_RES_ID+3

#define     NEW_ITEM                1
#define     CLOSE_ITEM              2
#define     QUIT_ITEM               3

#define     UNDO_ITEM               1
#define     CUT_ITEM                3
#define     COPY_ITEM               4
#define     PASTE_ITEM              5
#define     CLEAR_ITEM              6

#define     DRAG_THRESHOLD          30

#define     WINDOW_HOME_LEFT        5
#define     WINDOW_HOME_TOP         45
#define     NEW_WINDOW_OFFSET       20

#define     MIN_SLEEP               0L
#define     NIL_MOUSE_REGION        0L

#define     LEAVE_WHERE_IT_IS       FALSE

#define     WNE_TRAP_NUM            0x60
#define     UNIMPL_TRAP_NUM         0x9F

#define     NIL_STRING              "\p"
#define     HOPELESSLY_FATAL_ERROR  "\pGame over, man!"
```

```
Boolean      gDone, gWNEImplemented;
EventRecord  gTheEvent;
MenuHandle   gAppleMenu, gEditMenu;
PicHandle    gMyPicture;
Rect         gDragRect;
int          gNewWindowLeft = WINDOW_HOME_LEFT, gNewWindowTop =
                 WINDOW_HOME_TOP;


/***************************** main *********/

main()
{
      ToolBoxInit();
      MenuBarInit();
      LoadPicture();
      SetUpDragRect();

      MainLoop();
}


/******************************** ToolBoxInit */

ToolBoxInit()
{
      InitGraf( &thePort );
      InitFonts();
      FlushEvents( everyEvent, REMOVE_ALL_EVENTS );
      InitWindows();
      InitMenus();
      TEInit();
      InitDialogs( NIL_POINTER );
      InitCursor();
}


/********************************         MenuBarInit  */

MenuBarInit()
{
      Handle        myMenuBar;

      if ( ( myMenuBar = GetNewMBar( BASE_RES_ID ) ) == NIL_POINTER )
            ErrorHandler( NO_MBAR );
      SetMenuBar( myMenuBar );
      if ( ( gAppleMenu = GetMHandle( APPLE_MENU_ID ) ) == NIL_POINTER )
            ErrorHandler( NO_MENU );
      AddResMenu( gAppleMenu, 'DRVR' );
      if ( ( gEditMenu = GetMHandle( EDIT_MENU_ID ) ) == NIL_POINTER )
      ErrorHandler( NO_MENU );
      DrawMenuBar();
}
```

```
/****************************** LoadPicture *********/

LoadPicture()
{
      if ( ( gMyPicture = GetPicture( BASE_RES_ID ) ) == NIL_POINTER )
            ErrorHandler( NO_PICTURE );
}


/****************************** SetUpDragRect *********/

SetUpDragRect()
{
      gDragRect = screenBits.bounds;
      gDragRect.left += DRAG_THRESHOLD;
      gDragRect.right -= DRAG_THRESHOLD;
      gDragRect.bottom -= DRAG_THRESHOLD;
}


/****************************** MainLoop *********/

MainLoop()
{
      gDone = FALSE;
      gWNEImplemented = ( NGetTrapAddress( WNE_TRAP_NUM, ToolTrap ) !=
                  NGetTrapAddress( UNIMPL_TRAP_NUM, ToolTrap ) );
      while ( gDone == FALSE )
      {
            HandleEvent();
      }
}


/******************************** HandleEvent      */

HandleEvent()
{
      char     theChar;
      GrafPtr  oldPort;
      if ( gWNEImplemented )
            WaitNextEvent( everyEvent, &gTheEvent, MIN_SLEEP,
                  NIL_MOUSE_REGION );
      else
      {
            SystemTask();
            GetNextEvent( everyEvent, &gTheEvent );
      }

      switch ( gTheEvent.what )
      {
```

```
                case mouseDown:
                        HandleMouseDown();
                        break;
                case keyDown:
                case autoKey:
                        theChar = gTheEvent.message & charCodeMask;
                        if (( gTheEvent.modifiers & cmdKey ) != 0)
                        {
                                AdjustMenus();
                                HandleMenuChoice( MenuKey( theChar ) );
                        }
                        break;
                case updateEvt :
                        if    (!IsDAWindow ( gTheEvent.message) )
                        {
                        GetPort ( &oldPort ) ;
                        SetPort ( gTheEvent.message ) ;
                        BeginUpdate ( gTheEvent.message ) ;
                        DrawMyPicture ( gMyPicture, gTheEvent.message );
                        EndUpdate ( gTheEvent.message ) ;
                        SetPort (oldPort );
                        }
                        break;
        }
}
/************************************         HandleMouseDown    */

HandleMouseDown()
{
        WindowPtr       whichWindow;
        short int       thePart;
        long int        menuChoice, windSize;

        thePart = FindWindow( gTheEvent.where, &whichWindow );
        switch ( thePart )
        {
                case inMenuBar:
                        AdjustMenus();
                        menuChoice = MenuSelect( gTheEvent.where );
                        HandleMenuChoice( menuChoice );
                        break;
                case inSysWindow:
                        SystemClick( &gTheEvent, whichWindow );
                        break;
                case inDrag:
                        DragWindow( whichWindow, gTheEvent.where, &gDragRect );
                        break;
                case inGoAway:
                        DisposeWindow( whichWindow );
                        break;
                case inContent:
                        SelectWindow( whichWindow );
                        break;

        }
}
```

```
/*********************************** AdjustMenus */

AdjustMenus()
{
        if ( IsDAWindow( FrontWindow() ) )
        {
                EnableItem( gEditMenu, UNDO_ITEM );
                EnableItem( gEditMenu, CUT_ITEM );
                EnableItem( gEditMenu, COPY_ITEM );
                EnableItem( gEditMenu, PASTE_ITEM );
                EnableItem( gEditMenu, CLEAR_ITEM );
        }
        else
        {
                DisableItem( gEditMenu, UNDO_ITEM );
                DisableItem( gEditMenu, CUT_ITEM );
                DisableItem( gEditMenu, COPY_ITEM );
                DisableItem( gEditMenu, PASTE_ITEM );
                DisableItem( gEditMenu, CLEAR_ITEM );
        }
}


/*********************************** IsDAWindow */

IsDAWindow( whichWindow )
WindowPtr       whichWindow;
{
        if ( whichWindow == NIL_POINTER )
                return( FALSE );
        else    /* DA windows have negative windowKinds */
                return( ( (WindowPeek)whichWindow )->windowKind < 0 );
}


/*********************************** HandleMenuChoice */

HandleMenuChoice( menuChoice )
long int        menuChoice;
{
        int     theMenu;
        int     theItem;

        if ( menuChoice != 0 )
        {
                theMenu = HiWord( menuChoice );
                theItem = LoWord( menuChoice );
                switch ( theMenu )
                {
```

```
                            case APPLE_MENU_ID :
                                    HandleAppleChoice( theItem );
                                    break;
                            case FILE_MENU_ID :
                                    HandleFileChoice( theItem );
                                    break;
                            case EDIT_MENU_ID :
                                    HandleEditChoice( theItem );
                                    break;
                    }
                HiliteMenu( 0 );
        }
}


/*****************************          HandleAppleChoice    *******/

HandleAppleChoice( theItem )
int     theItem;
{
        Str255          accName;
        int             accNumber;

        switch ( theItem )
        {
                case ABOUT_ITEM :
                        NoteAlert( ABOUT_ALERT, NIL_POINTER );
                        break;
                default :
                        GetItem( gAppleMenu, theItem, accName );
                        accNumber = OpenDeskAcc( accName );
                        break;
        }
}


/******************************          HandleFileChoice    *******/

HandleFileChoice( theItem )
int     theItem;
{
        WindowPtr       whichWindow;
        switch ( theItem )
        {
                case NEW_ITEM :
                        CreateWindow();
                        break;
                case CLOSE_ITEM :
                        if ( ( whichWindow = FrontWindow() ) != NIL_POINTER )
                                DisposeWindow( whichWindow );
                        break;
                case QUIT_ITEM :
                        gDone = TRUE;
                        break;
        }
}
```

```
/******************************        HandleEditChoice      *******/

HandleEditChoice( theItem )
int    theItem;
{
       SystemEdit( theItem - 1 );
}


/*********************************** CreateWindow */

CreateWindow()
{
       WindowPtr      theNewestWindow;

       if ( ( theNewestWindow = GetNewWindow( BASE_RES_ID, NIL_POINTER,
                                MOVE_TO_FRONT ) ) == NIL_POINTER )
              ErrorHandler( NO_WIND );
       if ( ( (screenBits.bounds.right - gNewWindowLeft) < DRAG_THRESHOLD )
||
                ( ( screenBits.bounds.bottom - gNewWindowTop) < DRAG_THRESHOLD
) )
       {
              gNewWindowLeft = WINDOW_HOME_LEFT;
              gNewWindowTop = WINDOW_HOME_TOP;
       }

       MoveWindow( theNewestWindow, gNewWindowLeft,
gNewWindowTop,LEAVE_WHERE_IT_IS );
       gNewWindowLeft += NEW_WINDOW_OFFSET;
       gNewWindowTop += NEW_WINDOW_OFFSET;
       ShowWindow( theNewestWindow );
}


/******************************* DrawMyPicture *********/

DrawMyPicture( thePicture, pictureWindow )
PicHandle     thePicture;
WindowPtr     pictureWindow;
{
       Rect   myRect;

       myRect = pictureWindow->portRect;
       CenterPict( thePicture, &myRect );
       SetPort( pictureWindow );
       DrawPicture( thePicture, &myRect );
}
```

```
/***************************** CenterPict ********/

CenterPict( thePicture, myRectPtr )
PicHandle       thePicture;
Rect            *myRectPtr;
{
        Rect    windRect, pictureRect;

        windRect = *myRectPtr;
        pictureRect = (**( thePicture )).picFrame;
        myRectPtr->top = (windRect.bottom - windRect.top -
                        (pictureRect.bottom - pictureRect.top))
                        / 2 + windRect.top;
        myRectPtr->bottom = myRectPtr->top + (pictureRect.bottom -
                        pictureRect.top);
        myRectPtr->left = (windRect.right - windRect.left -
                        (pictureRect.right - pictureRect.left))
                        / 2 + windRect.left;
        myRectPtr->right = myRectPtr->left + (pictureRect.right -
                        pictureRect.left);

}


/***************************** ErrorHandler ********/

ErrorHandler( stringNum )
int     stringNum;
{
        StringHandle errorStringH;

        if ( ( errorStringH = GetString( stringNum ) ) == NIL_POINTER )
            ParamText( HOPELESSLY_FATAL_ERROR, NIL_STRING,
            NIL_STRING,NIL_STRING );
        else
        {
            HLock( errorStringH );
            ParamText( *errorStringH, NIL_STRING, NIL_STRING, NIL_STRING );
            HUnlock( errorStringH );
        }
        StopAlert( ERROR_ALERT_ID, NIL_POINTER );
        ExitToShell();
}
```

Running WindowMaker

Now that your source code is done, you're ready to run WindowMaker. Select Run from the Project menu. When asked to `Bring the project` up to date, click Yes. If you run into any compilation problems, consult the debugging tips found in Appendix E. When asked to Save changes before running, click Yes. The menu bar should display the , File, and Edit menus. Desk accessories should work. The File menu should contain three new menu items: New, Close, and Quit. The Edit menu contains the standard menu items but is dimmed. Select New from the File menu a few times: You should see something like Figure 7.8.

Each window can be selected and dragged around the screen. Selecting Close closes the currently selected window.

Try selecting New about a dozen times (or until you've created enough windows to cause window wrap). You should see something like Figure 7.9. Each new window is placed below and to the right of the previous window. When the new windows reach the bottom or the right of the screen, the window wraps back to the top left corner. Select a window and drag it partially off and then back onto the screen. An `updateEvt` will cause the `PICT` to be redrawn. Click in the close box of a window to close it. Now, choose Quit from the File menu. Let's take a look at the code.

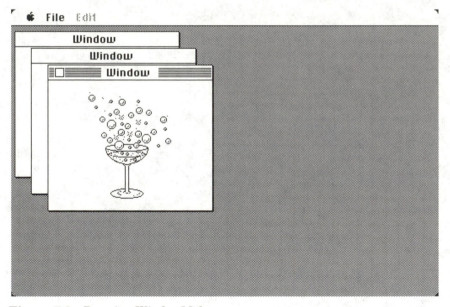

Figure 7.8 Running WindowMaker.

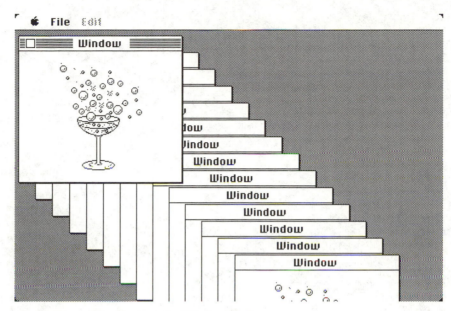

Figure 7.9 Window wrap in WindowMaker.

How WindowMaker Works

WindowMaker.c starts off with the #define statements. BASE_RES_ID, NIL_POINTER, MOVE_TO_FRONT, and REMOVE_ALL_EVENTS are the familiar assignments used in the initialization phase of the program. APPLE_MENU_ID, EDIT_MENU_ID, and FILE_MENU_ID are the resource ID numbers for the MENU resources. ABOUT_ITEM, ABOUT_ALERT, and ERROR_ALERT_ID are used for the alert section and resources. The names NO_MBAR, NO_MENU, NO_PICTURE, and NO_WIND are used to identify the resource ID of the four strings used in the error-handling routine. NEW_ITEM, CLOSE_ITEM, and QUIT_ITEM are used in the case statement in the menu-handling routines. UNDO_ITEM, CUT_ITEM, COPY_ITEM, PASTE_ITEM, and CLEAR_ITEM will be used to control the Edit menu items for desk accessories. The DRAG_THRESHOLD is used to set the distance from the edge, in pixels, that the windows may be moved or new windows created. WINDOW_HOME_LEFT and WINDOW_HOME_TOP are the default positions for a new window on the screen. The NEW_WINDOW_OFFSET is set to the number of pixels that a new window will be offset from the previous window. MIN_SLEEP and NIL_MOUSE_REGIONS are the parameters for WaitNextEvent(); LEAVE_WHERE_IT_IS is a constant for MoveWindow(). WNE_TRAP_NUM and UNIMPL_TRAP_NUM are used to determine the availability of WaitNextEvent() on the user's Mac. Finally, set up NIL_STRING and HOPELESSLY_FATAL_ERROR for use in the error-handling alert.

```
#define        BASE_RES_ID          400
#define        NIL_POINTER          0L
#define        MOVE_TO_FRONT        -1L
#define        REMOVE_ALL_EVENTS    0

#define        APPLE_MENU_ID        400
#define        FILE_MENU_ID         401
#define        EDIT_MENU_ID         402


#define        ABOUT_ITEM           1
#define        ABOUT_ALERT          400
#define        ERROR_ALERT_ID       401

#define        NO_MBAR              BASE_RES_ID
#define        NO_MENU              BASE_RES_ID+1
#define        NO_PICTURE           BASE_RES_ID+2
#define        NO_WIND              BASE_RES_ID+3

#define        NEW_ITEM             1
#define        CLOSE_ITEM           2
#define        QUIT_ITEM            3
#define        UNDO_ITEM            1
#define        CUT_ITEM             3
#define        COPY_ITEM            4
#define        PASTE_ITEM           5
#define        CLEAR_ITEM           6

#define        DRAG_THRESHOLD       30

#define        WINDOW_HOME_LEFT     5
#define        WINDOW_HOME_TOP      45
#define        NEW_WINDOW_OFFSET    20

#define        MIN_SLEEP            0L
#define        NIL_MOUSE_REGION     0L

#define        LEAVE_WHERE_IT_IS    FALSE

#define        WNE_TRAP_NUM         0x60
#define        UNIMPL_TRAP_NUM      0x9F

#define        NIL_STRING                    "\p"
#define        HOPELESSLY_FATAL_ERROR        "\pGame over, man!"
```

Then define your global variables:

```
Boolean        gDone, gWNEImplemented;
EventRecord    gTheEvent;
MenuHandle     gAppleMenu, gEditMenu;
PicHandle      gMyPicture;
Rect           gDragRect;
int            gNewWindowLeft = WINDOW_HOME_LEFT, gNewWindowTop =
                    WINDOW_HOME_TOP;
```

gDone, as always, is used as a flag for program completion. gWNEImplemented is the flag used when evaluating whether WaitNextEvent() is available. gAppleMenu and gEditMenu are handles to the MENU resource; gMyPicture, the handle to the PICT resource. gDragRect is the rectangle within the user's screen in which the window can be dragged around. gNewWindowLeft and gNewWindowTop are the left and top coordinates for new windows, and are initialized for the first window.

main() starts with the familiar calls to ToolBoxInit() and MenuInit(); then LoadPicture() loads your PICT resource, and SetUpDragRect() defines the dragging limits for windows. Next, go to MainLoop().

```
main()
{
    ToolBoxInit();
    MenuBarInit();
    LoadPicture();
    SetUpDragRect();

    MainLoop();
}
```

You haven't made any changes to ToolBoxInit():

```
/******************************** ToolBoxInit */

ToolBoxInit()
{
    InitGraf( &thePort );
    InitFonts();
    FlushEvents( everyEvent, REMOVE_ALL_EVENTS );
    InitWindows();
    InitMenus();
    TEInit();
    InitDialogs( NIL_POINTER );
    InitCursor();
}
```

In MenuBarInit(), load your menu resources and draw the menu bar. Everything is standard operating procedure except for the new error handling. If GetNewMBar(BASE_RES_ID) returns a NIL_POINTER, it indicates that the operating system could not find the MBAR resource in your resource file; the error-handling routine, ErrorHandler(), will then display an alert containing the string('STR ') resource with an ID number of NO_MBAR. The same thing happens if the ⌘ or Edit menu resource cannot be found:

```
/*******************************        MenuBarInit  */

MenuBarInit()
{
      Handle        myMenuBar;

      if ( ( myMenuBar = GetNewMBar( BASE_RES_ID ) ) == NIL_POINTER )
            ErrorHandler( NO_MBAR );
      SetMenuBar( myMenuBar );
      if ( ( gAppleMenu = GetMHandle( APPLE_MENU_ID ) ) == NIL_POINTER )
            ErrorHandler( NO_MENU );
      AddResMenu( gAppleMenu, 'DRVR' );
      if ( ( gEditMenu = GetMHandle( EDIT_MENU_ID ) ) == NIL_POINTER )
      ErrorHandler( NO_MENU );
      DrawMenuBar();
}
```

LoadPicture() gets the PICT resource out of your resource file. This
version of LoadPicture() also checks to see if the resource was available.
If not, the error-handling routine is run with the 'STR' resource string
possessing ID number NO_PICTURE.

```
/*****************************  LoadPicture  *********/

LoadPicture()
{
      if ( ( gMyPicture = GetPicture( BASE_RES_ID ) ) == NIL_POINTER )
            ErrorHandler( NO_PICTURE );
}
```

SetUpDragRect() initializes the region within which windows can be
dragged and new windows created. The initial Rect is set to the size of the
screen (screenBits.bounds); the left, right, and bottom of the Rect are
then decremented by DRAG_THRESHOLD. (Try changing DRAG_THRESHOLD
to a number other than 30 and see what happens to the application.)

```
/*****************************  SetUpDragRect  *********/

SetUpDragRect()
{
      gDragRect = screenBits.bounds;
      gDragRect.left += DRAG_THRESHOLD;
      gDragRect.right -= DRAG_THRESHOLD;
      gDragRect.bottom -= DRAG_THRESHOLD;
}
```

MainLoop() checks to see if WaitNextEvent() is implemented.

```
/****************************          MainLoop      *********/
MainLoop()
{
        gDone = FALSE;
        gWNEImplemented = ( NGetTrapAddress( WNE_TRAP_NUM, ToolTrap ) !=
                     NGetTrapAddress( UNIMPL_TRAP_NUM, ToolTrap ) );
        while ( gDone == FALSE )
        {
                HandleEvent();
        }
}
```

HandleEvent() is similar to the earlier event handlers, except that cut, copy, and paste operations are now supported in desk accessories. AdjustMenus() is now called if a command key equivalent event has occurred, to change the state of the Edit menu. updateEvts are handled with a call to DrawMyPicture().

```
/*********************************** HandleEvent      */
HandleEvent()
{
        char    theChar;
        GrafPtr oldPort;
        if ( gWNEImplemented )
                WaitNextEvent( everyEvent, &gTheEvent, MIN_SLEEP,
                        NIL_MOUSE_REGION );
        else
        {
                SystemTask();
                GetNextEvent( everyEvent, &gTheEvent );
        }

        switch ( gTheEvent.what )
        {
                case mouseDown:
                        HandleMouseDown();
                        break;
                case keyDown:
                case autoKey:
                        theChar = gTheEvent.message & charCodeMask;
                        if (( gTheEvent.modifiers & cmdKey ) != 0)
                        {
                                AdjustMenus();
                                HandleMenuChoice( MenuKey( theChar ) );
                        }
                        break;
                case updateEvt :
                        if    (!IsDAWindow ( gTheEvent.message) )
                        {
                                GetPort ( &oldPort ) ;
                                SetPort ( gTheEvent.message ) ;
                                BeginUpdate ( gTheEvent.message ) ;
                                DrawMyPicture ( gMyPicture, gTheEvent.message );
                                EndUpdate ( gTheEvent.message ) ;
                                SetPort (oldPort );
                        }
                        break;
        }
}
```

Now, HandleMouseDown() supports desk accessory use of the Edit menu. AdjustMenus() is also called to activate the Edit menu if a mouseDown has occurred in the menu bar. Clicking in the close box calls DisposeWindow(), which will close and free up the memory used for the window.

```
/*************************************** HandleMouseDown */

HandleMouseDown()
{
        WindowPtr       whichWindow;
        short int       thePart;
        long int        menuChoice, windSize;

        thePart = FindWindow( gTheEvent.where, &whichWindow );
        switch ( thePart )
        {
                case inMenuBar:
                        AdjustMenus();
                        menuChoice = MenuSelect( gTheEvent.where );
                        HandleMenuChoice( menuChoice );
                        break;
                case inSysWindow:
                        SystemClick( &gTheEvent, whichWindow );
                        break;
                case inDrag:
                        DragWindow( whichWindow, gTheEvent.where, &gDragRect );
                        break;
                case inGoAway:
                        DisposeWindow( whichWindow );
                        break;
                case inContent:
                        SelectWindow( whichWindow );
                        break;
        }
}
```

AdjustMenus() and IsDAWindow() work together: AdjustMenus() enables and disables the items in the Edit menu, depending on whether the current window is a desk accessory window or a WindowMaker window. To determine this we look into the structure of the current window: One of the fields of a window, windowKind, is positive if the window is an application window and negative if it is a desk accessory window. So, in IsDAWindow(), FALSE is returned if there is no window, or if the window belongs to WindowMaker, and all items in the Edit menu are disabled (dimmed). If TRUE is returned, the Edit items are enabled so that desk accessories can use them.

```
/********************************** AdjustMenus */

AdjustMenus()
{
        if ( IsDAWindow( FrontWindow() ) )
        {
                EnableItem( gEditMenu, UNDO_ITEM );
                EnableItem( gEditMenu, CUT_ITEM );
                EnableItem( gEditMenu, COPY_ITEM );
                EnableItem( gEditMenu, PASTE_ITEM );
                EnableItem( gEditMenu, CLEAR_ITEM );
        }
        else
        {
                DisableItem( gEditMenu, UNDO_ITEM );
                DisableItem( gEditMenu, CUT_ITEM );
                DisableItem( gEditMenu, COPY_ITEM );
                DisableItem( gEditMenu, PASTE_ITEM );
                DisableItem( gEditMenu, CLEAR_ITEM );
        }
}


/********************************** IsDAWindow */

IsDAWindow( whichWindow )
WindowPtr       whichWindow;
{
        if ( whichWindow == NIL_POINTER )
                return( FALSE );
        else    /* DA windows have negative windowKinds */
                return( ( (WindowPeek)whichWindow )->windowKind < 0 );
}
```

HandleMenuChoice( ) **hasn't changed from the earlier programs with
menus, except that you now handle Edit menu selections:**

```
/********************************** HandleMenuChoice */

HandleMenuChoice( menuChoice )
long int        menuChoice;
{
        int     theMenu;
        int     theItem;

        if ( menuChoice != 0 )
        {
                theMenu = HiWord( menuChoice );
                theItem = LoWord( menuChoice );
                switch ( theMenu )
                {
```

```
                        case APPLE_MENU_ID :
                                HandleAppleChoice( theItem );
                                break;
                        case FILE_MENU_ID :
                                HandleFileChoice( theItem );
                                break;
                        case EDIT_MENU_ID :
                                HandleEditChoice( theItem );
                                break;
                }
            HiliteMenu( 0 );
        }
}
```

HandleAppleChoice() works the same way as Chapter 6's Reminder program. The about item calls NoteAlert(), which displays the ALRT and the DITL you set up for the about box.

```
/*******************************          HandleAppleChoice    *******/

HandleAppleChoice( theItem )
int     theItem;
{
        Str255          accName;
        int             accNumber;

        switch ( theItem )
        {
                case ABOUT_ITEM :
                        NoteAlert( ABOUT_ALERT, NIL_POINTER );
                        break;
                default :
                        GetItem( gAppleMenu, theItem, accName );
                        accNumber = OpenDeskAcc( accName );
                        break;
        }
}
```

HandleFileChoice() takes care of the File menu choices. The New menu item runs the routine CreateWindow(), and the Close menu item closes the active window by calling DisposeWindow(). Using the Close menu item is the same as clicking in the active window's close box. Quit sets gDone to TRUE, which halts execution of the main event loop.

```
/*******************************        HandleFileChoice       *******/

HandleFileChoice( theItem )
int    theItem;
{
      WindowPtr    whichWindow;
      switch ( theItem )
      {
            case NEW_ITEM :
                  CreateWindow();
                  break;
            case CLOSE_ITEM :
                  if ( ( whichWindow = FrontWindow() ) != NIL_POINTER )
                        DisposeWindow( whichWindow );
                  break;
            case QUIT_ITEM :
                  gDone = TRUE;
                  break;
      }
}
```

HandleEditChoice() calls SystemEdit(). If the active window belongs to a desk accessory, SystemEdit() passes the appropriate edit command to the accessory. Otherwise, it returns FALSE, and your application should then handle the edit command. Since the Edit menu items are disabled in WindowMaker, HandleEditChoice() just takes care of desk accessories.

```
********************************* HandleEditChoice     *******/

HandleEditChoice( theItem )
int    theItem;
{
      SystemEdit( theItem - 1 );
}
```

CreateWindow() controls the creation and placing of new windows for WindowMaker. First, use GetNewWindow() with your WIND resource to create a new window. If the WIND is missing, GetNewWindow() returns a NIL_POINTER, so you can call ErrorHandler() with a 'STR ' resource of NO_WIND.

```
/********************************** CreateWindow */

CreateWindow()
{
      WindowPtr    theNewestWindow;

      if ( ( theNewestWindow = GetNewWindow( BASE_RES_ID, NIL_POINTER,
                              MOVE_TO_FRONT ) ) == NIL_POINTER )
            ErrorHandler( NO_WIND );
```

Next, check to see if the left edge or the top of the new window is within DRAG_THRESHOLD pixels of the edge of the screen. If so, reset gNewWindowLeft and gNewWindowTop to the home position.

```
if ( ( (screenBits.bounds.right - gNewWindowLeft)
                                    < DRAG_THRESHOLD ) ||
        ( ( screenBits.bounds.bottom - gNewWindowTop)
                                    < DRAG_THRESHOLD ) )
{
        gNewWindowLeft = WINDOW_HOME_LEFT;
        gNewWindowTop = WINDOW_HOME_TOP;
}

MoveWindow( theNewestWindow, gNewWindowLeft,
                            gNewWindowTop,LEAVE_WHERE_IT_IS );
gNewWindowLeft += NEW_WINDOW_OFFSET;
gNewWindowTop += NEW_WINDOW_OFFSET;
ShowWindow( theNewestWindow );
}
```

Normally, you'd use the position of a window as specified in the WIND resource. In this case, however, the position of each new window is defined by the globals gNewWindowLeft and gNewWindowTop. Whenever a new window is defined, MoveWindow() is called to move the window from the original WIND-based position to the position described by gNewWindowLeft and gNewWindowTop. The final parameter to MoveWindow() is a Boolean that determines whether the window, once moved, is moved to the front of all other windows or is left in the same layer. LEAVE_WHERE_IT_IS tells MoveWindow() not to move the window to the front. Since the window was created in the front, this parameter will have no effect.

Next, gNewWindowLeft and gNewWindowTop are incremented by NEW_WINDOW_OFFSET, so the next new window won't appear directly on top of the previous one. Finally, the window is made visible.

DrawMyPicture() passes gMyPicture to CenterPict() and then draws the centered PICT in pictureWindow.

The real value of parameter passing is seen here. By passing the WindowPtr embedded in gTheEvent.message as a parameter to DrawMyPicture(), you avoid hard-coded variable names that would limit the flexibility of this routine.

```
/****************************** DrawMyPicture *********/

DrawMyPicture( thePicture, pictureWindow )
PicHandle      thePicture;
WindowPtr      pictureWindow;
{
        Rect    myRect;

        myRect = pictureWindow->portRect;
        CenterPict( thePicture, &myRect );
        SetPort( pictureWindow );
        DrawPicture( thePicture, &myRect );
}
```

CenterPict() **is the same routine you've used in your other** PICT **drawing programs:**

```
/****************************** CenterPict *********/

CenterPict( thePicture, myRectPtr )
PicHandle      thePicture;
Rect    *myRectPtr;
{
        Rect    windRect, pictureRect;

        windRect = *myRectPtr;
        pictureRect = (**( thePicture )).picFrame;
        myRectPtr->top = (windRect.bottom - windRect.top -
                        (pictureRect.bottom - pictureRect.top))
            / 2 + windRect.top;
        myRectPtr->bottom = myRectPtr->top + (pictureRect.bottom -
                        pictureRect.top);
        myRectPtr->left = (windRect.right - windRect.left -
                        (pictureRect.right - pictureRect.left))
            / 2 + windRect.left;
        myRectPtr->right = myRectPtr->left + (pictureRect.right -
                        pictureRect.left);
}
```

Finally, there's the ErrorHandler() routine. ErrorHandler() **takes an error ID as input, loads the** 'STR' **resource with that ID, and uses** StopAlert() **to display the error message. If the program can't find the** 'STR' **resource it needs, it calls** StopAlert() **with the** HOPELESSLY_FATAL_ERROR **string defined at the beginning of Window-Maker** (Game Over, Man), **to inform the user that the situation is exceedingly grim.**

Finally, ExitToShell() **returns control of the Macintosh to the Finder.**

```
/******************************* ErrorHandler ********/

ErrorHandler( stringNum )
int     stringNum;
{
        StringHandle errorStringH;

        if ( ( errorStringH = GetString( stringNum ) ) == NIL_POINTER )
                ParamText( HOPELESSLY_FATAL_ERROR, NIL_STRING,
                NIL_STRING,NIL_STRING );
        else
        {
                HLock( errorStringH );
                ParamText( *errorStringH, NIL_STRING, NIL_STRING, NIL_STRING );
                HUnlock( errorStringH );
        }
        StopAlert( ERROR_ALERT_ID, NIL_POINTER );
        ExitToShell();
}
```

There are many solutions to error handling on the Macintosh. Whenever you make a Toolbox function call, check to see if an error has occurred. This is called passive error handling. Sometimes this is good enough, sometimes it's not.

You can also go out of your way to avoid errors by checking everything you can possibly check. For example, take another look at this code fragment from the `MenuInit()` routine:

```
MenuBarInit()
{
        Handle          myMenuBar;

        if ( ( myMenuBar = GetNewMBar( BASE_RES_ID ) ) == NIL_POINTER )
                ErrorHandler( NO_MBAR );
        SetMenuBar( myMenuBar );
        if ( ( gAppleMenu = GetMHandle( APPLE_MENU_ID ) ) == NIL_POINTER )
                ErrorHandler( NO_MENU );
        AddResMenu( gAppleMenu, 'DRVR' );
        DrawMenuBar();
}
```

Although you check the return codes from both function calls in `Menu-Init()`, you still missed something. What happens if the File or Edit MENU resources are not found? The program will not function properly and will most probably crash. Checking all your resources may be time-consuming, but in the end, it's well worth it.

Here's a version of `MenuInit()` with proactive error handling:

```
MenuBarInit()
{
        Handle          myMenuBar;

        if ( ( myMenuBar = GetNewMBar( BASE_RES_ID ) ) == NIL_POINTER )
                ErrorHandler( NO_MBAR );
        if ( ( gAppleMenu = GetMHandle( APPLE_MENU_ID ) ) == NIL_POINTER )
                ErrorHandler( NO_MENU );
        if ( ( gFileMenu = GetMHandle( FILE_MENU_ID ) ) == NIL_POINTER )
                ErrorHandler( NO_MENU );
        if ( ( gEditMenu = GetMHandle( EDIT_MENU_ID ) ) == NIL_POINTER )
                ErrorHandler( NO_MENU );
        AddResMenu( gAppleMenu, 'DRVR' );
        SetMenuBar( myMenuBar );
        DrawMenuBar();
}
```

You can take error handling one step further and also check your resources just before you use them. For example, you could call `GetMHandle()` immediately before `MenuSelect()` in case the `MENU` was somehow corrupted.

You'll decide on the appropriate amount of error handling to perform. Error handling bulks code up but provides a higher level of reliability for your program. We highly recommend the inclusion of error-handling code early in the programming cycle.

The Scrap Manager

Whenever you use the Mac's copy, cut, or paste facilities, you're making use of the **Scrap Manager**. The Scrap Manager manages the **desk scrap**, more commonly known as the **Clipboard**. The second program, **ShowClip**, will use the Scrap Manager Toolbox routines to open the Clipboard and display the contents in a window.

Scrap Manager Basics

Data copied to the desk scrap is stored in two basic flavors, `TEXT` and `PICT`. Data stored in `TEXT` format consist of a series of ASCII characters. Data stored in `PICT` format consist of a QuickDraw picture. ShowClip will handle both `TEXT` and `PICT` data types.

The Scrap Manager consists of six routines: `InfoScrap()`, `UnloadScrap()`, `LoadScrap()`, `ZeroScrap()`, `PutScrap()`, and `GetScrap()`. Each of these functions returns a long integer containing a result code (I:457).

InfoScrap()

InfoScrap() is a function (of type PScrapStuff) that returns information about the desk scrap in a struct of type ScrapStuff:

```
typedef struct  ScrapStuff
{
   long        scrapSize;
   Handle      scrapHandle;
   int         scrapCount;
   int         scrapState;
   StringPtr   scrapName;
} ScrapStuff, *PScrapStuff;
```

The scrapSize field contains the actual size, in bytes, of the desk scrap. The scrapHandle field contains a handle to the desk scrap (if it currently resides in memory). The scrapCount field is changed every time ZeroScrap() is called (we'll get to ZeroScrap() in a bit). The scrapState field is positive if the desk scrap is memory resident, zero if the scrap is on disk, and negative if the scrap has not yet been initialized. The scrapName field contains a pointer to the name of the scrap disk file (usually called the Clipboard file).

UnloadScrap() and LoadScrap()

If the scrap is currently in memory, UnloadScrap() copies the scrap to disk and releases the scrap's memory. If the scrap is currently disk-based, UnloadScrap() does nothing.

If the scrap is currently on disk, LoadScrap() allocates memory for the scrap and copies it from disk. If the scrap is currently memory-resident, LoadScrap() does nothing.

ZeroScrap()

If the desk scrap does not yet exist, ZeroScrap() creates it in memory. If it does exist, ZeroScrap() clears it. As we mentioned before, ZeroScrap() always changes the scrapCount field of the ScrapStuff struct.

PutScrap()

PutScrap() puts the data pointed to by source into the scrap:

```
long PutScrap( length, theType, source )
long      length;
ResType   theType;
Ptr       source;
```

The parameter `length` specifies the length of the data, and `theType` specifies its type (whether it's `PICT` or `TEXT` data). You must call `ZeroScrap()` immediately before each call to `PutScrap()`.

GetScrap()

`GetScrap()` resizes the handle `hDest` and stores a copy of the scrap in this resized block of memory:

```
long GetScrap( hDest, theType, offset )
Handle  hDest;
ResType theType;
long    *offset;
```

Specify the type of data you want in the parameter `theType`. The `offset` parameter is set to the returned data's offset in bytes from the beginning of the desk scrap. `GetScrap()` returns a long containing the length of the data in bytes.

You can actually put and get data types other than `TEXT` and `PICT` to and from the scrap (I:461). For the most part, however, the `TEXT` and `PICT` data types should serve your needs.

ShowClip

The ability to use the Clipboard is basic to Mac applications. ShowClip shows you how to add this capability to your applications. If you cut or copy text or a picture in an application or in the Finder and then run ShowClip, it will display the cut or copied text in a window.

ShowClip Specifications

The structure of ShowClip works like this:

- It initializes the Toolbox.
- It initializes a window.
- It puts whatever is in the Clipboard into the window.
- It quits.

ShowClip also does error checking. It warns if the `WIND` resource is missing, or if the scrap is empty.

Setting Up the ShowClip Project

Start by creating a folder for this project, called **ShowClip**. Use ResEdit to create a new file called **ShowClip Proj.Rsrc** and, within that, a WIND with an ID of 400. Figure 7.10 shows the specifications of this WIND.

Add the DITL in Figure 7.11 (this is the same ALRT as the "hopelessly fatal" DITL in WindowMaker, so use the WindowMaker DITL if you have it.

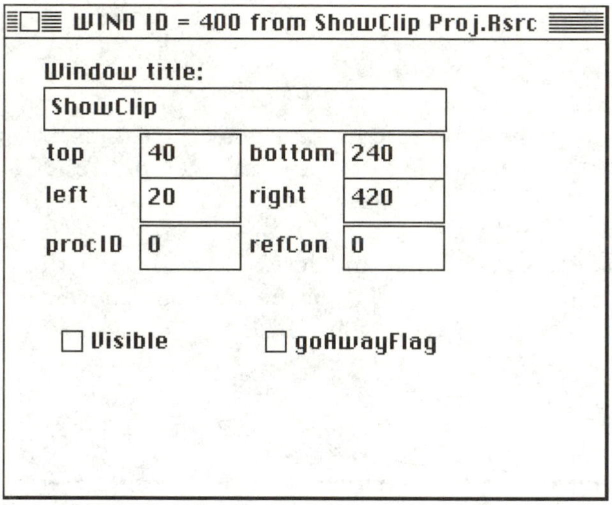

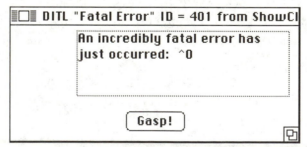

Figure 7.10   WIND resource for ShowClip.

Figure 7.11   DITL resource for ShowClip.

Item#	Type	Enabled	top	left	bottom	right	Text/Resource ID
1	Button	Yes	86	117	106	177	Gasp!
2	Static Text	Yes	5	67	71	283	An incredibly fatal error has just occurred: ^0

Figure 7.11   DITL resource for ShowClip (*continued*).

Next, create an ALRT resource for your new error-checking routines (Figure 7.12). Add the two 'STR' resources shown in Figure 7.13 to the ShowClip Proj.rsrc file. Again, be sure to change the resource IDs of each resource to those shown in the figure. When you're done, the resource ShowClip Proj.rsrc should look like Figure 7.14.

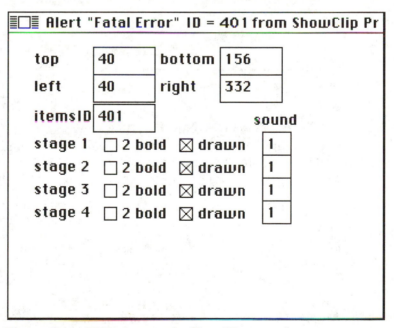

Figure 7.12   DITL resource for ShowClip.

```
          STR  ID = 400 from ShowClip Proj.Rsrc
  theStr        Can't load the WIND resource!!!
  Data      $
```

```
          STR  ID = 401 from ShowClip Proj.Rsrc
  theStr        Clipboard is Empty!!!
  Data      $
```

Figure 7.13 STR resources for ShowClip.

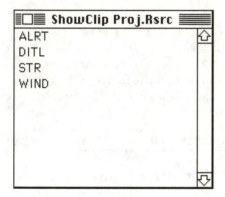

Figure 7.14 ShowClip
resources completed.

Now you're ready to launch THINK C. When prompted for a project to open, create a new project in the `ShowClip` folder and call it `ShowClip Proj`. Add `MacTraps` to your project. Create a new source file called `ShowClip.c` and add it to `ShowClip Proj`. Here's the source code for `ShowClip.c`:

```
#define        BASE_RES_ID            400
#define        NIL_POINTER            0L
#define        MOVE_TO_FRONT          -1L
#define        REMOVE_ALL_EVENTS      0

#define        ERROR_ALERT_ID               BASE_RES_ID+1
#define        NO_WIND                      BASE_RES_ID
#define        EMPTY_SCRAP                  BASE_RES_ID+1

#define        NIL_STRING                   "\p"
#define        HOPELESSLY_FATAL_ERROR       "\pGame over, man!"

WindowPtr      gClipWindow;
```

```
/***************************** main ********/

main()
{
      ToolBoxInit();
      WindowInit();
      MainLoop();
}


/***************************** ToolBoxInit ********/

ToolBoxInit()
{
      InitGraf( &thePort );
      InitFonts();
      FlushEvents( everyEvent, REMOVE_ALL_EVENTS );
      InitWindows();
      InitMenus();
      TEInit();
      InitDialogs( NIL_POINTER );
      InitCursor();
}


/***************************** WindowInit ********/

WindowInit()
{
      if ( ( gClipWindow = GetNewWindow( BASE_RES_ID, NIL_POINTER,
                      MOVE_TO_FRONT ) ) == NIL_POINTER )
                      ErrorHandler( NO_WIND );
      ShowWindow( gClipWindow );
      SetPort( gClipWindow );
}


/***************************** MainLoop ********/

MainLoop()
{
      Rect        myRect;
      Handle      clipHandle;
      long int    length, offset;

      clipHandle = NewHandle( 0 );
      if ( ( length = GetScrap( clipHandle, 'TEXT', &offset ) ) < 0 )
      {
            if ( ( length = GetScrap( clipHandle, 'PICT', &offset ) ) < 0 )
                  ErrorHandler( EMPTY_SCRAP );
            else
            {
```

```
                        myRect = gClipWindow->portRect;
                        CenterPict( clipHandle, &myRect );
                        DrawPicture( clipHandle, &myRect );
                }
        }
        else
        {
                HLock( clipHandle );
                TextBox( *clipHandle, length, &(thePort->portRect),
                        teJustLeft );
                HUnlock( clipHandle );
        }

        while ( !Button() ) ;
}


/****************************** CenterPict *********/

CenterPict( thePicture, myRectPtr )
PicHandle      thePicture;
Rect    *myRectPtr;
{
        Rect    windRect, pictureRect;

        windRect = *myRectPtr;
        pictureRect = (**( thePicture )).picFrame;
        myRectPtr->top = (windRect.bottom - windRect.top -
                (pictureRect.bottom - pictureRect.top))
                / 2 + windRect.top;
        myRectPtr->bottom = myRectPtr->top + (pictureRect.bottom -
                pictureRect.top);
        myRectPtr->left = (windRect.right - windRect.left -
                (pictureRect.right - pictureRect.left))
                / 2 + windRect.left;
        myRectPtr->right = myRectPtr->left + (pictureRect.right -
                pictureRect.left);
}


/****************************** ErrorHandler *********/

ErrorHandler( stringNum )
int     stringNum;
{
        StringHandle errorStringH;

        if ( ( errorStringH = GetString( stringNum ) ) == NIL_POINTER )
                ParamText( HOPELESSLY_FATAL_ERROR, NIL_STRING, NIL_STRING,
                                NIL_STRING );
        else
        {
```

```
        HLock( errorStringH );
        ParamText( *errorStringH, NIL_STRING, NIL_STRING,
NIL_STRING );
        HUnlock( errorStringH );
    }
    StopAlert( ERROR_ALERT_ID, NIL_POINTER );
    ExitToShell();
}
```

Running ShowClip

Now that your source code is done, you're ready to run ShowClip. Before you run the program, however, do a cut or copy operation on the `ShowClip.c` file, or copy a picture from the Scrapbook; otherwise, you'll get an alert telling you that the scrap is empty. Now run ShowClip. It should immediately display the text or picture that you cut or copied (Figure 7.15).

Quit by clicking the mouse. Try copying varying sizes of text, or different pictures and running ShowClip again. This code should point out the ease with which you can add the Clipboard functions to your applications.

Now, let's see how it's done.

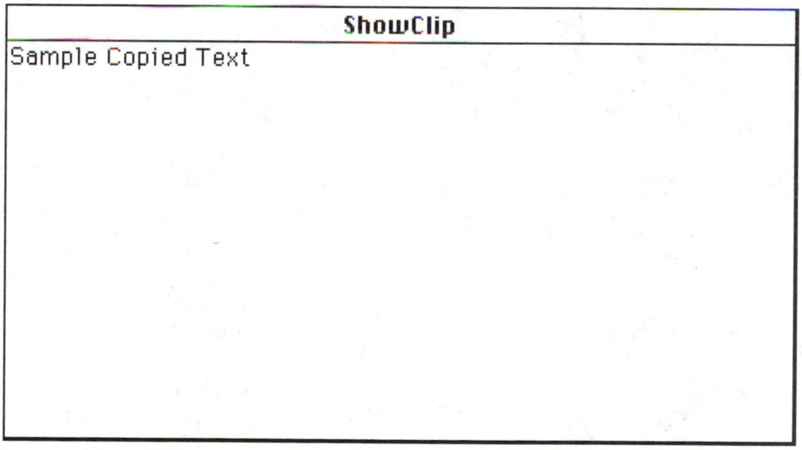

Figure 7.15   Running ShowClip.

How ShowClip Works

ShowClip.c starts off with the #define constants that you'll be using. (You saw these in WindowMaker already.) Next, declare your only global variable:

```
#define          BASE_RES_ID          400
#define          NIL_POINTER          0L
#define          MOVE_TO_FRONT        -1L
#define          REMOVE_ALL_EVENTS    0

#define          ERROR_ALERT_ID       BASE_RES_ID+1

#define          NO_WIND              BASE_RES_ID
#define          EMPTY_SCRAP          BASE_RES_ID+1

#define          NIL_STRING                   "\p"
#define          HOPELESSLY_FATAL_ERROR       "\pGame over, man!"
```

gClipWindow is the pointer to the window you'll use to display your scrap.

```
WindowPtr        gClipWindow;
```

main() calls ToolBoxInit(), WindowInit(), and then MainLoop(). No excitement here.

```
/****************************** main *********/

main()
{
     ToolBoxInit();
     WindowInit();
     MainLoop();
}
```

There aren't any changes in ToolBoxInit():

```
/****************************** ToolBoxInit *********/

ToolBoxInit()
{
     InitGraf( &thePort );
     InitFonts();
     FlushEvents( everyEvent, REMOVE_ALL_EVENTS );
     InitWindows();
     InitMenus();
     TEInit();
     InitDialogs( NIL_POINTER );
     InitCursor();
}
```

In WindowInit(), use GetNewWindow() to get gClipWindow from the resource file. Then call ShowWindow() to make gClipWindow visible, and SetPort() so that all drawing is done in gClipWindow:

```
/****************************** WindowInit ********/

WindowInit()
{
    if ( ( gClipWindow = GetNewWindow( BASE_RES_ID, NIL_POINTER,
                    MOVE_TO_FRONT ) ) == NIL_POINTER )
        ErrorHandler( NO_WIND );
    ShowWindow( gClipWindow );
    SetPort( gClipWindow );
}
```

MainLoop() is where the action is. You use NewHandle() (II:32) to create minimum-size blocks of storage for your PICT and TEXT data. Remember, GetScrap() will resize these memory blocks for you, as needed.

```
/****************************** MainLoop ********/

MainLoop()
{
    Rect          myRect;
    Handle        clipHandle;
    long int      length, offset;

    clipHandle = NewHandle( 0 );
```

Now, call GetScrap(), looking first for some TEXT data. If there are no TEXT data in the scrap, call GetScrap() to look for PICT data. If you find no PICT data, call ErrorHandler() with the EMPTY_SCRAP string. If you do find PICT data, call CenterPict() to center the picture in gClipWindow, and then call DrawPicture() to draw the picture:

```
if ( ( length = GetScrap( clipHandle, 'TEXT', &offset ) ) < 0 )
{
    if ( ( length = GetScrap( clipHandle, 'PICT', &offset ) ) < 0 )
        ErrorHandler( EMPTY_SCRAP );
    else
    {
        myRect = gClipWindow->portRect;
        CenterPict( clipHandle, &myRect );
        DrawPicture( clipHandle, &myRect );
    }
}
```

If you found the TEXT data in the scrap, lock clipHandle with Hlock(), then call TextBox() to draw the text in gClipWindow.

```
    else
    {
        HLock( clipHandle );
        TextBox( *clipHandle, length, &(thePort->portRect), teJustLeft
);
        HUnlock( clipHandle );
    }
```

Finally, wait for a mouse click to exit the program:

```
    while ( !Button() ) ;
}
```

CenterPict() is the same routine you've used in the other *Primer* PICT drawing programs:

```
/******************************* CenterPict ********/

CenterPict( thePicture, myRectPtr )
PicHandle       thePicture;
Rect            *myRectPtr;
{
    Rect    windRect, pictureRect;

    windRect = *myRectPtr;
    pictureRect = (**( thePicture )).picFrame;
    myRectPtr->top = (windRect.bottom - windRect.top -(pictureRect.bottom
            - pictureRect.top))
            / 2 + windRect.top;
    myRectPtr->bottom = myRectPtr->top + (pictureRect.bottom -
            pictureRect.top);
    myRectPtr->left = (windRect.right - windRect.left -
            (pictureRect.right - pictureRect.left))
            / 2 + windRect.left;
    myRectPtr->right = myRectPtr->left + (pictureRect.right -
            pictureRect.left);
}
```

ErrorHandler() is the same routine that's part of WindowMaker. Here, you get the string you need, then display it with StopAlert(). ExitToShell() halts program execution and brings up the Finder.

```
/******************************* ErrorHandler ********/

ErrorHandler( stringNum )
int     stringNum;
{
    StringHandle errorStringH;
```

```
if ( ( errorStringH = GetString( stringNum ) ) == NIL_POINTER )
      ParamText( HOPELESSLY_FATAL_ERROR, NIL_STRING, NIL_STRING,
            NIL_STRING );
else
{
      HLock( errorStringH );
      ParamText( *errorStringH, NIL_STRING, NIL_STRING, NIL_STRING );
      HUnlock( errorStringH );
}
StopAlert( ERROR_ALERT_ID, NIL_POINTER );
ExitToShell();
}
```

Inside the Printing and File Managers

The next program, PrintPICT, makes use of both the **Printing Manager** and the **File Manager**. PrintPICT uses the **Standard File Package** (IV:71) to prompt for the name of a PICT file to print. It opens the file, reads in a chunk of data, builds a page, and sends the page to the current printer. The power of the File and Printing Managers makes this task a simple one. Let's take a look at the Standard File Package.

The Standard File Package

The Standard File Package is used by most Macintosh applications to support the Open, Save, and Save As... File menu items. Figure 7.16 shows examples of calls to SFGetFile() and SFPutFile(). SFGetFile() is used to get a file name from the user. It can be called with a list of file types, limiting the user's choices to files of the types specified on the list. PrintPICT prints a single PICT file. By calling SFGetFile(), PrintPICT allows the user to select the print file from a list limited to PICT files.

The File Manager was totally remade when the Mac Plus came out. The original Macintosh Filing System (MFS) was inadequate to handle the number of files that hard disks could hold. The Hierarchical Filing System (HFS) replaced it, and Volume IV details the new Toolbox calls. So, if you need information about the File Manager, use Chapter 19 of Volume IV, not Chapter 4 of Volume II, which has been superseded.

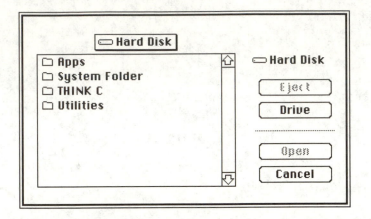

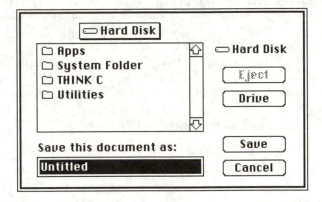

Figure 7.16 SFGetFile() and SFPutFile().

Here's the calling sequence for SFGetFile():

```
SFGetFile( where, prompt, fileFilter, numTypes, typeList,
dlgHook, reply );
Point          where;
Str255         prompt;
ProcPtr fileFilter;
int            numTypes;
SFTypeList     typeList;
ProcPtr dlgHook;
SFReply *reply;
```

SFGetFile() displays the standard open dialog on the screen at the point where. The prompt string is ignored. numTypes and typeList allow you to specify up to four distinct file types (like PICT or TEXT) for the user to choose from.

> Actually, you can specify as many file types as you like by creating your own data type, instead of SFTypeList. SFGetFile() looks in typeList for numTypes types.

fileFilter is a pointer to a filtering routine called by SFGetFile() after the file list is built from the typeList. This filtering routine can modify the file list before it's displayed to the user.

dlgHook also points to a function. The dlgHook function you write allows you to add extra items (like pop-up menus) to the standard open dialog.

Once the user selects a file, SFGetFile() fills in the struct pointed to by reply with information about the selected file:

```
typedef   struct SFReply
{
  char          good;
  char          copy;
  long          fType;   /* array[1..4] of char; */
  int           vRefNum;
  int           version;
  unsigned charfName[64];
} SFReply;
```

The good field contains FALSE if the user pressed the Cancel button, TRUE otherwise. The copy field is not currently used. The fType field contains the file type selected (if the good field contains TRUE). The version field always contains 0. The vRefNum and fName fields specify the selected file. You'll see how to use these last two fields in the next section.

Using the File Manager

Once the user has picked a file to open (via SFGetFile()), you'll use the File Manager routines FSOpen() to open the file, FSRead() to read a block of data, and FSClose() to close the file.

There are a few key terms you should know before you use the File Manager. **Volumes** are the media used to store files. When the user presses the Drive button in the SFGetFile() dialog box, they look at the files on the next available volume. Macintosh floppy and hard disks are both examples of volumes. In the original Macintosh (the one with 64K ROMs), all the files on a volume were organized in a flat file format called the Macintosh File System (MFS) (Figure 7.17).

The concept of **folders** existed on these "flat" Macs, but internally the files on a volume were all stored in one big list. The folders were an illusion maintained by the Finder. On flat volumes, users can't have two files with the same name, even if they're in different folders. The Mac Plus (with 128K ROMs) introduced a new method for organizing files: the Hierarchical File System (HFS) (Figure 7.18).

> Within each HFS volume is a set of files and directories. Within each directory, there can be still more files and directories. You'll use the File Manager Toolbox calls to open, read, write, and close these files and directories.

FSOpen( ) opens the specified file for reading and/or writing, depending on the file's open permission:

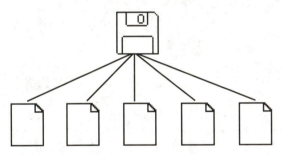

Figure 7.17   Flat files.

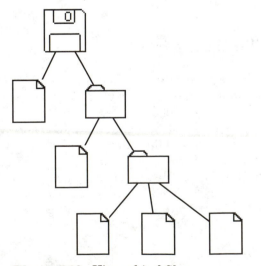

Figure 7.18   Hierarchical files.

```
OSErr    FSOpen( fileName, vRefNum, refNum )
Str255   fileName;
int      vRefNum, *refNum;
```

> SFGetFile() translates the user's file selection into a vRefNum and an fName. The vRefNum specifies the file's volume and directory, and the fName specifies the file name. FSOpen() gets open permission from a file control block stored on the file's volume.

Use the fileName and vRefnum fields of the reply record returned by SFGetFile() as parameters to FSOpen(). FSOpen() will return a path reference number in the refNum parameter that you can use in FSRead():

```
OSErr FSRead( refNum, count, buffPtr )
int       refNum;
long      *count;
Ptr       buffPtr;
```

> The refNum returned by FSOpen() is known as an **access path**, specifying the file's volume and the file's location on the volume all in one variable.

Specify the file to be read from using the parameter refNum, and specify the number of bytes to be read using the parameter count. The bytes will be read into the space pointed to by the parameter buffPtr (make sure you allocate the memory to which buffPtr points), and the number of bytes actually read will be returned in count.

Finally, close the file by calling FSClose():

```
OSErr FSClose( refNum )
int       refNum;
```

Specify the file to be closed via the parameter refNum.

For a detailed discussion of the File Manager, turn to *Inside Macintosh* (Volume IV, Chapter 1) and *Tech Notes* 47, 77, 80, and 190. You'll need this for any substantial development effort.

Now, let's take a look at the Printing Manager.

Using the Printing Manager

Prepare the Printing Manager for use by calling `PrOpen()`. Then, allocate a new print record using `NewHandle()`. The print record contains information the Printing Manager needs to print your job, including **page setup** information and information specific to the **print job**.

You can prompt the user to fill in the page setup information by calling `PrStlDialog()`. Prompt the user for job-specific information via a call to `PrJobDialog()`. Each of these routines displays the appropriate dialog box and fills the newly allocated print record with the results.

Then, call `PrOpenDoc()` to set up a printing `grafPort`. The printing `grafPort` is made up of pages. `PrOpenDoc()` calls `SetPort()`, so you don't need to do so. You'll call `PrOpenPage()` to start a new page, then make a set of QuickDraw calls (like `DrawPicture()`) to fill the page with graphics. Next, call `PrClosePage()` to close the current page. Call `PrOpenPage()` and `PrClosePage()` for each page you want to create.

When you've drawn all your pages, close the document with a call to `PrCloseDoc()`. Now, it's time to print our document. Do this with a call to `PrPicFile()`. When you're done with the Printing Manager, call `PrClose()`.

The Printing Manager is described in detail in *Inside Macintosh,* Volume II, Chapter 5. If you plan on writing an application that supports printing, read this chapter thoroughly.

Now, let's look at PrintPICT.

PrintPICT

Since the "paperless society" seems to be rapidly receding into the distance, it's reasonable to expect a Mac application to be able to print. PrintPICT shows you how to print `PICT` files.

> PrintPICT reads in the contents of a `PICT` file. Reading in the contents of a `TEXT` file is no different. Instead of interpreting the data as a `PICT`, you would run the data through a parser that handles pagination, line breaks, hyphenation, and so on, before you draw it on the print `grafPort`.

PrintPICT Specifications

PrintPICT works like this:

- It initializes the Toolbox.
- It uses the Standard File Package to locate a file of type PICT.
- It uses the File Manager to open a file of type PICT.
- It uses the Printing Manager to print the PICT file.
- It quits.

PrintPICT also has error checking. It puts up an alert if the printing operation goes astray at a number of different points.

Setting up the PrintPICT Resources

Start by creating a folder for this project, called PrintPICT. Then, use ResEdit to create a new file called **PrintPICT Proj.Rsrc**.

Create a DITL resource for your error alert (Figure 7.19). Add the same old ALRT (Figure 7.20). Next, add the six 'STR' resources shown in Figure

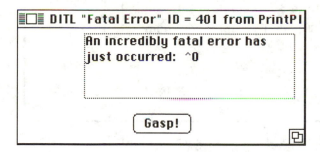

Item#	Type	Enabled	top	left	bottom	right	Text/Resource ID
1	Button	Yes	86	117	106	177	Gasp!
2	Static Text	Yes	5	67	71	283	An incredibly fatal error has just occurred: ^0

Figure 7.19 DITL Resource for PrintPICT.

7.21 to the PrintPICT resource file. Be sure to change the resource IDs of each resource to those shown in the figures. When you're done, the resource window of `PrintPICT Proj.rsrc` should look like Figure 7.22.

Once again, it's time to code.

Setting Up the PrintPICT Project

Start up THINK C. Create a new project in the `PrintPICT` folder. Call it `PrintPICT Proj`. Make sure to add the `MacTraps` library to your project. Create a new source file called `PrintPICT.c` and add it to `PrintPICT Proj`. The source code for `PrintPICT.c` follows on page 316.

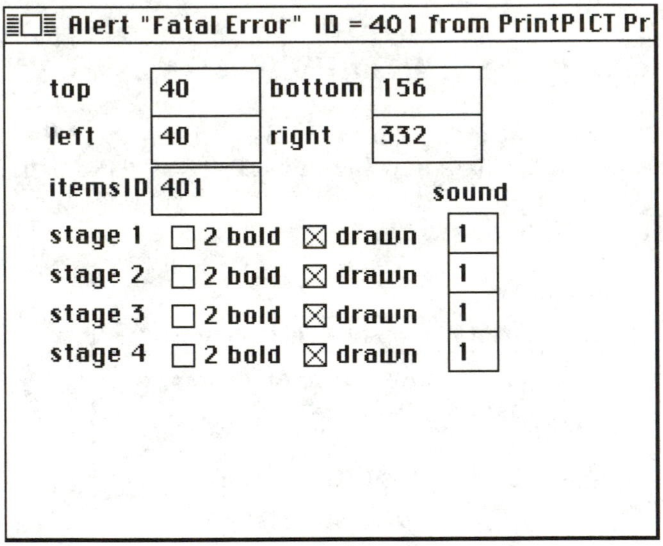

Figure 7.20   `ALRT` resource for PrintPICT.

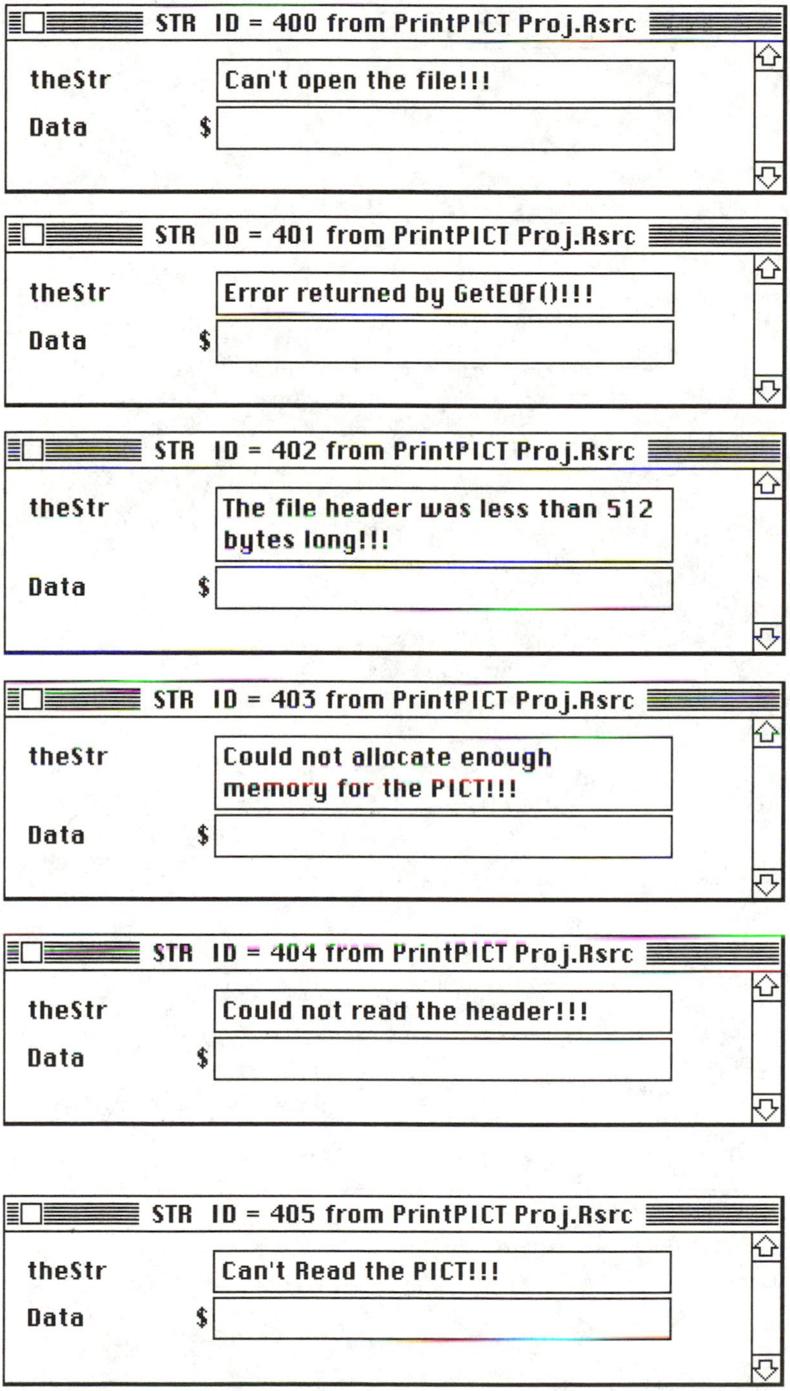

```
 STR  ID = 400 from PrintPICT Proj.Rsrc

theStr        Can't open the file!!!

Data      $
```

```
 STR  ID = 401 from PrintPICT Proj.Rsrc

theStr        Error returned by GetEOF()!!!

Data      $
```

```
 STR  ID = 402 from PrintPICT Proj.Rsrc

theStr        The file header was less than 512
              bytes long!!!

Data      $
```

```
 STR  ID = 403 from PrintPICT Proj.Rsrc

theStr        Could not allocate enough
              memory for the PICT!!!

Data      $
```

```
 STR  ID = 404 from PrintPICT Proj.Rsrc

theStr        Could not read the header!!!

Data      $
```

```
 STR  ID = 405 from PrintPICT Proj.Rsrc

theStr        Can't Read the PICT!!!

Data      $
```

Figure 7.21   STR resources for PrintPICT.

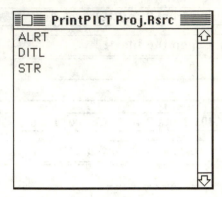

Figure 7.22 PrintPICT resources completed.

```
#include "PrintMgr.h"

#define        HEADER_SIZE          512
#define        NIL_POINTER          0L
#define        BASE_RES_ID          400
#define        REMOVE_ALL_EVENTS    0

#define        ERROR_ALERT_ID       BASE_RES_ID+1
#define        CANT_OPEN_FILE       BASE_RES_ID
#define        GET_EOF_ERROR        BASE_RES_ID+1
#define        HEADER_TOO_SMALL     BASE_RES_ID+2
#define        OUT_OF_MEMORY        BASE_RES_ID+3
#define        CANT_READ_HEADER     BASE_RES_ID+4
#define        CANT_READ_PICT       BASE_RES_ID+5

#define        NIL_PRPORT           NIL_POINTER
#define        NIL_IOBUFFER         NIL_POINTER
#define        NIL_DEVBUF           NIL_POINTER

#define        NIL_STRING                   "\p"
#define        IGNORED_STRING               NIL_STRING
#define        NIL_FILE_FILTER              NIL_POINTER
#define        NIL_DIALOG_HOOK              NIL_POINTER
#define        DONT_SCALE_OUTPUT            NIL_POINTER
#define        HOPELESSLY_FATAL_ERROR       "\pGame over, man!"


Boolean        DoDialogs();
THPrint        gPrintRecordH;
```

```
/****************************** main ********/

main()
{
      SFReply            reply;

      ToolBoxInit();
      PrintInit();
      GetFileName( &reply );
      if ( reply.good ) /* The User didn't hit Cancel */
      {
            if ( DoDialogs() )
            {
                  PrintPictFile( &reply );
            }
      }
}


/********************************* ToolBoxInit */

ToolBoxInit()
{
      InitGraf( &thePort );
      InitFonts();
      FlushEvents( everyEvent, REMOVE_ALL_EVENTS );
      InitWindows();
      InitMenus();
      TEInit();
      InitDialogs( NIL_POINTER );
      InitCursor();
}


/****************************** PrintInit ********/

PrintInit()
{
      gPrintRecordH = (THPrint)NewHandle( sizeof( TPrint ) );
      PrOpen();
      PrintDefault( gPrintRecordH );
}
```

```
/*******************************            GetFileName    *******/

GetFileName( replyPtr )
SFReply              *replyPtr;
{
      Point          myPoint;
      SFTypeList     typeList;
      int            numTypes;

      myPoint.h = 100;
      myPoint.v = 100;
      typeList[ 0 ] = 'PICT';
      numTypes = 1;
      SFGetFile( myPoint, IGNORED_STRING, NIL_FILE_FILTER, numTypes,
                      &typeList, NIL_DIALOG_HOOK, replyPtr );
}


/******************************            DoDialogs      *******/

Boolean     DoDialogs()
{
      PrStlDialog( gPrintRecordH );
      return( PrJobDialog( gPrintRecordH ) );
}


/******************************            PrintPictFile*******/

PrintPictFile( replyPtr )
SFReply              *replyPtr;
{
      int            srcFile;
      TPPrPort       printPort;
      TPrStatus      printStatus;
      PicHandle      thePict;
      char           pictHeader[ HEADER_SIZE ];
      long           pictSize, headerSize;

      if ( FSOpen( (*replyPtr).fName, (*replyPtr).vRefNum, &srcFile ) !=
              noErr )
              ErrorHandler( CANT_OPEN_FILE );

      if ( GetEOF( srcFile, &pictSize ) != noErr )
              ErrorHandler( GET_EOF_ERROR );

      headerSize = HEADER_SIZE;
      if ( FSRead( srcFile, &headerSize, pictHeader ) != noErr )
              ErrorHandler( CANT_READ_HEADER );

      if ( ( pictSize -= HEADER_SIZE ) <= 0 )
      {
              ErrorHandler( HEADER_TOO_SMALL );
      }
```

```
            if ( ( thePict = (PicHandle)NewHandle( pictSize ) ) == NIL_POINTER )
            {
                    ErrorHandler( OUT_OF_MEMORY );
            }

        HLock( thePict );

        if ( FSRead( srcFile, &pictSize, *thePict ) != noErr )
                ErrorHandler( CANT_READ_PICT );

        FSClose( srcFile );

        printPort = PrOpenDoc( gPrintRecordH, NIL_POINTER, NIL_POINTER );
        PrOpenPage( printPort, DONT_SCALE_OUTPUT );
        DrawPicture( thePict, &(**( thePict )).picFrame );
        PrClosePage( printPort );
        PrCloseDoc( printPort );

        PrPicFile( gPrintRecordH, NIL_PRPORT, NIL_IOBUFFER, NIL_DEVBUF,
&printStatus );
}


/******************************* ErrorHandler *********/

ErrorHandler( stringNum )
int     stringNum;
{
        StringHandle errorStringH;

        if ( ( errorStringH = GetString( stringNum ) ) == NIL_POINTER )
                ParamText( HOPELESSLY_FATAL_ERROR, NIL_STRING, NIL_STRING,
NIL_STRING );
        else
        {
                HLock( errorStringH );
                ParamText( *errorStringH, NIL_STRING, NIL_STRING, NIL_STRING );
                HUnlock( errorStringH );
        }
        StopAlert( ERROR_ALERT_ID, NIL_POINTER );
        ExitToShell();
}
```

Running PrintPICT

Now that your source code is entered, you're ready to run PrintPICT. PrintPICT will bring up the `SFGetFile()` dialog box (Figure 7.23).

Select a `PICT` file to be printed. The Page Setup dialog box will then be displayed (Figure 7.24). After you click OK, the Print Job dialog box appears (Figure 7.25). If you click on OK, or press <RETURN>, PrintPICT will print your `PICT` file and quit. Let's see how it's done.

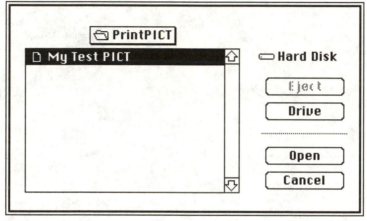

Figure 7.23   `SFGetFile()` dialog box.

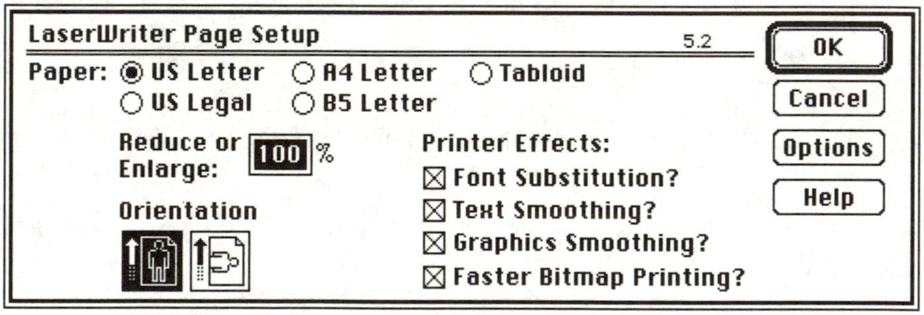

Figure 7.24   PrintPICT calls the Page Setup dialog box.

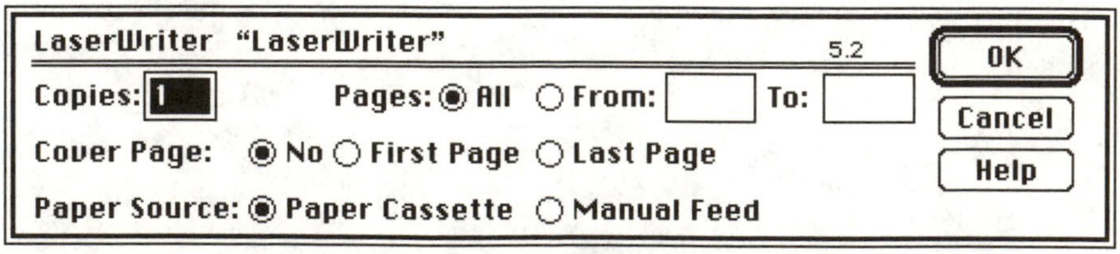

Figure 7.25   PrintPICT calls the Print Job dialog box.

How PICTPrinter Works

Start by #include-ing the Printing Manager's #include file. THINK C normally #includes everything you'll need, but there are a few exceptions. In this case, #include PrintMgr.h.

```
#include "PrintMgr.h"
```

Here's a list of files that are *not* included automatically:

```
#include "Appletalk.h"
#include "nAppletalk.h"
#include "Color.h"
#include "ColorToolbox.h"
#include "DeskBus.h"
#include "DiskDvr.h"
#include "PrintMgr.h"
#include "ScriptMgr.h"
#include "SCSIMgr.h"
#include "SerialDvr.h"
#include "SlotMgr.h"
#include "SoundDvr.h"
#include "SoundMgr.h"
#include "StartMgr.h"
#include "TimeMgr.h"
#include "VRetraceMgr.h"
```

How can you tell if you need to #include one of these? If you get a compiler error, like invalid declaration, and it refers to a THINK C defined global or type, check your code for typos. If the problem still exists, look through these #include files (use the Find command) until you find the type or variable's declaration. Finally, #include that file.

Next come your #defines:

```
#define        HEADER_SIZE           512
#define        NIL_POINTER           0L
#define        BASE_RES_ID           400
#define        REMOVE_ALL_EVENTS     0

#define        ERROR_ALERT_ID        BASE_RES_ID+1
#define        CANT_OPEN_FILE        BASE_RES_ID
#define        GET_EOF_ERROR         BASE_RES_ID+1
#define        HEADER_TOO_SMALL      BASE_RES_ID+2
#define        OUT_OF_MEMORY         BASE_RES_ID+3
#define        CANT_READ_HEADER      BASE_RES_ID+4
#define        CANT_READ_PICT        BASE_RES_ID+5

#define        NIL_PRPORT            NIL_POINTER
#define        NIL_IOBUFFER          NIL_POINTER
#define        NIL_DEVBUF            NIL_POINTER

#define        NIL_STRING            "\p"
#define        IGNORED_STRING        NIL_STRING
#define        NIL_FILE_FILTER       NIL_POINTER
#define        NIL_DIALOG_HOOK       NIL_POINTER
#define        DONT_SCALE_OUTPUT     NIL_POINTER
#define        HOPELESSLY_FATAL_ERROR    "\pGame over, man!"
```

HEADER_SIZE is used for removing the header at the top of PICT files. BASE_RES_ID, NIL_POINTER, and REMOVE_ALL_EVENTS are the initialization-related #defines you've seen earlier. ERROR_ALERT_ID, CANT_OPEN_FILE, GET_EOF_ERROR, HEADER_TOO_SMALL, OUT_OF_MEMORY, CANT_READ_HEADER, and CANT_READ_PICT are all used for the appropriate error strings in the error-handling routines. NIL_PRPORT, NIL_IOBUFFER, NIL_DEVBUF, NIL_STRING, IGNORED_STRING, NIL_FILE_FILTER, NIL_DIALOG_HOOK, and DONT_SCALE_OUTPUT are the arguments in the Printing Manager routines. Finally, HOPELESSLY_FATAL_ERROR is for your ALRT of last resort.

Next, declare your globals:

```
char           DoDialogs();
THPrint gPrintRecordH;
```

DoDialogs() returns either TRUE or FALSE, so declare it to be of type Boolean. gPrintRecordH is the handle to the print record you'll create.

As usual, main() starts off with a call to ToolBoxInit(). Then, PrintInit() is run and SFGetFile() is invoked. If the user doesn't click on the Cancel button, DoDialogs() is called.

```
/***************************** main *********/

main()
{
      SFReply        reply;

      ToolBoxInit();
      PrintInit();
      GetFileName( &reply );
      if ( reply.good ) /* The User didn't hit Cancel */
      {
            if ( DoDialogs() )
            {
                  PrintPictFile( &reply );
            }
      }
}
```

ToolBoxInit() is the same as always:

```
/******************************** ToolBoxInit */

ToolBoxInit()
{
      InitGraf( &thePort );
      InitFonts();
      FlushEvents( everyEvent, REMOVE_ALL_EVENTS );
      InitWindows();
      InitMenus();
      TEInit();
      InitDialogs( NIL_POINTER );
      InitCursor();
}
```

> The information entered by the user in the Page Setup and Print Job dialog boxes is stored in a print record. `PrintDefault()` fills the print record with default print values. A handle to the print record is passed to `PrPicFile()` at print time.

`PrintInit()` uses `NewHandle()` to allocate a block of memory the size of a print record, and makes `gPrintRecordH` a handle to that memory. Call `PrOpen()` to start up the Printing Manager, then set the default print record to `gPrintRecordH` by calling `PrintDefault()`. Doing this ensures that any changes you make to the Page Setup and Job dialogs will be implemented when you print.

```
/************************ PrintInit ********/

PrintInit()
{
      gPrintRecordH = (THPrint)NewHandle( sizeof( TPrint ) );
      PrOpen();
      PrintDefault( gPrintRecordH );
}
```

GetFileName() sets up the arguments and calls SFGetFile().
numTypes was defined as 1, so you need to set up a single entry in the
typeList array. Display only files of type PICT. The pointer to the reply
from SFGetFile() will be placed in replyPtr:

```
/***************************    GetFileName  *******/

GetFileName( replyPtr )
SFReply              *replyPtr;
{
      Point         myPoint;
      SFTypeList    typeList;
      int           numTypes;

      myPoint.h = 100;
      myPoint.v = 100;
      typeList[ 0 ] = 'PICT';
      numTypes = 1;
      SFGetFile( myPoint, IGNORED_STRING, NIL_FILE_FILTER, numTypes,
                    &typeList, NIL_DIALOG_HOOK, replyPtr );
}
```

DoDialogs() calls PrStlDialog() to do the Page Setup dialog, then
calls PrJobDialog() to do the Job dialog. If the user hits the cancel button
in the Print Job dialog box, DoDialogs() returns FALSE. The value returned by PrJobDialog() is returned by DoDialogs().

Normally, your application would bring up the Page Setup dialog in
response to a Page Setup... menu selection and the Print Job dialog in
response to a Print... menu selection. PrintPICT calls both dialogs for
demonstration purposes only

```
/****************************        DoDialogs    *******/

Boolean       DoDialogs()
{
      PrStlDialog( gPrintRecordH );
      return( PrJobDialog( gPrintRecordH ) );
}
```

PrintPictFile() starts off with a call to FSOpen() to get the access path of the file selected by SFGetFile(). If the file can be opened, GetEOF() is called, returning the size of the file in the parameter pictSize. Next, FSRead() attempts to read the 512-byte header that describes the rest of the file. The actual number of bytes read is returned in the parameter headerSize. If less than 512 bytes was read, or if you run out of memory while trying to read the picture in, call the ErrorHandler(). Since PrintPICT won't need the 512-byte PICT header, pictSize is decremented by 512. This reduced version of pictSize will be used to read in the headerless PICT.

```
/********************************          PrintPictFile*******/

PrintPictFile( replyPtr )
SFReply           *replyPtr;
{
      int         srcFile;
      TPPrPort    printPort;
      TPrStatus   printStatus;
      PicHandle   thePict;
      char        pictHeader[ HEADER_SIZE ];
      long        pictSize, headerSize;

      if ( FSOpen( (*replyPtr).fName, (*replyPtr).vRefNum, &srcFile ) !=
noErr )
            ErrorHandler( CANT_OPEN_FILE );

      if ( GetEOF( srcFile, &pictSize ) != noErr )
            ErrorHandler( GET_EOF_ERROR );

      headerSize = HEADER_SIZE;
      if ( FSRead( srcFile, &headerSize, pictHeader ) != noErr )
            ErrorHandler( CANT_READ_HEADER );

      if ( ( pictSize -= HEADER_SIZE ) <= 0 )
      {
            ErrorHandler( HEADER_TOO_SMALL );
      }

      if ( ( thePict = (PicHandle)NewHandle( pictSize ) ) == NIL_POINTER )
      {
            ErrorHandler( OUT_OF_MEMORY );
      }
```

If you've passed through these trials successfully, you're ready to read in the PICT data. Since FSRead() requires a pointer to the read buffer, and you allocated a handle (thePict), you'll have to HLock() the handle before you pass its pointer (*thePict) to FSRead(). Call FSRead() to read in the PICT. If this fails (IV:109), ErrorHandler() is run yet again. Assuming that you finally have the PICT in memory at this point, close the PICT file with FSClose(). Next, PrOpenDoc() is called, returning a pointer (printPort) to the printing grafPort. Open a new page with PrOpenPage(), and draw the PICT with DrawPicture(). When you're done PrClosePage() closes the page, and PrCloseDoc() closes the printing grafPort.

Finally, print the file with PrPicFile().

```
    HLock( thePict );

    if ( FSRead( srcFile, &pictSize, *thePict ) != noErr )
        ErrorHandler( CANT_READ_PICT );

    FSClose( srcFile );

    printPort = PrOpenDoc( gPrintRecordH, NIL_POINTER, NIL_POINTER );
    PrOpenPage( printPort, DONT_SCALE_OUTPUT );
    DrawPicture( thePict, &(**( thePict )).picFrame );
    PrClosePage( printPort );
    PrCloseDoc( printPort );

    PrPicFile( gPrintRecordH, NIL_PRPORT, NIL_IOBUFFER, NIL_DEVBUF,
        &printStatus );
}
```

ErrorHandler() is the same as in the earlier programs. Take the alert string resource ID and set up ParamText() with it. Then, display the alert with StopAlert() and quit with ExitToShell().

```
/******************************* ErrorHandler ********/

ErrorHandler( stringNum )
int     stringNum;
{
    StringHandle errorStringH;

    if ( ( errorStringH = GetString( stringNum ) ) == NIL_POINTER )
        ParamText( HOPELESSLY_FATAL_ERROR, NIL_STRING, NIL_STRING,
            NIL_STRING );
    else
    {
        HLock( errorStringH );
        ParamText( *errorStringH, NIL_STRING, NIL_STRING, NIL_STRING );
        HUnlock( errorStringH );
    }
    StopAlert( ERROR_ALERT_ID, NIL_POINTER );
    ExitToShell();
}
```

Scroll Bars! We're Gonna Do Scroll Bars!

Scroll bars are a common control used in Macintosh applications. This section shows you how to set one up to control paging between a series of pictures in a window.

Making Use of Scroll Bars

Scroll bars are a common control used in Macintosh applications (Figure 7.26). The routines that create and control scroll bars are part of the Control Manager. NewControl() is used to create a new control:

```
FUNCTION NewControl( theWindow : WindowPtr; boundsRect : Rect;
                title : Str255; visible : BOOLEAN;
                value : INTEGER; min,max : INTEGER;
                procID : INTEGER; refCon : LONGINT ) :
                ControlHandle;
```

Figure 7.26 Window with scroll bar (Pager).

327

The parameter `procID` specifies the type of control to be created. To create a new scroll bar, pass the constant `scrollBarProc` to `NewControl()`. Every scroll bar has a minimum, maximum, and current value. For example, a scroll bar may go from 1 to 20, and currently be at 10 (Figure 7.27).

Once the scroll bar is created, call `DrawControls()` to draw it in your window:

```
PROCEDURE DrawControls( theWindow : WindowPtr );
```

> As the calls to Window Manager routines (such as `ShowWindow()` or `MoveWindow()`) do not redraw controls in a window, `DrawControls()` must be called whenever the window receives an update event.

When a `mouseDown` event occurs `FindWindow()` is called, returning a part code describing the part of the window in which the `mouseDown` occurred. If the `mouseDown` was `inContent`, call `FindControl()`.

```
FUNCTION FindControl( thePoint : Point; theWindow : WindowPtr;
                      VAR whichControl : ControlHandle ) :
                      INTEGER;
```

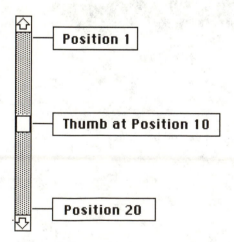

Figure 7.27   Scroll bar positioning.

Like `FindWindow()`, `FindControl()` returns a part code. This time, the part code specifies which part of the scroll bar was clicked in (Figure 7.28). Pass the part code returned by `FindControl()` to `TrackControl()`.

```
FUNCTION TrackControl( theControl : ControlHandle;
                       startPt : Point; actionProc : ProcPtr ) :
                       INTEGER;
```

`TrackControl()` will perform the action appropriate to that part of the scroll bar. For example, if the `mouseDown` was in the thumb of the scroll bar, an outline of the thumb is moved up and down (or across) the scroll bar until the mouse button is released. Once `TrackControl()` returns, take the appropriate action, depending on the new value of the scroll bar.

Next, let's look at Pager, a program that uses a scroll bar to page between `PICT` drawings in a window.

Pager

Pager demonstrates the use of scroll bars in a Macintosh application. It works like this:

- It initializes the Toolbox.
- It initializes a window.
- It creates a new scroll bar, using the number of available `PICT` resources to determine the number of position in the scroll bar.
- When a `mouseDown` occurs in the scroll bar, it loads the appropriate `PICT` and displays it in the window.
- It quits when the close box is clicked.

Pager also warns if the `WIND` or `PICT` resources are unavailable.

Setting Up the Pager Project

Start by creating a folder for this project, called `Pager`. Use ResEdit to create a new file called `Pager Proj.Rsrc`. You might want to save some time by just copying and pasting the `WIND`, `ALRT`, and `DITL` resources from the `WindowMaker Proj.Rsrc` file.

The `WIND` resource info appears in Figure 7.29.

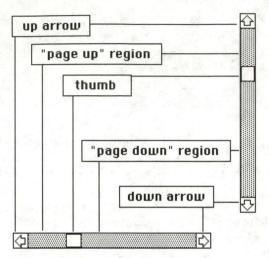

Figure 7.28 Parts of scroll bars.

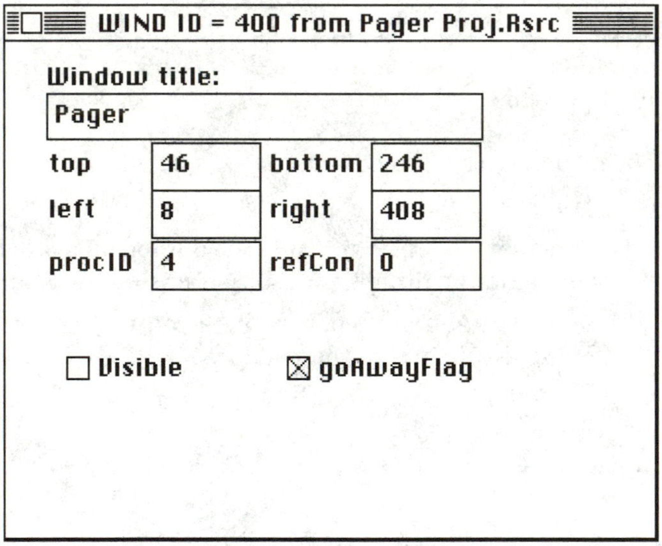

Figure 7.29 WIND resource for Pager.

Next, create a DITL resource (Figure 7.30). Add the ALRT (Figure 7.31). Then, add the three 'STR' resources shown in Figure 7.32 to the Pager Proj.Rsrc. Change the resource IDs of each resource to those shown in the figures.

Next, create some PICT resources from your favorite clip art and paste them into the Pager Proj.Rsrc. Paste in as many as you like. Don't worry about changing resource IDs for the PICT resources. We'll display every available PICT, regardless of race, creed, or resource ID. When you're done, the resource window of Pager Proj.Rsrc should look like Figure 7.33.

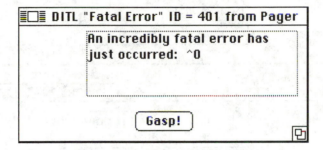

Item#	Type	Enabled	top	left	bottom	right	Text/Resource ID
1	Button	Yes	86	117	106	177	Gasp!
2	Static Text	Yes	5	67	71	283	An incredibly fatal error has just occurred: ^0

Figure 7.30 DITL resource for Pager.

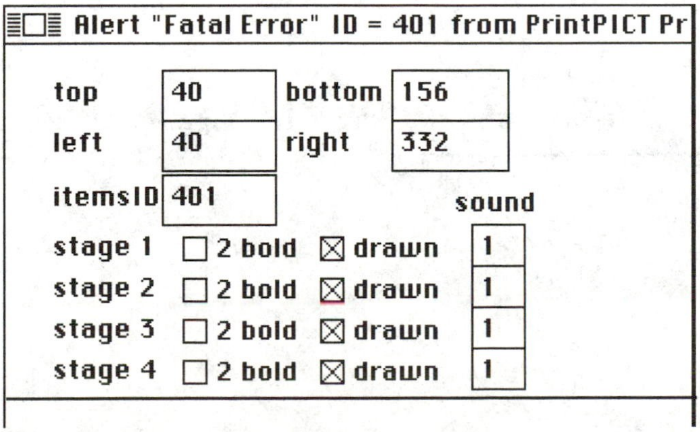

Figure 7.31 ALRT resource for Pager.

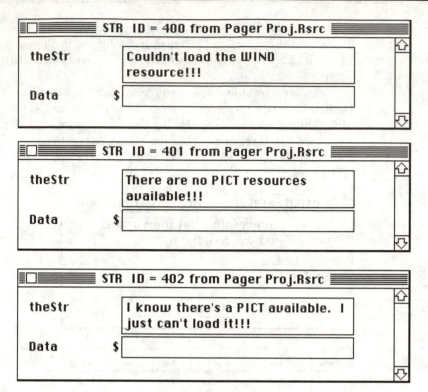

Figure 7.32   STR resources for Pager.

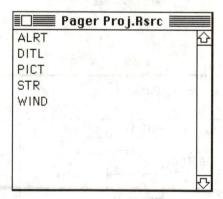

Figure 7.33   Pager resources completed.

Now you're ready to launch THINK C. Create a new project in the Pager folder. Call it **Pager Proj**. Make sure to add the MacTraps library to your project. Create **Pager.c** and add it to Pager Proj. Here's the source code for Pager.c:

```
#define     BASE_RES_ID          400
#define     NIL_POINTER          0L
#define     MOVE_TO_FRONT        -1L
#define     REMOVE_ALL_EVENTS    0
#define     SCROLL_BAR_PIXELS    16
#define     DRAG_THRESHOLD       30
#define     NIL_ACTION_PROC      NIL_POINTER

#define     MIN_SLEEP            0L
#define     NIL_MOUSE_REGION     0L

#define     WNE_TRAP_NUM         0x60
#define     UNIMPL_TRAP_NUM      0x9F

#define     ERROR_ALERT_ID       BASE_RES_ID+1
#define     NO_WIND              BASE_RES_ID
#define     NO_PICTS             BASE_RES_ID+1
#define     CANT_LOAD_PICT       BASE_RES_ID+2

#define     NIL_STRING           "\p"
#define     NIL_TITLE            NIL_STRING
#define     VISIBLE              TRUE
#define     START_VALUE          1
#define     MIN_VALUE            1
#define     NIL_REF_CON          NIL_POINTER
#define     HOPELESSLY_FATAL_ERROR   "\pGame over, man!"


WindowPtr       gPictWindow;
ControlHandle   gScrollBarHandle;
Boolean         gDone, gWNEImplemented;
EventRecord     gTheEvent;
Rect            gDragRect;
pascal void     ScrollProc();


/******************************* main *********/

main()
{
    ToolBoxInit();
    WindowInit();
    SetUpDragRect();
    SetUpScrollBar();
    MainLoop();
}
```

```
/********************************* ToolBoxInit */

ToolBoxInit()
{
      InitGraf( &thePort );
      InitFonts();
      FlushEvents( everyEvent, REMOVE_ALL_EVENTS );
      InitWindows();
      InitMenus();
      TEInit();
      InitDialogs( NIL_POINTER );
      InitCursor();
}


/******************************* WindowInit ********/

WindowInit()
{
      if ( ( gPictWindow = GetNewWindow( BASE_RES_ID, NIL_POINTER,
             MOVE_TO_FRONT ) ) == NIL_POINTER )
             ErrorHandler( NO_WIND );
      SelectWindow( gPictWindow );
      ShowWindow( gPictWindow );
      SetPort( gPictWindow );
}


/****************************** SetUpDragRect ********/

SetUpDragRect()
{
      gDragRect = screenBits.bounds;
      gDragRect.left += DRAG_THRESHOLD;
      gDragRect.right -= DRAG_THRESHOLD;
      gDragRect.bottom -= DRAG_THRESHOLD;
}
/******************************     SetUpScrollBar      *******/

SetUpScrollBar()
{
      Rect    vScrollRect;
      int     numPictures;

      if ( ( numPictures = CountResources( 'PICT' ) ) <= 0 )
             ErrorHandler( NO_PICTS );
      vScrollRect = gPictWindow->portRect;
      vScrollRect.top -= 1;
      vScrollRect.bottom +=1;
      vScrollRect.left = vScrollRect.right-SCROLL_BAR_PIXELS+1;
      vScrollRect.right += 1;
      gScrollBarHandle = NewControl( gPictWindow, &vScrollRect,
                         NIL_TITLE, VISIBLE, START_VALUE, MIN_VALUE,
                         numPictures, scrollBarProc, NIL_REF_CON);
}
```

```
/******************************** MainLoop ********/

MainLoop()
{
      gDone = FALSE;
      gWNEImplemented = ( NGetTrapAddress( WNE_TRAP_NUM, ToolTrap ) !=
      NGetTrapAddress( UNIMPL_TRAP_NUM, ToolTrap ) );
      while ( gDone == FALSE )
      {
             HandleEvent();
      }
}


/*********************************** HandleEvent    */

HandleEvent()
{
      if ( gWNEImplemented )
             WaitNextEvent( everyEvent, &gTheEvent, MIN_SLEEP,
                    NIL_MOUSE_REGION );
      else
      {
             SystemTask();
             GetNextEvent( everyEvent, &gTheEvent );
      }

      switch ( gTheEvent.what )
      {
             case mouseDown:
                    HandleMouseDown();
                    break;
             case updateEvt:
                    BeginUpdate( gTheEvent.message );
                    DrawControls( gTheEvent.message );
                    UpdateMyWindow( gTheEvent.message );
                    EndUpdate( gTheEvent.message );
                    break;
      }
}


/*********************************** HandleMouseDown */

HandleMouseDown()
{
      WindowPtr     whichWindow;
      short int     thePart;
      Point         thePoint;
      ControlHandle theControl;

      thePart = FindWindow( gTheEvent.where, &whichWindow );
      switch ( thePart )
      {
```

```
                case inSysWindow :
                        SystemClick( &gTheEvent, whichWindow );
                        break;
                case inDrag :
                        DragWindow( whichWindow, gTheEvent.where, &gDragRect );
                        break;
                case inContent:
                        thePoint = gTheEvent.where;
                        GlobalToLocal( &(thePoint) );
                        thePart = FindControl( thePoint, whichWindow,
                                    &theControl );
                        if ( theControl == gScrollBarHandle )
                        {
                                if ( thePart == inThumb )
                                {
                                        thePart = TrackControl( theControl,
                                        thePoint, NIL_ACTION_PROC );
                                        UpdateMyWindow( whichWindow );
                                }
                                else
                                {
                                        thePart = TrackControl( theControl,
                                        thePoint, &ScrollProc );
                                        UpdateMyWindow( whichWindow );
                                }
                        }
                        break;
                case inGoAway :
                        gDone = TRUE;
                        break;
        }
}


/*******************************        ScrollProc      *******/

pascal void ScrollProc(theControl, theCode)
ControlHandle           theControl;
int                     theCode;
{
        int             curControlValue, maxControlValue, minControlValue;

        maxControlValue = GetCtlMax( theControl );
        curControlValue = GetCtlValue( theControl );
        minControlValue = GetCtlMin( theControl );

        switch ( theCode )
        {
                case inPageDown:
                case inDownButton:
```

```
                    if ( curControlValue < maxControlValue )
                    {
                            curControlValue += 1;
                    }
                    break;
            case inPageUp:
            case inUpButton:
                    if ( curControlValue > minControlValue )
                    {
                            curControlValue -= 1;
                    }
        }
        SetCtlValue( theControl, curControlValue );
}


/********************************     UpdateMyWindow     *******/

UpdateMyWindow( drawingWindow )
WindowPtr     drawingWindow;
{
        PicHandle     currentPicture;
        Rect          drawingClipRect, myRect;
        RgnHandle     tempRgn;

        tempRgn = NewRgn();
        GetClip( tempRgn );

        myRect = drawingWindow->portRect;
        myRect.right -= SCROLL_BAR_PIXELS;
        EraseRect( &myRect );

        currentPicture = (PicHandle)GetIndResource( 'PICT', GetCtlValue(
                gScrollBarHandle ) );

        if ( currentPicture == NIL_POINTER )
                ErrorHandler( CANT_LOAD_PICT );

        CenterPict( currentPicture, &myRect );

        drawingClipRect = drawingWindow->portRect;
        drawingClipRect.right -= SCROLL_BAR_PIXELS;
        ClipRect( &drawingClipRect );

        DrawPicture( currentPicture, &myRect );

        SetClip( tempRgn );
        DisposeRgn( tempRgn );
}
```

```
/****************************** CenterPict *********/

CenterPict( thePicture, myRectPtr )
PicHandle     thePicture;
Rect          *myRectPtr;
{
        Rect    windRect, pictureRect;

        windRect = *myRectPtr;
        pictureRect = (**( thePicture )).picFrame;
        myRectPtr->top = (windRect.bottom - windRect.top -
                (pictureRect.bottom -pictureRect.top))
                / 2 + windRect.top;
        myRectPtr->bottom = myRectPtr->top + (pictureRect.bottom -
                pictureRect.top);
        myRectPtr->left = (windRect.right - windRect.left -
                (pictureRect.right - pictureRect.left))
                / 2 + windRect.left;
        myRectPtr->right = myRectPtr->left + (pictureRect.right -
                pictureRect.left);
}


/****************************** ErrorHandler *********/
ErrorHandler( stringNum )
int     stringNum;
{
        StringHandle errorStringH;

        if ( ( errorStringH = GetString( stringNum ) ) == NIL_POINTER )
                ParamText( HOPELESSLY_FATAL_ERROR, NIL_STRING, NIL_STRING,
                        NIL_STRING );
        else
        {
                HLock( errorStringH );
                ParamText( *errorStringH, NIL_STRING, NIL_STRING, NIL_STRING );
                HUnlock( errorStringH );
        }
        StopAlert( ERROR_ALERT_ID, NIL_POINTER );
        ExitToShell();
}
```

Running Pager

When you've finished typing in your source code, run Pager. You should see
something like Figure 7.26, except with the PICTs that you put in the Pager
Proj.Rsrc. The scroll bar should allow you to page back and forth between
the PICTs. Clicking in the close box ends Pager's execution.

How Pager Works

You've seen most of this program before. You'll create a window with
GetNewWindow() and get and handle events just as you did in Window-
Maker. Now, let's look at the code.

Pager starts off with #defines and global variable declarations. We'll discuss these in context.

```
#define     BASE_RES_ID          400
#define     NIL_POINTER          0L
#define     MOVE_TO_FRONT        -1L
#define     REMOVE_ALL_EVENTS    0
#define     SCROLL_BAR_PIXELS    16
#define     DRAG_THRESHOLD       30
#define     NIL_ACTION_PROC      NIL_POINTER

#define     MIN_SLEEP            0L
#define     NIL_MOUSE_REGION     0L

#define     WNE_TRAP_NUM         0x60
#define     UNIMPL_TRAP_NUM      0x9F

#define     ERROR_ALERT_ID       BASE_RES_ID+1
#define     NO_WIND              BASE_RES_ID
#define     NO_PICTS             BASE_RES_ID+1
#define     CANT_LOAD_PICT       BASE_RES_ID+2

#define     NIL_STRING                   "\p"
#define     NIL_TITLE                    NIL_STRING
#define     VISIBLE                      TRUE
#define     START_VALUE                  1
#define     MIN_VALUE                    1
#define     NIL_REF_CON                  NIL_POINTER
#define     HOPELESSLY_FATAL_ERROR       "\pGame over, man!"


WindowPtr       gPictWindow;
ControlHandlegScrollBarHandle;
Boolean         gDone, gWNEImplemented;
EventRecord     gTheEvent;
Rect            gDragRect;
pascal void     ScrollProc();
```

Main() calls the ToolboxInit() and WindowInit() routines, uses SetUpDragRect() to set the bounds for moving the window around on the screen and SetUpScrollBar() to initialize the scroll bar control, and then runs MainLoop() to start the main event loop.

```
/****************************** main *********/

main()
{
     ToolBoxInit();
     WindowInit();
     SetUpDragRect();
     SetUpScrollBar();
     MainLoop();
}
```

Nope. Still looks the same.

```
/********************************* ToolBoxInit */

ToolBoxInit()
{
        InitGraf( &thePort );
        InitFonts();
        FlushEvents( everyEvent, REMOVE_ALL_EVENTS );
        InitWindows();
        InitMenus();
        TEInit();
        InitDialogs( NIL_POINTER );
        InitCursor();
}
```

WindowInit() is uneventful. The WIND resource is loaded and displayed, with the customary call to ErrorHandler() if the WIND resource is missing.

```
/******************************** WindowInit *********/

WindowInit()
{
        if ( ( gPictWindow = GetNewWindow( BASE_RES_ID, NIL_POINTER,
                        MOVE_TO_FRONT ) ) == NIL_POINTER )
            ErrorHandler( NO_WIND );
        SelectWindow( gPictWindow );
        ShowWindow( gPictWindow );
        SetPort( gPictWindow );
}
```

As you saw in WindowMaker, SetUpDragRect() sets up the bounds for the dragging routine used in the HandleEvent() loop.

```
/******************************** SetUpDragRect *********/

SetUpDragRect()
{
        gDragRect = screenBits.bounds;
        gDragRect.left += DRAG_THRESHOLD;
        gDragRect.right -= DRAG_THRESHOLD;
        gDragRect.bottom -= DRAG_THRESHOLD;
}
```

SetUpScrollBar() calls CountResources() to find out how many PICT resources are available.

> Every application has access to resources from two different places: the resource fork of the application itself and the resource fork of the system file. In addition, an application may use the Resource Manager to open additional resource files. When looking for a resource, the Resource Manager searches the most recently opened resource file first.

If no `PICT` resources are available, the `ErrorHandler()` is called. Otherwise, `SetUpScrollBar()` creates a `Rect` the proper size for your scroll bar, then creates the scroll bar with a call to `NewControl()`. The scroll bar ranges in value from `MIN_VALUE` to `numPictures`, the number of available `PICT` resources. `START_VALUE` is the initial value of the scroll bar and determines the initial position of the scroll bar thumb. The final parameter is a reference value available for your application's convenience. You can use these four bytes as scratch pad space.

```
/********************************         SetUpScrollBar        *******/

SetUpScrollBar()
{
     Rect    vScrollRect;
     int     numPictures;

     if ( ( numPictures = CountResources( 'PICT' ) ) <= 0 )
          ErrorHandler( NO_PICTS );
     vScrollRect = gPictWindow->portRect;
     vScrollRect.top -= 1;
     vScrollRect.bottom +=1;
     vScrollRect.left = vScrollRect.right-SCROLL_BAR_PIXELS+1;
     vScrollRect.right += 1;
     gScrollBarHandle = NewControl( gPictWindow, &vScrollRect,
                      NIL_TITLE, VISIBLE, START_VALUE, MIN_VALUE,
                      numPictures, scrollBarProc, NIL_REF_CON);
}
```

`MainLoop()` **sets the flag for** `GetNextEvent()` **or** `WaitNextEvent()`, **then calls** `HandleEvent()`.

```
/******************************* MainLoop *********/

MainLoop()
{
     gDone = FALSE;
     gWNEImplemented = ( NGetTrapAddress( WNE_TRAP_NUM, ToolTrap ) !=
     NGetTrapAddress( UNIMPL_TRAP_NUM, ToolTrap ) );
     while ( gDone == FALSE )
     {
          HandleEvent();
     }
}
```

Pager handles two different events. mouseDowns are handled by HandleMouseDown(). updateEvts are handled in line. First, BeginUpdate() is called. Then, DrawControls() draws the scroll bar with the thumb in the proper position. Finally, EndUpdate() is called.

```
/*********************************** HandleEvent    */

HandleEvent()
{
      if ( gWNEImplemented )
            WaitNextEvent( everyEvent, &gTheEvent, MIN_SLEEP,
NIL_MOUSE_REGION );
      else
      {
            SystemTask();
            GetNextEvent( everyEvent, &gTheEvent );
      }

      switch ( gTheEvent.what )
      {
            case mouseDown:
                  HandleMouseDown();
                  break;
            case updateEvt:
                  BeginUpdate( gTheEvent.message );
                  DrawControls( gTheEvent.message );
                  UpdateMyWindow( gTheEvent.message );
                  EndUpdate( gTheEvent.message );
                  break;
      }
}
```

HandleMouseDown() looks the same at the start:

```
/*********************************** HandleMouseDown */

HandleMouseDown()
{
      WindowPtr     whichWindow;
      short int     thePart;
      Point         thePoint;
      ControlHandletheControl;

      thePart = FindWindow( gTheEvent.where, &whichWindow );
      switch ( thePart )
      {
            case inSysWindow :
                  SystemClick( &gTheEvent, whichWindow );
                  break;
            case inDrag :
                  DragWindow( whichWindow, gTheEvent.where, &gDragRect );
                  break;
```

The big change comes when a mouseDown occurs in the content region (inContent) of a window. The mouseDown's location (gEvent.where) is translated into the window's local coordinate system. The localized point is passed to FindControl(), which returns a Handle to the selected control (in the parameter theControl) and a part code indicating what part of the control was selected. If theControl is your scroll bar, find out if it was in the thumb. If it was, call TrackControl() to drag an outline of the thumb up and down the scroll bar. When the thumb is released, update the window using the new scroll bar value. If any other part of the control was used, call TrackControl() with a pointer to ScrollProc(). ScrollProc() scrolls the scroll bar until the mouse button is released.

Call TrackControl() with a pointer to an action procedure if you want the control to change while the mouse button is still down. If you pass a NIL_ACTION_PROC, the control will animate, but its value will not change until the mouse button is released.

```
case inContent:
        thePoint = gTheEvent.where;
        GlobalToLocal( &(thePoint) );
        thePart = FindControl( thePoint, whichWindow,
            &theControl );
        if ( theControl == gScrollBarHandle )
        {
                if ( thePart == inThumb )
                {
                        thePart = TrackControl( theControl,
                        thePoint, NIL_ACTION_PROC );
                        UpdateMyWindow( whichWindow );
                }
                else
                {
                        thePart = TrackControl( theControl,
                        thePoint, &ScrollProc );
                        UpdateMyWindow( whichWindow );
                }
        }
        break;
case inGoAway :
        gDone = TRUE;
        break;
    }
}
```

ScrollProc() handles mouseDowns in the page up, page down, up button, and down button regions of the scroll bar. maxControlValue, curControlValue, and minControlValue are set to the maximum, current, and minimum values of theControl. If the mouse click was inPageDown or inDownButton, increase the value of the control. If the mouse click was inPageUp or inUpButton areas were pressed, decrease the value of the control. Finally, update the control to this new value with SetCtlValue().

```
/********************************   ScrollProc   *******/
pascal void ScrollProc(theControl, theCode)
ControlHandletheControl;
int          theCode;
{
      int     curControlValue, maxControlValue, minControlValue;

      maxControlValue = GetCtlMax( theControl );
      curControlValue = GetCtlValue( theControl );
      minControlValue = GetCtlMin( theControl );

      switch ( theCode )
      {
            case inPageDown:
            case inDownButton:
                  if ( curControlValue < maxControlValue )
                  {
                        curControlValue += 1;
                  }
                  break;
            case inPageUp:
            case inUpButton:
                  if ( curControlValue > minControlValue )
                  {
                        curControlValue -= 1;
                  }
      }
      SetCtlValue( theControl, curControlValue );
}
```

UpdateMyWindow() works in a similar fashion to the DrawPicture() routine in EventTutor (Chapter 4). The algorithm works so: Temporarily reset the window's clipping region so it does not include the area covered by the scroll bar. Center the picture, draw it, and reset the original clip region. The call to GetIndResource() uses the current value of the scroll bar (GetCtlValue(gScrollBarHandle)) to load the appropriate PICT resource.

> For example, if there were 30 PICT resources available, the scroll bar would run from 1 to 30. If the current thumb setting was 10, the call to GetIndResource() would return a handle to the tenth PICT resource. Since GetIndResource() returns a handle, you can use C's type-casting mechanism to convert it to a PicHandle.

Note that only one PICT at a time is ever loaded into memory. When the scroll bar's value changes, a replacement PICT is loaded, not an additional one.

```
/********************        UpdateMyWindow        *******/

UpdateMyWindow( drawingWindow )
WindowPtr     drawingWindow;
{
      PicHandle      currentPicture;
      Rect           drawingClipRect, myRect;
      RgnHandle      tempRgn;

      tempRgn = NewRgn();
      GetClip( tempRgn );

      myRect = drawingWindow->portRect;
      myRect.right -= SCROLL_BAR_PIXELS;
      EraseRect( &myRect );

      currentPicture = (PicHandle)GetIndResource( 'PICT', GetCtlValue(
gScrollBarHandle ) );

      if ( currentPicture == NIL_POINTER )
            ErrorHandler( CANT_LOAD_PICT );

      CenterPict( currentPicture, &myRect );

      drawingClipRect = drawingWindow->portRect;
      drawingClipRect.right -= SCROLL_BAR_PIXELS;
      ClipRect( &drawingClipRect );

      DrawPicture( currentPicture, &myRect );

      SetClip( tempRgn );
      DisposeRgn( tempRgn );
}
```

CenterPict() is the same as it ever was.

```
/******************************* CenterPict ********/

CenterPict( thePicture, myRectPtr )
PicHandle    thePicture;
Rect         *myRectPtr;
{
    Rect    windRect, pictureRect;

    windRect = *myRectPtr;
    pictureRect = (**( thePicture )).picFrame;
    myRectPtr->top = (windRect.bottom - windRect.top -
(pictureRect.bottom -pictureRect.top))
            / 2 + windRect.top;
    myRectPtr->bottom = myRectPtr->top + (pictureRect.bottom -
pictureRect.top);
    myRectPtr->left = (windRect.right - windRect.left -
(pictureRect.right - pictureRect.left))
            / 2 + windRect.left;
    myRectPtr->right = myRectPtr->left + (pictureRect.right -
pictureRect.left);
}
```

ErrorHandler() should be familiar by now. ParamText() to StopAlert() to ExitToShell(), leaving nothing to chance.

```
/******************************* ErrorHandler ********/

ErrorHandler( stringNum )
int    stringNum;
{
    StringHandle errorStringH;

    if ( ( errorStringH = GetString( stringNum ) ) == NIL_POINTER )
            ParamText( HOPELESSLY_FATAL_ERROR, NIL_STRING, NIL_STRING,
                    NIL_STRING );
    else
    {
        HLock( errorStringH );
        ParamText( *errorStringH, NIL_STRING, NIL_STRING, NIL_STRING );
        HUnlock( errorStringH );
    }
    StopAlert( ERROR_ALERT_ID, NIL_POINTER );
    ExitToShell();
}
```

The Sound Manager

If you're tired of the same old `SysBeep()`, there is an alternative. Within the system file is a set of `'snd'` resources, commonly known as beep sounds. The `'snd'` with resource ID = 1 is the familiar Beep. The current system comes with three additional `'snd'`s: Monkey, Clink-Klank, and Boing. Hundreds more are available on electronic bulletin boards throughout the country.

Using the Sound Manager, you can add these sounds to your applications. The final Mac Primer application, Sounder, shows you how.

Sounder

Sounder works like this:

- It initializes the Toolbox.
- It loads the `'SND'` resources from the system file.
- It plays them (assuming you have the volume set above 0).
- It quits.

Sounder also performs error checking. It puts up an alert if the `'SND'` resources can't be accessed.

Setting Up the Sounder Project

Start by creating a folder for this project, called `Sounder`. Use ResEdit to create a new file called `Sounder Proj.Rsrc`. Sounder uses the same `DITL` and `ALRT` resources as all the other Chapter 7 programs, so you can cut and paste if you've typed in the other programs. If not, use Figures 7.34 and 7.35 for those resources. Add the four `'STR'` resources shown in Figure 7.36 to the `Sounder Proj.Rsrc` file. Again, be sure to change the resource IDs of each resource to those shown in the figure. When you're done, the resource window of `Sounder Proj.Rsrc` should look like Figure 7.37.

347

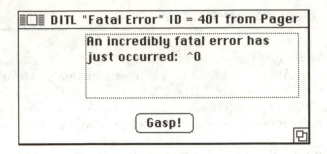

Item#	Type	Enabled	top	left	bottom	right	Text/Resource ID
1	Button	Yes	86	117	106	177	Gasp!
2	Static Text	Yes	5	67	71	283	An incredibly fatal error has just occurred: ^0

Figure 7.34   DITL resource for Sounder.

```
≣□≣ Alert "Fatal Error" ID = 401 from Sounder Pro

   top      [ 40 ]    bottom  [ 156 ]

   left     [ 40 ]    right   [ 332 ]

   itemsID  [ 401 ]            sound

   stage 1   ☐ 2 bold  ☒ drawn   [ 1 ]
   stage 2   ☐ 2 bold  ☒ drawn   [ 1 ]
   stage 3   ☐ 2 bold  ☒ drawn   [ 1 ]
   stage 4   ☐ 2 bold  ☒ drawn   [ 1 ]
```

Figure 7.35   ALRT resource for Sounder.

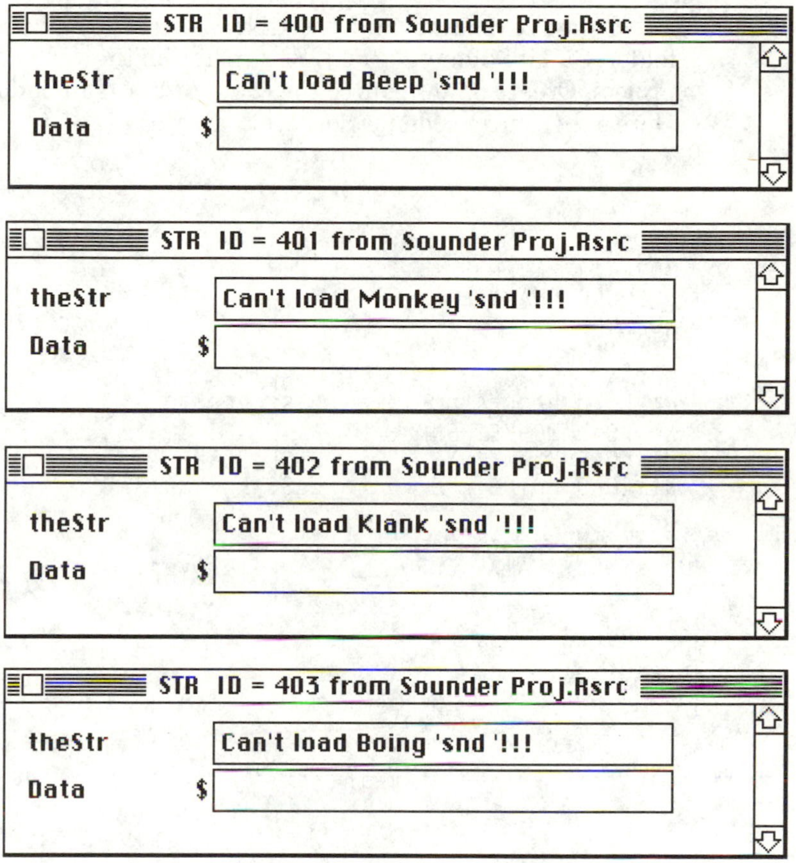

STR ID = 400 from Sounder Proj.Rsrc

theStr   Can't load Beep 'snd '!!!

Data $

STR ID = 401 from Sounder Proj.Rsrc

theStr   Can't load Monkey 'snd '!!!

Data $

STR ID = 402 from Sounder Proj.Rsrc

theStr   Can't load Klank 'snd '!!!

Data $

STR ID = 403 from Sounder Proj.Rsrc

theStr   Can't load Boing 'snd '!!!

Data $

Figure 7.36 STR resources for Sounder.

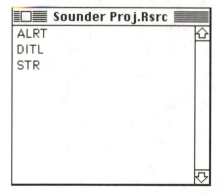

Sounder Proj.Rsrc

ALRT
DITL
STR

Figure 7.37 Sounder resources completed.

Now you're ready to launch THINK C. Create a new project in the Sounder folder. Call it Sounder Proj. Be sure to add the MacTraps library to your project. Create a new source file (Sounder.c), and add it to Sounder Proj. Here's the source code for Sounder.c:

```
#define          NIL_POINTER          0L
#define          BASE_RES_ID          400
#define          REMOVE_ALL_EVENTS    0
#define          NIL_SOUND_CHANNEL    NIL_POINTER
#define          SYNCHRONOUS          FALSE

#define          ERROR_ALERT_ID            BASE_RES_ID+1
#define          CANT_LOAD_BEEP_SND        BASE_RES_ID
#define          CANT_LOAD_MONKEY_SND      BASE_RES_ID+1
#define          CANT_LOAD_KLANK_SND       BASE_RES_ID+2
#define          CANT_LOAD_BOING_SND       BASE_RES_ID+3

#define          NIL_STRING                "\p"
#define          HOPELESSLY_FATAL_ERROR    "\pGame over, man!"

#define          BEEP_SND                  1
#define          MONKEY_SND                2
#define          KLANK_SND                 3
#define          BOING_SND                 4


/****************************** main *********/

main()
{
     ToolBoxInit();
     MakeSound();
}


/********************************** ToolBoxInit */

ToolBoxInit()
{
     InitGraf( &thePort );
     InitFonts();
     FlushEvents( everyEvent, REMOVE_ALL_EVENTS );
     InitWindows();
     InitMenus();
     TEInit();
     InitDialogs( NIL_POINTER );
     InitCursor();
}
```

```
/******************************* MakeSound *********/

MakeSound()
{
    Handle soundHandle;

    if ( ( soundHandle = GetResource( 'snd ', BEEP_SND ) ) == NIL_POINTER
)
            ErrorHandler( CANT_LOAD_BEEP_SND );
    SndPlay( NIL_SOUND_CHANNEL, soundHandle, SYNCHRONOUS );

    if ( ( soundHandle = GetResource( 'snd ', MONKEY_SND ) ) ==
            NIL_POINTER )
            ErrorHandler( CANT_LOAD_MONKEY_SND );
    SndPlay( NIL_SOUND_CHANNEL, soundHandle, SYNCHRONOUS );

    if ( ( soundHandle = GetResource( 'snd ', KLANK_SND ) ) ==
            NIL_POINTER )
            ErrorHandler( CANT_LOAD_KLANK_SND );
    SndPlay( NIL_SOUND_CHANNEL, soundHandle, SYNCHRONOUS );

    if ( ( soundHandle = GetResource( 'snd ', BOING_SND ) ) ==
            NIL_POINTER )
            ErrorHandler( CANT_LOAD_BOING_SND );
    SndPlay( NIL_SOUND_CHANNEL, soundHandle, SYNCHRONOUS );
}


/******************************* ErrorHandler *********/

ErrorHandler( stringNum )
int     stringNum;
{
    StringHandle errorStringH;

    if ( ( errorStringH = GetString( stringNum ) ) == NIL_POINTER )
            ParamText( HOPELESSLY_FATAL_ERROR, NIL_STRING, NIL_STRING,
                    NIL_STRING );
    else
    {
        HLock( errorStringH );
        ParamText( *errorStringH, NIL_STRING, NIL_STRING, NIL_STRING );
        HUnlock( errorStringH );
    }
    StopAlert( ERROR_ALERT_ID, NIL_POINTER );
    ExitToShell();
}
```

Walking through the Sounder Code

Sounder is short and sweet. These #defines should be familiar to you Chapter 7 *cognoscenti*.

```
#define      NIL_POINTER           OL
#define      BASE_RES_ID           400
#define      REMOVE_ALL_EVENTS     0
#define      NIL_SOUND_CHANNEL     NIL_POINTER
#define      SYNCHRONOUS           FALSE

#define      ERROR_ALERT_ID              BASE_RES_ID+1
#define      CANT_LOAD_BEEP_SND          BASE_RES_ID
#define      CANT_LOAD_MONKEY_SND        BASE_RES_ID+1
#define      CANT_LOAD_KLANK_SND         BASE_RES_ID+2
#define      CANT_LOAD_BOING_SND         BASE_RES_ID+3

#define      NIL_STRING                  "\p"
#define      HOPELESSLY_FATAL_ERROR      "\pGame over, man!"

#define      BEEP_SND           1
#define      MONKEY_SND         2
#define      KLANK_SND          3
#define      BOING_SND          4
```

Make the usual call to `ToolBoxInit()`. Then call `MakeSound()`.

```
/******************************** main *********/

main()
{
      ToolBoxInit();
      MakeSound();
}


/********************************* ToolBoxInit */

ToolBoxInit()
{
      InitGraf( &thePort );
      InitFonts();
      FlushEvents( everyEvent, REMOVE_ALL_EVENTS );
      InitWindows();
      InitMenus();
      TEInit();
      InitDialogs( NIL_POINTER );
      InitCursor();
}
```

The key to this program is the Sound Manager routine `SndPlay()`. Load each of the four `'snd '` resources normally found in the system file, and play them with `SndPlay()`.

> Since the Mac System file didn't always use `'snd '` resources, older systems may cause an error `ALRT` to appear. Check out the Sound Manager (Chapter 27) in *Inside Macintosh,* Volume V, for more detail.

The first parameter to `SndPlay()` is the `SndChannelPtr`. By passing `NIL_POINTER`, you've told `SndPlay()` to allocate a channel for you. The second parameter is the `'snd'` handle. The third parameter tells `SndPlay()` whether or not to play the sound asynchronously. When you pass `NIL` as the `SndChannelPtr`, you must pass `FALSE` as the third parameter. That is, if you ask `SndPlay()` to allocate a channel for you, you must play the sound synchronously. If you cannot find the `'snd '` resource, go to the beloved `ErrorHandler()`.

```
/****************************** MakeSound ********/

MakeSound()
{
     Handle soundHandle;

     if ( ( soundHandle = GetResource( 'snd ', BEEP_SND ) )
               == NIL_POINTER )
          ErrorHandler( CANT_LOAD_BEEP_SND );
     SndPlay( NIL_SOUND_CHANNEL, soundHandle, SYNCHRONOUS );

     if ( ( soundHandle = GetResource( 'snd ', MONKEY_SND ) ) ==
               NIL_POINTER )
          ErrorHandler( CANT_LOAD_MONKEY_SND );
     SndPlay( NIL_SOUND_CHANNEL, soundHandle, SYNCHRONOUS );

     if ( ( soundHandle = GetResource( 'snd ', KLANK_SND ) ) ==
               NIL_POINTER )
          ErrorHandler( CANT_LOAD_KLANK_SND );
     SndPlay( NIL_SOUND_CHANNEL, soundHandle, SYNCHRONOUS );

     if ( ( soundHandle = GetResource( 'snd ', BOING_SND ) ) ==
               NIL_POINTER )
          ErrorHandler( CANT_LOAD_BOING_SND );
     SndPlay( NIL_SOUND_CHANNEL, soundHandle, SYNCHRONOUS );
}
```

The error-handling routine is similar to what you've seen in the other Chapter 7 programs:

```
/****************************** ErrorHandler *********/

ErrorHandler( stringNum )
int    stringNum;
{
     StringHandle errorStringH;

     if ( ( errorStringH = GetString( stringNum ) ) == NIL_POINTER )
          ParamText( HOPELESSLY_FATAL_ERROR, NIL_STRING, NIL_STRING,
          NIL_STRING );
     else
     {
          HLock( errorStringH );
          ParamText( *errorStringH, NIL_STRING, NIL_STRING, NIL_STRING );
          HUnlock( errorStringH );
     }
     StopAlert( ERROR_ALERT_ID, NIL_POINTER );
     ExitToShell();
}
```

In Review

We covered a lot of ground in this chapter. Each of the four programs we presented involved a different part of the Mac Toolbox. If you're unsure about any of the concepts discussed, take the time to read about them in their respective *Inside Macintosh* chapters. The Scrap Manager is covered in Volume I, Chapter 15. The Standard File Package is covered in Volume I, Chapter 20 and updated in Volume IV, Chapter 15. The File Manager is covered in Volume IV, Chapter 19. (*Warning:* Don't be fooled by imitations! The File Manager section in Volume II, Chapter 4, has been completely replaced by Chapter 19 of Volume IV.) The Printing Manager is covered in Volume II, Chapter 5.

The Control Manager is covered in Volume I, Chapter 10. Scroll bars make up a small part of this chapter, but the concepts implemented in Pager will carry through to other types of controls.

Finally, the Sound Manager is covered in Volume V, Chapter 27. An authoritative version of this chapter has been published by Macintosh Developer Technical Support under the title "The Sound Manager." If you're really interested in sound on the Mac, read the Sound Driver chapter (Volume I, Chapter 8). This was the way sound originally worked on the Mac, and many of the basic concepts are still supported.

Chapter 8 introduces the wonderful world of ResEdit. See you there!

Using ResEdit

ResEdit provides a simple, yet powerful way to edit resources. This chapter shows you how to use this tool to create the Finder resources necessary to turn your projects into standalone applications.

By Now, You should have a good grip on the most important aspects of Macintosh application programming. We've described how to handle events, access files, and display pictures and text. You've worked with menus, windows, and dialogs. In this chapter we'll discuss some issues that become important after you have your basic programming problems in hand.

After you compile your debugged application, but before you announce your first stock offering, you need to take care of a few loose ends. For example, you'll want to turn your code into a standalone application. You'll want to design your own custom icon. These finishing touches require the creation of six resources known as the Finder resources. These resources do not affect the operation of the application; rather, they affect the way your application interfaces with the Finder. This chapter discusses how to add the six Finder resources to your application.

If any readers are still shaky about the use of ResEdit, this discussion on the installation of Finder resources is for you. After installing the resources in this chapter, you should feel comfortable using ResEdit.

Why use ResEdit to edit resources? Because ResEdit creates resources graphically, whereas the others build resources by describing them textually. For example, here is a text description of a `WIND` resource:

```
TYPE WIND
  ,128                      ;; the resource number
My Window                   ;; the window title
40 40 200 472               ;; the window rect (top left
                            bottom right)
Visible GoAway              ;; resource flags
0                           ;; window definition ID
0                           ;; refcon (points to user call)
```

This is the way that RMaker, another Apple resource editor, makes resources. RMaker also comes with THINK C.

ResEdit's `WIND` editor looks like Figure 8.1. When you're creating resources for the first time, ResEdit's graphic approach has many advantages: It's more intuitive, and it gives you a chance—with many resource types—to examine the appearance of a resource without actually running your program. You can use RMaker and ResEdit interchangeably; see the appendix in THINK C's *User Manual* if you're interested in using RMaker.

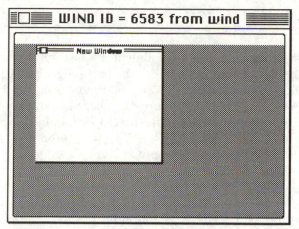

Figure 8.1   Graphic representation of
`WIND` resource.

First, you'll compile an application in THINK C. Then, you'll use
ResEdit to add the six Finder resources to it. You can use the procedure in
this chapter for any project you wish; the tutorial uses the Hello2 project
that we created in Chapter 3.

The Finder Resources

Apple recommends that software developers install six special resources in
their applications. Each resource plays an essential role in your application's interface to the Finder. They are grouped into three categories:

- **Application icon:** The `ICN#`, `FREF`, `BNDL`, and **signature** resources are
  used to add a unique icon to an application as it appears on the desktop.
- **Application version information:** The `vers` resource contains general information used by the Finder, including the specific version of an
  application, the country for which it is localized, and its creation date.
- **Application MultiFinder requirements:** The `SIZE` resource designates the recommended and minimum application memory size needed
  for an application, and also contains further details on the application's
  level of MultiFinder compatibility.

Completing a Standalone Application: Hello2 Revisited

The first step is to create a standalone application from a working project. You'll do this by compiling Hello2, the first program in Chapter 3. Open up the Hello2 Project. Select Set Project Type... from the Project menu. You should see something like Figure 8.2. There are four project options in the dialog box. Make sure the **Application** radio button is selected in the dialog; click on OK. See THINK C's *User Manual* or Appendix C for a description of the other three project types.

Now choose Build Application from the Project menu. If the project is up to date, it should prompt you for an application name (Figure 8.3). Call the application Hello2. (The Smart Link check box should be checked.) When you click on Save, THINK C will build the Hello2 application. When it's completed, quit THINK C and try double-clicking on the Hello2 application created in your Hello2 folder. It should display the text Hello, World in a window (Figure 8.4).

Now that you have a working standalone program, you're ready to add the Finder resources. Click the mouse button to quit Hello2.

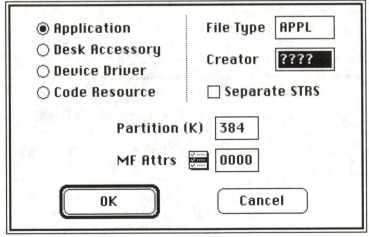

Figure 8.2   Project Type dialog box.

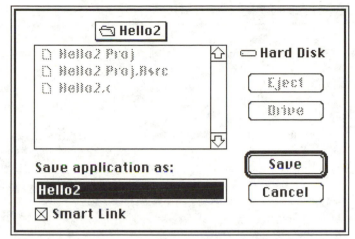

Figure8.3 Build Application dialog box.

Figure 8.4 Running Hello2.

Notes on Using ResEdit

Although you can use ResEdit in MultiFinder, it is more robust (i.e., doesn't crash as much) in the regular Finder. We suggest that you not use MultiFinder when creating resources for this book. If you do, make sure that the application memory size used by ResEdit is at least 512K (Figure 8.5).

You can't edit resources in files that are currently in use, such as the Finder file. This is not much of a disadvantage, as editing open files is not recommended anyway.

It's a good idea to make a copy of any file you plan to edit. It is very easy to modify resources irrevocably. Be careful. If you're planning on entering more than one or two resources in a single ResEdit session, save your file periodically.

Although ResEdit works with all resource types, it may have difficulty performing some operations on large resources, such as sound resources ('snd') that exceed a few hundred K in size. In these cases, proceed with caution.

These guidelines are a little like the sign posted at swimming pools about waiting 30 minutes after you eat: Most of the time, they're not necessary. ResEdit is generally quite well-mannered and will quickly become an indispensable programming tool.

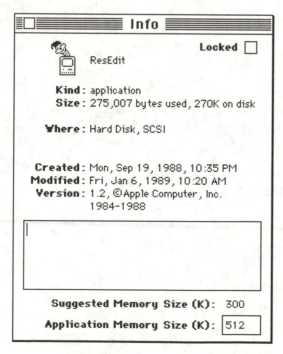

Figure 8.5 Setting ResEdit to 512K.

How ResEdit Works

Before you start using ResEdit to install the Finder resources, let's examine how ResEdit accomplishes the job of creating, editing, and deleting resources in files. Double-click on ResEdit to start it up.

A window is displayed for every storage device currently available. Each window lists all the folders and files on that storage device (see Figure 8.6). To open a folder, double-click on the folder name. To close a folder, click on the close box of the folder's window.

The Macintosh has a number of different types of storage devices available for use. If files are available on a storage device (known as a volume), it's called a mounted volume. Mounted volumes include:

- Floppy disks currently in an internal or external drive
- Hard disk drives, both serial and SCSI
- Tapes currently mounted on or in a tape drive
- Remote file systems, currently mounted via AppleShare, TOPS, and so on

Notice that an empty floppy disk drive is not a mounted volume. An initialized floppy disk, however, once inserted into the drive, is a mounted volume.

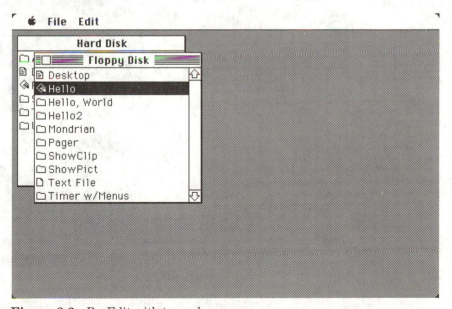

Figure 8.6 ResEdit with two volumes open.

ResEdit has two menus, **File** and **Edit**. When you're editing some resources, an additional menu will appear. As you've seen in earlier chapters, you can create new resource files by selecting New from the File menu.

To create a new resource, create a new resource file or open an existing one. To open an existing file, double-click on its name. Figure 8.7 shows the resource window for Hello2. Choose New from the File menu to add a new resource to the current file. The Type dialog box (Figure 8.8) appears: This allows you to select the type of resource you wish to build. You can either select from the scrolling window or type in the name of the new resource type.

If you have just selected a new resource type, or have double-clicked on an existing resource type, the Resource Picker window is displayed. This window shows all resources of the selected type in the resource file. To create an individual resource of the type indicated in the Picker window (Figure 8.9), select New from the File menu again.

An editor window will now appear. The methods by which the editor works vary with the resource type. Some resource types have a MacPaint "fat bits" editor (ICON, ICN#). Many types simply display named fields for you to input (FREF, BNDL, MENU, MBAR). Other resource types can be resized and positioned graphically (WIND, DITL, DLOG). If ResEdit doesn't know how to handle a certain resource type, it defaults to a hexadecimal editor.

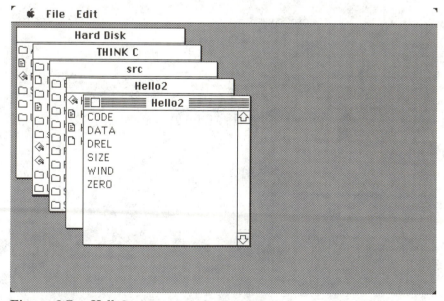

Figure 8.7   Hello2 resource window.

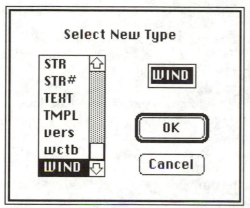

Figure 8.8 The Resource Type dialog box.

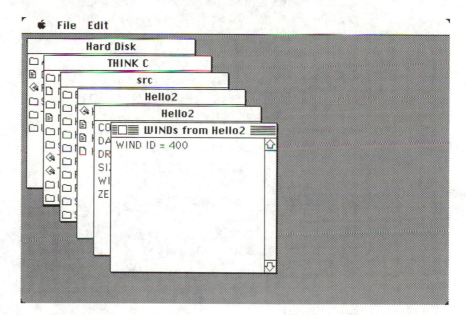

Figure 8.9 WIND Picker window in the Hello2 application.

To get things started, let's take a look at the way you'd create a WIND resource. Start by creating a new resource file or opening an existing one. Figure 8.10 shows the empty Hello2 Proj.Rsrc file. Select New from the File menu. The Type dialog box is displayed, which allows you to select the type of resource that you plan to create (Figure 8.11). Type in WIND, or select WIND from the scrolling list. Click on OK.

The WIND Picker window is now displayed. This shows all the WIND resources currently in the file. Since we haven't added any to Hello2.Rsrc yet, the window should be empty. Select New from the File menu again to create your first WIND resource (Figure 8.12). The WIND editor displays the new window in a miniaturized version of the screen. Click and drag the window around the mini desktop to change its global coordinates (Figure 8.13). Click and drag on the lower right corner of the window to resize it (Figure 8.14).

Finally, select the **Display as Text** item in the WIND menu. This shows another way to enter the parameters for your WIND resource. If you make changes here and select **Display Graphically** from the WIND menu, the adjusted window will be positioned correctly on the mini desktop.

Certain information about each resource can be edited in the resource's Get Info window. To edit this information, click on the resource in the Resource Picker window and select Get Info from the File menu. ResEdit assigns new resources a random resource ID number. The most important piece of information in this window is the resource ID. Because you use the resource ID number to specify the resource you plan to use, it's important to change the resource ID number to match your program design.

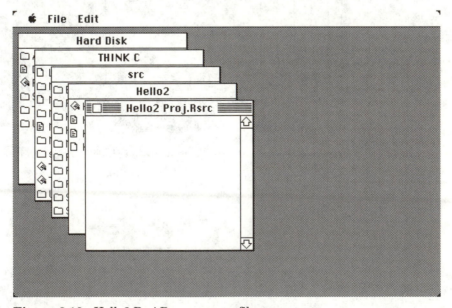

Figure 8.10   Hello2 Proj.Rsrc resource file.

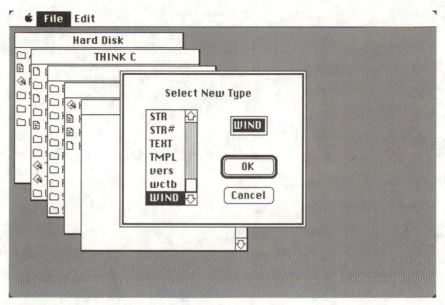

Figure 8.11 The Resource Type dialog Box.

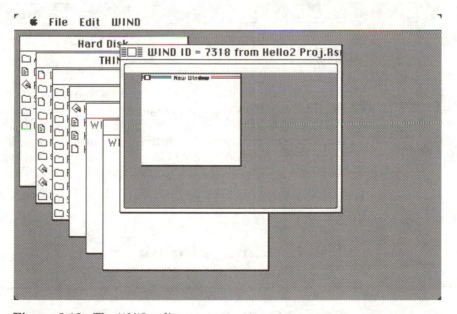

Figure 8.12 The WIND editor.

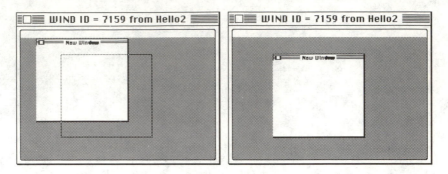

Figure 8.13   Changing the WIND coordinates.

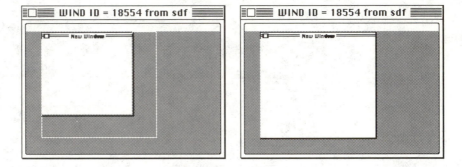

Figure 8.14   Resizing the WIND resource.

This is all you need to know to use most of ResEdit's functionality. ResEdit is probably the most popular resource editor available. Apple has constantly updated it and has published a manual called *Using ResEdit*. If you'd like more technical information about how ResEdit works, you can procure the manual from APDA (see Chapter 9 for more information).

That's the end of the ResEdit overview. Next, we'll talk about the six special Finder resources, and add them to your application.

The ResEdit Tutorial: Installing the Finder Resources

Completing a Standalone Application

Double-click on ResEdit. Double-click on the THINK C folder to open it up. Then, double-click on the source code folder inside the THINK C folder ('src' in our figures). Finally, double-click on the Hello2 folder that you created back in Chapter 3. You should see something like Figure 8.15.

If you double-click on the new Hello2 application file that you built earlier, the resource window of the application will appear. These are the resources that THINK C created when it compiled the application (Figure 8.16). The CODE resources are your executable code. The WIND resource (which you built with ResEdit) is used to build Hello2's window. The DATA, DREL, and ZERO resources are created by the compiler: Don't mess with them. The SIZE resource is one of the Finder resources; THINK C created it for you, so you don't need to. We'll look at it later.

Click on the close box to close the resource list window. Make sure Hello2 is still highlighted, and select Get Info from the File menu (Figure 8.17). This dialog contains information that the system has on your new application. APPL is short for application. Files having type APPL are recognized as applications by the Finder.

Start the installation of your Finder resources by changing the Creator from ???? to HELO. Be careful: ResEdit discriminates between upper and lower case. Now close the window by clicking in the close box and save your changes.

The four-charactor Creator name HELO will be used when the Finder looks for the application's icon. If, by chance, another application with a defined icon has the same Creator, the first icon the Finder finds will be used. Be careful in your choice of Creator names. If you plan to market a Macintosh application, register the Creator name with Macintosh Developer Technical Support, who can tell you whether or not others have used this Creator tag. We registered HELO, so go ahead and use it for Primer applications.

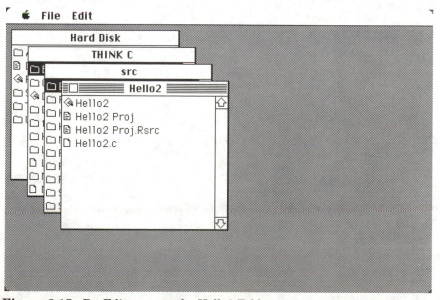

Figure 8.15   ResEdit, open to the Hello2 Folder.

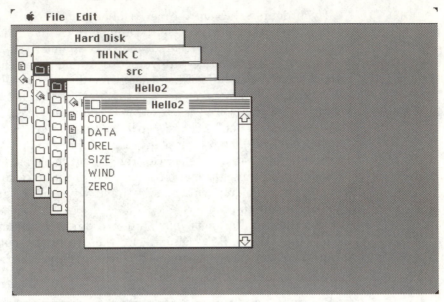

Figure 8.16   Hello2's resource window.

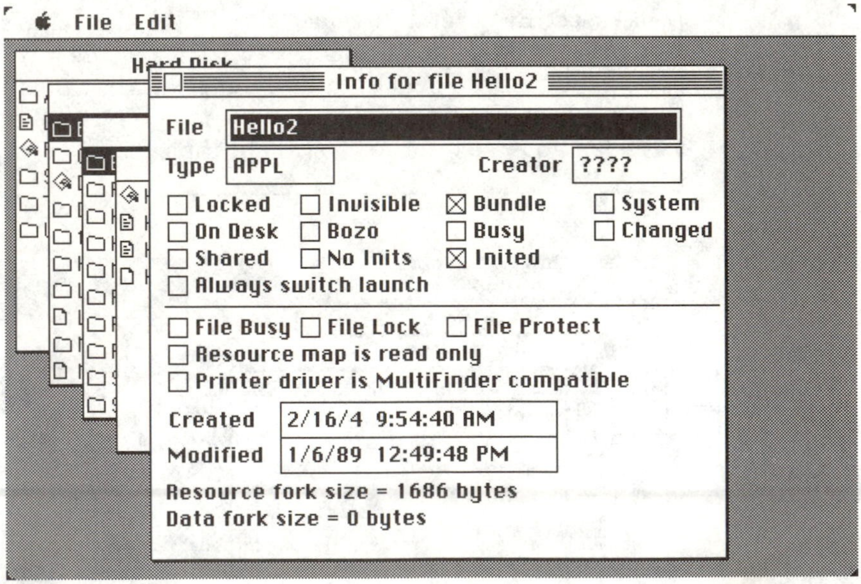

Figure 8.17   Hello2's Get Info window.

The flags displayed in the File Information window are information that the Finder keeps regarding your application. Normally, you should not change them.

Here is a brief description of the Finder flags found in the File Info box (see Figure 8.18).

The **Locked** flag is no longer implemented.

If the **Invisible** bit is set, the file is not displayed by the Finder. ResEdit can see it, however, as well as Finder substitutes like DiskTop.

The **Bundle** flag is set by the Finder if you have a BNDL resource in the file. We'll talk more about BNDLs later in this chapter.

The **System** bit indicates that the file cannot be renamed, and that a warning will be given when the file is dragged to the trash.

If the file is on the Desktop (i.e., not in any folder), then the **On Desk** flag is set.

The **Bozo** flag was an early attempt to implement copy protection on the Mac. If it is set, the Finder will not copy the file. Since ResEdit can turn the Bozo bit off, however, you can defeat this copy protection scheme. Current protected software uses more sophisticated copy protection schemes.

The **Busy** bit is currently not implemented.

The **Changed** flag tells you that your file has been modified since it was opened. ResEdit uses that information to prompt you to save your changes when you quit.

If the **Shared** flag is set, the application can be opened more than once.

The **Inited** bit is set by the Finder when it determines the file's location and window.

If the **File Busy** bit is set, the file is open. You see this if you examine a running application with ResEdit while in MultiFinder.

If the **File Lock** bit is set, the file cannot be renamed (although it can be thrown away).

The **File Protect** flag is not currently used.

If the **Resource map is read only** check box is checked, the resources in the file cannot be changed.

The **Printer driver is MultiFinder compatible** is set only for printer drivers that work with MultiFinder.

The **File Information** dialog box also contains **created** and **modified** dates for the application.

At the bottom, the dialog box displays the size of the **resource fork** and the **data fork**. As was discussed in Chapter 2, all Macintosh applications have a resource fork and a data fork. The resource fork contains resources. The data fork may store information about user preferences or anything else you desire.

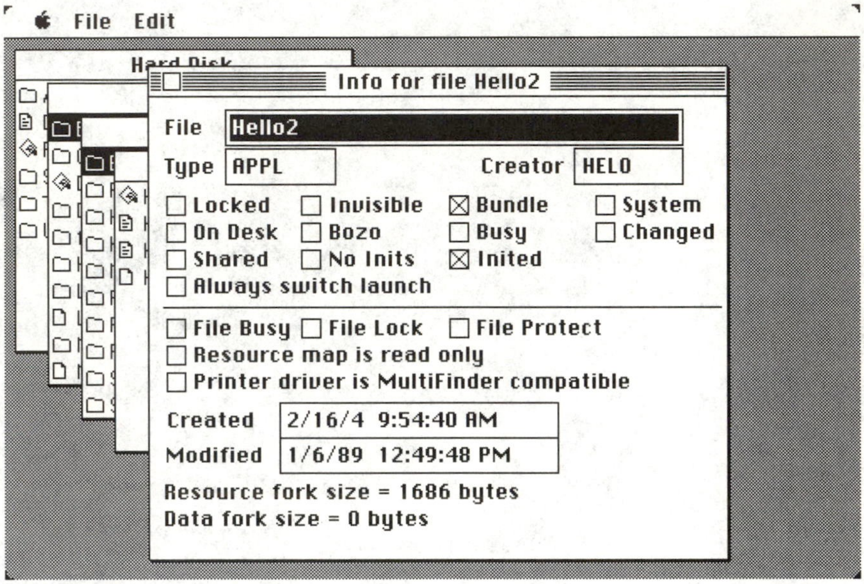

Figure 8.18 Finder flags.

As stated earlier, the Finder resources are broken down into three groups. One set of resources sets up the icon, another resource contains version information, and the last resource contains MultiFinder information. First, you'll create the resources that add an icon to the Hello2 application.

Adding an Icon to Hello2

Adding your own icon to Hello2 is an involved procedure. Four resources must be placed into your application file to get the Finder to replace the generic application icon with a unique icon.

Begin by creating the graphic icon used to identify the application on the desktop. Open up Hello2 with ResEdit, and choose New from the File menu. The Type dialog box appears. Either key in ICN# or select it from the scrolling list. Figure 8.19 shows the ICN# Picker window.

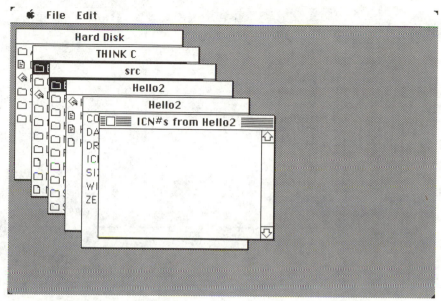

Figure 8.19 ICN# Picker window.

A desktop icon (ICN#) actually consists of an icon and its mask. The mask is used to change the appearance of the icon to indicate a change in condition (TN:55). Resources that contain an icon without the mask are of resource type ICON.

Build your first icon by again selecting New in the File Menu. An ICN# editing window should be displayed. The special editor for ICN# resources allows you to build your icon graphically. With a little experimentation, you should be able to draw lines and circles with the mouse (Figure 8.20).

The ICN# Resource Editor in ResEdit allows you to preview the icon on both a light and a dark background. It also shows you what the icon will look like if the application is unavailable. (This commonly occurs if you ejected the disk with the program on it using Command E. If the application was on the desktop, it will still show up but will be dimmed, indicating that it can't be used).

The ICN# editor is like the Fat Bits mode in MacPaint. The pane on the left is the icon displayed by the application. The pane on the right is the

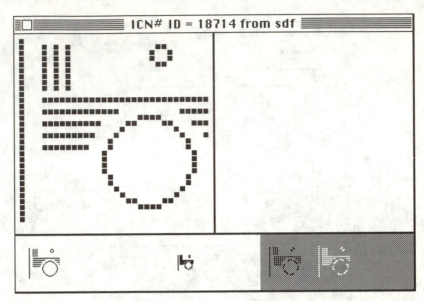

Figure 8.20   The ICN# editor.

mask, and governs the change in the application's icon when selected. Figure 8.21 shows how THINK C's application icon looks in the ICN# editor.

When you're comfortable drawing figures with the bit map editor, try creating an icon for your application. If you prefer, use the icon in Figure 8.22, which will be used in the rest of the tutorial screen shots. When you're done with your icon, select Data->Mask from the ICN# menu. This will automatically draw a mask for your application in the right pane of the window. When the icon is complete, examine the title bar. You should see something like the text in Figure 8.23, except that the resource ID number will probably be different. Click on the close window of your Hello2 icon, and select Get Info in the File menu (Figure 8.24). Change the ID to 128. It is a Macintosh convention to use 128 as the application's ICN# ID number.

Your version of ResEdit may contain a second ICN# menu item that rotates between Display Using Old Method and Display Using New Method. Make sure it shows Display Using New Method. This will ensure that your icon looks good on the desktop. With system Version 6, changes were made that could cause the old method of displaying icons on the desktop to be aesthetically unappealing (TN:147).

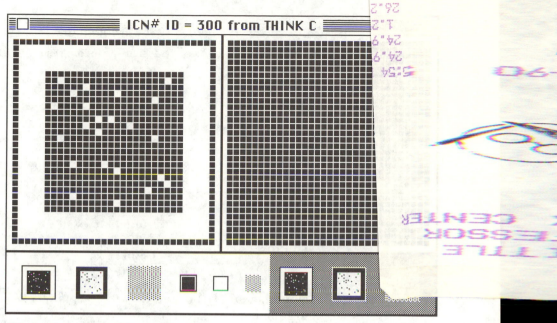

Figure 8.21   The THINK C ICN#.

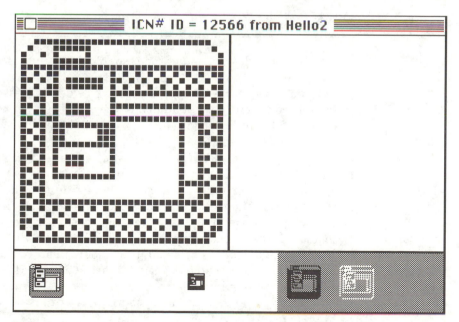

Figure 8.22   The Primer ICN#.

ICN# ID = 12566 from Hello2

Figure 8.23 New resources are assigned random resource IDs.

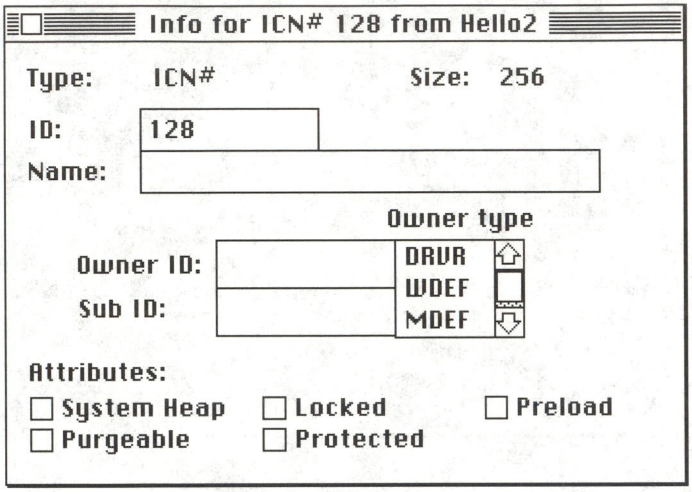

Info for ICN# 128 from Hello2

Type: ICN#   Size: 256

ID: 128

Name:

                                        Owner type

Owner ID: DRVR
                                 WDEF
Sub ID: MDEF

Attributes:
☐ System Heap   ☐ Locked   ☐ Preload
☐ Purgeable   ☐ Protected

Figure 8.24 Get Info window of ICN# resource.

Here's a brief description of the resource fields in this window.

Owner Type: Special programs such as desk accessories must be handled differently. If you click on Owner Type, your resource ID changes. Resources in desk accessories must have IDs within certain ranges to work properly.

Owner ID and **Sub ID** are used when you are sharing the resource with other programs.

The Hello2 icon is automatically set to **Preload** and **Purgeable** by the Finder. PreLoad resources are loaded into memory as soon as your application starts running. Purgeable resources are removed from memory if the Memory Manager needs to reclaim that space.

If **System Heap** is selected, the resource will be loaded into the **System Heap** instead of the **Application Heap**. If the resource is **Locked**, the Memory Manager cannot move it around when it is rearranging memory. If the resource is **Protected**, the Resource Manager can't modify it.

Now that you've created an icon for your application, you have to create the resources that will link your icon to your application's creator name.

Building the File Reference Resource

Now we'll build the FREF (short for File Reference) resource. First, close the ICN# Get Info window, then close the ICN# Picker window. Select New from the File menu and select FREF from the scrolling window (or type it in).

While you're in the FREF Picker window, select New from the File menu again. The FREF resource appears. It contains three pieces of information about the application:

- **File Type:** You saw this in the Get Info dialog box of your application.
- **icon local ID:** The local ID number that other resources (like BNDL) will use when looking for the icon. Don't confuse this with the ICN# resource ID.
- **fileName:** This field is not currently used.

Type APPL for file type. Put a 0 in the icon Local ID field. The fileName is not currently used; you can leave it blank. Click in the close box to close the FREF window (Figure 8.25). Now, select Get Info so that you can change the FREF resource number ID. As you did with the ICN# resource, change the ID of the FREF to 128 (Figure 8.26). You have now completed the ICN# and FREF resources of Hello2.

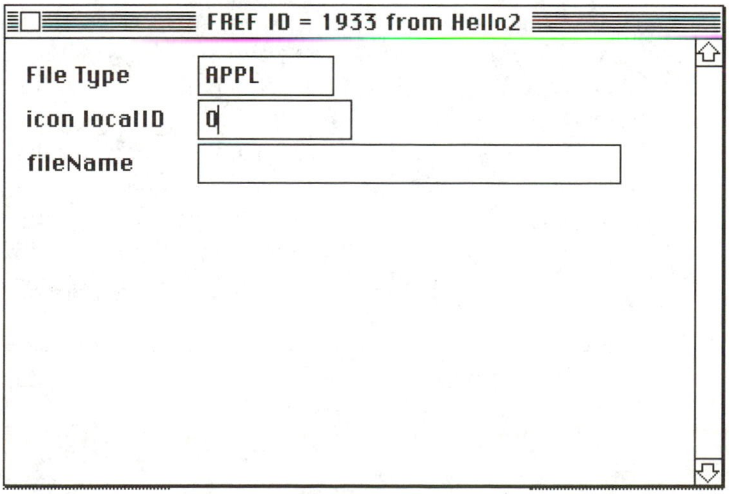

Figure 8.25   Completed FREF fields.

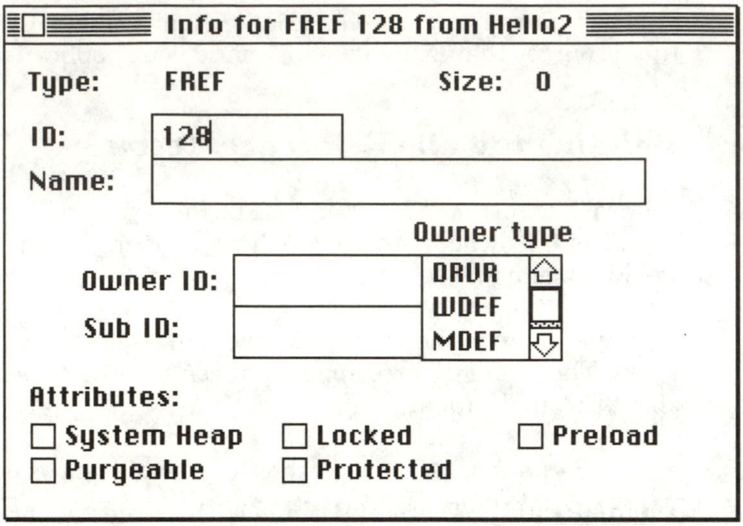

Figure 8.26   Get Info window of `FREF 128`.

Remember, the resource ID is not the same as the **local ID**. Your application's code will call a resource by its resource ID; the local ID is used by the Finder to correctly load Finder resources into the Desktop file (TN:48).

Building the Bundle Resource

Your next task is to build a bundle resource. The `BNDL` keeps track of the resource IDs and local IDs used by the application.

Select New from the File menu. Key in `BNDL`, or click on it in the scrolling window (Figure 8.27). Click on OK.

The BNDL resource, like the FREF you just built, is edited with the text editor. `BNDL`s, however, have a variable number of fields, depending on how many resources are being bundled together. This particular editing operation is not intuitive for most people, so we'll go very slowly. The next time you need to create a resource with a variable number of fields, you'll be ready.

To create the `BNDL` resource, select New again from the File menu. Type in `HELO` for OwnerName. Put a `0` into the `ownerID` field (Figure 8.28).

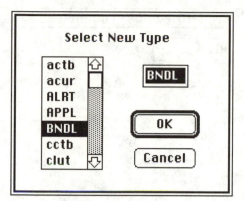

Figure 8.27 `BNDL` selected Resource Type dialog box.

BNDL ID = 5400 from Hello2

OwnerName	HELO
ownerID	0
numTypes	-1

*****

8.28 `BNDL` fields, part 1.

`HELO` is `Hello2`'s Creator name. The `BNDL` field OwnerName corresponds to the application's Creator name. The `BNDL` field owner-erID is the resource ID of the signature resource (which you'll build next).

Click on the row of asterisks at the bottom of the listing. The asterisks should be highlighted by a rectangle (Figure 8.29). Select New from the File menu bar. You can now add the first resource that the `BNDL` is supposed to track. Enter `ICN#` in the new type field. Then, click on the row of dashes.

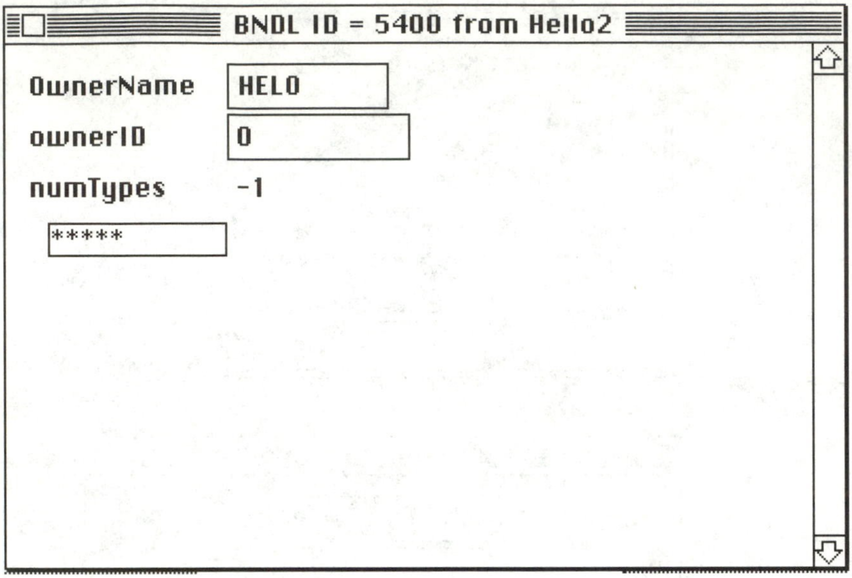

Figure 8.29   Highlighted asterisks.

It should be highlighted with a rectangle (Figure 8.30). Select New from the
File menu again. Type in 0 for the Local ID and 128 for the rsrcID for the
ICN# resource. Scroll down to the bottom of the window using the scroll bar
on the right. Select the asterisks again (Figure 8.31). (Since the windows in
ResEdit are not resizable, you will often need to scroll down to find
additional fields in a resource. This is the only time we'll discuss scrolling
in the text.)

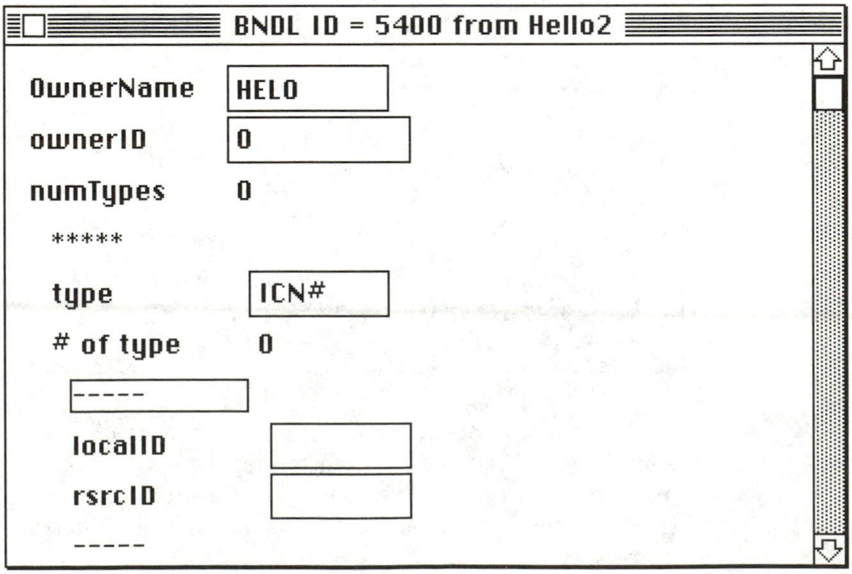

Figure 8.30   Highlighted dashes.

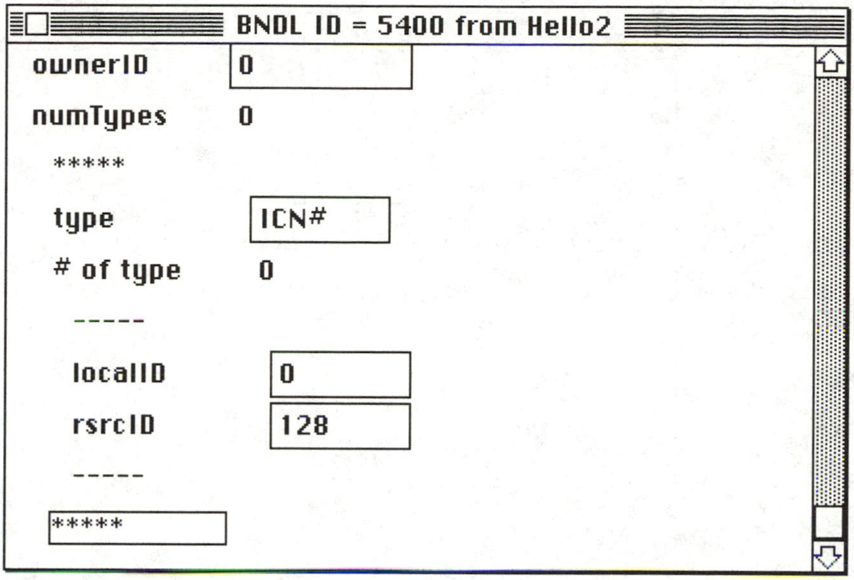

Figure 8.31 Asterisks highlighted again.

Now that you've put the ICN# information into the BNDL, let's add the FREF resource information. Use the same techniques that you just used for the ICN# information to complete the BNDL as shown in Figure 8.32. Select Get Info from the File menu and change the BNDL's resource ID to 128. By convention, Macintosh applications have a single BNDL with resource ID = 128. Now, close the edit window and save your changes.

ResEdit does some basic error checking with the data that you type in, so it's possible that you will get an alert box complaining about something. For example, ResEdit will check to make sure you have no more than four characters in your type fields; if you get the alert in Figure 8.33 when you close the resource, go back to the two type fields and make sure you have only four characters (including spaces).

One way to make sure your fields are clear of nonprinting characters is to double-click on the field to highlight it and then clear the field with the backspace/delete key. Then, input the field again. Use the tab key or the mouse to get between fields, not the <Return> key.

Click on the close box and you're done with bundles. Now, you're just one resource away from iconization.

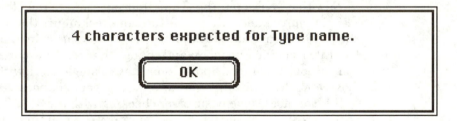

```
┌──────────────────────────────────────────────────┐
│ □ ▤▤▤▤▤▤ BNDL ID = 5400 from Hello2 ▤▤▤▤▤ │
├──────────────────────────────────────────────────┤
│      rsrcID            ┌─────────┐           ⇧    │
│                        │ 128     │                │
│                        └─────────┘                │
│      ─ ─ ─ ─ ─                                     │
│                                                    │
│      *****                                         │
│                                                    │
│      type              ┌─────────┐                │
│                        │ FREF    │                │
│                        └─────────┘                │
│      # of type           0                        │
│                                                    │
│      ─ ─ ─ ─ ─                                     │
│                                                    │
│      localID           ┌─────────┐                │
│                        │ 0       │                │
│                        └─────────┘                │
│      rsrcID            ┌─────────┐                │
│                        │ 128     │                │
│                        └─────────┘                │
│                                                    │
│      ─ ─ ─ ─ ─                                     │
│                                                    │
│      *****                                    ⇩    │
└──────────────────────────────────────────────────┘
```

8.32   Completed BNDL fields.

```
┌──────────────────────────────────────────────────┐
│ ┌──────────────────────────────────────────────┐ │
│ │                                                │ │
│ │     4 characters expected for Type name.      │ │
│ │                                                │ │
│ │            ╭──────────────────╮                │ │
│ │            ║        OK         ║                │ │
│ │            ╰──────────────────╯                │ │
│ │                                                │ │
│ └──────────────────────────────────────────────┘ │
└──────────────────────────────────────────────────┘
```

8.33   ResEdit error alert.

Adding the Signature Resource

You've now added three of the four resources needed to attach an icon to
Hello2. The last one to be added is the **signature** resource. The signature
resource is somewhat different from the other resources, which all have
fixed names. The signature resource type is actually the Creator name that
you assigned to Hello2 at the beginning of this chapter.

At this point, use ResEdit to display the resources that you've already
installed (Figure 8.34). Select New from the File menu. Since the Creator
name you used was HELO, type HELO and click on OK. (Because HELO is not
a standard resource, it's not in the scrolling window; you'll have to type it
in, as shown in Figure 8.35.)

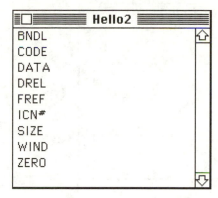

Figure 8.34 Hello2 resources.

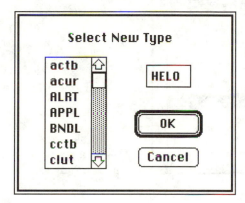

Figure 8.35 Type dialog box with 'HELO' typed in.

With the HELO Picker window open, select New from the File menu. So far, you've edited resources textually (like FREF and BNDL), and you've used a bit map editor (ICN#). Each resource in ResEdit has a **template** that specifies how the resource should be edited. If ResEdit does not have a template for the resource selected, it defaults to the hexadecimal editor (Figure 8.36). This general-purpose editor allows you to type in hexadecimal information on the left side of the window and ASCII text on the right side. You can force the use of the hexadecimal editor on any resource by choosing Open General instead of Open in the File menu.

The signature resource is used to supply the Creator ID name to the Finder, so you don't actually type anything in. Close the window and select Get Info from the File menu while the HELO resource is selected. Change the resource ID to 0 and close the Get Info Box. You should have the resources shown in Figure 8.37 displayed in Hello2.

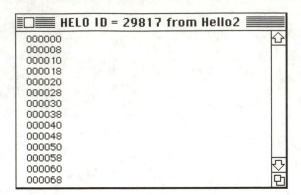

Figure 8.36   ResEdit's hexadecimal editor.

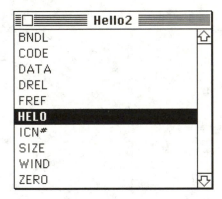

Figure 8.37   Hello2 with
Finder resources.

You're done! The four required Finder resources are installed into your
Hello2 application. To see if it worked, save your changes and quit ResEdit.
If you succeeded (Figure 8.43), you may proceed to the `vers` resource
discussion. If the situation resembles Figure 8.38, read on.

The `signature` resource used to have an additional function. If you
typed text into it, the text would be displayed when the Get Info menu
item was selected in the Finder with the application highlighted. This
function has been eliminated by the `vers` resource, which now
supports the Get Info call in the Finder. If the `vers` resource is missing
in a file, the Finder will alternatively use the information in your
signature resource. For example, if you typed the text of Figure 8.39
into Hello2's `HELO` resource, the Finder would display the Get Info
window in Figure 8.40. The first character in the `HELO` resource
(shown as a hex `36` or an ASCII `6`) is the length of the Get Info text.

Figure 8.38 Hello2 application icon (unchanged).

```
 Helo ID = 0 from Hello2
000000   3648 656C 6C6F 3220   6Hello2
000008   312E 3020 6973 2061   1.0 is a
000010   2073 616D 706C 6520   sample
000018   6170 706C 6963 6174   applicat
000020   696F 6E20 6672 6F6D   ion from
000028   2074 6865 204D 6163   the Mac
000030   2050 7269 6D65 72     Primer
000038
000040
000048
000050
000058
000060
000068
```

Figure 8.39 A complete `HELO` resource.

Info

Locked ☐

Hello2

Kind: application
Size: 2,672 bytes used, 3K on disk

Where: Hard Disk, SCSI

Created: Tue, Feb 16, 1904, 9:54 AM
Modified: Fri, Jan 6, 1989, 2:59 PM
Version: Hello2 1.0 is a sample application
from the Mac Primer

Suggested Memory Size (K): 384

Application Memory Size (K): 384

Figure 8.40 The Get Info window corresponding to Figure 8.39.

If your new icon appeared, great! If not, don't despair; use ResEdit to check each of the four resources you created. Make sure the resource IDs are correct. If this is true and the icon still doesn't appear, try rebooting your machine. This almost always works. The final alternative is rebuilding your Desktop. Before you go downstairs for the hammer and nails, read the next section.

Rebuilding the Desktop

The icon you made failed to show up in the Finder when you quit ResEdit. The reason was that the Desktop file needs to be rebuilt after you modify the Finder resources. The Desktop file is the Finder's application database. Among other things, the Desktop file holds information about the volume's file bundles. When a volume's Desktop is rebuilt, the entire volume is searched, and the Desktop database is reconstructed. One way to rebuild the Desktop is to clear the Desktop file using ResEdit (you can't do this in MultiFinder). Rebuilding the Desktop does one irrevocable thing, (so if you're not a person who likes to do seven irrevocable things before breakfast, please read carefully); *it causes the loss of the information that has been placed in the text box of the Get Info window for all your applications.*

> One way to avoid rebuilding your Desktop file is to add the resources to a copy of Hello2 on a floppy and then copy it to the target disk. This should cause the Desktop file on the target disk to update itself.

In ResEdit, highlight the Desktop file by clicking on it once. If you have two storage devices mounted, each disk will contain a Desktop file that keeps track of things for that disk. Make sure you've chosen the Desktop file that's on the diskette or hard drive containing Hello2. Select Clear from the Edit menu (Figure 8.41). At this point, you'll be asked to confirm the file deletion (Figure 8.42). Click on OK if everything looks right. Select Quit from the File menu. After a few moments (the bigger your drive, the longer it will take), the Desktop file will be rebuilt with the new information about Hello2 (Figure 8.43).

Did your icon show up correctly? If not, you might want to check the resources again. Each step is crucial in making sure the Finder figures out

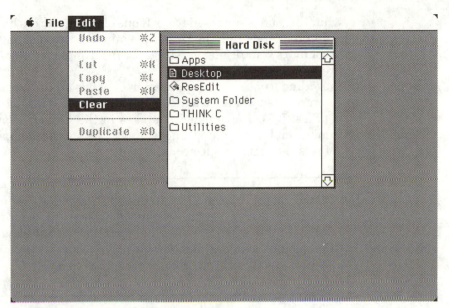

Figure 8.41 Deleting the Desktop file.

Figure 8.42 Last chance alert.

Figure 8.43 The new Hello2 icon is displayed.

what the icon is supposed to be. If one of the resources has an error, correct it and try rebuilding the Desktop again. One good debugging technique is to compare your resources with those in an application that displays its icon properly, like THINK C.

Adding icons to your application depends on the correct relationship of the resources you have added. One mistake in a resource ID or field is all it takes. If you have made mistakes in the Finder resources, the Finder won't complain; it will just go on using the standard application icon until it finds the resources it needs.

> Once you understand how to install the Finder resources, you'll find it easier to add them directly to your .rsrc file of your project, instead of adding them to completed applications. That way, each time you build a standalone application from your project, THINK C will automatically add the Finder resources to it.

The vers Resource

The next Finder resource that you'll add is the vers resource, which stores information about the current version of an application. Fire up ResEdit and open up Hello2. Create a new resource of type vers (Figure 8.44). As you can see, the vers is edited like the FREFs or BNDLs you have already seen. Key in the fields as shown in Figure 8.45. Then close the vers edit window and change the resource ID to 1.

The information you put in tells the Finder more about your application. Most of this additional information refers to the application's version. The version is designated using Apple's intricate numbering system for program releases, which works like this. A new program has Version 1.0. If there is a minor revision to the program, it is then labeled Version 1.1. If there's a **bug fix** to Version 1.1, it's designated 1.1.1. So, if you have a program that just had a second bug fix to a third minor revision, it would be Version 1.3.2. If there's a **major revision** to the program, the first number is incremented. If the program has gone through a major revision, four minor revisions, and six bug fixes, the current version is 2.4.6.

There's also a **development suffix,** which is added to indicate how far along the product is. There are three different stages: The earliest is **d** for "development" (for example, 1.0d). The next level is **a** (for "alpha"—1.0a). Then, the **b** ("beta") version comes out (1.0b). Theoretically, the released version would then be 1.0. If you have a product labeled 1.3d1.2, it's the second bug fix of the first development version of the third revision of the first release of the product.

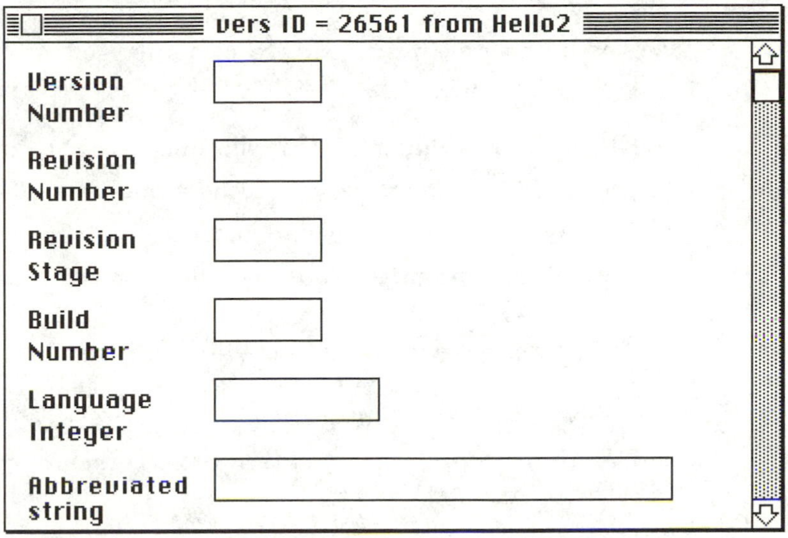

Figure 8.44 vers resource editor.

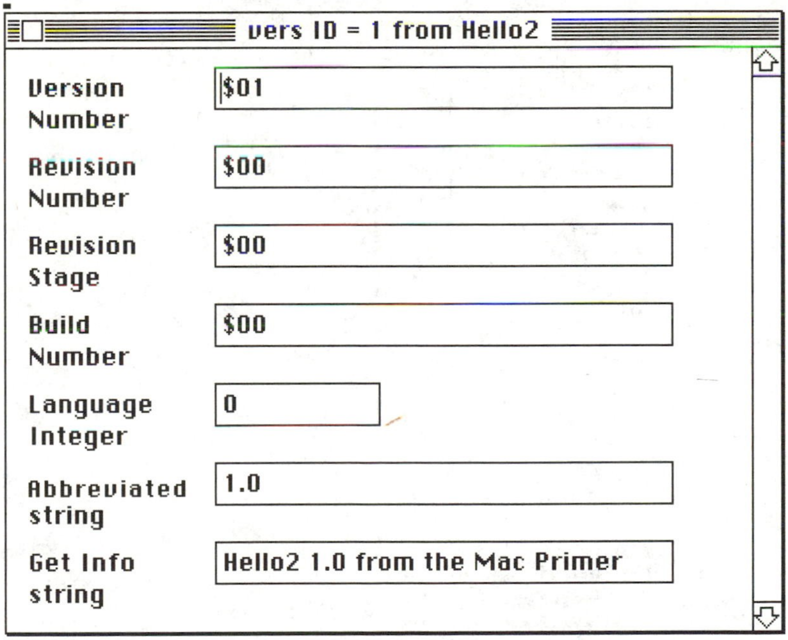

Figure 8.45 Completed vers resource.

Now that we've said all that, it's unlikely that you'll need as complex a version number as that, unless you own Microsoft.

This relates to the `vers` resource fields as follows:

- The **version number** is the first number, the "1" in 1.0.
- The **revision number** is the second number, the "3" in 4.3.1.
- The **revision stage** is the development level, the "b" in 1.0b2.
- The **build number** is the number following the development suffix, the "5" in 2.3a5.
- The **language integer** refers to the country to which this version of the program is headed. The United States is 0; see Figure 8.46 for a list of numbers for other countries.
- The **abbreviated string** is the whole version strung together, like 1.2b1.1.
- The **Get Info string** is the text that is put in the Get Info box when you're in the Finder.

US	**0**
France	**1**
Britian	**2**
Germany	**3**
Italy	**4**
Netherlands	**5**
Belgium	**6**
Sweden	**7**
Spain	**8**
Denmark	**9**
Portugal	**10**
French Canada	**11**
Norway	**12**
Israel	**13**
Japan	**14**
Australia	**15**
Arabia	**16**
Finland	**17**
French Swiss	**18**
German Swiss	**19**
Greece	**20**
Iceland	**21**
Malta	**22**
Cyprus	**23**
Turkey	**24**
Yugoslavia	**25**

Figure 8.46   Country numbers.

Test the resource by saving and quitting ResEdit. Then, click on the Hello2 application and choose Get Info from the File menu of the Finder (Figure 8.47). The dialog box should show what you put into the `vers` resource. Currently, the Finder doesn't use any of the information except for the Get Info string, which is placed in the Get Info box. The `vers` resource type is a relatively recent addition to the Finder resources; Apple will have plans for it in the future, so put it in your applications (TN:189).

Some of you may be confused by the fact that the `signature` resource seems to put information into the Get Info box in the same way that the `vers` resource does. You're right, and here's what happened: The `signature` resource was the old way of attaching the icon to the application and putting information in the Get Info box. The `vers` resource type is intended to supply the Finder with extra information, including the Get Info data, about your application. If there is no `vers` resource, the Get Info information in the `signature` resource is used. If there is, the `signature` resource is ignored, and the vers Get Info field is used. In any event, don't dump the `signature` resource! It still is used to identify the desktop icon for the application. There doesn't have to be anything in it however; just create it, change the resource ID to 0, and close it.

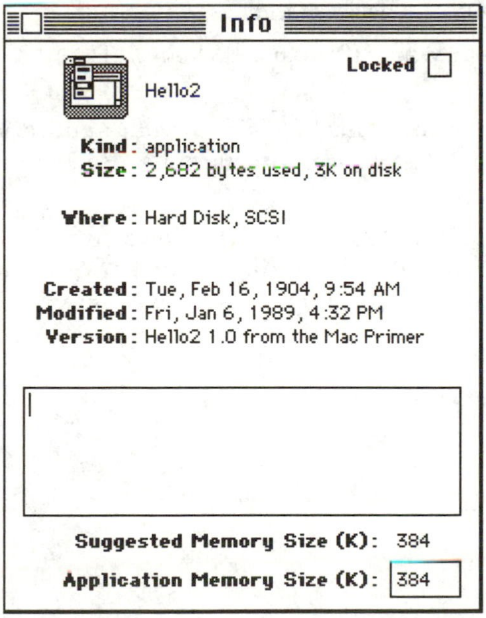

Figure 8.47 Hello2's Get Info window.

If you have a `vers` resource with a resource ID number of 2, it can be used to link a set of files together. Apple has used this number to identify the current system level of the files in their disks. Figure 8.48 shows how this system information is displayed.

In the bottom of the Get Info box, there are two other fields, Mininum and Suggested Memory Size for the application. These fields are filled by the SIZE resource, which is discussed next.

Last of the Finder Resources: The SIZE Resource

The last Finder resource is the `SIZE` resource, which contains MultiFinder information. As you saw earlier, THINK C installs the `SIZE` resource for you when it compiles your application. Open the `SIZE` resource in Hello2 and examine the fields. Figure 8.49, suitably elongated, shows the fields that the `SIZE` resource contains.

The following is a brief description of these fields:

- **Save screen (Switcher):** A flag used by the Switcher, an early version of MultiFinder.

- **Accept Suspend/Resume events:** If your application handles Suspend/Resume events, set this flag.

- **Disable option:** Another flag used by Switcher.

  Can Background: A MultiFinder flag set if your application uses null events while in the background.

- **MultiFinder aware:** If you use `WaitNextEvent()` in your programs, set this flag.

- **Only Background:** This flag is set if your application runs only in the background and has no user interface (i.e., Backgrounder in the System folder).

- **Get Front Clicks:** If set, this flag allows your applications to receive mouse clicks even if it is working in the background. If this is not set, clicking on your application window will only make the application active, and not pass on the click.

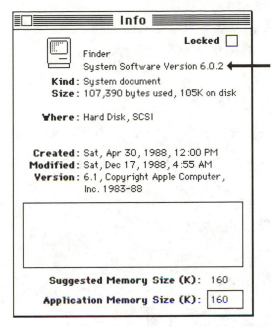

Figure 8.48 Illustration of `vers` 2 resource.

The rest of the bits are reserved by Apple. This is just a brief description of the flags in the `SIZE` resource. For a detailed discussion of the `SIZE` resource, read *The Programmer's Guide to MultiFinder*, available from Apple through APDA.

In most cases, the only bits that need concern you are the ones that you can set from THINK C in the Project dialog box.

> As we go to press, two `SIZE` resource flags have been reserved by Apple (the two Switcher flags), and two new flags: getChildDiedEvents and 32Bitcompatible. The `SIZE` editor in your copy of ResEdit may be updated to include these changes. (TN:180,205).

The next section demonstrates how intrinsic resources are to the Macintosh. We now present Minimalist, a program that contains *nothing* except two `CODE` resources and a `WIND` resource, all created with ResEdit.

Minimalist, the ResEdit Program

Minimalist could be charitably described as a very small, useless program. It demonstrates, however, how resources make Macintosh programs work.

In ResEdit, create a new file named Minimalist. Using the Get Info menu item, change the file type to `APPL`. Then, create a new resource of type `CODE` (Figure 8.50). The general hexadecimal editor appears.

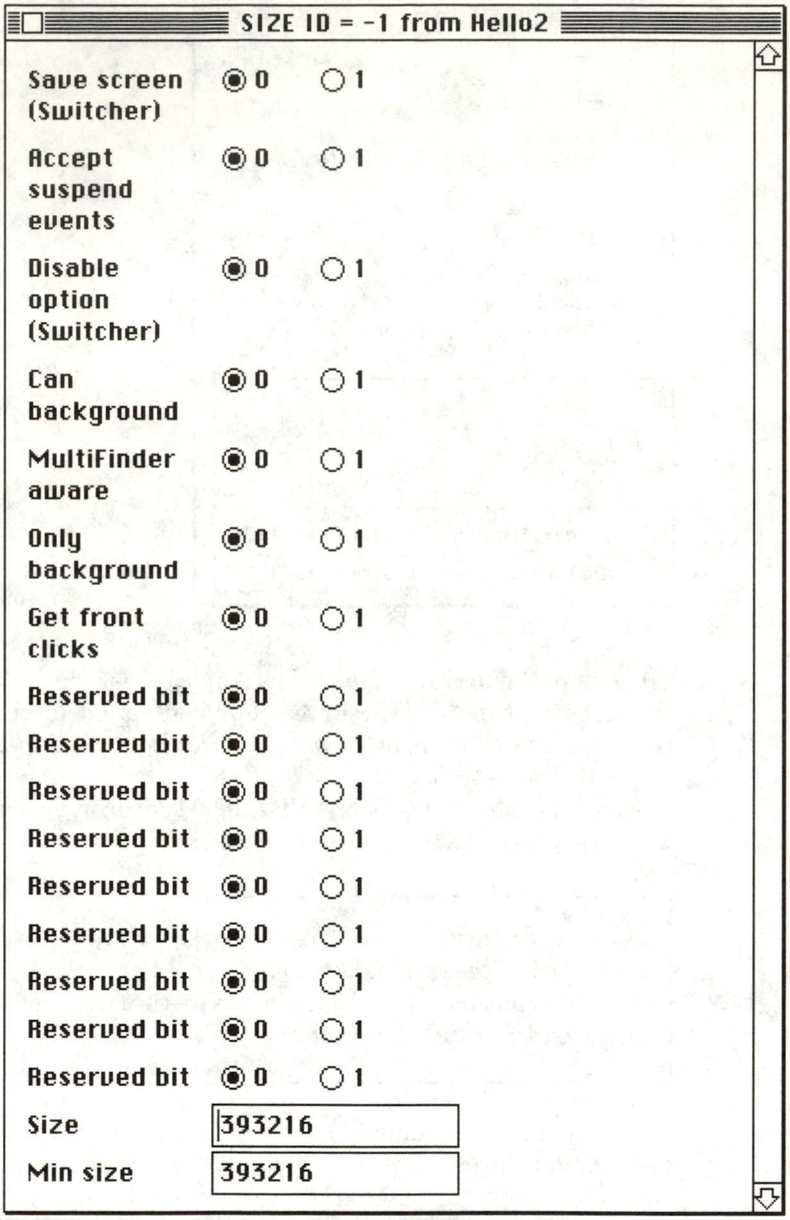

SIZE ID = -1 from Hello2		
Save screen (Switcher)	◉ 0	○ 1
Accept suspend events	◉ 0	○ 1
Disable option (Switcher)	◉ 0	○ 1
Can background	◉ 0	○ 1
MultiFinder aware	◉ 0	○ 1
Only background	◉ 0	○ 1
Get front clicks	◉ 0	○ 1
Reserved bit	◉ 0	○ 1
Reserved bit	◉ 0	○ 1
Reserved bit	◉ 0	○ 1
Reserved bit	◉ 0	○ 1
Reserved bit	◉ 0	○ 1
Reserved bit	◉ 0	○ 1
Reserved bit	◉ 0	○ 1
Reserved bit	◉ 0	○ 1
Reserved bit	◉ 0	○ 1
Size	393216	
Min size	393216	

Figure 8.49   The SIZE resource fields.

Type in the hex in Figure 8.51. As you're typing, alphanumeric characters will appear on the right. When you're done, click on the close box. Change the ID of the resource by choosing Get Info from the File menu. Change the ID to 0. Build the second `CODE` resource with the hex in Figure 8.52. Change the resource ID number of the second `CODE` resource ID to 1. Finally, build a `WIND` resource with a resource ID of 400. Use any size or window type that you prefer, but make sure that the `Visible` and `goAwayFlag` checkboxes are checked. Save the `WIND` and the two `CODE` resources.

You now have an application. If you double-click on Minimalist, it will display the window you created. Clicking anywhere on the screen will return you to the Finder.

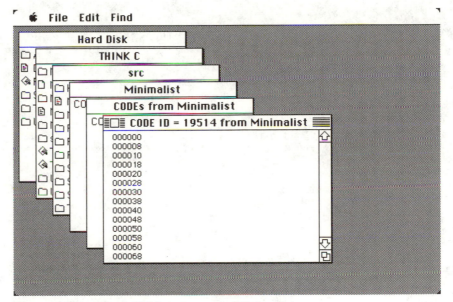

Figure 8.50 Blank `CODE` resource in Minimalist.

```
▓□≡  CODE ID = 0 from Minimalist  ≡▓
000000    0000 0028 0000 0200   □□□<□□□□  ⬆
000008    0000 0008 0000 0020   □□□□□□□
000010    0000 3F3C 0001 A9F0   □□?<□□Ͻ□
000018
000020
000028
000030
000038
000040
000048
000050
000058                                    ⬇
000060
000068                                    🗇
```

Figure 8.51 Minimalist's `CODE` 0 resource.

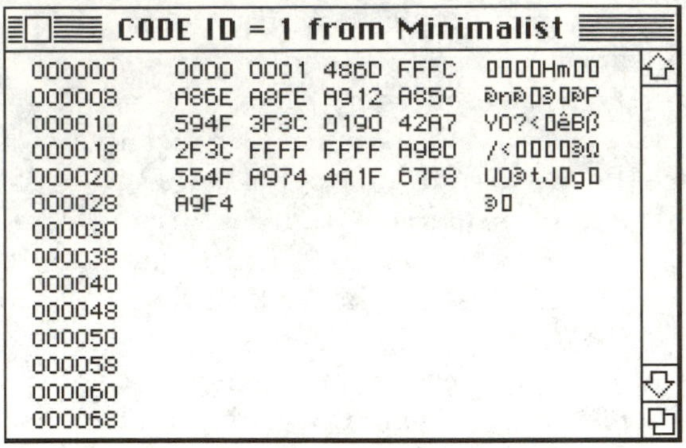

```
▭▤▥▤  CODE ID = 1 from Minimalist  ▥▤▥
000000    0000 0001 486D FFFC    ▯▯▯▯Hm▯▯    ⇧
000008    A86E A8FE A912 A850    ⓐⓝⓟ▯▯▯▯ⓟ
000010    594F 3F3C 0190 42A7    YO?<▯êBß
000018    2F3C FFFF FFFF A9BD    /<▯▯▯▯3Ω
000020    554F A974 4A1F 67F8    UO⊅tJ▯g▯
000028    A9F4                   ⊅▯
000030
000038
000040
000048
000050
000058                                      ⇩
000060
000068
```

Figure 8.52 Minimalist's CODE 1 resource.

To get the CODE hex, we wrote a short assembly language program that does initialization, draws a window, and quits on a mouse click. Here's the code:

```
include 'Traps.a'
main
pea -4(A5)
_InitGraf
_InitFonts
_InitWindows
_InitCursor

subq #4,sp
move #400,-(sp)
clr.l -(sp)
move.l #-1,-(sp)
_GetNewWindow

TryButton
subq #2,sp
_Button
tst.b (sp)+
beq.s TryButton
_ExitToShell

end
```

We don't, in general, recommend this strategy for program development. It's best to leave CODE resources to THINK C.

In Review

Chapter 8 discussed the steps necessary to install the Finder resources into your applications. It provided a tutorial for new ResEdit users.

Chapter 9 discusses the issues you'll face as you start developing your own Macintosh applications. We'll start by taking a look at a few Mac periodicals you may find useful. We'll talk about *Inside Macintosh* and other Apple technical references. We'll look at Apple's support apparatus for Macintosh programmers and developers.

The Final Chapter

To successfully develop software for the Macintosh, you need current technical information. You need to know how to use the standard Macintosh references effectively. You also need to know about the different technical support programs Apple offers. In this chapter, we'll discuss these and other Macintosh development issues.

THE BASICS OF programming the Macintosh have been laid out in the eight preceding chapters. Familiarity with these basics is half the job of becoming a successful developer. The other half is understanding how the Macintosh programming world works and knowing where to get the information you, as a Macintosh software developer, will need.

To succeeed in developing software for the Macintosh, you need current technical information. You need to be able to use the standard Macintosh references effectively. You also need to know about the different technical support programs Apple offers.

In this chapter, we'll investigate the periodicals that are your link to the Macintosh community. We'll look at *Inside Macintosh* and other Mac technical texts. We'll look at software tools, from compilers to debuggers. We'll also examine Apple's support programs for Macintosh software developers.

The *Macintosh Programming Primer* is your passport to Mac application programming. When you've finished reading this book, join a local Macintosh user's group, and buy a copy of the best Mac programmer's magazine, *MacTutor*. Get involved and write some code!

Macintosh Periodicals

Whether you're interested in making a commercial product or a shareware product, or just want to know the inside stories of the Mac community, get the trades. *MacWeek* is great, and *PCWeek* and *InfoWorld* are good, if less oriented to the Macintosh computer line. All three magazines deliver timely dollops of news: the new software packages, scoops on company goings-on, and juicy industry gossip.

The Macintosh programming journal is *MacTutor*, an invigorating monthly discourse on the art of Mac programming. Popular Mac magazines include *MacUser* and *MacWorld*. Their broad viewpoint can show you what is of interest to Macintosh users, and what's available.

While you wait for the idea that will make you the seventh richest person in the world, you need to learn the Macintosh inside out. To do this, you need *Inside Macintosh*.

The Essential Inside Macintosh

The *Inside Macintosh* technical reference series is written by Apple and published by Addison-Wesley. There are six books in the *Inside Mac* series (Volumes I-V and the I*nside Macintosh X-Ref*). In Chapter 1, we suggested that you could get by with Volumes I and V.

We lied. Get them all.

Volumes I, II, and III represent the Mac technical world as it was before the Mac Plus was introduced. All three volumes focus on the original 128K Mac, describing interfaces to the ROM routines, memory management, hardware specs, and more.

Volume IV was released after the Mac Plus and the Mac 512KE were introduced. Both of these new Macs sported 128K ROMs (as opposed to the 128K Macintoshes' 64K ROMs). These larger ROMs contain the routines that handle the new, hierarchical file system (HFS), routines that interface to the SCSI (Small Computer System Interface) port, and updates to most of the 64K ROM routines. Volume IV covers all these changes.

Volume V was released after the introduction of the Mac SE and the Mac II. The Mac II and the SE have 256K ROMs and support features like pop-up, hierarchical, and scrolling menus; a sophisticated sound manager; new text edit routines; and more. Perhaps the biggest change of all was the addition of color support to the Mac II ROMs. Volume V covers both the Mac SE and the Mac II.

The Typical *Inside Mac* Chapter

One of the best features of the *Inside Mac* volumes is their consistency. Each chapter starts with a table of contents, followed by the "About This Chapter" section which gives an overview of what the chapter covers and what you should already be familiar with before you continue.

The next section or sections give an overview of the chapter's technical premise—for example, "About the Event Manager" or "About the Window Manager." The fundamental concepts are explained in great detail. At first, you may be overwhelmed by the wealth of detail, but after a few readings (and a little experimentation), you'll warm to the concept.

Then the chapter's data structures, constants, and essential variables are detailed. These are presented in Pascal and/or assembly language. Back in Chapter 2, we presented a set of rules for translating *Inside Mac*'s Pascal data structures and calling sequences into C.

Next come the chapter's Toolbox routines. Each routine's calling sequence is presented in Pascal, along with a detailed explanation of the uses of the routine. This section includes notes and warnings, as appropriate.

Some chapters follow the Toolbox routines section with a few additional sections. Among these extras are a description of the resources pertinent to that chapter and, perhaps, a description of extensions available to the advanced programmer.

Finally, there's a chapter summary, with its unadorned lists of constants, data types, routines, and variables.

Appendices and Special Sections

Inside Macintosh, Volume I, Chapter 1, contains a road map that gives you a feel for the basics of the Macintosh and how the *Inside Mac* volumes work. The road map suggests you read Chapters 1 through 4, then read the chapters that are relevant to your current development effort. This is sage advice. These chapters offer an excellent grounding in Mac basics (or an excellent review if you've been at it for awhile).

Volume III contains three chapters, some appendixes, a glossary, and an index. Chapter 1 discusses the Finder (with an emphasis on Finder-related resources). Chapter 2 discusses the pre-Mac Plus hardware. Chapter 3 is a compendium of all the summary sections from Volumes I and II. Appendix A is a handy, if occasionally inaccurate, table of result codes from the functions defined in Volumes I and II. The rest of the appendixes in Volume III have been superseded by the appendices in the *Inside Macintosh X-Ref*.

The *Inside Mac X-Ref* starts off with a general index covering all five *Inside Mac* volumes, the Macintosh *Technical Notes, Programmer's Introduction to the Macintosh Family, Technical Introduction to the Macintosh Family,* and *Designing Cards and Drivers for the Macintosh II and Macintosh SE*. The general index is followed by an index of constants and field names. Appendix A of the *X-Ref* lists every Toolbox routine that may move or purge memory.

Appendix B of *Inside Mac* consists of two lists. The first is a list of Toolbox routines presented alphabetically by name, with each name followed by the routine's **trap address**, which is the four-byte instruction the compiler generates to call the routine. The second is a list of the trap addresses, in order, with each trap address followed by the routine name. This information is extremely useful if you ever have to look at code in hexadecimal format, a likely event if you use TMON or MacsBug, two Mac debuggers.

Appendix C lists most of the operating system global variables, with their memory location and a brief description. Finally, Appendix C is followed by a glossary of terms presented in Volumes I through V.

Apple Technical References

In the first few years of the Mac era, *Inside Macintosh* was the only definitive reference on the Macintosh. Recently, however, Apple has published some additional reference texts for the Macintosh, including *Technical Introduction to the Macintosh Family*, *Programmer's Introduction to the Macintosh Family*, and *Designing Cards and Drivers for the Macintosh II and Macintosh SE*. These books are all part of Addison-Wesley's Apple

Technical Library. Another excellent source of technical information are the Macintosh *Technical Notes*.

Macintosh Technical Notes

Macintosh Technical Notes are published on a regular basis by Apple and distributed to developers free of charge. The *Tech Notes* are a necessity for serious Mac developers. They contain technical information that was not yet available when the latest volume of *Inside Macintosh* went to press. For example, *Tech Note* #184 describes the Notification Manager (used in chapter 6). Without this *Tech Note,* developers wouldn't even know the Notification Manager existed, let alone know how to use it.

A timely way to receive Tech Notes if you are not a developer is to become a member of APDA, the Apple Programmer's and Developer's Association (developers are automatically members of APDA). APDA charges $20 per year for membership and they sell most of the technical references mentioned in this chapter. They sell the Tech Notes in both hard copy and disk formats. For more information on APDA, contact:

Apple Programmer's and Developer's Association
Apple Computer, Inc.
20525 Mariani Avenue, MS: 33-G
Cupertino, CA 95014-6299

APDA was formerly an organization independent of Apple and has just recently been returned to the fold, so changes in its operation may be imminent.

If you're not either a developer of a member of APDA, you can still get Tech Notes by downloading them from Mac-oriented bulletin boards around the country.

Other Books

There are a number of excellent books on Mac programming. One of the most popular is the *Macintosh Revealed* series, written by Stephen Chernicoff. Volume I of *Macintosh Revealed* dives right into the Toolbox, providing an in-depth tour of the Mac ROM routines. Volume II continues the exploration of ROM routines, and additional texts are planned.

Another excellent reference is Scott Knaster's *How to Write Macintosh Software*. This book is little too advanced for the beginner, but it's worth the struggle to get through it. If you plan on writing a lot of Mac code, read this book.

We're also hard at work on a sequel to the *Macintosh Programming Primer*. We'll address concepts like color QuickDraw, INITs, CDEVs, and other interesting Toolbox routines with lots of examples and code walkthroughs.

Apple's Developer Programs

Apple has recently replaced the Certified Developer Program with the Apple Partners program. This new program provides additional technical support from Apple. Developers accepted into the new Apple Partners program receive complete Apple technical documentation, system software updates, membership in APDA, access to training classes, and discounts on Apple hardware and software. Developers also get a year's subscription to AppleLink, Apple's electronic communication network, and access to Macintosh Developer Technical Support (see below). However, the original Certified Developer yearly rate ($0) has also been enhanced to cover the services provided ($600).

You don't have to be a Fortune 500 company to qualify as an Apple Partner, but Apple is looking specifically for developers of Apple hardware and software who intend to resell their products. It you are interested in developing software, but don't have an immediate plan to market it, you might consider the Apple Associates Program, a new support program from Apple.

The Apple Associates Program is aimed at educators, in-house developers and shareware programmers. It provides a basic level of support, including AppleLink (one month prepaid), system software upgrades, APDA, Tech Notes, and access to other technical information. The Associates program has a yearly charge of $350.

If you plan on writing a product for the Mac, the information that you receive in either program is invaluable. Call the Developer Programs Hotline at (408) 974-4897 and ask them to send you an application.

As a developer, there's nothing more satisfying than talking to people who have solved, or at least are aware of the technical programs you encounter in writing programs. At Apple, these people come from Macintosh Developer Technical Support, or MacDTS.

Macintosh Developer Technical Support and AppleLink

Macintosh Developer Technical Support is composed of talented Mac software engineers dedicated to helping developers with their technical problems. To work with MacDTS, send them a message via MCI Mail. Or you can use AppleLink.

AppleLink is Apple's electronic communication network. It gives access to information about Apple products, prices, programs, and policy information. You can write to Developer Technical Support at MacDTS on AppleLink, and they will make every possible effort to answer your question within twenty-four hours. (If they can't solve the problem, they'll give you a very chic button to wear.)

Both Apple Partners and Apple Associates receive subscriptions to AppleLink: Apple Partners receive a full year's subscription with the minimum monthly fees prepaid; Apple Associates receive one month of the minimum monthly fee prepaid.

Besides access to MacDTS, AppleLink affords access to a lot of other services. You can download the new system utilities or look at the Help Wanted ads posted on the bulletin board. You can send beta versions of your products to your evangelist at Apple or to other developers. AppleLink makes you a part of the developer community.

Software Development Tools

All the applications presented in this book were written in C using the THINK C development environment from Symantec. The advantages of THINK C lie primarily in its ease of use and the THINK C Debugger. Symantec also makes a powerful, yet friendly, Pascal development environment called THINK Pascal.

Both THINK environments are basically nonextensible. This means that you can't create shell scripts to back up your files automatically, or rebuild an older version of your project. You also can't create custom menu items that automate your development process. Lightspeed handles most of the development cycle so thoroughly that you may not miss these features. If you do, you may want to take a look at the Macintosh Programmer's Workshop (MPW) from Apple.

MPW from Apple

MPW is an extremely powerful development environment that is totally extensible—so extensible, in fact, that several third parties have produced compilers that run under MPW. MPW is like a Mac-based UNIX shell. You can write shell scripts, tie them to your own menus, and create tools that have total access to the Toolbox, yet run inside the Toolbox environment with access to all your data. The catch is that MPW is more complex than THINK C and, therefore, more difficult to master. MPW also is not cheap, typically costing more than three times as much as THINK C or Pascal.

Both MPW and THINK have a lot of followers and are supported by MacDTS. Whichever way you go, you'll be in good company.

The THINK C Debugger, TMON, and MacsBug

Debugging on any computer can be a tedious and frustrating experience. Luckily, there are some excellent tools that you can use to fix up your code.

THINK C 3.0 comes with a source-level debugger. Assuming you use MultiFinder with at least two megabytes of RAM, this debugger fits the bill for most bugs. We discuss its capabilities in Appendix D.

MacsBug is an object-level debugger developed by Motorola for the 68000 family of processors. For a long time, it was the only debugger available for the Mac. If, however, you need a little more horsepower, consider TMON.

TMON is the pro's debugger. Instead of running as a separate program under MultiFinder, TMON takes over the processor when it runs. TMON preserves your program's run-time environment by not calling any of the Mac Toolbox routines (which might alter the state of your program). Instead, the folks at ICOM Simulations cleverly wrote their own window and menu handlers. Although TMON is somewhat difficult to learn, it's worth it. When you run into an exasperatingly unexplainable bug, pop into TMON and step through your program. You can set breakpoints, disassemble your executable image, and even make changes to your program and data. For debugging drivers, `INIT`s, and `DA`s, TMON can't be beat.

To Boldly Go

The Macintosh world is accelerating.

New hardware and software are being designed and marketed faster than ever before. Each successive system software version paves the way to wonderful things: multimedia, image processing, CD-quality sound, voice recognition. There's a feeling that everything is finally arriving. This vision may seem daunting, but remember—a few years ago, the Mac was an intriguing experiment; the people who gambled on it won big.

The changes that Apple is making are setting the stage for machines that will be as big a jump as the Macintosh was from the Apple II line. In the Mac world, you're close to the edge.

Enjoy it!

Appendix A

Glossary

access path: A description of the route that the File Manager follows to access a file; created when a file is opened.

access path buffer: Memory used by the File Manager to transfer data between an application and a file.

action procedure: A procedure, used by the Control Manager function TrackControl, that defines an action to be performed repeatedly for as long as the mouse button is held down.

activate event: An event generated by the Window Manager when a window changes from active to inactive or vice versa.

active control: A control that will respond to the user's actions with the mouse.

active end: In a selection, the location to which the insertion point moves to complete the selection.

active window: The frontmost window on the desktop.

address: A number used to identify a location in the computer's address space. Some locations are allocated to memory, others to I/O devices.

alert: A warning or report of an error, in the form of an alert box, sound from the Macintosh's speaker, or both.

alert box: A box that appears on the screen to give a warning or report an error during a Macintosh application.

alert template: A resource that contains information from which the Dialog Manager can create an alert.

alert window: The window in which an alert box is displayed.

allocate: To reserve an area of memory for use.

application font: The font your application will use unless you specify otherwise—Geneva, by default.

application list: A data structure, kept in the Desktop file, for launching applications from their documents in the hierarchical file system. For

Source: *Inside Macintosh X-Ref* © 1988 Apple Computer, Inc. Reprinted with permission of Addison-Wesley Publishing Company.

each application in the list, an entry is maintained that includes the name and signature of the application, as well as the directory ID of the folder containing it.

application window: A window created as the result of something done by the application, either directly or indirectly (as through the Dialog Manager).

asynchronous execution: After calling a routine asynchronously, an application is free to perform other tasks until the routine is completed.

auto-key event: An event generated repeatedly when the user presses and holds down a character key on the keyboard or keypad.

auto-key rate: The rate at which a character key repeats after it's begun to do so.

auto-key threshold: The length of time a character key must be held down before it begins to repeat.

background activity: A program or process that runs while the user is engaged with another application.

bit image: A collection of bits in memory that have a rectilinear representation. The screen is a visible bit image.

bit map: A set of bits that represent the position and state of a corresponding set of items; in QuickDraw, a pointer to a bit image, the row width of that image, and its boundary rectangle.

boundary rectangle: A rectangle, defined as part of a QuickDraw bit map, that encloses the active area of the bit image and imposes a coordinate system on it. Its top left corner is always aligned around the first bit in the bit image.

bundle: A resource that maps local IDs of resources to their actual resource IDs; used to provide mappings for file references and icon lists needed by the Finder.

button: A standard Macintosh control that causes some immediate or continuous action when clicked or pressed with the mouse. See also **radio button**.

catalog tree file: A file that maintains the relationships between the files and directories on a hierarchical directory volume. It corresponds to the file directory on a flat directory volume.

cdev: A resource file containing device information, used by the Control Panel.

channel: A queue that's used by an application to send commands to the Sound Manager.

character code: An integer representing the character that a key or combination of keys on the keyboard or keypad stands for.

character key: A key that generates a keyboard event when pressed; any key except Shift, Caps Lock, Command, or Option.

character style: A set of stylistic variations, such as bold, italic, and underline. The empty set indicates plain text (no stylistic variations).

character width: The distance to move the pen from one character's origin to the next character's origin.

check box: A standard Macintosh control that displays a setting, either checked (on) or unchecked (off). Clicking inside a check box reverses its setting.

Chooser: A desk accessory that provides a standard interface for device drivers to solicit and accept specific choices from the user.

clipping: Limiting drawing to within the bounds of a particular area.

clipping region: Same as **clipRgn**.

`clipRgn:` The region to which an application limits drawing in a `grafPort`.

closed file: A file without an access path. Closed files cannot be read from or written to.

compaction: The process of moving allocated blocks within a heap zone in order to collect the free space into a single block.

content region: The area of a window that the application draws in.

control: An object in a window on the Macintosh screen with which the user, moving the mouse, can cause instant action with visible results or change settings to modify a future action.

Control Manager: The part of the Toolbox that provides routines for creating and manipulating controls (such as buttons, check boxes, and scroll bars).

control definition function: A function called by the Control Manager when it needs to perform type-dependent operations on a particular type of control, such as drawing the control.

control definition ID: A number passed to control-creation routines to indicate the type of control. It consists of the control definition function's resource ID and a variation code.

control list: A list of all the controls associated with a given window.

control record: The internal representation of a control, where the Control Manager stores all the information it needs for its operations on that control.

control template: A resource that contains information from which the Control Manager can create a control.

coordinate plane: A two-dimensional grid. In QuickDraw, the grid coordinates are integers ranging from -32,767 to 32,767, and all grid lines are infinitely thin.

current resource file: The last resource file opened, unless you specify otherwise with a Resource Manager routine.

cursor: A 16-by-16 bit image that appears on the screen and is controlled by the mouse; called the "pointer" in Macintosh user manuals.

cursor level: A value, initialized by InitCursor, that keeps track of the number of times the cursor has been hidden.

data fork: The part of a file that contains data accessed via the File Manager.

data mark: In a sector, information that primarily contains data from an application.

date/time record: An alternate representation of the date and time (which is stored on the clock chip in seconds since midnight, January 1, 1904).

default button: In an alert box or modal dialog, the button whose effect will occur if the user presses Return or Enter. In an alert box, it's boldly outlined; in a modal dialog, it's boldly outlined or the OK button.

default directory: A directory that will be used in File Manager routines whenever no other directory is specified. It may be the root directory, in which case the default directory is equivalent to the default volume.

default volume: A volume that will receive I/O during a File Manager routine call, whenever no other volume is specified.

dereference: To refer to a block by its master pointer instead of its handle.

Desk Manager: The part of the Toolbox that supports the use of desk accessories from an application.

desk accessory: A "mini-application," implemented as a device driver, that can be run at the same time as a Macintosh application.

desk scrap: The place where data is stored when it's cut (or copied) and pasted among applications and desk accessories.

desktop: The screen as a surface for doing work on the Macintosh.

Desktop file: A resource file in which the Finder stores the version data, bundle, icons, and file references for each application on the volume.

device driver event: An event generated by one of the Macintosh's device drivers.

device driver: A program that controls the exchange of information between an application and a device.

dial: A control with a moving indicator that displays a quantitative setting or value. Depending on the type of dial, the user may be able to change the setting by dragging the indicator with the mouse.

dialog: Same as **dialog box**.

dialog box: A box that a Macintosh application displays to request information it needs to complete a command, or to report that it's waiting for a process to complete.

Dialog Manager: The part of the Toolbox that provides routines for implementing dialogs and alerts.

dialog record: The internal representation of a dialog, where the Dialog Manager stores all the information it needs for its operations on that dialog.

dialog template: A resource that contains information from which the Dialog Manager can create a dialog.

dialog window: The window in which a dialog box is displayed.

dimmed: Drawn in gray rather than black.

directory ID: A unique number assigned to a directory, which the File Manager uses to distinguish it from other directories on the volume. (It's functionally equivalent to the file number assigned to a file; in fact, both directory IDs and file numbers are assigned from the same set of numbers.)

directory: A subdivision of a volume that can contain files as well as other directories; equivalent to a folder.

disabled: A disabled menu item or menu is one that cannot be chosen; the menu item or menu title appears dimmed. A disabled item in a dialog or alert box has no effect when clicked.

Disk Initialization Package: A Macintosh package for initializing and naming new disks; called by the Standard File Package.

disk-inserted event: An event generated when the user inserts a disk in a disk drive or takes any other action that requires a volume to be mounted.

display rectangle: A rectangle that determines where an item is displayed within a dialog or alert box.

document window: The standard Macintosh window for presenting a document.

double-click time: The greatest interval between a mouse-up and mouse-down event that would qualify two mouse clicks as a double-click.

draft printing: Printing a document immediately as it's drawn in the printing grafPort.

drag delay: A length of time that allows a user to drag diagonally across a main menu, moving from a submenu title into the submenu itself without the submenu disappearing.

drag region: A region in a window frame. Dragging inside this region moves the window to a new location and makes it the active window unless the Command key was down.

drive number: A number used to identify a disk drive. The internal drive is number 1, the external drive is number 2, and any additional drives will have larger numbers.

empty handle: A handle that points to a NIL master pointer, signifying that the underlying relocatable block has been purged.

end-of-file: See **logical end-of-file** or **physical end-of-file**.

event: A notification to an application of some occurrence that the application may want to respond to.

event code: An integer representing a particular type of event.

Event Manager: See **Toolbox Event Manager**.

event mask: A parameter passed to an Event Manager routine to specify which types of events the routine should apply to.

event message: A field of an event record containing information specific to the particular type of event.

event queue: The Operating System Event Manager's list of pending events.

event record: The internal representation of an event, through which your program learns all pertinent information about that event.

exception: An error or abnormal condition detected by the processor in the course of program execution; includes interrupts and traps.

external reference: A reference to a routine or variable defined in a separate compilation or assembly.

file: A named, ordered sequence of bytes; a principal means by which data is stored and transmitted on the Macintosh.

file catalog: A hierarchical file directory.

file control block: A fixed-length data structure, contained in the file-control-block buffer, where information about an access path is stored.

file directory: The part of a volume that contains descriptions and locations of all the files and directories on the volume. There are two types of file directories: hierarchical file directories and flat file directories.

File Manager: The part of the Operating System that supports file I/O.

file name: A sequence of up to 255 printing characters, excluding colons (:), that identifies a file.

file number: A unique number assigned to a file, which the File Manager uses to distinguish it from other files on the volume. A file number specifies the file's entry in a file directory.

file reference: A resource that provides the Finder with file and icon information about an application.

file type: A four-character sequence, specified when a file is created, that identifies the type of file.

Finder information: Information that the Finder provides to an application upon starting it up, telling it which documents to open or print.

font: A complete set of characters of one typeface, which may be restricted to a particular size and style, or may comprise multiple sizes, or multiple sizes and styles, as in the context of menus.

Font Manager: The part of the Toolbox that supports the use of various character fonts for QuickDraw when it draws text.

font number: The number by which you identify a font to QuickDraw or the Font Manager.

font size: The size of a font in points; equivalent to the distance between the ascent line of one line of text and the ascent line of the next line of single-spaced text.

fork: One of the two parts of a file; see **data fork** and **resource fork**.

free block: A memory block containing space available for allocation.

full pathname: A pathname beginning from the root directory.

global coordinate system: The coordinate system based on the top left corner of the bit image being at (0,0).

go-away region: A region in a window frame. Clicking inside this region of the active window makes the window close or disappear.

grafPort: A complete drawing environment, including such elements as a bit map, a subset of it in which to draw, a character font, patterns for drawing and erasing, and other pen characteristics.

graphics device: A video card, a printer, a display device, or an offscreen pixel map. Any of these device types may be used with Color Quick-Draw.

GrayRgn: The global variable that in the multiple screen desktop describes and defines the desktop, the area on which windows can be dragged.

grow image: The image pulled around when the user drags inside the grow region; whatever is appropriate to show that the window's size will change.

grow region: A window region, usually within the content region, where dragging changes the size of an active window.

handle: A pointer to a master pointer, which designates a relocatable block in the heap by double indirection.

heap: The area of memory in which space is dynamically allocated and released on demand, using the Memory Manager.

hierarchical menu: A menu that includes, among its various menu choices, the ability to display a submenu. In most cases the submenu appears to the right of the menu item used to select it, and is marked with a filled triangle indicator.

highlight: To display an object on the screen in a distinctive visual way, such as inventing it.

hotSpot: The point in a cursor that's aligned with the mouse location.

icon: A 32-by-32 bit image that graphically represents an object, concept, or message.

icon list: A resource consisting of a list of icons.

icon number: A digit from 1 to 255 to which the Menu Manager adds 256 to get the resource ID of an icon associated with a menu item.

inactive control: A control that won't respond to the user's actions with the mouse. An inactive control is highlighted in some special way, such as dimmed.

inactive window: Any window that isn't the frontmost window on the desktop.

indicator: The moving part of a dial that displays its current setting.

interface routine: A routine called from Pascal whose purpose is to trap to a certain Toolbox or Operating System routine.

International Utilities Package: A Macintosh package that gives you access to country-dependent information such as the formats for numbers, currency, dates, and times.

invert: To highlight by changing white pixels to black and vice versa.

invisible control: A control that's not drawn in its window.

invisible window: A window that's not drawn in its plane on the desktop.

item: In dialog and alert boxes, a control, icon, picture, or piece of text, each displayed inside its own display rectangle. See also **menu item**.

item list: A list of information about all the items in a dialog or alert box.

item number: The index, starting from 1, of an item in an item list.

IWM: "Integrated Woz Machine"; the custom chip that controls the 3 1/2-inch disk drives.

job dialog: A dialog that sets information about one printing job; associated with the Print command.

jump table: A table that contains one entry for every routine in an application and is the means by which the loading and unloading of segments is implemented.

key code: An integer representing a key on the keyboard or keypad, without reference to the character that the key stands for.

key-down event: An event generated when the user presses a character key on the keyboard or keypad.

key-up event: An event generated when the user releases a character key on the keyboard or keypad.

keyboard equivalent: The combination of the Command key and another key, used to invoke a menu item from the keyboard.

keyboard event: An event generated when the user presses, releases, or holds down a character key on the keyboard or keypad; any key-down, key-up, or auto-key event.

List Manager: The part of the Operating System that provides routines for creating, displaying, and manipulating lists.

local coordinate system: The coordinate system local to a `grafPort`, imposed by the boundary rectangle defined in its bit map.

local `ID`: A number that refers to an icon list or file reference in an application's resource file and is mapped to an actual resource `ID` by a bundle.

localization: The process of adapting an application to different languages, including converting its user interface to a different script.

lock: To temporarily prevent a relocatable block from being moved during heap operation.

lock bit: A bit in the master pointer to a relocatable block that indicates whether the block is currently locked.

locked file: A file whose data cannot be changed.

locked volume: A volume whose data cannot be changed. Volumes can be locked by either a software flag or a mechanical setting.

logical end-of-file: The position of one byte past the last byte in a file; equal to the actual number of bytes in the file.

main event loop: In a standard Macintosh application program, a loop that repeatedly calls the Toolbox Event Manager to get events and then responds to them as appropriate.

main screen: On a system with multiple display devices, the screen with the menu bar is called the main screen.

main segment: The segment containing the main program.

master pointer: A single pointer to a relocatable block, maintained by the Memory Manager and updated whenever the block is moved, purged, or reallocated. All handles to a relocatable block refer to it by double indirection through the master pointer.

Memory Manager: The part of the Operating System that dynamically allocates and releases memory space in the heap.

menu: A list of menu items that appears when the user points to a menu title in the menu bar and presses the mouse button. Dragging through the menu and releasing over an enabled menu item chooses that item.

menu bar: The horizontal strip at the top of the Macintosh screen that contains the menu titles of all menus in the menu list.

menu definition procedure: A procedure called by the Menu Manager when it needs to perform type-dependent operations on a particular type of menu, such as drawing the menu.

menu ID: A number in the menu record that identifies the menu.

menu item: A choice in a menu, usually a command to a current application.

menu list: A list containing menu handles for all menus in the menu bar, along with information on the position of each menu.

Menu Manager: The part of the Toolbox that deal with setting up menus and letting the user choose from them.

menu title: A word or phrase in the menu bar that designates one menu.

modal dialog: A dialog that requires the user to respond before doing any other work on the desktop.

modeless dialog: A dialog that allows the user to work elsewhere on the desktop before responding.

mounted volume: A volume that previously was inserted into a disk drive and had descriptive information read from it by the File Manager.

mouse-down event: An event generated when the user presses the mouse button.

mouse-up event: An event generated when the user releases the mouse button.

network event: An event generated by the AppleTalk Manager.

null event: An event reported when there are no other events to report.

offspring: For a given directory, the set of files and directories for which it is the parent.

on-line volume: A mounted volume with its volume buffer and descriptive information contained in memory.

open file: A file with an access path. Open files can be read from and written to.

open permission: Information about a file that indicates whether the file can be read from, written to, or both.

Operating System: The lowest-level software in the Macintosh. It does basic tasks such as I/O, memory management, and interrupt handling.

Operating System Utilities: Operating System routines that perform miscellaneous tasks such as getting the date and time, finding out the user's preferred speaker volume and other preferences, and doing simple string comparison.

page rectangle: The rectangle marking the boundaries of a printed page image. The boundary rectangle, portRect, and clipRgn of the printing grafPort are set to this rectangle.

panel: An area of a window that shows a different interpretation of the same part of a document.

part code: An integer between 1 and 253 that stands for a particular part of a control (possibly the entire control).

partial pathname: A pathname beginning from any directory other than the root directory.

path reference number: A number that uniquely identifies an individual access path; assigned when the access path is created.

pathname: A series of concatenated directory and file names that identifies a given file or directory. See also **partial pathname** and **full pathname**.

pattern: An 8-by-8 bit image, used to define a repeating design (such as stripes) or tone (such as gray).

physical end-of-file: The position of one byte past the last allocation block of a file; equal to 1 more than the maximum number of bytes the file can contain.

picture: A saved sequence of QuickDraw drawing commands (and, optionally, picture comments) that you can play back later with a single procedure call; also, the image resulting from these commands.

pixel: A dot on a display screen. Pixel is short for picture element.

plane: The front-to-back position of a window on the desktop.

point: The intersection of a horizontal grid line and a vertical grid line on the coordinate plane, defined by a horizontal and a vertical coordinate; also, a typographical term meaning approximately 1/72 inch.

polygon: A sequence of connected lines, defined by QuickDraw line-drawing commands.

pop-up menu: A menu not located in the menu bar, which appears when the user presses the mouse button in a particular place.

port: See **grafPort**.

portBits: The bit map of a grafPort.

portRect: A rectangle, defined as part of a grafPort, that encloses a subset of the bit map for use by the grafPort.

post: To place an event in the event queue for later processing.

print record: A record containing all the information needed by the Printing Manager to perform a particular printing job.

Printer Driver: The device driver for the currently installed printer.

printer resource file: A file containing all the resources needed to run the Printing Manager with a particular printer.

Printing Manager: The routines and data types that enable applications to communicate with the Printer Driver to print on any variety of printer via the same interface.

printing grafPort: A special grafPort customized for printing instead of drawing on the screen.

purgeable block: A relocatable block that can be purged from the heap.

queue: A list of identically structured entries linked together by pointers.

QuickDraw: The part of the Toolbox that performs all graphic operations on the Macintosh screen.

radio button: A standard Macintosh control that displays a setting, either on or off, and is part of a group in which only one button can be on at a time.

RAM: The Macintosh's random access memory, which contains exception vectors, buffers used by hardware devices, the system and application heaps, the stack, and other information used by applications.

reallocate: To allocate new space in the heap for a purged block, updating its master pointer to point to its new location.

reference number: A number greater than 0, returned by the Resource Manager when a resource file is opened, by which you can refer to that file. In Resource Manager routines that expect a reference number, 0 represents the system resource file.

region: An arbitrary area or set of areas on the QuickDraw coordinate plane. The outline of a region should be one or more closed loops.

release. To free an allocated area of memory, making it available for reuse.

relocatable block: A block that can be moved within the heap during compaction.

resource: Data or code stored in a resource file and managed by the Resource Manager.

resource attribute: One of several characteristics, specified by bits in a resource reference, that determine how the resource should be dealt with.

resource data: In a resource file, the data that comprises a resource.

resource file: The resource fork of a file.

resource fork: The part of a file that contains data used by an application (such as menus, fonts, and icons). The resource fork of an application file also contains the application code itself.

resource header: At the beginning of a resource file, data that gives the offsets to and lengths of the resource data and resource map.

resource ID: A number that, together with the resource type, identifies a resource in a resource file. Every resource has an ID number.

Resource Manager: The part of the Toolbox that reads and writes resources.

resource name: A string that, together with the resource type, identifies a resource in a resource file. A resource may or may not have a name.

resource specification: A resource type and either a resource ID or a resource name.

resource type: The type of a resource in a resource file, designated by a sequence of four characters (such as 'MENU' for a menu).

result code: An integer indicating whether a routine completed its task successfully or was prevented by some error condition (or other special condition, such as reaching the end of a file).

resume procedure: A procedure within an application that allows the application to recover from system errors.

ROM: The Macintosh's permanent Read-Only Memory, which contains the routines for the Toolbox and Operating System, and the various system traps.

root directory: The directory at the base of a file catalog.

row width: The number of bytes in each row of a bit image.

Scrap Manager: The part of the Toolbox that enables cutting and pasting between applications, desk accessories, or an application and a desk accessory.

scrap: A place where cut or copied data is stored.

scrap file: The file containing the desk scrap (usually named "Clipboard File").

SCSI: See **Small Computer Standard Interface**.

SCSI Manager: The part of the Operating System that controls the exchange of information between a Macintosh and peripheral devices connected through the Small Computer Standard Interface (SCSI).

segment: One of several parts into which the code of an application may be divided. Not all segments need to be in memory at the same time.

selection range: The series of characters (inversely highlighted), or the character position (marked with a blinking caret), at which the next editing operation will occur.

signature: A four-character sequence that uniquely identifies an application to the Finder.

Small Computer Standard Interface (SCSI): A specification of mechanical, electrical, and functional standards for connecting small computers with intelligent peripherals such as hard disks, printers, and optical disks.

solid shape: A shape that's filled in with any pattern.

Sound Driver: The device driver that controls sound generation in an application.

sound procedure: A procedure associated with an alert that will emit one of up to four sounds from the Macintosh's speaker. Its integer parameter ranges from 0 to 3 and specifies which sound.

source transfer mode: One of eight transfer modes for drawing text or transferring any bit image between two bit maps.

stack: The area of memory in which space is allocated and released in LIFO (last-in-first-out) order.

Standard File Package: A Macintosh package for presenting the standard user interface when a file is to be saved or opened.

startup screen: When the system is started up, one of the display devices is selected as the **startup screen,** the screen on which the "happy Macintosh" icon appears.

structure region: An entire window; its complete "structure."

style: See **character style**.

style dialog: A dialog that sets options affecting the page dimensions; associated with the Page Setup command.

subdirectory: Any directory other than the root directory.

submenu delay: The length of time before a submenu appears as a user drags through a hierarchical main menu; it prevents rapid flashing of submenus.

System Error Handler: The part of the Operating System that assumes control when a fatal system error occurs.

system error alert: An alert box displayed by the System Error Handler.

system error ID: An ID number that appears in a system error alert to identify the error.

system event mask: A global event mask that controls which types of events get posted into the event queue.

system font: The font that the system uses (in menus, for example). Its name is Chicago.

system font size: The size of text drawn by the system in the system font; 12 points.

system heap: The portion of the heap reserved for use by the Operating System.

system resource: A resource in the system resource file.

system resource file: A resource file containing standard resources, accessed if a requested resource wasn't found in any of the other resource files that were searched.

system window: A window in which a desk accessory is displayed.

target device: An SCSI device (typically an intelligent peripheral) that receives a request from an initiator device to perform a certain operation.

thumb: The Control Manager's term for the scroll box (the indicator of a scroll bar).

tick: A sixtieth of a second.

Toolbox: Same as **User Interface Toolbox**.

Toolbox Event Manager: The part of the Toolbox that allows your application program to monitor the user's actions with the mouse, keyboard, and keypad.

Toolbox Utilities: The part of the Toolbox that performs generally useful operations such as fixed-point arithmetic, string manipulation, and logical operations on bits.

transfer mode: A specification of which Boolean operation QuickDraw should perform when drawing or when transferring a bit image from one bit map to another.

trap dispatcher: The part of the Operating System that examines a trap word to determine what operation it stands for, looks up the address of the corresponding routine in the trap dispatch table, and jumps to the routine.

trap word: An unimplemented instruction representing a call to a Toolbox or Operating System routine.

type coercion: Many compilers feature type coercion (also known as typecasting), which allows a data structure of one type to be converted to another type. In many cases, this conversion is simply a relaxation of type-checking in the compiler, allowing the substitution of a differently typed but equivalent data structure.

unlock: To allow a relocatable block to be moved during heap compaction.

unmounted volume: A volume that hasn't been inserted into a disk drive and had descriptive information read from it, or a volume that previously was mounted and has since had the memory used by it released.

unpurgeable block: A relocatable block that can't be purged from the heap.

update event: An event generated by the Window Manager when a window's contents need to be redrawn.

update region: A window region consisting of all areas of the content region that have to be redrawn.

User Interface Toolbox: The software in the Macintosh ROM that helps you implement the standard Macintosh user interface in your application.

version data: In an application's resource file, a resource that has the application's signature as its resource type; typically a string that gives the name, version number, and date of the application.

vertical blanking interval: The time between the display of the last pixel on the bottom line of the screen and the first one on the top line.

virtual key codes: The key codes that appear in keyboard events.

visible control: A control that's drawn in its window (but may be completely overlapped by another window or other object on the screen).

visible window: A window that's drawn in its plane on the desktop (but may be completely overlapped by another window or object on the screen).

visRgn: The region of the grafPort, manipulated by the Window Manager, that's actually visible on the screen.

volume: A piece of storage medium formatted to contain files; usually a disk or part of a disk. A 3.5-inch Macintosh disk is one volume.

volume attributes: Information contained on volumes and in memory indicating whether the volume is locked, whether it's busy (in memory only), and whether the volume control block matches the volume information (in memory only).

volume name: A sequence of up to 27 printing characters that identifies a volume; followed by a colon (:) in File Manager routine calls, to distinguish it from a file name.

window: An object on the desktop that presents information, such as a document or a message.

window class: In a window record, an indication of whether a window is a system window, a dialog or alert window, or a window created directly by the application.

window definition function: A function called by the Window Manager when it needs to perform certain type-dependent operations on a particular type of window, such as drawing the window frame.

window definition ID: A number passed to window-creation routines to indicate the type of window. It consists of the window definition function's resource ID and a variation code.

window frame: The structure region of a window minus its content region.

window list: A list of all windows ordered by their front-to-back positions on the desktop.

Window Manager: The part of the Toolbox that provides routines for creating and manipulating windows.

Window Manager port: A grafPort that has the entire screen as its portRect and is used by the Window Manager to draw window frames.

window record: The internal representation of a window, where the Window Manager stores all the information it needs for its operations on that window.

window template: A resource from which the Window Manager can create a window.

word wraparound: Keeping words from being split between lines when text is drawn.

working directory: An alternative way of referring to a directory. When opened as a working directory, a directory is given a working directory reference number that's used to refer to it in File Manager calls.

working directory control block: A data structure that contains the directory ID of a working directory, as well as the volume reference number of the volume on which the directory is located.

working directory reference number: A temporary reference number used to identify a working directory. It can be used in place of the volume reference number in all File Manager calls; the File Manager uses it to get the directory ID and volume reference number from the working directory control block.

Appendix B

Code Listings

The following pages contain complete listings of all the source code presented in Chapters 1-9. The listings are presented in order by Chapter. Each listing contains comments detailing the new features found in that program. Remember, you can send in the coupon in the back of the book for a disk containing the complete set of Macintosh Primer applications.

Chapter 2, Hello.c

```
#include <stdio.h>

main()
{
        printf ("Hello, World");  /*  The Unix way...  */
}
```

Chapter 3, Hello2.c

```
#define BASE_RES_ID             400
#define NIL_POINTER             0L
#define MOVE_TO_FRONT           -1L
#define REMOVE_ALL_EVENTS       0

#define HORIZONTAL_PIXEL        30
#define VERTICAL_PIXEL          50


WindowPtr       gPictureWindow; /*  We'll draw in this window  */


/********************** Main *************/

main()
{
        ToolBoxInit(); /*  Standard Toolbox initialization  */
        WindowInit();  /*  Setup the window  */

        while ( !Button() ) ; /*  Wait for a press of the mouse */
                              /*      button...                 */
}


/******************************** ToolBoxInit */

ToolBoxInit()
{
        InitGraf( &thePort );
        InitFonts();
        FlushEvents( everyEvent, REMOVE_ALL_EVENTS );
        InitWindows();
        InitMenus();
        TEInit();
        InitDialogs( NIL_POINTER );
        InitCursor();
}


/*******************WindowInit*************/

WindowInit()
{
        gPictureWindow = GetNewWindow( BASE_RES_ID , NIL_POINTER,
                MOVE_TO_FRONT );      /*  Load the WIND resource  */
```

420

```
ShowWindow( gPictureWindow );  /*  Make the WIND
visible  */
        SetPort( gPictureWindow );     /*  We'll start drawing in
                                                gPictureWindow */

        MoveTo( HORIZONTAL_PIXEL, VERTICAL_PIXEL );
        DrawString("\pHello, World");
}
```

Chapter 3, Mondrian.c

```
#define BASE_RES_ID            400
#define NIL_POINTER            0L
#define MOVE_TO_FRONT          -1L
#define REMOVE_ALL_EVENTS      0


WindowPtr       gDrawWindow;
long            gFillColor = blackColor;


/***************************** main *********/

main()
{
        ToolBoxInit();
        WindowInit();
        MainLoop();
}


/******************************** ToolBoxInit */

ToolBoxInit()
{
        InitGraf( &thePort );
        InitFonts();
        FlushEvents( everyEvent, REMOVE_ALL_EVENTS );
        InitWindows();
        InitMenus();
        TEInit();
        InitDialogs( NIL_POINTER );
        InitCursor();
}


/***************************** WindowInit *********/

WindowInit()
{
        gDrawWindow = GetNewWindow( BASE_RES_ID, NIL_POINTER,
                                            MOVE_TO_FRONT );

        ShowWindow( gDrawWindow );
        SetPort( gDrawWindow );
}
```

```
/******************************* MainLoop ********/

MainLoop()
{
        GetDateTime( &randSeed );   /* Use the current time as a
                                       seed for the random number generator  */
        while ( ! Button() )
        {
                DrawRandomRect();               /*  Draw a random shape */
                if ( gFillColor == blackColor )    /* Alternate drawing */
                        gFillColor = whiteColor;   /* between black and */
                else                                       /* white...        */
                        gFillColor = blackColor;
        }
}


/******************************* DrawRandomRect ********/

DrawRandomRect()
{
        Rect    myRect;

        RandomRect( &myRect, gDrawWindow );  /* Generate a random rectangle
                                that fits within the bounds of gDrawWindow  */
        ForeColor( gFillColor );
        PaintOval( &myRect ); /*  Paint an oval filled with gFillColor,
                                   the size of myRect.  We could call
                                   other shape drawing routines (like
                                   PainRect()) instead of PaintOval()...
                              */
}


/******************************* RandomRect ********/

RandomRect( myRectPtr, boundingWindow )
Rect            *myRectPtr;
WindowPtr       boundingWindow;
{
/*
 *     A window's portRect is a Rect the size of the window...
 */
        myRectPtr->left = Randomize( boundingWindow->portRect.right
                - boundingWindow->portRect.left );
        myRectPtr->right = Randomize( boundingWindow->portRect.right
                - boundingWindow->portRect.left );
        myRectPtr->top = Randomize( boundingWindow->portRect.bottom
                - boundingWindow->portRect.top );
        myRectPtr->bottom = Randomize( boundingWindow->portRect.bottom
                - boundingWindow->portRect.top );
}


/******************************* Randomize ********/

Randomize( range )
int     range;
{
        long    rawResult;
        rawResult = Random(); /*  Random() returns a random number
                                   between -32767 and 32767  */
```

```
        if ( rawResult < 0 ) rawResult *= -1;  /*  We could call abs(),
                            but abs() is not part of the Toolbox.  If
                            you need it, make sure to add the math
                            library to your project.  Otherwise, your
                            project won't link...  */
        return( (rawResult * range) / 32768 );  /*  We'll return a number
                            between 0 and range-1    */
}
```

Chapter 3, ShowPict.c

```
#define BASE_RES_ID          400
#define NIL_POINTER          0L
#define MOVE_TO_FRONT        -1L
#define REMOVE_ALL_EVENTS    0


PicHandle       gThePicture;
WindowPtr       gPictureWindow;


/******************************** main ********/

main()
{
        ToolBoxInit();
        WindowInit();
        LoadPicture();
        DrawMyPicture( gThePicture, gPictureWindow );

        while ( !Button() ) ;
}


/********************************** ToolBoxInit */

ToolBoxInit()
{
        InitGraf( &thePort );
        InitFonts();
        FlushEvents( everyEvent, REMOVE_ALL_EVENTS );
        InitWindows();
        InitMenus();
        TEInit();
        InitDialogs( NIL_POINTER );
        InitCursor();
}


/****************************** WindowInit ********/

WindowInit()
{
        gPictureWindow = GetNewWindow( BASE_RES_ID, NIL_POINTER,
                                            MOVE_TO_FRONT );

        ShowWindow( gPictureWindow );
        SetPort( gPictureWindow );
}
```

```
/******************************* LoadPicture ********/

LoadPicture()
{
        gThePicture = GetPicture( BASE_RES_ID );
}


/******************************* DrawMyPicture ********/

DrawMyPicture( thePicture, pictureWindow )
PicHandle       thePicture;
WindowPtr       pictureWindow;
{
        Rect    myRect;

        myRect = pictureWindow->portRect;
        CenterPict( thePicture, &myRect );  /*  Pass the window's portRect
                                to CenterPict() via myRect, as well as a handle
                                to the picture to be centered.  CenterPict()
                                will modify myRect to be a Rect the size of the
                                Picture, centered in the window.  */
        DrawPicture( thePicture, &myRect );
}


/******************************* CenterPict ********/

CenterPict( thePicture, myRectPtr )
PicHandle       thePicture;
Rect            *myRectPtr;
{
        Rect    windRect, pictureRect;

        windRect = *myRectPtr;
        pictureRect = (**( thePicture )).picFrame;  /*  Two interesting
                                facts:
                                1)  picFrame is a field in the picture
                                        data structure.  It is a Rect, the
                                        size of the picture, with the same
                                        coordinates as the picture had when
                                        it was created.
                                2)  ANSI C allows the direct assignment of
                                        one data structure to another of the
                                        same type.  This allows us to copy
                                        one Rect to another with one
                                        statement.  Some compilers may not
                                        support this feature.  It sure makes
                                        life easier!  */
        myRectPtr->top = (windRect.bottom - windRect.top -
                        (pictureRect.bottom - pictureRect.top))/ 2 +
                        windRect.top;
        myRectPtr->bottom = myRectPtr->top +
                        (pictureRect.bottom - pictureRect.top);
        myRectPtr->left = (windRect.right - windRect.left -
(pictureRect.right - pictureRect.left))/ 2 +
                        windRect.left;
        myRectPtr->right = myRectPtr->left + (pictureRect.right -
                        pictureRect.left);
}
```

Chapter 3, Flying Line.c

```
/*
 *      Try using different values for NUM_LINES, gDeltaTop, gDeltaBottom,
 *      gDeltaLeft, and gDeltaRight.  This will alter the shape and
 *      behavior of the Flying Line.
 */

#define NUM_LINES               50        /*  Try 100 or 150  */
#define NIL_POINTER             0L
#define MOVE_TO_FRONT           -1L
#define REMOVE_ALL_EVENTS       0
#define NIL_STRING              "\p"
#define NIL_TITLE               NIL_STRING
#define VISIBLE                 TRUE
#define NO_GO_AWAY              FALSE
#define NIL_REF_CON             NIL_POINTER


WindowPtr       gLineWindow;
Rect            gLines[ NUM_LINES ];
int             gDeltaTop=3, gDeltaBottom=3; /* These four are the  */
int             gDeltaLeft=2, gDeltaRight=6; /* key to flying line! */
int             gOldMBarHeight;

/******************************* main ********/

main()
{
        ToolBoxInit();
        WindowInit();
        LinesInit();
        MainLoop();
}


/********************************* ToolBoxInit */

ToolBoxInit()
{
        InitGraf( &thePort );
        InitFonts();
        FlushEvents( everyEvent, REMOVE_ALL_EVENTS );
        InitWindows();
        InitMenus();
        TEInit();
        InitDialogs( NIL_POINTER );
        InitCursor();
}


/******************************* WindowInit ********/

WindowInit()
{
        Rect            totalRect, mBarRect;
        RgnHandle       mBarRgn;
```

```
        gOldMBarHeight = MBarHeight;
        MBarHeight = 0;
        gLineWindow = NewWindow( NIL_POINTER, &(screenBits.bounds),
                NIL_TITLE, VISIBLE, plainDBox, MOVE_TO_FRONT, NO_GO_AWAY,
                NIL_REF_CON );
/*
 *      We use NewWindow() instead of GetNewWindow() because we want a
 *      window the size of the screen.  NewWindow() allows you to specify
 *      the size of your window.  With GetNewWindow(), the window size is
 *      pulled from the WIND resource.
 */

        SetRect( &mBarRect, screenBits.bounds.left, screenBits.bounds.top,
            screenBits.bounds.right, screenBits.bounds.top+gOldMBarHeight );
/*
 *      The following 4 lines of code are for demonstration purposes only.
 *      The thought police have prohibited the modification of a window's
 *      visRgn under MultiFinder.  Reuse this code at your own risk!!!
 */

        mBarRgn = NewRgn();
        RectRgn( mBarRgn, &mBarRect );
        UnionRgn( gLineWindow->visRgn, mBarRgn, gLineWindow->visRgn );
        DisposeRgn( mBarRgn );

        SetPort( gLineWindow );
        FillRect( &(gLineWindow->portRect), black ); /*  Change black to
                                              ltGray,  */
        PenMode( patXor );      /*   <— and comment out this line  */
}


/****************************** LinesInit ********/

LinesInit()
{
        int i;

        HideCursor();
        GetDateTime( &randSeed ); /* Reseed the random number generator */
        RandomRect( &(gLines[ 0 ]), gLineWindow );
        DrawLine( 0 );   /* Generate and draw the first line */
        for ( i=1; i<NUM_LINES; i++ )
        {
                gLines[ i ] = gLines[ i-1 ];   /*  Copy the previous line, */
                RecalcLine( i );               /*   modify it,  */
                DrawLine( i ); /* and draw the new line */
        }
}


/****************************** MainLoop ********/

MainLoop()
{
        int i;

        while ( ! Button() )
        {
                DrawLine( NUM_LINES - 1 );  /* Erase the last line (because
                                                we used patXor mode)  */
```

```
                          for ( i=NUM_LINES-1; i>0; i--)
                                  gLines[ i ] = gLines[ i-1 ];   /* Bump each line one */
                          RecalcLine( 0 );                /* Modify the first line and  */
                          DrawLine( 0 ); /*  redraw it  */
                  }
            MBarHeight = gOldMBarHeight;  /*  Once the button is clicked,
                                                we better reset the menubar
                                                height, else we won't be able
                                                to click in it  */

}


/****************************** RandomRect ********/

RandomRect( myRectPtr, boundingWindow )
Rect            *myRectPtr;
WindowPtr       boundingWindow;
{
        myRectPtr->left = Randomize( boundingWindow->portRect.right
                          - boundingWindow->portRect.left );
        myRectPtr->right = Randomize( boundingWindow->portRect.right
                          - boundingWindow->portRect.left );
        myRectPtr->top = Randomize( boundingWindow->portRect.bottom
                          - boundingWindow->portRect.top );
        myRectPtr->bottom = Randomize( boundingWindow->portRect.bottom
                          - boundingWindow->portRect.top );
}


/****************************** Randomize ********/

Randomize( range )
int     range;
{
        long    rawResult;

        rawResult = Random();
        if ( rawResult < 0 ) rawResult *= -1;
        return( (rawResult * range) / 32768 );
}


/****************************** RecalcLine ********/

RecalcLine( i )
int i;
{
        gLines[ i ].top += gDeltaTop;
        if ( ( gLines[ i ].top < gLineWindow->portRect.top ) ||
             ( gLines[ i ].top > gLineWindow->portRect.bottom ) )
        {
                gDeltaTop *= -1;
                gLines[ i ].top += 2*gDeltaTop;
        }

        gLines[ i ].bottom += gDeltaBottom;
        if ( ( gLines[ i ].bottom < gLineWindow->portRect.top ) ||
             ( gLines[ i ].bottom > gLineWindow->portRect.bottom ) )
        {
                gDeltaBottom *= -1;
                gLines[ i ].bottom += 2*gDeltaBottom;
        }
```

```
        gLines[ i ].left += gDeltaLeft;
        if ( ( gLines[ i ].left < gLineWindow->portRect.left ) ||
               ( gLines[ i ].left > gLineWindow->portRect.right ) )
        {
                gDeltaLeft *= -1;
                gLines[ i ].left += 2*gDeltaLeft;
        }

        gLines[ i ].right += gDeltaRight;
        if ( ( gLines[ i ].right < gLineWindow->portRect.left ) ||
               ( gLines[ i ].right > gLineWindow->portRect.right ) )
        {
                gDeltaRight *= -1;
                gLines[ i ].right += 2*gDeltaRight;
        }
}


/******************************* DrawLine ********/

DrawLine( i )
int     i;
{
        MoveTo( gLines[ i ].left, gLines[ i ].top ); /* Move to first
                                                                point */
        LineTo( gLines[ i ].right, gLines[ i ].bottom );  /*  Draw line to
                                                        second point */
}
```

Chapter 4, EventTutor.c

```
#define BASE_RES_ID             400
#define NIL_POINTER             0L
#define MOVE_TO_FRONT           -1L
#define REMOVE_ALL_EVENTS       0

#define LEAVE_WHERE_IT_IS       FALSE
#define NORMAL_UPDATES          TRUE

#define SLEEP                   0L
#define NIL_MOUSE_REGION        0L
#define WNE_TRAP_NUM            0x60
#define UNIMPL_TRAP_NUM         0x9F
#define SUSPEND_RESUME_BIT      0x0001
#define ACTIVATING              1
#define RESUMING                1

#define TEXT_FONT_SIZE          12

#define DRAG_THRESHOLD          30
#define MIN_WINDOW_HEIGHT       50
#define MIN_WINDOW_WIDTH        50
#define SCROLL_BAR_PIXELS       16

#define ROWHEIGHT               15
#define LEFTMARGIN              10
#define STARTROW                0
#define HORIZONTAL_OFFSET       0
```

```
PicHandle        gPictureHandle;
WindowPtr        gPictWindow, gEventWindow;
Boolean          gDone, gWNEImplemented;
EventRecord      gTheEvent;
int              gCurRow, gMaxRow;
Rect             gDragRect, gSizeRect;


/***************************** main ********/

main()
{
        ToolBoxInit();
        WindowInit();
        LoadPicture();
        SetUpDragRect();
        SetUpSizeRect();

        MainLoop();
}


/********************************* ToolBoxInit */

ToolBoxInit()
{
        InitGraf( &thePort );
        InitFonts();
        FlushEvents( everyEvent, REMOVE_ALL_EVENTS );
        InitWindows();
        InitMenus();
        TEInit();
        InitDialogs( NIL_POINTER );
        InitCursor();
}


/****************************** WindowInit ********/

WindowInit()
{
/*
 * Start by loading the two windows from the resource file...
 */
        gPictWindow = GetNewWindow( BASE_RES_ID, NIL_POINTER,
                                                MOVE_TO_FRONT );
        gEventWindow = GetNewWindow( BASE_RES_ID+1, NIL_POINTER,
                                                MOVE_TO_FRONT );

        SetPort( gEventWindow );
        SetupEventWindow();

/*
 *      Make both windows visible...
 */
        ShowWindow( gEventWindow );
        ShowWindow( gPictWindow );

/*
 *      Finally, make gEventWindow the active window...
 */
        SelectWindow( gEventWindow );
}
```

```
/****************************** SetupEventWindow *********/

SetupEventWindow()
{
        Rect    eventRect;

/*
 *      Set up gMaxRow:  it determines when gEventWindow is scrolled.
 * Set up gCurRow: it holds the current vertical pixel value.
 */
        eventRect = gEventWindow->portRect;
        gMaxRow = eventRect.bottom - eventRect.top - ROWHEIGHT;
        gCurRow = STARTROW;

/*
 *      Set the gEventWindow font to monaco, and the gEventWindow
 *      text size to TEXT_FONT_SIZE...
 */
        TextFont( monaco );
        TextSize( TEXT_FONT_SIZE );
}


/****************************** LoadPicture *********/

LoadPicture()
{
/*      Load the picture (to center in gPictWindow)   */
        gPictureHandle = GetPicture( BASE_RES_ID );
}


/****************************** SetUpDragRect *********/

SetUpDragRect()
{
/*
 *      We'll use gDragRect to limit the dragging area of a window.  This
 *      means that when a user clicks on the title bar of a window and
 *      drags it around the screen, they will be forced to leave
 *      DRAG_THRESHOLD pixels of the window on the screen.  This prevents
 *      the user from dragging all but a few pixels of a window off the
 *      screen (which makes that window mighty tough to find later on).
 */
        gDragRect = screenBits.bounds;
        gDragRect.left += DRAG_THRESHOLD;
        gDragRect.right -= DRAG_THRESHOLD;
        gDragRect.bottom -= DRAG_THRESHOLD;
}


/****************************** SetUpSizeRect *********/

SetUpSizeRect()
{
/*
 *      We'll use gSizeRect to control the size of a window.  This
 *      means that when a user tries to resize a window with a grow box
 *      (like gPictWindow) gSizeRect will determine the minimum height
 *      and width of the window, and the maximum height and width of the
 *      window.
 */
```

```
            gSizeRect.top = MIN_WINDOW_HEIGHT;
            gSizeRect.left = MIN_WINDOW_WIDTH;

            gSizeRect.bottom = screenBits.bounds.bottom -
                                       screenBits.bounds.top;
            gSizeRect.right = screenBits.bounds.right -
                                       screenBits.bounds.left;
}


/****************************** MainLoop ********/

MainLoop()
{
        gDone = FALSE;
/*
 *      Is WaitNextEvent() implemented?  If it is, the address of the
 *      WaitNextEvent() trap will be different than the standard,
 *      "unimplemented" trap...
 */
        gWNEImplemented = ( NGetTrapAddress( WNE_TRAP_NUM, ToolTrap ) !=
                            NGetTrapAddress( UNIMPL_TRAP_NUM, ToolTrap ) );

/*
 * Don't wait for a mouse click.  Retrieve and process events
 *      instead!
 */
        while ( gDone == FALSE )
        {
                HandleEvent();
        }
}


/************************************** HandleEvent   */

HandleEvent()
{
/*
 *      We'll see this routine in all "proper" Macintosh applications.
 *      First, we'll retrieve an event...
 */
        if ( gWNEImplemented )
                WaitNextEvent( everyEvent, &gTheEvent, SLEEP,
                                       NIL_MOUSE_REGION );
        else
        {
                SystemTask();
                GetNextEvent( everyEvent, &gTheEvent );
        }

/*
 *      ...then, we'll process the event.
 */
        switch ( gTheEvent.what )
        {
                case nullEvent:
                        /*DrawEventString( "\pnullEvent" );*/
                        /*      Uncomment the previous line for a burst of
                                       flavor!  */
                        break;
```

```
              case mouseDown:
                      DrawEventString( "\pmouseDown" );
                      HandleMouseDown();
                      break;
              case mouseUp:
                      DrawEventString( "\pmouseUp" );
                      break;
              case keyDown:
                      DrawEventString( "\pkeyDown" );
                      break;
              case keyUp:
                      DrawEventString( "\pkeyUp" );
                      break;
              case autoKey:
                      DrawEventString( "\pautoKey" );
                      break;
              case updateEvt:
                      if ( (WindowPtr)gTheEvent.message == gPictWindow )
                      {
                              DrawEventString( "\pupdateEvt:  gPictWindow" );
                              BeginUpdate( gTheEvent.message );
                              DrawMyPicture(gTheEvent.message,gPictureHandle);
                              EndUpdate( gTheEvent.message );
                      } else
                      {
                              DrawEventString( "\pupdateEvt:  gEventWindow" );
                              BeginUpdate( gTheEvent.message );
                              /*
                               *      We won't handle updates to gEventWindow,
                               * but we still need to empty the gEventWindow
                               * Update Region so the Window Manager will stop
                               * queueing UpdateEvts.
                               *      We do this with calls to BeginUpdate()
                               * and EndUpdate().
                               */
                              EndUpdate( gTheEvent.message );
                      }
                      break;
              case diskEvt:
                      DrawEventString( "\pdiskEvt" );
                      break;
              case activateEvt:
                      if ( (WindowPtr)gTheEvent.message == gPictWindow )
                      {
/*
 *      If gPictWindow was activated or deactivated, we better redraw the
 *      grow box (as well as the scroll bar outlines.  We do this because
 *      active and inactive windows have different looking grow boxes.
 */
                              DrawGrowIcon( gTheEvent.message );
                              if ( ( gTheEvent.modifiers & activeFlag ) ==
                                          ACTIVATING )
                              {
                                      DrawEventString(
                                      "\pactivateEvt:  activating gPictWindow");
                              }
                              else
                                      DrawEventString(
                                      "\pactivateEvt:  deactivating gPictWindow"
                                      );
```

```
                    } else
                    {
                            if ( ( gTheEvent.modifiers & activeFlag ) ==
                                        ACTIVATING )
                                DrawEventString(
                                "\pactivateEvt:  activating gEventWindow"
                                );
                            else
                                DrawEventString(
                                "\pactivateEvt:  deactivating gEventWindow"
                                );
                    }
                    break;
            case networkEvt:
                    DrawEventString( "\pnetworkEvt" );
                    break;
            case driverEvt:
                    DrawEventString( "\pdriverEvt" );
                    break;
            case app1Evt:
                    DrawEventString( "\papp1Evt" );
                    break;
            case app2Evt:
                    DrawEventString( "\papp2Evt" );
                    break;
            case app3Evt:
                    DrawEventString( "\papp3Evt" );
                    break;
            case app4Evt:
/*
 *      app4Evts are like Trojan horses for suspend, resume, and mouse
 *      moved events.  The actual event type is specified by the
 *      appropriate bit in the event's message field.  For more info
 *      on these events (especially on mouse moved events) read Apple's
 *      "Programmer's Guide to MultiFinder".
 */
                    if ( ( gTheEvent.message & SUSPEND_RESUME_BIT ) ==
                                RESUMING )
                            DrawEventString( "\pResume event" );
                    else
                            DrawEventString( "\pSuspend event" );
                    break;
        }
}


/******************************  DrawEventString      *******/

DrawEventString( s )
Str255 s;
{
/*  if we're at the bottom of gEventWindow, scroll the window.  */
        if ( gCurRow > gMaxRow )
        {
                ScrollWindow();
        }
        else
        {
                gCurRow += ROWHEIGHT;
        }
        MoveTo( LEFTMARGIN, gCurRow );
        DrawString( s );
}
```

```
/********************************    ScrollWindow    *******/

ScrollWindow()
{
        RgnHandle        tempRgn;

        tempRgn = NewRgn();
/*
 *      We use ScrollRect() to scroll all the pixels in gEventWindow
 *      up one row.  The newly created rectangular region at the bottom of
 *      the window will be stored in tempRgn.  We could use tempRgn to
 *      do some smart updating of our window, only refreshing the area
 *      of the window specified by tempRgn.
 */
        ScrollRect( &gEventWindow->portRect, HORIZONTAL_OFFSET, -
                                        ROWHEIGHT, tempRgn );
        DisposeRgn( tempRgn );   /* Free up the memory used by tempRgn */
}


/************************************** HandleMouseDown */

HandleMouseDown()
{
        WindowPtr        whichWindow;
        short int        thePart;
        long             windSize;
        GrafPtr          oldPort;

/*
 *      First, find out which window the mouse click occurred in.
 * Then, find out what part of the window the mouse click
 *      occurred in.
 */
        thePart = FindWindow( gTheEvent.where, &whichWindow );
        switch ( thePart )
        {
                case inSysWindow :
/*
 *      Probably a desk accessory window...
 */
                        SystemClick( &gTheEvent, whichWindow );
                        break;
                case inDrag :
/*  Drag the window around the screen, limited by gDragRect   */
                        DragWindow( whichWindow, gTheEvent.where, &gDragRect);
                        break;
                case inContent:
/*  Bring the clicked on window to the front   */
                        SelectWindow( whichWindow );
                        break;
                case inGrow:
/*  First, let the user specify the new size of the window...   */
                        windSize = GrowWindow( whichWindow, gTheEvent.where,
                                                        &gSizeRect );
                        if ( windSize != 0 )
                        {
/*
 * ...If they resize the window, temporarily make the window the
 *      window the current port, erase the window, and use InvalRect()
 *      to make sure an update event is generated for the window.
 */
```

```
                                GetPort( &oldPort );
                                SetPort( whichWindow );
                                EraseRect( &whichWindow->portRect );
                                SizeWindow( whichWindow, LoWord( windSize ),
                                        HiWord( windSize ), NORMAL_UPDATES );
                                InvalRect( &whichWindow->portRect );
                                SetPort( oldPort );
                        }
                        break;
                case inGoAway :
/*
 *      Important!!!  Normally, we'll only set gDone to TRUE when Quit is
 *      selected from the File menu.  For the currect handling of
 *      the inGoAway case, refer to the WindowMaker application in
 *      Chapter 7.
 */

                        gDone = TRUE;
                        break;
                case inZoomIn:
                case inZoomOut:
/*
 *      Handling a click in the zoom box is similar to handling the
 *      resizing of a window.
 */
                        if ( TrackBox(whichWindow, gTheEvent.where, thePart) )
                        {
                                GetPort( &oldPort );
                                SetPort( whichWindow );
                                EraseRect( &whichWindow->portRect );
                                ZoomWindow( whichWindow, thePart,
                                                LEAVE_WHERE_IT_IS );
                                InvalRect( &whichWindow->portRect );
                                SetPort( oldPort );
                        }
                        break;
        }
}


/******************************** DrawMyPicture *********/

DrawMyPicture( drawingWindow, thePicture )
WindowPtr       drawingWindow;
PicHandle       thePicture;
{
        Rect    drawingClipRect, myRect;
        GrafPtr oldPort;
        RgnHandle       tempRgn;

/*
 *      We start by temporarily making the window specified in the
 *      drawingWindow parameter the current port.  We also store the
 *      window's clipping region in tempRgn.  Next, we erase the window
 *      and redraw the GrowIcon.
 */
        GetPort( &oldPort );
        SetPort( drawingWindow );
        tempRgn = NewRgn();
        GetClip( tempRgn );
        EraseRect( &drawingWindow->portRect );
        DrawGrowIcon( drawingWindow );
```

```
/*
 *      Next, we create a clip rectangle that doesn't cover the scroll
 *      bar areas (or the size box either).  We use this rectangle as
 *      our clipping region and center and draw the picture.
 */
        drawingClipRect = drawingWindow->portRect;
        drawingClipRect.right -= SCROLL_BAR_PIXELS;
        drawingClipRect.bottom -= SCROLL_BAR_PIXELS;

        myRect = drawingWindow->portRect;
        CenterPict( thePicture, &myRect );
        ClipRect( &drawingClipRect );
        DrawPicture( thePicture, &myRect );

/*
 *      Finally, we restore the original clip region, free up the memory
 *      used by tempRgn, and reset the original port.
 */
        SetClip( tempRgn );
        DisposeRgn( tempRgn );
        SetPort( oldPort );
}


/****************************** CenterPict *********/

CenterPict( thePicture, myRectPtr )
PicHandle       thePicture;
Rect            *myRectPtr;
{
        Rect    windRect, pictureRect;

        windRect = *myRectPtr;
        pictureRect = (**( thePicture )).picFrame;
        myRectPtr->top = (windRect.bottom - windRect.top -
                    (pictureRect.bottom - pictureRect.top))/ 2 +
                    windRect.top;
        myRectPtr->bottom = myRectPtr->top +
                    (pictureRect.bottom - pictureRect.top);
        myRectPtr->left = (windRect.right - windRect.left -
(pictureRect.right - pictureRect.left))/ 2 +
                    windRect.left;
        myRectPtr->right = myRectPtr->left + (pictureRect.right -
                    pictureRect.left);
}
```

Chapter 5, Timer.c

```
#define BASE_RES_ID             400
#define NIL_POINTER             0L
#define MOVE_TO_FRONT           -1L
#define REMOVE_ALL_EVENTS       0

#define PLAIN                   0
#define PLAIN_ITEM              1
#define BOLD_ITEM               2
#define ITALIC_ITEM             3
#define UNDERLINE_ITEM          4
#define OUTLINE_ITEM            5
#define SHADOW_ITEM             6
```

```
#define INCLUDE_SECONDS          TRUE

#define ADD_CHECK_MARK           TRUE
#define REMOVE_CHECK_MARK        FALSE

#define DRAG_THRESHOLD           30

#define MIN_SLEEP                0L
#define NIL_MOUSE_REGION         0L

#define WNE_TRAP_NUM             0x60
#define UNIMPL_TRAP_NUM          0x9F

#define QUIT_ITEM                1
#define ABOUT_ITEM               1
#define NOT_A_NORMAL_MENU        -1
#define APPLE_MENU_ID            BASE_RES_ID
#define FILE_MENU_ID             BASE_RES_ID+1
#define FONT_MENU_ID             100
#define STYLE_MENU_ID            101

#define CLOCK_LEFT               12
#define CLOCK_TOP                25
#define CLOCK_SIZE               24

#define ABOUT_ALERT              400


WindowPtr       gClockWindow;
Boolean         gDone, gWNEImplemented;
long            gCurrentTime, gOldTime;
EventRecord     gTheEvent;
MenuHandle      gAppleMenu, gFontMenu, gStyleMenu;
int             gLastFont;
Rect            gDragRect;
Style           gCurrentStyle = PLAIN;


/***************************** main ********/

main()
{
        ToolBoxInit();
        WindowInit();
        SetUpDragRect();
        MenuBarInit();
        MainLoop();
}


/******************************* ToolBoxInit */

ToolBoxInit()
{
        InitGraf( &thePort );
        InitFonts();
        FlushEvents( everyEvent, REMOVE_ALL_EVENTS );
```

```
        InitWindows();
        InitMenus();
        TEInit();
        InitDialogs( NIL_POINTER );
        InitCursor();
}


/*********************************** WindowInit   */

WindowInit()
{
        gClockWindow = GetNewWindow( BASE_RES_ID, NIL_POINTER,
                                                MOVE_TO_FRONT );
        SetPort( gClockWindow );
        ShowWindow( gClockWindow );

        TextSize( CLOCK_SIZE );
}


/****************************** SetUpDragRect ********/

SetUpDragRect()
{
        gDragRect = screenBits.bounds;
        gDragRect.left += DRAG_THRESHOLD;
        gDragRect.right -= DRAG_THRESHOLD;
        gDragRect.bottom -= DRAG_THRESHOLD;
}


/********************************** MenuBarInit    */

MenuBarInit()
{
        Handle          myMenuBar;
/*
 *      First, we'll load the MBAR resource, which specifies the MENUs
 *      to use in myMenuBar.  Next, make myMenuBar the current menu bar.
 *      Put handles to their respective menus in the globals gAppleMenu,
 *      gFontMenu, and gStyleMenu for later use.
 */

        myMenuBar = GetNewMBar( BASE_RES_ID );
        SetMenuBar( myMenuBar );
        gAppleMenu = GetMHandle( APPLE_MENU_ID );
        gFontMenu = GetMenu( FONT_MENU_ID );
        gStyleMenu = GetMenu( STYLE_MENU_ID );
/*
 *      Add the heirarchical menu, gFontMenu, to the menu list.
 *      We set up the Special MENU resource so that the Font and
 *      Style menus would automatically be added as hierarchical
 *      submenus to the Special menu.
 */

        InsertMenu( gFontMenu, NOT_A_NORMAL_MENU );
/*
 *      We also add all the FONTs to the font menu.
 */

        AddResMenu( gFontMenu, 'FONT' );
        InsertMenu( gStyleMenu, NOT_A_NORMAL_MENU );
```

```
/*
 *      Put a check mark next to Plain on the Style submenu and
 *      Add all the desk accessory names to the apple menu.
 */
        CheckItem( gStyleMenu, PLAIN_ITEM, TRUE );
        AddResMenu( gAppleMenu, 'DRVR' );
        DrawMenuBar();
/*
 *      We'll start off using the first font on the menu.  By
 *      calling HandleFontChoice(), we simulate the user selecting
 *      the first font from the font menu...
 */
        gLastFont = 1;
        HandleFontChoice( gLastFont );
}


/******************************* MainLoop ********/

MainLoop()
{
        gDone = FALSE;
        gWNEImplemented = ( NGetTrapAddress( WNE_TRAP_NUM, ToolTrap ) !=
                            NGetTrapAddress( UNIMPL_TRAP_NUM, ToolTrap ) );
        while ( gDone == FALSE )
        {
                HandleEvent();
        }
}


/*********************************** HandleEvent   */

HandleEvent()
{
        char    theChar;

        if ( gWNEImplemented )
                WaitNextEvent( everyEvent, &gTheEvent, MIN_SLEEP,
                                                NIL_MOUSE_REGION );
        else
        {
                SystemTask();
                GetNextEvent( everyEvent, &gTheEvent );
        }


        switch ( gTheEvent.what )
        {
                case nullEvent:
/*
 *      Since the clock needs to be updated on a regular basis (and not
 *      just when an update event is generated), we'll check the clock
 *      every time we get a null event.
 */
                        HandleNull();
                        break;
                case mouseDown:
                        HandleMouseDown();
                        break;
                case keyDown:
```

```
                      case autoKey:
                            theChar = gTheEvent.message & charCodeMask;
                            if (( gTheEvent.modifiers & cmdKey ) != 0)
                                    HandleMenuChoice( MenuKey( theChar ) );
                            break;
                      case updateEvt:
/*
 *      We don't need to do anything about updateEvts but we must
 *      call Begin and EndUpdate() so the Window Manager won't keep
 *      generating update events.  The problem is, if the Window
 *      Manager keeps generating updateEvts, the event queue will
 *      eventually fill up, and the Event Manager won't be able to
 *      generate any nullEvts.
 */

                            BeginUpdate( gTheEvent.message );
                            EndUpdate( gTheEvent.message );
                            break;
            }
}


/******************************* HandleNull *********/

HandleNull()
{
/*
 *      Check the time, compare it against the last time you
 *      checked.  If the time (which is measured in seconds)
 *      changed, update the clock.
 */

        GetDateTime( &gCurrentTime );
        if ( gCurrentTime != gOldTime )
        {
                DrawClock( gClockWindow );
        }
}


/******************************* DrawClock *********/

DrawClock( theWindow )
WindowPtr       theWindow;
{
        Str255          myTimeString;

        IUTimeString( gCurrentTime, INCLUDE_SECONDS, myTimeString );
        EraseRect( &( theWindow->portRect ) );
        MoveTo( CLOCK_LEFT, CLOCK_TOP );
        DrawString( myTimeString );
        gOldTime = gCurrentTime;
}


/********************************* HandleMouseDown */

HandleMouseDown()
{
        WindowPtr       whichWindow;
        short int       thePart;
        long int        menuChoice, windSize;
```

```
                thePart = FindWindow( gTheEvent.where, &whichWindow );
                switch ( thePart )
                {
                        case inMenuBar:
                                menuChoice = MenuSelect( gTheEvent.where );
                                HandleMenuChoice( menuChoice );
                                break;
                        case inSysWindow :
                                SystemClick( &gTheEvent, whichWindow );
                                break;
                        case inDrag :
                                DragWindow( whichWindow, gTheEvent.where, &gDragRect);
                                break;
                        case inGoAway :
                                gDone = TRUE;
                                break;
                }
}


/****************************** HandleMenuChoice */

HandleMenuChoice( menuChoice )
long int        menuChoice;
{
/*
 *      menuChoice is 4 bytes, 2 bytes of which contain the resource
 *      ID of the selected menu, and 2 bytes of which contain the
 *      selected item number.
 */
        int     theMenu;
        int     theItem;

        if ( menuChoice != 0 )
        {
                theMenu = HiWord( menuChoice );
                theItem = LoWord( menuChoice );
                switch ( theMenu )
                {
                        case APPLE_MENU_ID :
                                HandleAppleChoice( theItem );
                                break;
                        case FILE_MENU_ID :
                                HandleFileChoice( theItem );
                                break;
                        case FONT_MENU_ID :
                                HandleFontChoice( theItem );
                                break;
                        case STYLE_MENU_ID:
                                HandleStyleChoice( theItem );
                                break;
                }
                HiliteMenu( 0 );
        }
}


/****************************      HandleAppleChoice    *******/

HandleAppleChoice( theItem )
int     theItem;
{
```

```
        Str255    accName;
        int       accNumber;
        short int itemNumber;
        DialogPtr AboutDialog;

        switch ( theItem )
        {
                case ABOUT_ITEM :
/*
 *      Alerts are extremely easy to do.  Dialog boxes are
 *      much more complex (they're explained in Chapter 6).
 */
                        NoteAlert( ABOUT_ALERT, NIL_POINTER );
                        break;
                default :
/*
 *      If the selection was not "About ...", open the selected
 *      Desk Accessory...
 */
                        GetItem( gAppleMenu, theItem, accName );
                        accNumber = OpenDeskAcc( accName );
                        break;
        }
}


/******************************        HandleFileChoice        *******/

HandleFileChoice( theItem )
int     theItem;
{
        switch ( theItem )
        {
/*
 *      This is the correct way to exit an application:  by
 *      selecting Quit from the File menu!
 */
        case QUIT_ITEM :
                gDone = TRUE;
                break;
        }
}


/******************************        HandleFontChoice        *******/

HandleFontChoice( theItem )
int     theItem;
{
        int     fontNumber;
        Str255  fontName;

/*      Uncheck the old font, check the newly selected font  */
        CheckItem( gFontMenu, gLastFont, REMOVE_CHECK_MARK );
        CheckItem( gFontMenu, theItem, ADD_CHECK_MARK );
        gLastFont = theItem;
        GetItem( gFontMenu , theItem , fontName );
        GetFNum( fontName , &fontNumber );
/*  Change the font to the selected font...  */
        TextFont( fontNumber );
}
```

```
/******************************      HandleStyleChoice      *******/

HandleStyleChoice( theItem )
int     theItem;
{
/*
 *      gCurrentStyle accumulates the style changes made via the
 *      Style menu.
 */
        switch( theItem )
        {
                case PLAIN_ITEM:
                        gCurrentStyle = PLAIN;
                        break;
                case BOLD_ITEM:
                        if ( gCurrentStyle & bold )
                                gCurrentStyle -= bold;
                        else
                                gCurrentStyle |= bold;
                        break;
                case ITALIC_ITEM:
                        if ( gCurrentStyle & italic )
                                gCurrentStyle -= italic;
                        else
                                gCurrentStyle |= italic;
                        break;
                case UNDERLINE_ITEM:
                        if ( gCurrentStyle & underline )
                                gCurrentStyle -= underline;
                        else
                                gCurrentStyle |= underline;
                        break;
                case OUTLINE_ITEM:
                        if ( gCurrentStyle & outline )
                                gCurrentStyle -= outline;
                        else
                                gCurrentStyle |= outline;
                        break;
                case SHADOW_ITEM:
                        if ( gCurrentStyle & shadow )
                                gCurrentStyle -= shadow;
                        else
                                gCurrentStyle |= shadow;
                        break;
        }
/*
 *      Check or uncheck the appropriate items from the Style
 *      menu, then change the current text face to that encoded
 *      in gCurrentStyle.
 */
        CheckStyles();
        TextFace( gCurrentStyle );
}


/******************************      CheckStyles      *******/

CheckStyles()
{
/*
 *      Check or uncheck each item on the Style menu, depending on
 *      the contents of gCurrentStyle.
 */
```

```
        CheckItem( gStyleMenu, PLAIN_ITEM, gCurrentStyle == PLAIN );
        CheckItem( gStyleMenu, BOLD_ITEM, gCurrentStyle & bold );
        CheckItem( gStyleMenu, ITALIC_ITEM, gCurrentStyle & italic );
        CheckItem( gStyleMenu, UNDERLINE_ITEM, gCurrentStyle & underline);
        CheckItem( gStyleMenu, OUTLINE_ITEM, gCurrentStyle & outline );
        CheckItem( gStyleMenu, SHADOW_ITEM, gCurrentStyle & shadow );
}
```

Chapter 5, Popup.c

```
#define BASE_RES_ID             400
#define NIL_POINTER             OL
#define MOVE_TO_FRONT           -1L
#define REMOVE_ALL_EVENTS       0

#define MIN_SLEEP               OL
#define NIL_MOUSE_REGION        OL

#define DRAG_THRESHOLD          30

#define WNE_TRAP_NUM            0x60
#define UNIMPL_TRAP_NUM         0x9F

#define POPUP_MENU_ID           BASE_RES_ID
#define NOT_A_NORMAL_MENU       -1

#define POPUP_LEFT              100
#define POPUP_TOP               35
#define POPUP_RIGHT             125
#define POPUP_BOTTOM            52
#define SHADOW_PIXELS           1
#define RIGHT_MARGIN            5
#define BOTTOM_MARGIN           4
#define LEFT_MARGIN             5
#define PIXEL_FOR_TOP_LINE      1


Boolean         gDone, gWNEImplemented;
int             gPopUpItem = 1, gPopUpLabelWidth;
MenuHandle      gPopUpMenu;
EventRecord     gTheEvent;
Rect            gPopUpRect, gLabelRect, gDragRect;


/********************** Main *************/

main()
{
        ToolBoxInit();
        WindowInit();
        SetUpDragRect();
        MenuBarInit();
        DrawPopUp();
        MainLoop();
}
```

```
/******************************** ToolBoxInit */

ToolBoxInit()
{
        InitGraf( &thePort );
        InitFonts();
        FlushEvents( everyEvent, REMOVE_ALL_EVENTS );
        InitWindows();
        InitMenus();
        TEInit();
        InitDialogs( NIL_POINTER );
        InitCursor();
}


/********************WindowInit************/

WindowInit()
{
        WindowPtr         popUpWindow;

        popUpWindow = GetNewWindow( BASE_RES_ID , NIL_POINTER,
                                                 MOVE_TO_FRONT );
        ShowWindow( popUpWindow );
        SetPort( popUpWindow );
        TextFont( systemFont );
        TextMode( srcCopy );
}


/****************************** SetUpDragRect ********/

SetUpDragRect()
{
        gDragRect = screenBits.bounds;
        gDragRect.left += DRAG_THRESHOLD;
        gDragRect.right -= DRAG_THRESHOLD;
        gDragRect.bottom -= DRAG_THRESHOLD;
}


/********************MenuBarInit************/

MenuBarInit()
{
/*
 *      Just as we did with the hierarchical menus in Timer,
 *      we load the MENU, and add it to the menu list via the
 *      call to InsertMenu().  Next, we get the popup label
 *      from the menu data structure and calculate its width in
 *      pixels.  We'll use this information later.
 */
        gPopUpMenu = GetMenu( POPUP_MENU_ID );
        InsertMenu( gPopUpMenu, NOT_A_NORMAL_MENU );
        HLock( gPopUpMenu );
        gPopUpLabelWidth = StringWidth( (**gPopUpMenu).menuData );
        HUnlock( gPopUpMenu );
}
```

```
/******************** DrawPopUp *************/

DrawPopUp()
{
/*
 *      DrawPopUp() will draw the popup outline, its 1-pixel
 *      drop shadow, the popup label, and set gLabelRect,
 *      which we'll invert when the popup is selected.  DrawPopUp()
 *      will also be called to handle updateEvts.
 */
        SetRect( &gPopUpRect, POPUP_LEFT, POPUP_TOP,
                                    POPUP_RIGHT, POPUP_BOTTOM );
        FrameRect( &gPopUpRect );

        MoveTo( gPopUpRect.left+SHADOW_PIXELS, gPopUpRect.bottom );
        LineTo( gPopUpRect.right, gPopUpRect.bottom );
        LineTo( gPopUpRect.right, gPopUpRect.top+SHADOW_PIXELS );

        MoveTo( gPopUpRect.left - gPopUpLabelWidth - RIGHT_MARGIN,
                        gPopUpRect.bottom - BOTTOM_MARGIN );
        HLock( gPopUpMenu );
        DrawString( (**gPopUpMenu).menuData );
        HUnlock( gPopUpMenu );

        gLabelRect.top = gPopUpRect.top + PIXEL_FOR_TOP_LINE;
        gLabelRect.left = gPopUpRect.left - gPopUpLabelWidth
                                    - LEFT_MARGIN - RIGHT_MARGIN;
        gLabelRect.right = gPopUpRect.left;
        gLabelRect.bottom = gPopUpRect.bottom;

/*
 *      After the background is drawn, we can draw the current
 *      menu value, in this case, a number.
 */
        DrawPopUpNumber();
}


/******************** DrawPopUpNumber *************/

DrawPopUpNumber()
{
        Str255  menuItem;
        int     itemLeftMargin;

/*
 *      Get the menu item corresponding to gPopUpItem,
 *      calculate the margin, and draw it...
 */
        GetItem( gPopUpMenu, gPopUpItem, &menuItem );
        itemLeftMargin = ( gPopUpRect.right - gPopUpRect.left -
                                    StringWidth( menuItem ) ) / 2;
        MoveTo( gPopUpRect.left + itemLeftMargin,
                                gPopUpRect.bottom - BOTTOM_MARGIN );
        DrawString( menuItem );
}
```

```
/****************************** MainLoop ********/

MainLoop()
{
        gDone = FALSE;
        gWNEImplemented = ( NGetTrapAddress( WNE_TRAP_NUM, ToolTrap ) !=
                            NGetTrapAddress( UNIMPL_TRAP_NUM, ToolTrap ) );
        while ( gDone == FALSE )
        {
                HandleEvent();
        }
}



/*********************************** HandleEvent   */

HandleEvent()
{
        if ( gWNEImplemented )
                WaitNextEvent( everyEvent, &gTheEvent, MIN_SLEEP,
                                            NIL_MOUSE_REGION );
        else
        {
                SystemTask();
                GetNextEvent( everyEvent, &gTheEvent );
        }

        switch ( gTheEvent.what )
        {
                case mouseDown:
                        HandleMouseDown();
                        break;
                case updateEvt:
                        BeginUpdate( gTheEvent.message );
                        DrawPopUp();
                        EndUpdate( gTheEvent.message );
                        break;

        }
}



/*********************************** HandleMouseDown */

HandleMouseDown()
{
        WindowPtr       whichWindow;
        short int       thePart, i;
        long int        theChoice;
        Point           myPoint, popUpUpperLeft;

        thePart = FindWindow( gTheEvent.where, &whichWindow );
        switch ( thePart )
        {
                case inContent:
/*
 *      If the mouse was clicked in the window, copy the Point,
 *      convert it to the window's local coordinate system, and
 *      check to see if its inside gPopUpRect.  If so...
 */
                        myPoint = gTheEvent.where;
                        GlobalToLocal( &myPoint );
```

```
                        if ( PtInRect( myPoint, &gPopUpRect ) )
                        {
/*
*       ...Invert the label, call PopUpMenuSelect, uninvert the
*       label.  Finally, handle the selection.
*/
                            InvertRect( &gLabelRect );
                            popUpUpperLeft.v = gPopUpRect.top +
                                            PIXEL_FOR_TOP_LINE;
                            popUpUpperLeft.h = gPopUpRect.left;
                            LocalToGlobal( &popUpUpperLeft );
                            theChoice = PopUpMenuSelect( gPopUpMenu,
                                    popUpUpperLeft.v, popUpUpperLeft.h,
                                    gPopUpItem );
                            InvertRect( &gLabelRect );
                            if ( LoWord( theChoice ) > 0 )
                            {
                                    gPopUpItem = LoWord( theChoice );
                                    DrawPopUpNumber();
                                    for ( i=0; i<gPopUpItem; i++ )
                                            SysBeep( 20 );
                            }
                        }
                        break;
                case inSysWindow:
                        SystemClick( &gTheEvent, whichWindow );
                        break;
                case inDrag:
                        DragWindow( whichWindow, gTheEvent.where, &gDragRect);
                        break;
                case inGoAway :
/*
*       Again, this is not the way "proper" Macintosh applications
*       exit.  We would normally use a Quit item in the File menu.
*/
                        gDone = TRUE;
                        break;
        }
}
```

Chapter 6, Reminder.c

```
#define BASE_RES_ID            400
#define ABOUT_ALERT            401
#define BAD_SYS_ALERT          402
#define NIL_POINTER            0L
#define MOVE_TO_FRONT          -1L
#define REMOVE_ALL_EVENTS      0

#define MIN_SLEEP              0L
#define NIL_MOUSE_REGION       0L

#define DRAG_THRESHOLD 30

#define SAVE_BUTTON            1
#define CANCEL_BUTTON          2
#define TIME_FIELD             4
#define S_OR_M_FIELD           5
#define SOUND_ON_BOX           6
```

```
#define ICON_ON_BOX              7
#define ALERT_ON_BOX             8
#define SECS_RADIO              10
#define MINS_RADIO              11

#define DEFAULT_SECS_ID        401
#define DEFAULT_MINS_ID        402

#define ON                       1
#define OFF                      0

#define SECONDS                  0
#define MINUTES                  1
#define SECONDS_PER_MINUTE      60

#define TOP                     25
#define LEFT                    12

#define MARK_APPLICATION         1

#define APPLE_MENU_ID           BASE_RES_ID
#define FILE_MENU_ID            BASE_RES_ID+1
#define ABOUT_ITEM_ID            1

#define CHANGE_ITEM              1
#define START_STOP_ITEM          2
#define KILL_ITEM                3
#define QUIT_ITEM                4

#define SYS_VERSION              1        /* Version Number of SysEnvirons */


DialogPtr       gSettingsDialog;
Rect            gDragRect;
Boolean         gDone, gCounting, gNotify_set;
char            gSeconds_or_minutes = SECONDS;
StringHandle    gNotifyStrH, gDefaultSecsH, gDefaultMinsH;
NMRec           gMyNMRec;
MenuHandle      gAppleMenu, gFileMenu;
EventRecord     gTheEvent;

struct
{
        Str255  timeString;
        int     sound;
        int     icon;
        int     alert;
        int     secsRadio;
        int     minsRadio;
} savedSettings;


/****************************** main ********/

main()
{
        ToolBoxInit();
/*
 *      Since we'll be using the Notification Manager, we have to make
 *      sure System 6.0 or later is installed.
 */
```

```
        if ( Sys6OrLater() )
        {
                DialogInit();
                MenuBarInit();
                SetUpDragRect();
                NotifyInit();
                MainLoop();
        }
}


/********************************* ToolBoxInit */

ToolBoxInit()
{
        InitGraf( &thePort );
        InitFonts();
        FlushEvents( everyEvent, REMOVE_ALL_EVENTS );
        InitWindows();
        InitMenus();
        TEInit();
        InitDialogs( NIL_POINTER );
        InitCursor();
}


/***************************** Sys6OrLater *********/

int     Sys6OrLater()
{
        OSErr           status;
        SysEnvRec       SysEnvData;

/*
 *      SysEnvirons() is documented in (V:5-6).  We're interested in
 *      the systemVersion field.
 */
        status = SysEnvirons( SYS_VERSION, &SysEnvData );
        if (( status != noErr ) || ( SysEnvData.systemVersion < 0x0600 ))
        {
                StopAlert( BAD_SYS_ALERT, NIL_POINTER );
                return( FALSE );
        }
        else
                return( TRUE );
}


/***************************** DialogInit *********/

DialogInit()
{
        int             itemType;
        Rect            itemRect;
        Handle          itemHandle;

/*  These 2 'STR 's hold the default values for minutes
            and seconds   */
        gDefaultSecsH = GetString( DEFAULT_SECS_ID );
        gDefaultMinsH = GetString( DEFAULT_MINS_ID );
```

```
/*
 *      Load gSettingsDialog with GetNewDialog().  You can treat
 *      it like a WindowPtr.  If you want to draw in the Dialog
 *      window, use SetPort first to make the dialog port the current
 *      port.
 */
        gSettingsDialog = GetNewDialog( BASE_RES_ID, NIL_POINTER,
                                                MOVE_TO_FRONT );
/*
 *      Get a handle to the dialog items to be initialized with
 *      GetDItem(), use SetCtlValue() to set the control's value.
 */
        GetDItem( gSettingsDialog, SECS_RADIO, &itemType, &itemHandle,
                                                &itemRect );
        SetCtlValue( itemHandle, ON );
        GetDItem( gSettingsDialog, SOUND_ON_BOX, &itemType, &itemHandle,
                                                &itemRect );
        SetCtlValue( itemHandle, ON );
        GetDItem( gSettingsDialog, ICON_ON_BOX, &itemType, &itemHandle,
                                                &itemRect );
        SetCtlValue( itemHandle, ON );
        GetDItem( gSettingsDialog, ALERT_ON_BOX, &itemType, &itemHandle,
                                                &itemRect );
        SetCtlValue( itemHandle, ON );
}


/******************************** MenuBarInit    */

MenuBarInit()
{
        Handle          myMenuBar;

        myMenuBar = GetNewMBar( BASE_RES_ID );
        SetMenuBar( myMenuBar );
        gAppleMenu = GetMHandle( APPLE_MENU_ID );
        AddResMenu( gAppleMenu, 'DRVR' );
        gFileMenu = GetMHandle( FILE_MENU_ID );
        DrawMenuBar();
}


/******************************* SetUpDragRect ********/

SetUpDragRect()
{
        gDragRect = screenBits.bounds;
        gDragRect.left += DRAG_THRESHOLD;
        gDragRect.right -= DRAG_THRESHOLD;
        gDragRect.bottom -= DRAG_THRESHOLD;
}


/******************************* NotifyInit ********/

NotifyInit()
{
/*  Initialize the notification data structure   */
        gNotifyStrH = GetString( BASE_RES_ID );  /*  The Alert string   */
        gMyNMRec.qType = nmType;      /*  All notifs use this type   */
```

```
        gMyNMRec.nmMark = MARK_APPLICATION;   /* mark the applications
              entry in the apple menu  */
        gMyNMRec.nmResp = NIL_POINTER;  /*  don't use a response
              routine  */
}


/****************************** MainLoop ********/

MainLoop()
{
/*
 *      gCounting is TRUE while the countdown is happening.  gNotify_set
 *      is TRUE while the notification is set.
 */
        gDone = FALSE;
        gCounting = FALSE;
        gNotify_set = FALSE;

        while ( gDone == FALSE )
        {
                HandleEvent();
        }
}


/********************************** HandleEvent   */

HandleEvent()
{
        char    theChar;

/*
 *      Because we're running System 6.0 or later, we don't need
 *      to check for WaitNextEvent().
 */
        WaitNextEvent( everyEvent, &gTheEvent, MIN_SLEEP,
                                        NIL_MOUSE_REGION );

        switch ( gTheEvent.what )
        {
                case mouseDown:
                        HandleMouseDown();
                        break;
                case keyDown:
                case autoKey:
                        theChar = gTheEvent.message & charCodeMask;
                        if (( gTheEvent.modifiers & cmdKey ) != 0 )
                             HandleMenuChoice( MenuKey( theChar ) );
                        break;
        }
}


/********************************** HandleMouseDown */

HandleMouseDown()
{
        WindowPtr       whichWindow;
        short int       thePart;
        long int        menuChoice, windSize;
```

```
                thePart = FindWindow( gTheEvent.where, &whichWindow );
                switch ( thePart )
                {
                        case inMenuBar:
                                menuChoice = MenuSelect( gTheEvent.where );
                                HandleMenuChoice( menuChoice );
                                break;
                        case inSysWindow :
                                SystemClick( &gTheEvent, whichWindow );
                                break;
                        case inDrag :
                                DragWindow( whichWindow, gTheEvent.where, &gDragRect);
                                break;
                        case inGoAway :
                                gDone = TRUE;
                                break;
                }
        }


/*********************************** HandleMenuChoice */

HandleMenuChoice( menuChoice )
long int        menuChoice;
{
        int     theMenu;
        int     theItem;

        if ( menuChoice != 0 )
        {
                theMenu = HiWord( menuChoice );
                theItem = LoWord( menuChoice );
                switch ( theMenu )
                {
                        case APPLE_MENU_ID :
                                HandleAppleChoice( theItem );
                                break;
                        case FILE_MENU_ID :
                                HandleFileChoice( theItem );
                                break;
                }
        }
        HiliteMenu( 0 );
}


/******************************       HandleAppleChoice       *******/

HandleAppleChoice( theItem )
int     theItem;
{
        Str255          accName;
        int             accNumber;
        short int       itemNumber;

        switch ( theItem )
        {
                case ABOUT_ITEM_ID :
                        NoteAlert( ABOUT_ALERT, NIL_POINTER );
                        break;
```

```
                default :
                        GetItem( gAppleMenu, theItem, accName );
                        accNumber = OpenDeskAcc( accName );
                        break;
        }
}


/*******************************          HandleFileChoice        *******/

HandleFileChoice( theItem )
int     theItem;
{
        Str255 timeString;
        long    countDownTime;
        int     itemType;
        Rect    itemRect;
        Handle  itemHandle;

        switch ( theItem )
        {
                case CHANGE_ITEM :
                        /*  Change Settings  */
                        HandleDialog();
                        break;
                case START_STOP_ITEM :
                        /*  Start or Stop the Countdown  */
                        if ( gCounting )  /*  Stop Countdown  */
                        {
                                SetItem( gFileMenu,theItem,"\pStart Countdown");
                                gCounting = FALSE;
                        } else                  /*  Start Countdown  */
                        {
/*
 *      Start the countdown by unhilighting the menu, getting the time
 *      field from the settings dialog, disabling the "Change Settings"
 *      menu item, changing "Start Countdown" to "Stop Countdown" and,
 *      finally, calling CountDown().
 */
                                HiliteMenu( 0 );
                                GetDItem( gSettingsDialog, TIME_FIELD,
                                        &itemType, &itemHandle, &itemRect );
                                GetIText( itemHandle, &timeString );
                                StringToNum( timeString, &countDownTime );

                                DisableItem( gFileMenu, CHANGE_ITEM );
                                        /*  Disable Change Settings  */
                                SetItem( gFileMenu, theItem,"\pStop Countdown");
                                CountDown( countDownTime );
/*  Once Countdown() returns, reenable "Change Settings",
        change "Stop Countdown" to "Start Countdown"  */
                                EnableItem( gFileMenu, CHANGE_ITEM );
                                        /*  Reenable Change Settings  */
                                SetItem( gFileMenu,theItem,"\pStart Countdown");
                        }
                        break;
                case KILL_ITEM :
                        /*  Kill Notification  */
                        NMRemove( &gMyNMRec );
                        HUnlock( gNotifyStrH );
```

```
                              DisableItem( gFileMenu, KILL_ITEM );
                              gNotify_set = FALSE;
                              break;
                      case QUIT_ITEM :
/*
 *      There is a call to HandleEvent() inside Countdown(), so the Quit
 *      item might be selected during the countdown.  Setting gCounting
 *      to FALSE will cause us to drop out of the Countdown() event
 *      loop.  Setting gDone to TRUE will drop us out of the main event
 *      loop.
 */
                              gCounting = FALSE;
                              gDone = TRUE;
                              break;
              }
}


/******************************* HandleDialog *********/

HandleDialog()
{
        int     itemHit, dialogDone = FALSE;
        long    alarmDelay;
        Str255  delayString;
        int     itemType;
        Rect    itemRect;
        Handle  itemHandle;

        ShowWindow( gSettingsDialog );
        SaveSettings();

        while ( dialogDone == FALSE )
                {
/*
 *      call ModalDialog() to find out which item was hit, then
 *      process that item.
 */
                ModalDialog( NIL_POINTER, &itemHit );
                switch ( itemHit )
                        {
                        case SAVE_BUTTON:
                                HideWindow( gSettingsDialog );
                                dialogDone = TRUE;
                                break;
                        case CANCEL_BUTTON:
                                HideWindow( gSettingsDialog );
                                RestoreSettings();
                                dialogDone = TRUE;
                                break;
                        case SOUND_ON_BOX:
                                GetDItem( gSettingsDialog, SOUND_ON_BOX,
                                        &itemType, &itemHandle, &itemRect );
/*      This is a nice technique for flipping the value of checkboxes */
                                SetCtlValue( itemHandle,
                                                ! GetCtlValue( itemHandle ) );
                                break;
                        case ICON_ON_BOX:
                                GetDItem( gSettingsDialog, ICON_ON_BOX,
                                        &itemType, &itemHandle, &itemRect );
                                SetCtlValue( itemHandle,
                                                ! GetCtlValue( itemHandle ) );
                                break;
```

```
                              case ALERT_ON_BOX:
                                      GetDItem( gSettingsDialog, ALERT_ON_BOX,
                                              &itemType, &itemHandle, &itemRect );
                                      SetCtlValue( itemHandle,
                                                      ! GetCtlValue( itemHandle ) );
                                      break;
                              case SECS_RADIO:
/*
 *      Turn off the minutes radio button, turn on the seconds
 *      radio button.  Change the string from "minutes" to "seconds".
 */
                                      gSeconds_or_minutes = SECONDS;
                                      GetDItem( gSettingsDialog, MINS_RADIO,
                                              &itemType, &itemHandle, &itemRect );
                                      SetCtlValue( itemHandle, OFF );
                                      GetDItem( gSettingsDialog, SECS_RADIO,
                                              &itemType, &itemHandle, &itemRect );
                                      SetCtlValue( itemHandle, ON );
                                      GetDItem( gSettingsDialog, S_OR_M_FIELD,
                                              &itemType, &itemHandle, &itemRect );
                                      SetIText( itemHandle, "\pseconds" );
                                      GetDItem( gSettingsDialog, TIME_FIELD,
                                              &itemType, &itemHandle, &itemRect );
                                      HLock( gDefaultSecsH );
                                      SetIText( itemHandle, *gDefaultSecsH );
                                      HUnlock( gDefaultSecsH );
                                      break;
                              case MINS_RADIO:
/*
 *      Turn off the seconds radio button, turn on the minutes
 *      radio button.  Change the string from "seconds" to "minutes".
 */
                                      gSeconds_or_minutes = MINUTES;
                                      GetDItem( gSettingsDialog, SECS_RADIO,
                                              &itemType, &itemHandle, &itemRect );
                                      SetCtlValue( itemHandle, OFF );
                                      GetDItem( gSettingsDialog, MINS_RADIO,
                                              &itemType, &itemHandle, &itemRect );
                                      SetCtlValue( itemHandle, ON );
                                      GetDItem( gSettingsDialog, S_OR_M_FIELD,
                                              &itemType, &itemHandle, &itemRect );
                                      SetIText( itemHandle, "\pminutes" );
                                      GetDItem( gSettingsDialog, TIME_FIELD,
                                              &itemType, &itemHandle, &itemRect );
                                      HLock( gDefaultMinsH );
                                      SetIText( itemHandle, *gDefaultMinsH );
                                      HUnlock( gDefaultMinsH );
                                      break;
                      }
              }
}


/*********************************** SaveSettings */

SaveSettings()
{
      int     itemType;
      Rect    itemRect;
      Handle  itemHandle;
```

```
/*
 *      Fill the savedSettings data structure with all the current
 *      settings.  If the user Cancels, we can restore the data.
 */
        GetDItem( gSettingsDialog, TIME_FIELD, &itemType, &itemHandle,
                                                        &itemRect );
        GetIText( itemHandle, &(savedSettings.timeString) );
        GetDItem( gSettingsDialog, SOUND_ON_BOX, &itemType, &itemHandle,
                                                        &itemRect );
        savedSettings.sound = GetCtlValue( itemHandle );
        GetDItem( gSettingsDialog, ICON_ON_BOX, &itemType, &itemHandle,
                                                        &itemRect );
        savedSettings.icon = GetCtlValue( itemHandle );
        GetDItem( gSettingsDialog, ALERT_ON_BOX, &itemType, &itemHandle,
                                                        &itemRect );
        savedSettings.alert = GetCtlValue( itemHandle );
        GetDItem( gSettingsDialog, SECS_RADIO, &itemType, &itemHandle,
                                                        &itemRect );
        savedSettings.secsRadio = GetCtlValue( itemHandle );
        GetDItem( gSettingsDialog, MINS_RADIO, &itemType, &itemHandle,
                                                        &itemRect );
        savedSettings.minsRadio = GetCtlValue( itemHandle );
}


/************************************** RestoreSettings */

RestoreSettings()
{
        int     itemType;
        Rect    itemRect;
        Handle  itemHandle;

/*
 *      Use the information in the savedSettings data structure to
 *      restore the fields in the settings dialog.  Usually occurs
 *      as the result of the user hitting the Cancel button.
 */
        GetDItem( gSettingsDialog, TIME_FIELD, &itemType, &itemHandle,
                                                        &itemRect );
        SetIText( itemHandle, savedSettings.timeString );
        GetDItem( gSettingsDialog, SOUND_ON_BOX, &itemType, &itemHandle,
                                                        &itemRect );
        SetCtlValue( itemHandle, savedSettings.sound );
        GetDItem( gSettingsDialog, ICON_ON_BOX, &itemType, &itemHandle,
                                                        &itemRect );
        SetCtlValue( itemHandle, savedSettings.icon );
        GetDItem( gSettingsDialog, ALERT_ON_BOX, &itemType, &itemHandle,
                                                        &itemRect );
        SetCtlValue( itemHandle, savedSettings.alert );
        GetDItem( gSettingsDialog, SECS_RADIO, &itemType, &itemHandle,
                                                        &itemRect );
        SetCtlValue( itemHandle, savedSettings.secsRadio );
        GetDItem( gSettingsDialog, MINS_RADIO, &itemType, &itemHandle,
                                                        &itemRect );
        SetCtlValue( itemHandle, savedSettings.minsRadio );

        if ( savedSettings.secsRadio == ON )
        {
                GetDItem( gSettingsDialog, S_OR_M_FIELD, &itemType,
                                                &itemHandle, &itemRect );
```

```
                          SetIText( itemHandle, "\pseconds" );
                } else
                {
                          GetDItem( gSettingsDialog, S_OR_M_FIELD, &itemType,
                                                        &itemHandle, &itemRect );
                          SetIText( itemHandle, "\pminutes" );
                }
        }


/*******************************     CountDown       *******/

CountDown( numSecs )
long numSecs;
{
        long            myTime, oldTime, difTime;
        Str255          myTimeString;
        WindowPtr       countDownWindow;

/*  Load the countDownWindow, set its attributes...  */
        countDownWindow = GetNewWindow( BASE_RES_ID, NIL_POINTER,
                                                        MOVE_TO_FRONT );

        SetPort( countDownWindow );
        ShowWindow( countDownWindow );
        TextFace( bold );
        TextSize( 24 );

/*
 *      Get the time in seconds.  Convert countdown time to seconds
 *      if it's in minutes.  Finally, turn on the countdown flag,
 *      so the rest of the program knows we're counting...
 */

        GetDateTime( &myTime );
        oldTime = myTime;
        if ( gSeconds_or_minutes == MINUTES )
                numSecs *= SECONDS_PER_MINUTE;
        gCounting = TRUE;

/*  The counting event loop...  */
        while ( ( numSecs > 0 ) && ( gCounting ) )
        {
                HandleEvent();
                if ( gCounting )
                {
                        MoveTo( LEFT, TOP );
                        GetDateTime( &myTime );
                        if ( myTime != oldTime )
                        {
                                difTime = myTime - oldTime;
                                numSecs = numSecs - difTime;
                                oldTime = myTime;
                                NumToString( numSecs , myTimeString );
                                EraseRect ( &(countDownWindow->portRect) );
                                DrawString( myTimeString );
                        }
                }
        }
```

```
/*  If we haven't canceled, set the notification, turn off
              the counting flag, hide the counting window...  */
       if ( gCounting )
              SetNotification();
       gCounting = FALSE;
       HideWindow( countDownWindow );
}


/*******************************    SetNotification      *******/

SetNotification()
{
       int     itemType;
       Rect    itemRect;
       Handle  itemHandle;

/*
 *      If there was already a notification set, remove it,
 *      unlock the notify string.
 */
       if ( gNotify_set )
       {
              NMRemove( &gMyNMRec );
              HUnlock( gNotifyStrH );
       }

/*  Set the various fields of the notification data structure...  */
       GetDItem( gSettingsDialog, ICON_ON_BOX, &itemType, &itemHandle,
                                                   &itemRect );
       if ( GetCtlValue( itemHandle ) )
              gMyNMRec.nmSIcon = GetResource( 'SICN', BASE_RES_ID );
       else
              gMyNMRec.nmSIcon = NIL_POINTER;

       GetDItem( gSettingsDialog, SOUND_ON_BOX, &itemType, &itemHandle,
                                                   &itemRect );
       if ( GetCtlValue( itemHandle ) )
              gMyNMRec.nmSound = GetResource( 'snd ', BASE_RES_ID );
       else
              gMyNMRec.nmSound = NIL_POINTER;

       GetDItem( gSettingsDialog, ALERT_ON_BOX, &itemType, &itemHandle,
                                                   &itemRect );
       if ( GetCtlValue( itemHandle ) )
       {
/*      Since we'll be dereferencing the Handle to a Pointer, we better
 *      lock gNotifyStrH.  First, we'll call MoveHHi() to defragment
 *      the heap as much as possible.  If we were using the handle as is,
 *      or using the handled data (as a value), we wouldn't need to lock
 *      the handle.
 */
              MoveHHi( gNotifyStrH );
              HLock( gNotifyStrH );
              gMyNMRec.nmStr = *gNotifyStrH;
       }
       else
              gMyNMRec.nmStr = NIL_POINTER;

/*
 *      Install the notification on the notification queue, enable the
 *      "Kill Notification" item, turn on the notification flag.
 */
```

```
        NMInstall( &gMyNMRec );
        EnableItem( gFileMenu, KILL_ITEM );
        gNotify_set = TRUE;
}
```

Chapter 7, WindowMaker.c

```
#define BASE_RES_ID              400
#define NIL_POINTER              0L
#define MOVE_TO_FRONT            -1L
#define REMOVE_ALL_EVENTS        0

#define APPLE_MENU_ID            400
#define FILE_MENU_ID             401

#define ABOUT_ITEM               1
#define ABOUT_ALERT              400
#define ERROR_ALERT_ID           401

#define NO_MBAR                  BASE_RES_ID
#define NO_MENU                  BASE_RES_ID+1
#define NO_PICTURE               BASE_RES_ID+2
#define NO_WIND                  BASE_RES_ID+3

#define NEW_ITEM                 1
#define CLOSE_ITEM               2
#define QUIT_ITEM                3

#define DRAG_THRESHOLD           30

#define WINDOW_HOME_LEFT         5
#define WINDOW_HOME_TOP          45
#define NEW_WINDOW_OFFSET        20

#define MIN_SLEEP                0L
#define NIL_MOUSE_REGION         0L

#define LEAVE_WHERE_IT_IS        FALSE

#define WNE_TRAP_NUM             0x60
#define UNIMPL_TRAP_NUM          0x9F

#define NIL_STRING               "\p"
#define HOPELESSLY_FATAL_ERROR          "\pGame over, man!"


Boolean        gDone, gWNEImplemented;
EventRecord    gTheEvent;
MenuHandle     gAppleMenu;
PicHandle      gMyPicture;
Rect           gDragRect;
int            gNewWindowLeft = WINDOW_HOME_LEFT,
                    gNewWindowTop = WINDOW_HOME_TOP;
```

```
/******************************* main ********/

main()
{
        ToolBoxInit();
        MenuBarInit();
        LoadPicture();
        SetUpDragRect();

        MainLoop();
}


/******************************** ToolBoxInit */

ToolBoxInit()
{
        InitGraf( &thePort );
        InitFonts();
        FlushEvents( everyEvent, REMOVE_ALL_EVENTS );
        InitWindows();
        InitMenus();
        TEInit();
        InitDialogs( NIL_POINTER );
        InitCursor();
}


/******************************** MenuBarInit    */

MenuBarInit()
{
        Handle          myMenuBar;

/*
 *      This is an example of error handling in a Macintosh program.
 *      If you want to write an application for public consumption,
 *      you must do error handling.  The question is, how much is
 *      enough?  The answer:  you should feel pretty certain that a
 *      user will never get the dreaded bomb box.  Even if your
 *      application reaches a point of no return, you should at the
 *      least put up a fatal error alert, then exit to the Finder.
 */
        if ( ( myMenuBar = GetNewMBar( BASE_RES_ID ) ) == NIL_POINTER )
                ErrorHandler( NO_MBAR );
        SetMenuBar( myMenuBar );
        if ( ( gAppleMenu = GetMHandle( APPLE_MENU_ID ) ) == NIL_POINTER )
                ErrorHandler( NO_MENU );
        AddResMenu( gAppleMenu, 'DRVR' );
        DrawMenuBar();
}


/****************************** LoadPicture ********/

LoadPicture()
{
/*
 *      Functions that return error codes are great candidates
 *      for error checking!
 */
        if ( ( gMyPicture = GetPicture( BASE_RES_ID ) ) == NIL_POINTER )
                ErrorHandler( NO_PICTURE );
}
```

```
/***************************** SetUpDragRect *********/

SetUpDragRect()
{
      gDragRect = screenBits.bounds;
      gDragRect.left += DRAG_THRESHOLD;
      gDragRect.right -= DRAG_THRESHOLD;
      gDragRect.bottom -= DRAG_THRESHOLD;
}


/***************************** MainLoop *********/

MainLoop()
{
      gDone = FALSE;
      gWNEImplemented = ( NGetTrapAddress( WNE_TRAP_NUM, ToolTrap ) !=
                          NGetTrapAddress( UNIMPL_TRAP_NUM, ToolTrap ) );
      while ( gDone == FALSE )
      {
            HandleEvent();
      }
}


/******************************* HandleEvent     */
HandleEvent()
{
      char     theChar;
      GrafPtr  oldPort;
      if ( gWNEImplemented )
            WaitNextEvent( everyEvent, &gTheEvent, MIN_SLEEP,
                  NIL_MOUSE_REGION );
      else
      {
            SystemTask();
            GetNextEvent( everyEvent, &gTheEvent );
      }

      switch ( gTheEvent.what )
      {
            case mouseDown:
                  HandleMouseDown();
                  break;
            case keyDown:
            case autoKey:
                  theChar = gTheEvent.message & charCodeMask;
                  if (( gTheEvent.modifiers & cmdKey ) != 0)
                  {
                        AdjustMenus();
                        HandleMenuChoice( MenuKey( theChar ) );
                  }
                  break;
            case updateEvt :
                  if    (!IsDAWindow ( gTheEvent.message) )
                  {
                        GetPort ( &oldPort ) ;
                        SetPort ( gTheEvent.message ) ;
                        BeginUpdate ( gTheEvent.message ) ;
                        DrawMyPicture ( gMyPicture, gTheEvent.message );
                        EndUpdate ( gTheEvent.message ) ;
                        SetPort (oldPort );
                  }
                  break;
      }
}
```

```
/*********************************** HandleMouseDown */

HandleMouseDown()
{
        WindowPtr       whichWindow;
        short int       thePart;
        long int        menuChoice, windSize;

        thePart = FindWindow( gTheEvent.where, &whichWindow );
        switch ( thePart )
        {
                case inMenuBar:
                        menuChoice = MenuSelect( gTheEvent.where );
                        HandleMenuChoice( menuChoice );
                        break;
                case inSysWindow:
                        SystemClick( &gTheEvent, whichWindow );
                        break;
                case inDrag:
                        DragWindow( whichWindow, gTheEvent.where, &gDragRect);
                        break;
                case inGoAway:
/*
 *      In previous programs, we've used the goAway box to exit the
 *      application.  This was evil and incorrect!  The goAway box is
 *      a signal to close the window and should behave just as if the
 *      user selected Close from the File menu.  We'll use
 *      DisposeWindow() to close the window and free up the memory used
 *      by the window.
 */
                        DisposeWindow( whichWindow );
                        break;
        }
}


/*********************************** HandleMenuChoice */

HandleMenuChoice( menuChoice )
long int        menuChoice;
{
        int     theMenu;
        int     theItem;

        if ( menuChoice != 0 )
        {
                theMenu = HiWord( menuChoice );
                theItem = LoWord( menuChoice );
                switch ( theMenu )
                {
                        case APPLE_MENU_ID :
                                HandleAppleChoice( theItem );
                                break;
                        case FILE_MENU_ID :
                                HandleFileChoice( theItem );
                                break;
                }
                HiliteMenu( 0 );
        }
}
```

```
/*****************************        HandleAppleChoice        *******/

HandleAppleChoice( theItem )
int     theItem;
{
        Str255          accName;
        int             accNumber;

        switch ( theItem )
        {
                case ABOUT_ITEM :
                        NoteAlert( ABOUT_ALERT, NIL_POINTER );
                        break;
                default :
                        GetItem( gAppleMenu, theItem, accName );
                        accNumber = OpenDeskAcc( accName );
                        break;
        }
}


/*****************************        HandleFileChoice        *******/

HandleFileChoice( theItem )
int     theItem;
{
        WindowPtr       whichWindow;
        switch ( theItem )
        {
                case NEW_ITEM :
                        CreateWindow();
                        break;
                case CLOSE_ITEM :
                        if ( ( whichWindow = FrontWindow() ) != NIL_POINTER )
                                DisposeWindow( whichWindow );
                        break;
                case QUIT_ITEM :
/*  This is the corect time to exit the application!  */
                        gDone = TRUE;
                        break;
        }
}


/********************************** CreateWindow   */

CreateWindow()
{
        WindowPtr       theNewestWindow;

/*
 *      One of the most important features of this application is its
 *      ability to create a large number of windows, limited only
 *      by the memory available on the machine.  We put up an error
 *      message if we can't allocate enough memory to open the window.
 *      Your application may want to put up an Alert, but allow the
 *      user to continue.  The true test of your application us, how
 *      well it performs under stress.
 */
```

```
            if ( ( theNewestWindow = GetNewWindow( BASE_RES_ID, NIL_POINTER,
                                            MOVE_TO_FRONT ) ) == NIL_POINTER )
                    ErrorHandler( NO_WIND );
/*
 *
 *      New windows are created down and to the right by NEW_WINDOW_OFFSET
 *      pixels.  If the new window will be created too close to the edge
 *      of the screen, move back to the upper left...
 */

        if (((screenBits.bounds.right-gNewWindowLeft) < DRAG_THRESHOLD) ||
                ((screenBits.bounds.bottom-gNewWindowTop) < DRAG_THRESHOLD))
        {
                gNewWindowLeft = WINDOW_HOME_LEFT;
                gNewWindowTop = WINDOW_HOME_TOP;
        }

        MoveWindow( theNewestWindow, gNewWindowLeft, gNewWindowTop,
                                            LEAVE_WHERE_IT_IS );
        gNewWindowLeft += NEW_WINDOW_OFFSET;
        gNewWindowTop += NEW_WINDOW_OFFSET;
        ShowWindow( theNewestWindow );
}



/****************************** DrawMyPicture ********/

DrawMyPicture( thePicture, pictureWindow )
PicHandle       thePicture;
WindowPtr       pictureWindow;
{
        Rect    myRect;

        myRect = pictureWindow->portRect;
        CenterPict( thePicture, &myRect );
        SetPort( pictureWindow );
        DrawPicture( thePicture, &myRect );
}



/****************************** CenterPict ********/

CenterPict( thePicture, myRectPtr )
PicHandle       thePicture;
Rect            *myRectPtr;
{
        Rect    windRect, pictureRect;

        windRect = *myRectPtr;
        pictureRect = (**( thePicture )).picFrame;
        myRectPtr->top = (windRect.bottom - windRect.top -
                    (pictureRect.bottom - pictureRect.top))/ 2 +
                    windRect.top;
        myRectPtr->bottom = myRectPtr->top +
                    (pictureRect.bottom - pictureRect.top);
        myRectPtr->left = (windRect.right - windRect.left -
(pictureRect.right - pictureRect.left))/ 2 +
                    windRect.left;
        myRectPtr->right = myRectPtr->left + (pictureRect.right -
                    pictureRect.left);
}
```

```
/****************************** ErrorHandler ********/

ErrorHandler( stringNum )
int     stringNum;
{
        StringHandle    errorStringH;

/*
 *      Load the error message from the resource fork.  Use ParamText()
 *      to make it the first parameter.  This will replace "^0" in a
 *      text item of a dialog box.  If we couldn't get the string, we're
 *      in deep trouble, so we put up the HOPELESSLY_FATAL_ERROR...
 */
        if ( ( errorStringH = GetString( stringNum ) ) == NIL_POINTER )
                ParamText( HOPELESSLY_FATAL_ERROR, NIL_STRING, NIL_STRING,
                                                             NIL_STRING );

        else
        {
                HLock( errorStringH );
                ParamText( *errorStringH, NIL_STRING, NIL_STRING,
                                                NIL_STRING );
                HUnlock( errorStringH );
        }
        StopAlert( ERROR_ALERT_ID, NIL_POINTER );
/*  ExitToShell() returns to the calling program immediately.  */
        ExitToShell();
}
```

Chapter 7, ShowClip.c

```
#define BASE_RES_ID             400
#define NIL_POINTER             0L
#define MOVE_TO_FRONT           -1L
#define REMOVE_ALL_EVENTS       0

#define ERROR_ALERT_ID          BASE_RES_ID
#define NO_WIND                 BASE_RES_ID
#define EMPTY_SCRAP             BASE_RES_ID+1

#define NIL_STRING                      "\p"
#define HOPELESSLY_FATAL_ERROR          "\pGame over, man!"


WindowPtr       gClipWindow;


/****************************** main ********/

main()
{
        ToolBoxInit();
        WindowInit();
        MainLoop();
}
```

```
/****************************** ToolBoxInit *********/

ToolBoxInit()
{
        InitGraf( &thePort );
        InitFonts();
        FlushEvents( everyEvent, REMOVE_ALL_EVENTS );
        InitWindows();
        InitMenus();
        TEInit();
        InitDialogs( NIL_POINTER );
        InitCursor();
}



/****************************** WindowInit *********/

WindowInit()
{
        if ( ( gClipWindow = GetNewWindow( BASE_RES_ID, NIL_POINTER,
                            MOVE_TO_FRONT ) ) == NIL_POINTER )
             ErrorHandler( NO_WIND );
        ShowWindow( gClipWindow );
        SetPort( gClipWindow );
}



/****************************** MainLoop *********/

MainLoop()
{
        Rect            myRect;
        Handle          clipHandle;
        long int        length, offset;

        clipHandle = NewHandle( 0 );
/*
 *      GetScrap() resizes clipHandle to hold the scrap data of the
 *      specified type.  While TEXT and PICT are the primary types, you
 *      can design your own scrap type or use other folks' types, but
 *      if you do, you better know what's at the other end of the handle.
 */
        if ( ( length = GetScrap( clipHandle, 'TEXT', &offset ) ) < 0 )
        {
                if (( length = GetScrap( clipHandle, 'PICT',&offset )) < 0 )
                        ErrorHandler( EMPTY_SCRAP );
                else
                {
                        myRect = gClipWindow->portRect;
                        CenterPict( clipHandle, &myRect );
                        DrawPicture( clipHandle, &myRect );
                }
        }
        else
        {
                HLock( clipHandle );
/*
 *      We used TextBox() to draw the text in the current port (that's
 *      why we used the QuickDraw global thePort), left justified.
 */
```

```
                TextBox( *clipHandle, length, &(thePort->portRect),
                                                        teJustLeft );
                HUnlock( clipHandle );
        }

        while ( !Button() ) ;
}


/******************************* CenterPict *********/

CenterPict( thePicture, myRectPtr )
PicHandle       thePicture;
Rect            *myRectPtr;
{
        Rect    windRect, pictureRect;

        windRect = *myRectPtr;
        pictureRect = (**( thePicture )).picFrame;
        myRectPtr->top = (windRect.bottom - windRect.top -
                        (pictureRect.bottom - pictureRect.top))/ 2 +
                        windRect.top;
        myRectPtr->bottom = myRectPtr->top +
                        (pictureRect.bottom - pictureRect.top);
        myRectPtr->left = (windRect.right - windRect.left -
(pictureRect.right - pictureRect.left))/ 2 +
                        windRect.left;
        myRectPtr->right = myRectPtr->left + (pictureRect.right -
                        pictureRect.left);
}


/******************************* ErrorHandler *********/

ErrorHandler( stringNum )
int     stringNum;
{
        StringHandle    errorStringH;

        if ( ( errorStringH = GetString( stringNum ) ) == NIL_POINTER )
                ParamText( HOPELESSLY_FATAL_ERROR, NIL_STRING, NIL_STRING,
                                                        NIL_STRING );
        else
        {
                HLock( errorStringH );
                ParamText( *errorStringH, NIL_STRING, NIL_STRING,
                                                NIL_STRING );
                HUnlock( errorStringH );
        }
        StopAlert( ERROR_ALERT_ID, NIL_POINTER );
        ExitToShell();
}
```

Chapter 7, PrintPICT.c

```c
/*
 *      Notice the #include of "PrintMgr.h".  LightspeedC will not
 *      automatically include this one for you.
 */
#include "PrintMgr.h"

#define HEADER_SIZE              512
#define NIL_POINTER              0L
#define BASE_RES_ID              400
#define REMOVE_ALL_EVENTS        0

#define ERROR_ALERT_ID           BASE_RES_ID
#define CANT_OPEN_FILE           BASE_RES_ID
#define GET_EOF_ERROR            BASE_RES_ID+1
#define HEADER_TOO_SMALL         BASE_RES_ID+2
#define OUT_OF_MEMORY            BASE_RES_ID+3
#define CANT_READ_HEADER         BASE_RES_ID+4
#define CANT_READ_PICT           BASE_RES_ID+5

#define NIL_PRPORT               NIL_POINTER
#define NIL_IOBUFFER             NIL_POINTER
#define NIL_DEVBUF               NIL_POINTER

#define NIL_STRING               "\p"
#define IGNORED_STRING           NIL_STRING
#define NIL_FILE_FILTER          NIL_POINTER
#define NIL_DIALOG_HOOK          NIL_POINTER
#define DONT_SCALE_OUTPUT        NIL_POINTER
#define HOPELESSLY_FATAL_ERROR   "\pGame over, man!"


Boolean      DoDialogs();
THPrint      gPrintRecordH;


/***************************** main *********/

main()
{
        SFReply       reply;

        ToolBoxInit();
        PrintInit();
        GetFileName( &reply );
        if ( reply.good )   /* The User didn't hit Cancel  */
        {
                if ( DoDialogs() ) /* Again, the User didn't hit Cancel  */
                {
                        PrintPictFile( &reply );
                }
        }
}
```

```
/******************************** ToolBoxInit */

ToolBoxInit()
{
        InitGraf( &thePort );
        InitFonts();
        FlushEvents( everyEvent, REMOVE_ALL_EVENTS );
        InitWindows();
        InitMenus();
        TEInit();
        InitDialogs( NIL_POINTER );
        InitCursor();
}


/****************************** PrintInit ********/

PrintInit()
{
/*
 *      Allocate a new print record, open the chosen printer driver and
 *      load the default values from the printer resource file...
 */
        gPrintRecordH = (THPrint)NewHandle( sizeof( TPrint ) );
        PrOpen();
        PrintDefault( gPrintRecordH );
}


/****************************** GetFileName    ******/

GetFileName( replyPtr )
SFReply        *replyPtr;
{
        Point          myPoint;
        SFTypeList     typeList;
        int            numTypes;

/*
 *      Prompt the user to open a file of type 'PICT', putting the dialog
 *      myPoint.  IGNORED_STRING is a prompt parameter that is ignored
 *      by SFGetFile().
 */
        myPoint.h = 100;
        myPoint.v = 100;
        typeList[ 0 ] = 'PICT';
        numTypes = 1;
        SFGetFile( myPoint, IGNORED_STRING, NIL_FILE_FILTER, numTypes,
                           &typeList, NIL_DIALOG_HOOK, replyPtr );
}


/****************************** DoDialogs      ******/

Boolean DoDialogs()
{
/*
 *      PrStlDialog() puts up the standard Page Setup dialog box,
 *      recording the changes in the print record handled by
 *      gPrintRecordH.  PrJobDialog() puts up the print job dialog box,
 *      letting the user set things like number of copies, page ranges,
```

```
 *      etc., depending on the printer type.  PrJobDialog() will return
 *      TRUE if the user wants to continue with the print (didn't
 *      hit the Cancel button).
 */
        PrStlDialog( gPrintRecordH );
        return( PrJobDialog( gPrintRecordH ) );
}


/*******************************        PrintPictFile *******/

PrintPictFile( replyPtr )
SFReply         *replyPtr;
{
        int             srcFile;
        TPPrPort        printPort;
        TPrStatus       printStatus;
        PicHandle       thePict;
        char            pictHeader[ HEADER_SIZE ];
        long            pictSize, headerSize;

/*
 *      FSOpen() opens the PICT file.  GetEOF() sets pictSize to the
 *      size of the file.  FSRead() attempts to read the 512 byte header
 *      that describes the rest of the file.  Once the header is read,
 *      we're ready to read the rest of the picture in.
 */
        if ( FSOpen( (*replyPtr).fName, (*replyPtr).vRefNum, &srcFile )
                        != noErr )
                ErrorHandler( CANT_OPEN_FILE );

        if ( GetEOF( srcFile, &pictSize ) != noErr )
                ErrorHandler( GET_EOF_ERROR );

        headerSize = HEADER_SIZE;
        if ( FSRead( srcFile, &headerSize, pictHeader ) != noErr )
                ErrorHandler( CANT_READ_HEADER );

/*
 *      Make sure there were at least HEADER_SIZE bytes in the file.  If
 *      not, exit via ErrorHandler().  We won't use the header info in
 *      this program, so we'll adjust pictSize to the size of the picture
 *      without the header.
 */
        if ( ( pictSize -= HEADER_SIZE ) <= 0 )
        {
                ErrorHandler( HEADER_TOO_SMALL );
        }

/*  Allocate enough memory for the picture...  */
        if ( ( thePict = (PicHandle)NewHandle( pictSize ) )
                        == NIL_POINTER )
        {
                ErrorHandler( OUT_OF_MEMORY );
        }

/*  Lock the picHandle, since we'll need to dereference it to a
                Pointer to use in the call to FSRead().  */
        HLock( thePict );

/*  Read in the Picture, and close the file...  */
```

```
        if ( FSRead( srcFile, &pictSize, *thePict ) != noErr )
                ErrorHandler( CANT_READ_PICT );

        FSClose( srcFile );

/*
 *      Open a new print document, and a new page within that doc.
 *      Draw the picture on the print page, close the page, and close
 *      the doc.  Finally, print the print doc.  Wasn't that easy!!!
 */
        printPort = PrOpenDoc( gPrintRecordH, NIL_POINTER, NIL_POINTER );
        PrOpenPage( printPort, DONT_SCALE_OUTPUT );
        DrawPicture( thePict, &(**( thePict )).picFrame );
        PrClosePage( printPort );
        PrCloseDoc( printPort );

        PrPicFile( gPrintRecordH, NIL_PRPORT, NIL_IOBUFFER, NIL_DEVBUF,
                                                        &printStatus );
}


/******************************* ErrorHandler ********/

ErrorHandler( stringNum )
int     stringNum;
{
        StringHandle    errorStringH;

        if ( ( errorStringH = GetString( stringNum ) ) == NIL_POINTER )
                ParamText( HOPELESSLY_FATAL_ERROR, NIL_STRING, NIL_STRING,
                                                        NIL_STRING );
        else
        {
                HLock( errorStringH );
                ParamText( *errorStringH, NIL_STRING, NIL_STRING,
                                                NIL_STRING );
                HUnlock( errorStringH );
        }
        StopAlert( ERROR_ALERT_ID, NIL_POINTER );
        ExitToShell();
}
```

Chapter 7, Pager.c

```
#define BASE_RES_ID             400
#define NIL_POINTER             0L
#define MOVE_TO_FRONT           -1L
#define REMOVE_ALL_EVENTS       0
#define SCROLL_BAR_PIXELS       16
#define DRAG_THRESHOLD          30
#define NIL_ACTION_PROC         NIL_POINTER

#define MIN_SLEEP               0L
#define NIL_MOUSE_REGION        0L

#define WNE_TRAP_NUM            0x60
#define UNIMPL_TRAP_NUM         0x9F
```

```
#define ERROR_ALERT_ID          BASE_RES_ID
#define NO_WIND                 BASE_RES_ID
#define NO_PICTS                BASE_RES_ID+1
#define CANT_LOAD_PICT          BASE_RES_ID+2

#define NIL_STRING              "\p"
#define NIL_TITLE               NIL_STRING
#define VISIBLE                 TRUE
#define START_VALUE             1
#define MIN_VALUE               1
#define NIL_REF_CON             NIL_POINTER
#define HOPELESSLY_FATAL_ERROR  "\pGame over, man!"


WindowPtr       gPictWindow;
ControlHandle   gScrollBarHandle;
Boolean         gDone, gWNEImplemented;
EventRecord     gTheEvent;
Rect            gDragRect;
pascal void     ScrollProc();


/****************************** main ********/

main()
{
        ToolBoxInit();
        WindowInit();
        SetUpDragRect();
        SetUpScrollBar();
        MainLoop();
}


/******************************** ToolBoxInit */

ToolBoxInit()
{
        InitGraf( &thePort );
        InitFonts();
        FlushEvents( everyEvent, REMOVE_ALL_EVENTS );
        InitWindows();
        InitMenus();
        TEInit();
        InitDialogs( NIL_POINTER );
        InitCursor();
}


/****************************** WindowInit ********/

WindowInit()
{
        if ( ( gPictWindow = GetNewWindow( BASE_RES_ID, NIL_POINTER,
                             MOVE_TO_FRONT ) ) == NIL_POINTER )
                ErrorHandler( NO_WIND );
        SelectWindow( gPictWindow );
        ShowWindow( gPictWindow );
        SetPort( gPictWindow );
}
```

```
/***************************** SetUpDragRect *********/

SetUpDragRect()
{
        gDragRect = screenBits.bounds;
        gDragRect.left += DRAG_THRESHOLD;
        gDragRect.right -= DRAG_THRESHOLD;
        gDragRect.bottom -= DRAG_THRESHOLD;
}


/******************************** SetUpScrollBar *******/

SetUpScrollBar()
{
        Rect    vScrollRect;
        int     numPictures;

/*
 *      Find out how many PICT resources are available.  Remember,
 *      resources will be available from any open resource files,
 *      including the System file and the application's resource
 *      fork.
 */
        if ( ( numPictures = CountResources( 'PICT' ) ) <= 0 )
                ErrorHandler( NO_PICTS );
/*  Set up the scroll bar Rect.  Make it fit within the window   */
        vScrollRect = gPictWindow->portRect;
        vScrollRect.top -= 1;
        vScrollRect.bottom +=1;
        vScrollRect.left = vScrollRect.right-SCROLL_BAR_PIXELS+1;
        vScrollRect.right += 1;
/*  Create a new scroll bar with NewControl()   */
        gScrollBarHandle = NewControl( gPictWindow, &vScrollRect,
                        NIL_TITLE, VISIBLE, START_VALUE, MIN_VALUE,
                        numPictures, scrollBarProc, NIL_REF_CON);
}


/****************************** MainLoop *********/

MainLoop()
{
        gDone = FALSE;
        gWNEImplemented = ( NGetTrapAddress( WNE_TRAP_NUM, ToolTrap ) !=
                        NGetTrapAddress( UNIMPL_TRAP_NUM, ToolTrap ) );
        while ( gDone == FALSE )
        {
                HandleEvent();
        }
}


/******************************** HandleEvent   */

HandleEvent()
{
        if ( gWNEImplemented )
                WaitNextEvent( everyEvent, &gTheEvent, MIN_SLEEP,
                                        NIL_MOUSE_REGION );
        else
        {
```

```
                        SystemTask();
                        GetNextEvent( everyEvent, &gTheEvent );
            }

        switch ( gTheEvent.what )
        {
                case mouseDown:
                        HandleMouseDown();
                        break;
                case updateEvt:
/*
 *      DrawControls() draws all the controls currently visible in the
 *      specified window.  We then update the window contents.
 */
                        BeginUpdate( gTheEvent.message );
                        DrawControls( gTheEvent.message );
                        UpdateMyWindow( gTheEvent.message );
                        EndUpdate( gTheEvent.message );
                        break;
        }
}


/************************************** HandleMouseDown */

HandleMouseDown()
{
        WindowPtr        whichWindow;
        short int        thePart;
        Point            thePoint;
        ControlHandle    theControl;

        thePart = FindWindow( gTheEvent.where, &whichWindow );
        switch ( thePart )
        {
                case inSysWindow :
                        SystemClick( &gTheEvent, whichWindow );
                        break;
                case inDrag :
                        DragWindow( whichWindow, gTheEvent.where, &gDragRect);
                        break;
                case inContent:
/*
 *      FindControl() is very similar to FindWindow() in that it
 *      determines which control, if any, thePoint was found in...
 */
                        thePoint = gTheEvent.where;
                        GlobalToLocal( &(thePoint) );
                        thePart = FindControl( thePoint, whichWindow,
                                                     &theControl );
                        if ( theControl == gScrollBarHandle )
                        {
/*
 *      If thePoint was in our control, find out if it was in the thumb.
 *      If it was, call TrackControl() to drag an outline of the thumb up
 *      and down (in this case) the scroll bar.  When the thumb is
 *      released, update the window using the new control value.  If any
 *      other part of the control was used, call TrackControl() with a
 *      pointer to ScrollProc(), since we may need to scroll before
 *      the user releases the mouse button (for example, if they click
 *      in the scroll bar arrows.
 */
```

```
                                if ( thePart == inThumb )
                                {
                                        thePart = TrackControl( theControl,
                                                        thePoint, NIL_ACTION_PROC );
                                        UpdateMyWindow( whichWindow );
                                }
                                else
                                {
                                        thePart = TrackControl( theControl,
                                                        thePoint, &ScrollProc );
                                        UpdateMyWindow( whichWindow );
                                }
                        }
                        break;
                case inGoAway :
                        gDone = TRUE;
                        break;
        }
}


/******************************   ScrollProc      *******/

pascal void ScrollProc(theControl, theCode)
ControlHandle  theControl;
int            theCode;
{
        int     curControlValue, maxControlValue, minControlValue;

/*
 *      Get the min, max, and current values of the scroll bar.  If the
 *      page down or down button areas were pressed, increase the value
 *      of the control.  If the page up or up button areas were pressed,
 *      decrease the value of the control.  Finally, update the control
 *      to this new value with SetCtlValue()...
 */

        maxControlValue = GetCtlMax( theControl );
        curControlValue = GetCtlValue( theControl );
        minControlValue = GetCtlMin( theControl );

        switch ( theCode )
        {
                case inPageDown:
                case inDownButton:
                        if ( curControlValue < maxControlValue )
                        {
                                curControlValue += 1;
                        }
                        break;
                case inPageUp:
                case inUpButton:
                        if ( curControlValue > minControlValue )
                        {
                                curControlValue -= 1;
                        }
        }
        SetCtlValue( theControl, curControlValue );
}
```

```
/*********************************     UpdateMyWindow *******/

UpdateMyWindow( drawingWindow )
WindowPtr        drawingWindow;
{
        PicHandle        currentPicture;
        Rect             drawingClipRect, myRect;
        RgnHandle        tempRgn;

/*
 *      UpdateMyWindow() works in a similar fashion to the DrawPicture()
 *      routine in EventTutor (Chapter 4).  Basically, we temporarily
 *      reset the windows clipping region to not include the area covered
 *      by the scroll bar.  We center the picture, draw it, and reset the
 *      original clip region.
 */
        tempRgn = NewRgn();
        GetClip( tempRgn );

        myRect = drawingWindow->portRect;
        myRect.right -= SCROLL_BAR_PIXELS;
        EraseRect( &myRect );

        currentPicture = (PicHandle)GetIndResource( 'PICT',
                                        GetCtlValue( gScrollBarHandle ) );

        if ( currentPicture == NIL_POINTER )
                ErrorHandler( CANT_LOAD_PICT );

        CenterPict( currentPicture, &myRect );

        drawingClipRect = drawingWindow->portRect;
        drawingClipRect.right -= SCROLL_BAR_PIXELS;
        ClipRect( &drawingClipRect );

        DrawPicture( currentPicture, &myRect );

        SetClip( tempRgn );
        DisposeRgn( tempRgn );
}


/*******************************  CenterPict *********/

CenterPict( thePicture, myRectPtr )
PicHandle       thePicture;
Rect            *myRectPtr;
{
        Rect    windRect, pictureRect;

        windRect = *myRectPtr;
        pictureRect = (**( thePicture )).picFrame;
        myRectPtr->top = (windRect.bottom - windRect.top -
                        (pictureRect.bottom - pictureRect.top))/ 2 +
                        windRect.top;
        myRectPtr->bottom = myRectPtr->top +
                        (pictureRect.bottom - pictureRect.top);
        myRectPtr->left = (windRect.right - windRect.left -
(pictureRect.right - pictureRect.left))/ 2 +
                        windRect.left;
        myRectPtr->right = myRectPtr->left + (pictureRect.right -
                        pictureRect.left);
}
```

```
/******************************* ErrorHandler ********/

ErrorHandler( stringNum )
int     stringNum;
{
        StringHandle   errorStringH;

        if ( ( errorStringH = GetString( stringNum ) ) == NIL_POINTER )
                ParamText( HOPELESSLY_FATAL_ERROR, NIL_STRING, NIL_STRING,
                                                       NIL_STRING );
        else
        {
                HLock( errorStringH );
                ParamText( *errorStringH, NIL_STRING, NIL_STRING,
                                                NIL_STRING );
                HUnlock( errorStringH );
        }
        StopAlert( ERROR_ALERT_ID, NIL_POINTER );
        ExitToShell();
}
```

Chapter 7, Sounder.c

```
#define NIL_POINTER             0L
#define BASE_RES_ID             400
#define REMOVE_ALL_EVENTS       0
#define NIL_SOUND_CHANNEL       NIL_POINTER
#define SYNCHRONOUS             FALSE

#define ERROR_ALERT_ID          BASE_RES_ID
#define CANT_LOAD_BEEP_SND      BASE_RES_ID
#define CANT_LOAD_MONKEY_SND    BASE_RES_ID+1
#define CANT_LOAD_KLANK_SND     BASE_RES_ID+2
#define CANT_LOAD_BOING_SND     BASE_RES_ID+3

#define NIL_STRING              "\p"
#define HOPELESSLY_FATAL_ERROR  "\pGame over, man!"

#define BEEP_SND                1
#define MONKEY_SND              2
#define KLANK_SND               3
#define BOING_SND               4


/******************************* main ********/

main()
{
        ToolBoxInit();
        MakeSound();
}


/******************************* ToolBoxInit */

ToolBoxInit()
{
        InitGraf( &thePort );
        InitFonts();
```

```
                FlushEvents( everyEvent, REMOVE_ALL_EVENTS );
                InitWindows();
                InitMenus();
                TEInit();
                InitDialogs( NIL_POINTER );
                InitCursor();
        }


/****************************** MakeSound *********/

MakeSound()
{
        Handle  soundHandle;

/*
 *      The key to this program is the sound routine SndPlay().  We
 *      are loading the 'snd ' resources normally found in the system
 *      file.  Since the Mac System file didn't always have these 'snd '
 *      resources, older systems may cause the error messages to appear.
 *      Check out the Sound Manager (Chapter 27) in Volume V for more
 *      detail...
 */
        if ( ( soundHandle = GetResource( 'snd ', BEEP_SND ) )
                                == NIL_POINTER )
                ErrorHandler( CANT_LOAD_BEEP_SND );
        SndPlay( NIL_SOUND_CHANNEL, soundHandle, SYNCHRONOUS );

        if ( ( soundHandle = GetResource( 'snd ', MONKEY_SND ) )
                                == NIL_POINTER )
                ErrorHandler( CANT_LOAD_MONKEY_SND );
        SndPlay( NIL_SOUND_CHANNEL, soundHandle, SYNCHRONOUS );

        if ( ( soundHandle = GetResource( 'snd ', KLANK_SND ) )
                                == NIL_POINTER )
                ErrorHandler( CANT_LOAD_KLANK_SND );
        SndPlay( NIL_SOUND_CHANNEL, soundHandle, SYNCHRONOUS );

        if ( ( soundHandle = GetResource( 'snd ', BOING_SND ) )
                                == NIL_POINTER )
                ErrorHandler( CANT_LOAD_BOING_SND );
        SndPlay( NIL_SOUND_CHANNEL, soundHandle, SYNCHRONOUS );
}


/****************************** ErrorHandler *********/

ErrorHandler( stringNum )
int     stringNum;
{
        StringHandle   errorStringH;

        if ( ( errorStringH = GetString( stringNum ) ) == NIL_POINTER )
                ParamText( HOPELESSLY_FATAL_ERROR, NIL_STRING, NIL_STRING,
                                                        NIL_STRING );
        else
        {
                HLock( errorStringH );
                ParamText( *errorStringH, NIL_STRING, NIL_STRING,
                                                NIL_STRING );
                HUnlock( errorStringH );
        }
        StopAlert( ERROR_ALERT_ID, NIL_POINTER );
        ExitToShell();
}
```

Appendix C

THINK C Command Summary

This appendix summarizes some of the basic operations of THINK C, Version 3.0

THINK C Is a simple but powerful programming environment. This appendix provides an overview of its operations.

The Project Menu

THINK C keeps track of all of the library files and code files that you are using in a **Project** file. To create a project, select **New Project** from the Project menu, and type in a project name. (Create a folder for your project first to keep your files together.) To open an existing project, use **Open Project**. If you have a project open, and you want to look at another project, use **Close Project**. If you choose **Close & Compact**, the project file will be compressed. This makes it smaller, but means that it takes longer to open. The **Set Project Type . . .** menu item brings up a dialog box, which allows you to define the kind of project that you want to have (Figure C.1). There are four types of projects: applications, desk accessories, device drivers and code resources.

APPLICATIONS

Normally, the first radio button should be clicked on, as standalone applications are usually what you'll be building in THINK C. You can key in the **File Type** and **Creator** for your application. The default for the File Type is APPL: your applications should use this. Other types of projects may have other File Types. In the *Primer,* we have been selecting the Creator name using ResEdit. You can do it here instead.

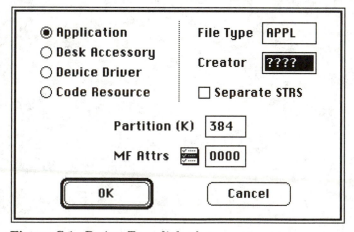

Figure C.1 Project Type dialog box.

482

The Project Type dialog box also lets you select the level of MultiFinder friendliness that you intend your application to have (Figure C.2).

The pop-up menu allows you to set three flags. **MultiFinder Aware** means that your application will conform to Apple's MultiFinder guidelines. This means that your application will respond properly to suspend/resume events. **Background Null Events** means that your program will get null events when it is running in the background, and **Suspend and Resume Events** means that your program will get suspend/resume events as well as the normal activate/deactivate events. The MultiFinder flags may also be keyed in hex in the field to the right.

> Early versions of THINK C 3.0 had a bug where the Suspend and Resume Events and the MultiFinder Aware flags were swapped. To check for this problem, examine the SIZE resource in your THINK C-created application. All MultiFinder options are currently stored in the SIZE resource, and may be easily changed in ResEdit.

In the Partition field, you can key in the preferred amounts of RAM that your application will need in MultiFinder. If the **Separate STRS** check box is checked, THINK C will place string literals and floating point constants in a STR# resource instead of a DATA resource. Do this if you think you'll have more than 32K worth of string literals or floating point constants.

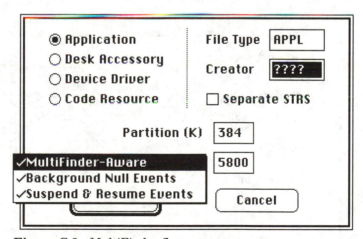

Figure C.2 MultiFinder flags pop up menu.

DESK ACCESSORIES AND DEVICE DRIVERS

If your project is a desk accessory, or a device driver (like a printer driver), your dialog box is somewhat different (Figure C.3).

Both desk accessories and device drivers have the same fields; desk accessories have a default **File Type** and **Creator** of DFIL and DMOV. The **Multi-Segment** check box allows you to have up to 31 segments on your device driver or desk accessory.

The **Name** field contains the name of the desk accessory or device driver resource. THINK C will add a null byte to the beginning of your desk accessory (a convention). It will also place a period before the device driver name if you don't put one there.

The **Type** of resource created is defaulted to DRVR for both kinds of projects. The ID of the resource for desk accessories is defaulted to 12. The **Font D/A Mover** will handle ID number conflicts, so this number need not be changed.

CODE RESOURCE

THINK C allows you to build CODE resources. This comes in really handy for building INITs, WDEFs and cdevs. The code resource project type has the same basic fields as the desk accessories. If the **Custom Header** check box is unchecked, THINK C builds a 16-byte header for your CODE resource that places the address of your resource into register AO and branches to your main() function. The Attrs field allows you to select the standard resource attributes for your code resource. You can also use ResEdit to set these flags.

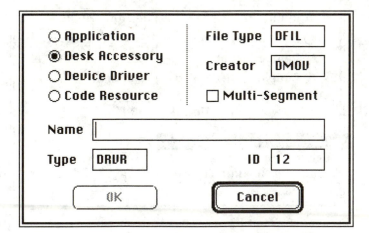

Figure C.3   Desk Accessories/Device Drivers dialog box.

MORE ON THE PROJECT MENU

The next few menu items on the Project menu are **Remove Objects**, **Bring up to Date** and **Check Link**.

Remove Objects will remove object code for all files in your project. Be sure to do this for all your projects built with older versions of THINK C. By removing all the objects from a project, you are dramatically reducing the size of the project (until you put the objects back in) and you are also ensuring that your project uses the current version of all your link libraries (like MacTraps). **Bring Up to Date** compiles source code and loads library files that haven't been compiled or loaded yet. **Check Link** checks the link-worthiness of your project without running it.

Build Library takes the current project and saves it as a binary library, so it can be used by other projects. **Build Application . . .** (or Desk Accessory, Device Driver, or Code Resource) saves the project as a standalone application (or desk accessory, device driver, or `CODE` resource), depending on the project type chosen.

If you set the **Use Debugger** flag, the debugger will automatically run when you run your application (in MultiFinder). The final menu item, **Run**, runs your application. If you run your application under MultiFinder, THINK C runs your application as a separate entity.

The File Menu

Once you've created your project, you're ready to type in your source code. THINK C has a number of formatting facilities that should save you some time. Most of the options in the **File** menu are self-explanatory (Figure C.4).

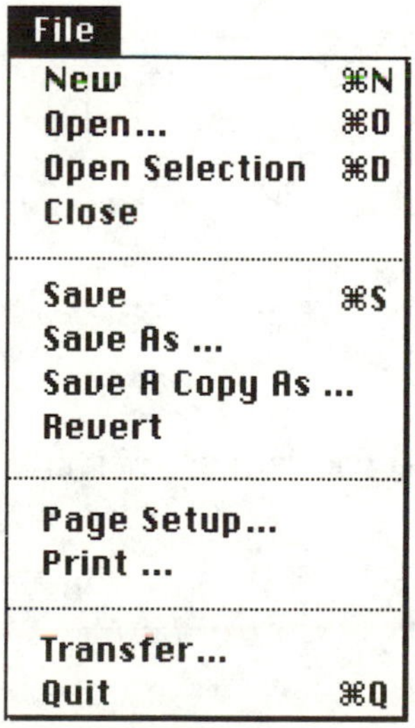

```
File
New              ⌘N
Open...           ⌘O
Open Selection    ⌘D
Close
.................................
Save              ⌘S
Save As ...
Save A Copy As ...
Revert
.................................
Page Setup...
Print ...
.................................
Transfer...
Quit              ⌘Q
```

Figure C.4   THINK C's File menu.

To create a new file, select **New**. To open an existing file, choose **Open**. You can also open a file by double-clicking its name in the Project window. If a file name is highlighted in an edit window, **Open Selection** will open the file. **Close** will close your file; you are prompted to save or discard your changes if any have been made. **Save** will save the current file you're working on. **Save As** will save your current file under a new name and change the name in the Project window. **Save A Copy As** will save your current file under a different name and use the original file. **Revert** will return the current file to the saved version of that file. **Print Setup** puts up the standard Print Setup dialog box to choose printing options. **Print** prints your current file with the name, date, time and page number at the top. **Transfer** allows you to go directly to another program without going back to the Finder. **Quit** allows you to leave THINK C; you are prompted to save changes in your current files.

The Edit Menu

The **Edit** Menu provides options for working on your current file (Figure C.5).

The **Undo**, **Cut**, **Copy**, **Paste**, **Clear**, and **Select All** menu items are the standard text editing options available on most Macintosh applications. **Set Tabs & Font . . .** (Figure C.6) puts up a dialog box that allows you to select the tab size (usually, one tab every four character positions), as well as the font type and size.

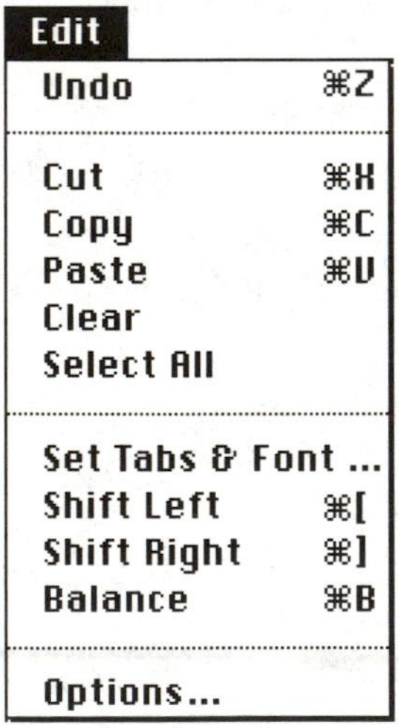

Figure C.5   THINK C's Edit menu.

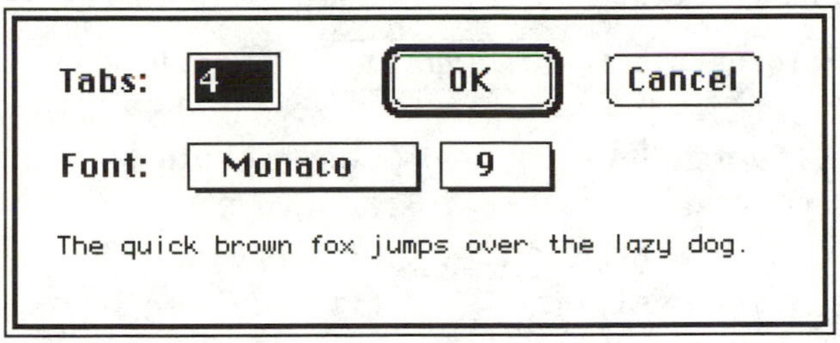

Figure C.6   Tabs & Font dialog box.

Shift Left and **Shift Right** will move selected text one tab to the right or left. **Balance** will highlight the code balanced by the nearest (), [], or {} before and after the cursor position.

The **Options . . .** menu item (Figure C.7) brings up a dialog box that allows you to set the default options for five different areas of THINK C.

Search Options has three options to set. These all affect the defaults used by options under the **Search** menu. Selecting the **Match Words** check box lets you search for whole words instead of parts of words. **Wrap Around** means that the entire file will be searched, not just from the cursor to the end of the file. **Ignore Case** lets you ignore upper and lower case in searching.

Preferences lets you set four options (Figure C.8). The **Confirm Auto-Make** check box, when checked, always brings up the `Bring Project up to Date?` dialog box when the project is being compiled. If it is not checked, THINK C will automatically update the project. When not checked, **Confirm Saves** always saves changes to the current document without asking. **Always Compact** always saves

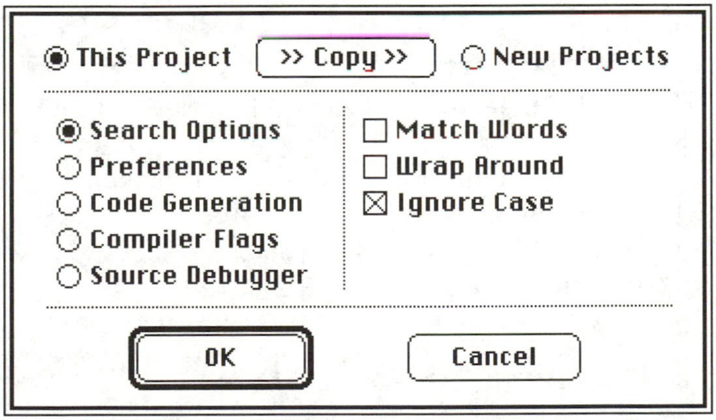

Figure C.7   Search options.

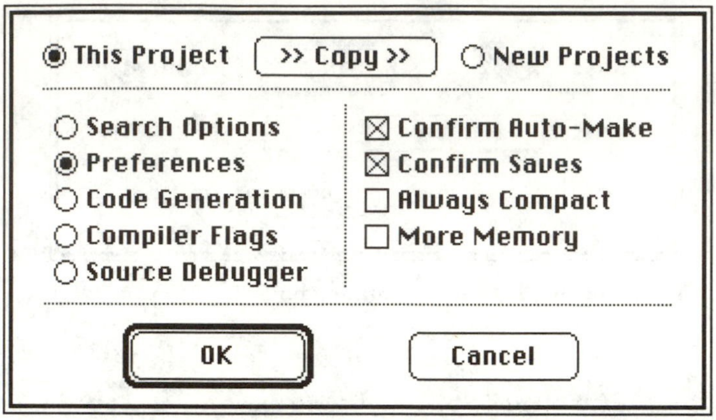

Figure C.8   Preferences.

the current project using a compression algorithm. When checked, **More Memory** will cause THINK C to try to work around a Mac that keeps running out of memory.

Code Generation (Figure C.9) allows you to set five options. The Macsbug Symbols should be set if you plan to use a symbolic debugger like MacsBug or TMON. When **Profile** is checked, THINK C collects timing statistics about your functions. If the **68020** flag is set, THINK C will use the 020 instruction set, when the **68881** flag is set, floating point coprocessor code will be generated as well. If the **<MacHeaders>** option is set, THINK C automatically uses the MacHeaders file for every project.

Compiler Flags (Figure C.10) has two options. If **Check Pointer Types** is selected, THINK C generates compiler errors for pointer types that don't match. The **Require Prototypes** flag makes THINK C strict about type checking with respect to function calls and their arguments.

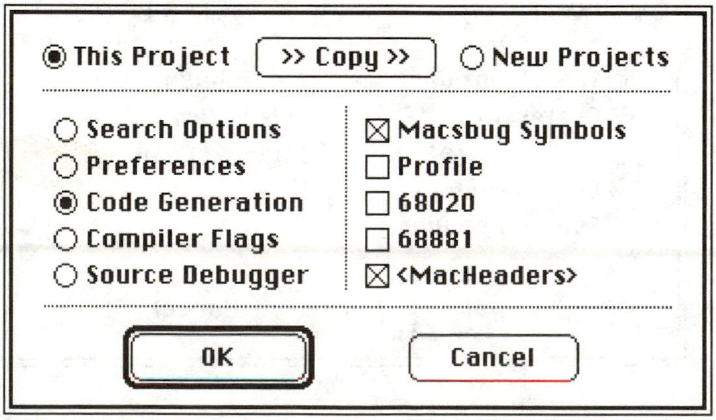

Figure C.9   Code generation.

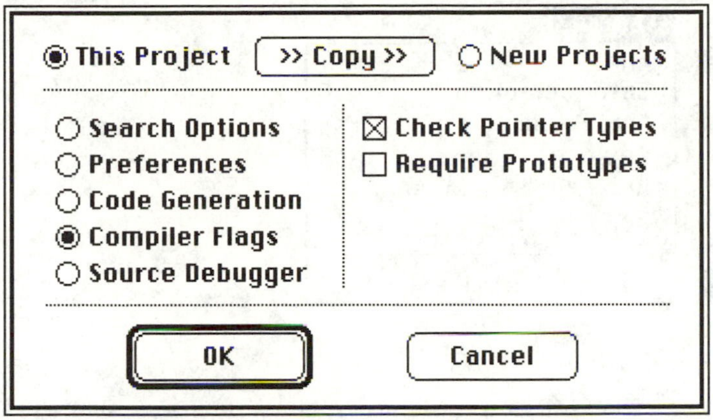

Figure C.10 Compiler flags.

Source Debugger (Figure C.11) has three options. **Use Debugger** starts your project off with the Use Debugger item checked under the Project menu. If **Use 2nd Screen** is checked, THINK C will place the debugger windows on a second monitor if the Mac being used is equipped with one. If **Update Windows** is set, the Debugger will try to update your windows for you when execution of the code is stopped. (This option really eats up memory, so you may want to increase the debugger's MultiFinder partition.)

The Search Menu

The **Search** menu (Figure C.12) has a number of functions that allow you to find and change text in your files.

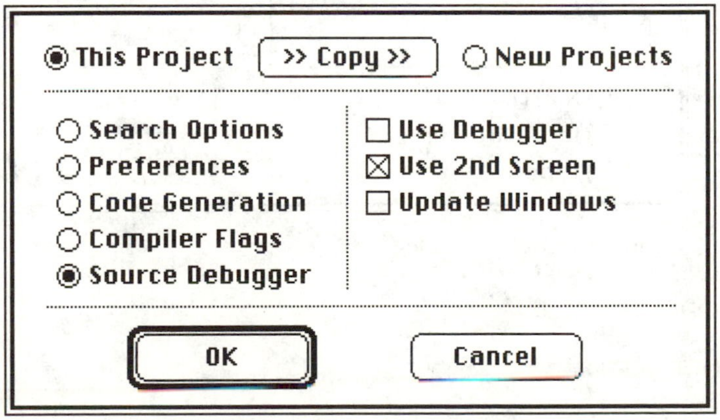

Figure C.11 Source debugger.

Figure C.12 Search menu.

The Find . . . menu item puts up a dialog box, as shown in Figure C.13. The Find dialog box allows you to enter in the string to search for and, optionally, the string to replace it with. The three search options, **Match Words**, **Wrap Around**, and **Ignore Case** were described in the discussion of Search Options. If **Grep** is checked, a utility similar to the Grep utility in UNIX is run. If **Multi-File Search** is checked, a dialog box is put up to allow you to select which files to search.

Enter Selection will take highlighted code and place it in the Search for field in the Find dialog box. **Find Again** searches for the next occurrence of the Search For: text without bringing up the dialog box again. **Replace** replaces the highlighted string; if there is no string in the Replace With field, the highlighted text is deleted. **Replace and Find Again** will replace the highlighted string in the code and highlights the next occurrence of the Search For: string. **Replace All** replaces all occurrences of the sought string. **Find In Next File** is used in conjunction with the **Multi-File Search** check box; it puts up a dialog box so the next files to search may be selected.

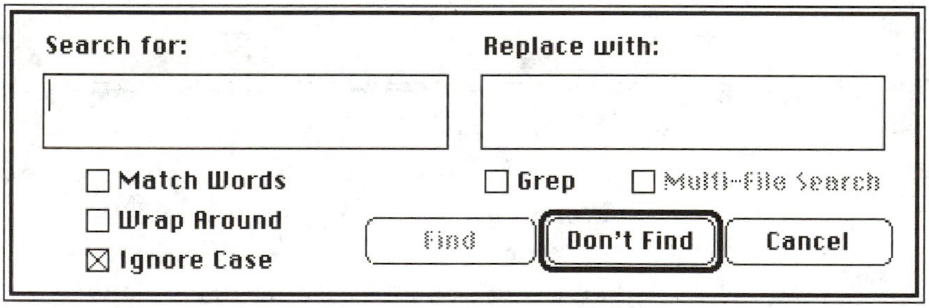

Figure C.13 Find dialog box.

The Source Menu

The **Source menu** (Figure C.14) deals with the files currently in the project. **Add** and **Remove** will add or remove the currently selected file in the Project window. If Add is dimmed, the current window has not been saved, or does not have the .c suffix. **Get Info** provides a dialog that displays information about the current file, such as number of lines of code and data and string resources used. Other files may be examined by clicking on the next or previous buttons. **Check Syntax** compiles a file to check syntax without adding it to the project. **Precompile . . .** creates a precompiled header (like <MacHeaders>) for your project. It may not have code or data definitions. **Debug** sends the currently edited file to the Source window of the debugger. **Compile** will compile the currently selected file and place it in the project window. **Load Library** will take the currently edited library and add it to the current project. **Add . . .** displays a dialog box that allows you to add other files into the project. **Make . . .** puts up a dialog box listing the current files in the project. You can then compile any file or load libraries directly instead of having THINK C figure it out for you.

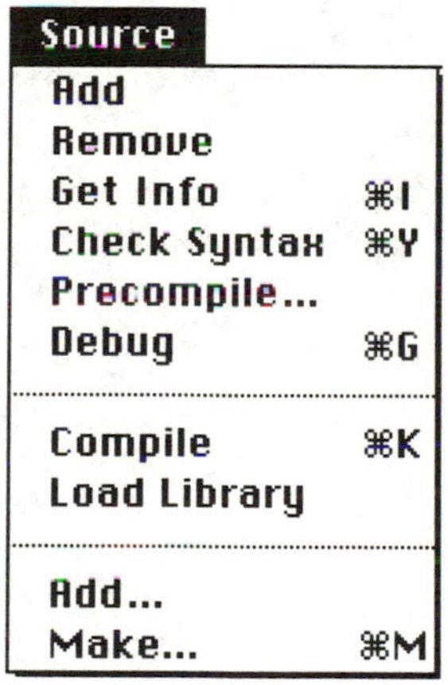

```
┌─────────────────────┐
│ Source              │
├─────────────────────┤
│ Add                 │
│ Remove              │
│ Get Info        ⌘I  │
│ Check Syntax    ⌘Y  │
│ Precompile...       │
│ Debug           ⌘G  │
│ ................... │
│ Compile         ⌘K  │
│ Load Library        │
│ ................... │
│ Add...              │
│ Make...         ⌘M  │
└─────────────────────┘
```

Figure C.14   THINK C's Source menu.

The Windows Menu

The Windows menu (Figure C.15) controls the windows of THINK C. **Clean Up** resizes and stacks currently opened windows. **Zoom** resizes the current window to fill the screen; if selected again, the window returns to the previous size. **Full Titles** puts the full path of each file on the top of its window. **Close All** closes all edit windows. **Save All** saves all edit windows. **Project window** brings the Project window to the front. The menu items will contain the project title (e.g., `Hello proj`). Following the Project windows is a list of all currently opened windows in the project. Selecting a window on the list will bring it to the front.

This appendix is meant to provide an overview to THINK C only. For detailed information about THINK C, read Think's THINK C *User's Manual* and *Standard Libraries Reference*.

Windows	
Clean Up	
Zoom	⌘/
Full Titles	
Close All	
Save All	
Sample	⌘0
Untitled	⌘1

Figure C.15   THINK C's Windows menu.

Appendix D

The Debugger Command Summary

This appendix summarizes some of the basic operations of the THINK C source-level code debugger. The descriptions are specific to Version 3.0 of THINK C.

THINKC NOW has a debugger that provides a powerful way to test applications. The Debugger runs exclusively under MultiFinder and needs at least two megabytes to work properly.

When an application is run inside THINK C, and the **Use Debugger** flag has been set, the windows shown in Figure D.1 are displayed. Each of the two windows that are part of the Debugger has a specific function. First, take a look at the Source window.

The Source Window of the Debugger

The **Source window** displays the code of the file that is currently being run. In Figure D.1, the arrow to the left of the code indicates where the Debugger has stopped. At this point, you can **Step** to the next line, step **In** to the function at which the arrow points, or step **Out** of the function to the next line of the calling function. If you click on **Go**, the program will run until it hits a breakpoint or until the **Stop** button is clicked on. The **Trace** button is like the Step button, except that it will step into the current function if the code is available for it; Step stays at the same level of your program.

To set up a breakpoint, just click on the diamond to the left of the statement at which you want to stop, then click **Go** (Figure D.2). The program will halt execution when it reaches the breakpoint. To clear a breakpoint, click on the diamond again. To set up a temporary breakpoint, hold down the command or option key when you click on the diamond of the statement at which you want to stop. When you reach the breakpoint and then click Go, the breakpoint is cleared.

If you want to examine a file other than the one in the Source window, select the Project window to bring it to the front, choose the file you want to debug, and select Debug from the Source menu of THINK C. The file will then appear in the Source window. The field in the bottom left-hand corner of the Source window displays the name of the current file.

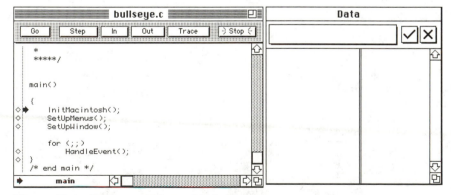

Figure D.1 Bullseye project with the Debugger running.

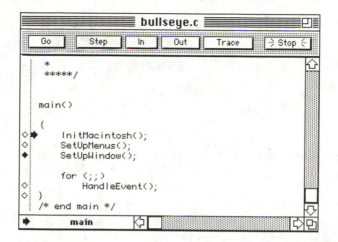

FigureD.2 Breakpoint selected.

The button actions can also be selected from the Debug menu of the Debugger. The debug menu also has some other debugging actions. **Go Until Here** is the same as setting a temporary breakpoint. If you click on a line of source code and select Go Until Here, the Debugger will run until that line of code is reached. **Skip To Here** allows you to skip execution of portions of your code. Be careful that whatever you are testing doesn't depend on the code you are skipping.

You can step or trace continuously through your program if you click on these buttons with either the command or the option key depressed. To cancel the action, click on the Stop button.

Monitor invokes the currently installed monitor (low-level debuggers like Macsbug or TMON). **ExitToShell** halts execution of your program and quits to THINK C.

If you want to get information about the values of your variables as your code executes, use the Debugger's Data window.

The Data Window of The Debugger

The **Data window** lets you find out the values of your variables as the program runs. To use it, type in a C expression in the data entry area just under the title bar, and the value of the expression will be displayed in the right-hand column. For example, Figure D.3 shows the value of a string variable. As you can see, the string variable was displayed in hex format. To view the data correctly, click on the variable of interest in the left column, pull down the Data menu, and select **Pascal String**. The data are now displayed as a Pascal string. Figure D.4 lists the possible data format types with examples.

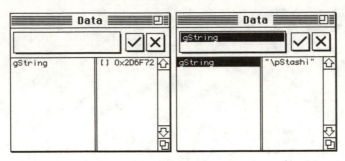

Figure D.3 Data window with expression.

Decimal	7569994, -5000
Hexadecimal	0xB11E1520
Character	'a', 'Chuck'
Pointer	0x7A7000
Address	[] 0x09FE44, struct 0x08FC14
C string	"GoodbyeCruel\nWorld\33"
Pascal string	"\pGoodbyeCruel\nWorld\33"
Floating Point	90983.611

Figure D.4 Data formats in the Debugger.

In the **Data** menu, you can also **Show Context**, which will display the context for the expression selected in the Data window in the Source window. If you select a line in the Source window, you can then **Set Context** to change the context to the line highlighted in the Source window. If you want to make sure that an expression doesn't change its value, select **Lock** in the Data menu with the desired variable highlighted (Figure D.6).

This appendix is meant to provide an overview of the Debugger. For more detailed information, read Symantec's *THINK C User's Manual* and *Standard Libraries Reference*.

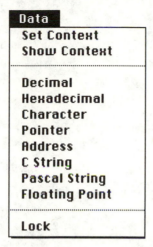

Figure D.5   Data menu in the Debugger.

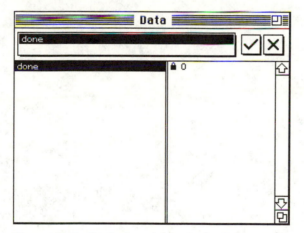

Figure D.6   Locked variables in the Debugger.

Appendix E

Debugging Techniques

One of the most frustrating experiences in programming is running up against a really tough bug. In this appendix, we'll discuss some techniques for hunting down bugs, and some others for avoiding them in the first place.

Compilation Errors

THE FIRST BUGS you're likely to encounter will pop up during compilation, when you've typed in your code and select Run from the Project menu. When THINK C asks you if you'd like to rebuild your project, click Yes.

THINK C is now compiling your code. You'll see a dialog box similar to the one in Figure E.1:

TYPING MISTAKES

The first sign that something's amiss is the appearance of a bug alert. The one in Figure E.2 crops up a lot and seems frustratingly uninformative. Syntax errors are usually indicative of a misspelled keyword or bad programming grammar. For example, if you misspell #define or type something like:

```
EventRecord = theEvent;
```

instead of

```
EventRecord      theEvent;
```

you'll end up with a syntax error. This happens frequently. Carefully review the line of code with the blinking cursor in the left-hand column. If you still can't find the bug, check the previous line. Is there a semicolon at the end of the line? Is there supposed to be one?

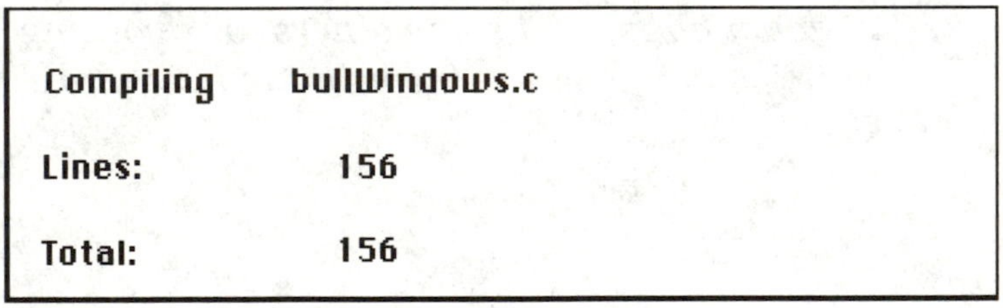

```
Compiling      bullWindows.c

Lines:            156

Total:            156
```

Figure E.1   Compiling dialog box.

Figure E.2   Syntax Error dialog box.

Missing semicolons can cause several different types of bugs. For example, in Chapter 4's `EventTutor.c`, we took the semicolon away from the end of three different lines and got three different errors—an `invalid declaration`, a `syntax error`, and finally, a `missing ;`. C compilers are very tricky.

Another popular error meassage is the `xxx has not been declared` alert. Sometimes this is the result of a missing declaration, but often it's the result of a misspelled variable name. Remember, in C, upper and lower case are crucially different when it comes to identifiers. The variables `myPicture` and `MyPicture` are completely different. Check your case.

Another indicator of a typing error is the `illegal token` error message. Usually, this means you have a character in your code that shouldn't be there. Here's an example:

```
myVar $ = 27;
```

In this case, the $ was the illegal token. If you try repeatedly but still can't find the illegal token, try deleting and retyping the line in question. If that doesn't work, check the previous line.

INDIRECT COMPILER ERRORS

An example of a indirect compiler error is caused by a missing `#include` file. For example, the printing program presented in Chapter 7 depended on the `#include` file `PrintMgr.h`. This file is not one of the standard `#include`s automatically included by THINK C. If you leave out this `#include`, you get an `invalid declaration` error, and the cursor moves to the line:

```
THPrint    printRecordH;
```

It turns out that `THPrint` is a special type declared in `PrintMgr.h`. The real trick is to figure out which file to `#include`. Chapter 7 lists all the `#include`s not automatically included by THINK C. You'll find these files in the `Mac #includes` folder on your THINK C disk. The files are well named, so picking a likely candidate shouldn't be too hard. Use the THINK C Find facility to search for the missing type or global variable.

Another indirect compiler error stems from not closing your comment blocks. For example:

```
/* my 1st comment *
int i;
/* my 2nd comment */
i = 10;
```

This code will lead to an `'i' was not declared` error. The declaration of i was swallowed up by the `my 1st comment` comment block, which was never closed.

LINKER ERRORS

If you call a procedure or function in your program that was never declared, you'll get a `link failed` error and a `FailedLinks` window will appear, listing the routines that were called but that the linker couldn't locate. This error is often the result of a misspelled procedure name. For example:

```
sysBeep( 20 );
```

The compiler will accept this line because it will assume that you've written a routine called sysBeep( ) that will be provided at link time.

Improving Your Debugging Technique

Once your program compiles, your next step is to get the bugs out. One of the best ways to debug a Mac program is to use a debugger like the THINK C Debugger described in Appendix D, or the TMON debugger from ICOM Simulations. Debuggers are real life-savers.

No matter which debugging tool you use, there are some things you can do to improve your debugging technique.

BEING A GOOD DETECTIVE

When your program crashes or exhibits some unusual behavior, you have to to be a detective. Did the system error occur just before your dialog box was scheduled to appear? Did those wavy lines start appearing immediately after you clicked on the OK button?

The key to being a good detective is having a good surveillance technique. Try to establish a definite pattern in your program's misbehavior. Can you pinpoint exactly where in your code things started to go awry? These clues will help you home in on the offending code.

If you can't tell by observation exactly when things went sour, don't give up. You can always use the binary method of bug control.

THE BINARY METHOD

The key to the binary method lies in establishing good boundary conditions for the bug. First, you'll need to establish a **lower limit**, a place in your code at which you feel fairly certain the bug has not yet occurred. You'd like the lower limit to be as close to the actual bug as possible, but make sure the bug has not yet happened.

Next, establish an **upper limit** in your code, a point by which you're certain the bug has occurred (because the system has crashed, or the screen has turned green, or whatever).

To use the binary method, split the difference between the upper and lower limits. If the bug still has not occurred, split the difference again. Now, if the bug has occurred, you have a new upper limit. By repeating this procedure, you'll eventually locate the exact line of source code where the bug occurs.

There are several different ways to split the difference between two lines of source code. If you're using a debugger, you can set a breakpoint halfway between the lines of code representing the upper and lower limits. Did you hit the breakpoint without encountering the bug? If so, set a new breakpoint, halfway between this one and the upper limit.

If you don't have a debugger, use a ROM call like `SysBeep()` to give you a clue. Did you hear the beep before the bug occurred? If so, put a new `SysBeep()` halfway between the old one and the upper limit. The nice thing about using `SysBeep()` is that it is reasonably nonintrusive, unlike putting up a new window and drawing some debugging information in it, which tends to interfere with your program's basic algorithm.

Recommended Reading

In closing, we'd like to recommend some good reading material: your THINK C *User's Manual!* The *User's Manual* is a treasure trove of valuable tips for writing and debugging Mac programs. The more you know about the Macintosh and the THINK C development environment, the better you'll be at debugging your programs.

Appendix F

Building Hypercard XCMDs

The introduction of HyperCard in August 1987 caused quite a stir in the Macintosh world. A complete programming environment in its own right, HyperCard became even richer with the addition of XCMDs and XFCNs. Now you can access the raw power of THINK C from inside HyperCard.

HyperCard ComesWith its own powerful programming language: **HyperTalk**. The designers of HyperTalk thoughtfully provided a mechanism for adding extensions to the HyperTalk command set. These extensions are code resources of type **XCMD** and **XFCN**.

XCMDs (X-Commands) take a parameter block as input from HyperCard, perform some calculations, put the results back into the parameter block, and return to the calling script. **XFCN**s (X-functions) take the same parameter block as input, perform the same types of calculations, but return the results as a C or Pascal function would.

We've written an XCMD (called XChooser) that puts the Chooser name in the parameter block and returns to HyperCard. A typical call of XChooser looks like this:

```
XChooser
Put the result into card field 1
```

We also created an XFCN (called FChooser) that performs the same service. A typical call of FChooser looks like this:

```
Put FChooser() into card field 1
```

The source code for FChooser and XChooser is identical. One is saved as an XFCN and the other as an XCMD. In addition to the XFCN.c and XCMD.c files, you'll also need a set of HyperCard service routines and the XCMD type definition include file. The service routines and the #include file were kindly provided by the THINK C folks. We've included all the source code (as well as a HyperCard test stack and a resource mover stack) on the *Mac Primer* source code disk (use the coupon on the last page). All the source code is also presented in this Appendix, however, so the more intrepid among you can type it right in.

There are 28 HyperCard service routines, each in its own source code file. You don't need to type in all 28 at once. In the example, you'll need only the routine in the file PasToZero.c. You may want to type that one in now. In addition, put the #include file, HyperXCmd.h, in the same folder as the other Mac #includes. All of the source code can be found later in this appendix.

The XChooser XCMD

Create a new project. Add MacTraps and the file PasToZero.c. Next, type in this source code, save it as XCMD.c, and add it to the project:

```
#include "HyperXCmd.h"

pascal void main(XCmdBlockPtr);

/****************************** main ********/

pascal void main( paramPtr )
XCmdBlockPtr    paramPtr;
{
        StringHandle   chooserStr255H;

        chooserStr255H = GetString( -16096 );
        HLock( chooserStr255H );
        paramPtr->returnValue = PasToZero( paramPtr, *chooserStr255H );
        HUnlock( chooserStr255H );
}
```

Start by loading the Chooser name from resource STR with ID = -16096. Lock the handle and pass it, along with the parameter block you receive from HyperCard, to PasToZero, which converts the Chooser name from a Pascal-based string to a zero-terminated string. Next, place the zero-terminated version of the Chooser name in the returnValue field of the parameter block, and return.

Building the XCMD

Before compiling XChooser, you must first tell LightspeedC that you're building an XCMD. Pull down the Project menu and select Set Project Type... When the dialog box appears, set the fields as they appear in Figure F.1:

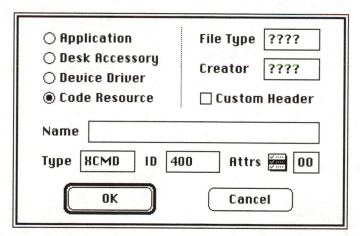

Figure F.1 Set Project Type dialog box.

Click the OK button. Pull down the Project menu and select Build Code
Resource... The standard file dialog will appear, asking you to name your new
resource file. Call it XChooser.

Copying the XCMD Into a Stack

Once XChooser is built, use ResEdit to copy it into a stack. You can also copy the
XCMD directly into HyperCard, but work with a copy to stay on the safe side. Once
the XCMD is copied, you'll be able to access it from within any script.

To create an XFCN, change XCMD to XFCN in the Set Project Type . . . dialog box.

HyperXCmd.h

```
/*
        HyperXCmd.h Definitions for calling all standard
        HyperCard callback routines from C.
        ©Apple Computer, Inc. 1987
        All Rights Reserved.

        See CFlash.C for an example of how to include this module in your
        C program.
*/

#include <MacTypes.h>

typedef struct XCmdBlock {
        short  paramCount;
  Handle params[16];
  Handle returnValue;
  Boolean    passFlag;

  void (*entryPoint)();  /* to call back to HyperCard */
  short        request;
  short        result;
  long inArgs[8];
  long outArgs[4];
  } XCmdBlock, *XCmdBlockPtr;

typedef unsigned char Str31[32];
/*
typedef struct Str31 {
        char   guts[32];
        } Str31, *Str31Ptr;
*/

enum {
        xresSucc = 0,
        xresFail,
        xresNotImp
};
```

```
/* request codes */
enum {
        xreqSendCardMessage = 1,
        xreqEvalExpr,
        xreqStringLength,
        xreqStringMatch,
        xreqSendHCMessage,
        xreqZeroBytes,
        xreqPasToZero,
        xreqZeroToPas,
        xreqStrToLong,
        xreqStrToNum,
        xreqStrToBool,
        xreqStrToExt,
        xreqLongToStr,
        xreqNumToStr,
        xreqNumToHex,
        xreqBoolToStr,
        xreqExtToStr,
        xreqGetGlobal,
        xreqSetGlobal,
        xreqGetFieldByName,
        xreqGetFieldByNum,
        xreqGetFieldByID,
        xreqSetFieldByName,
        xreqSetFieldByNum,
        xreqSetFieldByID,
        xreqStringEqual,
        xreqReturnToPas,
        xreqScanToReturn,
        xreqScanToZero = 39   /* was suppose to be 29! Oops! */
};


/* Forward definitions of glue routines. Main program
        must include XCmdGlue.inc.c. See XCmdGlue.inc.c for
        documentation of each routine. */

typedef void (*MyProcPtr) ();

pascal void        SendCardMessage(XCmdBlockPtr, StringPtr msg);
pascal Handle  EvalExpr(XCmdBlockPtr, StringPtr expr);
pascal long        StringLength(XCmdBlockPtr, StringPtr strPtr);
pascal Ptr         StringMatch(XCmdBlockPtr, StringPtr pattern, Ptr target);
pascal void        ZeroBytes(XCmdBlockPtr ,Ptr   dstPtr, long longCount);
pascal Handle  PasToZero(XCmdBlockPtr, StringPtr pasStr);
pascal void        ZeroToPas(XCmdBlockPtr, unsigned char *zeroStr, StringPtr
pasStr);
pascal long        StrToLong(XCmdBlockPtr, unsigned char * strPtr);
pascal long        StrToNum(XCmdBlockPtr, unsigned char *str);
pascal Boolean StrToBool(XCmdBlockPtr,unsigned char *str);
pascal void        StrToExt(XCmdBlockPtr,unsigned char *str, double *myext);
pascal void        LongToStr(XCmdBlockPtr, long posNum, unsigned char *mystr);
pascal void        NumToStr(XCmdBlockPtr, long num, unsigned char *mystr);
pascal void        NumToHex(XCmdBlockPtr, long num, short nDigits, unsigned char
*mystr);
pascal void        BoolToStr(XCmdBlockPtr, Boolean bool, unsigned char *mystr);
pascal void        ExtToStr(XCmdBlockPtr, double *myext, unsigned char *mystr);
pascal Handle  GetGlobal(XCmdBlockPtr, StringPtr globName);
```

```
pascal void          SetGlobal(XCmdBlockPtr, StringPtr globName, Handle globValue);
pascal Handle  GetFieldByName(XCmdBlockPtr, Boolean cardFieldFlag, StringPtr
fieldName);
pascal Handle  GetFieldByNum(XCmdBlockPtr, Boolean cardFieldFlag, short fieldNum);
pascal Handle  GetFieldByID(XCmdBlockPtr,Boolean cardFieldFlag, short fieldID);
pascal void          SetFieldByName(XCmdBlockPtr, Boolean cardFieldFlag, StringPtr
fieldName, Handle fieldVal);
pascal void          SetFieldByNum(XCmdBlockPtr, Boolean cardFieldFlag, short
fieldNum,Handle fieldVal);
pascal void          SetFieldByID(XCmdBlockPtr, Boolean cardFieldFlag, short
fieldID,Handle fieldVal);
pascal Boolean StringEqual(XCmdBlockPtr, unsigned char *str1, unsigned char *str2);
pascal void          ReturnToPas(XCmdBlockPtr, Ptr zeroStr, StringPtr pasStr);
pascal void          ScanToReturn(XCmdBlockPtr, Ptr *scanHndl);
pascal void          ScanToZero(XCmdBlockPtr, Ptr *scanHndl);
```

BoolToStr.c

```
#include "HyperXCmd.h"


 /* Convert a boolean to 'true' or 'false'. Instead of returning
  a new string, as Pascal does, it expects you to create mystr
        and pass it in to be filled. */
pascal void
BoolToStr(paramPtr,bool,mystr)
register XCmdBlockPtr paramPtr;
Boolean              bool;
Str31   mystr;
{
        paramPtr->inArgs[0] = (long)bool;
        paramPtr->inArgs[1] = (long)mystr;
        paramPtr->request = xreqBoolToStr;
   (*paramPtr->entryPoint)();
}
```

EvalExpr.c

```
#include <MacTypes.h>
#include "HyperXCmd.h"

/* Evaluate a HyperCard expression and return the answer. The answer is
  a handle to a zero-terminated string.
  */
pascal Handle
EvalExpr(paramPtr,expr)
register XCmdBlockPtr paramPtr;
StringPtr       expr;
{
        paramPtr->inArgs[0] = (long)expr;
        paramPtr->request = xreqEvalExpr;
   (*paramPtr->entryPoint)();
        return (Handle)paramPtr->outArgs[0];
}
```

ExtToStr.c

```
#include "HyperXCmd.h"

/* Original comment:
   Convert an extended long integer to decimal digits in a string.
   Instead of returning a new string, as Pascal does, it expects
        you to create mystr and pass it in to be filled. */

/* My comment:
        I assume that an extended is supposed to be an 80-byte double,
        which is declared as double in LSC. I've changed "extended" to
        "double" to reflect this
 */
pascal void
ExtToStr(paramPtr,myext,mystr)
register XCmdBlockPtr paramPtr;
double        *       myext;
Str31   mystr;
{
        paramPtr->inArgs[0] = (long)myext;
        paramPtr->inArgs[1] = (long)mystr;
        paramPtr->request = xreqExtToStr;
   (*paramPtr->entryPoint)();
}
```

GetFieldByID.c

```
#include "HyperXCmd.h"

/* Return a handle to a zero-terminated string containing the value of
   the field whise ID is fieldID. You must dispose of the handle.
 */
pascal Handle
GetFieldByID(paramPtr,cardFieldFlag,fieldID)
register XCmdBlockPtr paramPtr;
Boolean cardFieldFlag;
short   fieldID;
{
        paramPtr->inArgs[0] = (long)cardFieldFlag;
        paramPtr->inArgs[1] = fieldID;
        paramPtr->request = xreqGetFieldByID;
   (*paramPtr->entryPoint)();
        return (Handle)paramPtr->outArgs[0];
}
```

GetFieldByName.c

```
#include "HyperXCmd.h"

/* Return a handle to a zero-terminated string containing the value of
   field fieldName on the current card. You must dispose the handle.
 */
pascal Handle
GetFieldByName(paramPtr,cardFieldFlag,fieldName)
```

```
register XCmdBlockPtr paramPtr;
Boolean cardFieldFlag;
StringPtr      fieldName;
{
      paramPtr->inArgs[0] = (long)cardFieldFlag;
      paramPtr->inArgs[1] = (long)fieldName;
      paramPtr->request = xreqGetFieldByName;
  (*paramPtr->entryPoint)();
      return (Handle)paramPtr->outArgs[0];
}
```

GetFieldByNum.c

```
#include "HyperXCmd.h"

/* Return a handle to a zero-terminated string containing the value of
   field fieldNum on the current card. You must dispose of the handle.
 */
pascal Handle
GetFieldByNum(paramPtr, cardFieldFlag,fieldNum)
register XCmdBlockPtr paramPtr;
Boolean cardFieldFlag;
short   fieldNum;
{
      paramPtr->inArgs[0] = (long)cardFieldFlag;
      paramPtr->inArgs[1] = fieldNum;
      paramPtr->request = xreqGetFieldByNum;
  (*paramPtr->entryPoint)();
      return (Handle)paramPtr->outArgs[0];
}
```

GetGlobal.c

```
#include "HyperXCmd.h"

/* Return a handle to a zero-terminated string containing the value of
   the specified HyperTalk global variable.
 */
pascal Handle
GetGlobal(paramPtr,globName)
register XCmdBlockPtr paramPtr;
StringPtr      globName;
{
      paramPtr->inArgs[0] = (long)globName;
      paramPtr->request = xreqGetGlobal;
  (*paramPtr->entryPoint)();
      return (Handle)paramPtr->outArgs[0];
}
```

LongToStr.c

```c
#include "HyperXCmd.h"


/* Convert an unsigned long integer to a Pascal string. Instead of
        returning a new string, as Pascal does, it expects you to
        create mystr and pass it in to be filled.
 */
pascal void
LongToStr(paramPtr, posNum, mystr)
register XCmdBlockPtr paramPtr;
long                  posNum;
Str31   mystr;
{
        paramPtr->inArgs[0] = posNum;
        paramPtr->inArgs[1] = (long)mystr;
        paramPtr->request = xreqLongToStr;
   (*paramPtr->entryPoint)();
}
```

NumToHex.c

```c
#include "HyperXCmd.h"

/* Convert an unsigned long integer to a hexadecimal number and put it
   into a Pascal string. Instead of returning a new string, as
   Pascal does, it expects you to create mystr and pass it in to be filled.
 */
pascal void
NumToHex(paramPtr, num, nDigits, mystr)
register XCmdBlockPtr paramPtr;
long                  num;
short                 nDigits;
Str31   mystr;
{
        paramPtr->inArgs[0] = num;
        paramPtr->inArgs[1] = nDigits;
        paramPtr->inArgs[2] = (long)mystr;
        paramPtr->request = xreqNumToHex;
   (*paramPtr->entryPoint)();
}
```

NumToStr.c

```c
#include "HyperXCmd.h"

/* Convert a signed long integer to a Pascal string. Instead of
   returning a new string, as Pascal does, it expects you to
        create mystr and pass it in to be filled.
 */
pascal void
NumToStr(paramPtr,num,mystr)
register XCmdBlockPtr paramPtr;
long                  num;
Str31   mystr;
{
```

```
      paramPtr->inArgs[0] = num;
      paramPtr->inArgs[1] = (long)mystr;
      paramPtr->request = xreqNumToStr;
  (*paramPtr->entryPoint)();
}
```

PasToZero.c

```
#include "HyperXCmd.h"


/* Convert a Pascal string to a zero-terminated string. Returns a handle
   to a new zero-terminated string. The caller must dispose the handle.
   You'll need to do this for any result or argument you send from
   your XCMD to HyperTalk. Note that if you use C-format strings, you won't
   need to do this from C.
 */
pascal Handle
PasToZero(paramPtr,pasStr)
register XCmdBlockPtr paramPtr;
StringPtr      pasStr;
{
      paramPtr->inArgs[0] = (long)pasStr;
      paramPtr->request = xreqPasToZero;
  (*paramPtr->entryPoint)();
      return (Handle)paramPtr->outArgs[0];
}
```

ReturnToPas.c

```
#include "HyperXCmd.h"

/* zeroStr points into a zero-terminated string. Collect the
   characters from there to the next carriage Return and return
   them in the Pascal string pasStr. If a Return is not found,
   collect chars until the end of the string.
 */
pascal void
ReturnToPas(paramPtr,zeroStr,pasStr)
register XCmdBlockPtr paramPtr;
Ptr     zeroStr;
StringPtr      pasStr;
{
      paramPtr->inArgs[0] = (long)zeroStr;
      paramPtr->inArgs[1] = (long)pasStr;
      paramPtr->request = xreqReturnToPas;
  (*paramPtr->entryPoint)();
}
```

ScanToReturn.c

```c
#include "HyperXCmd.h"

/* Move the pointer scanPtr along a zero-terminated
   string until it points at a Return character
   or a zero byte.
 */
pascal void
ScanToReturn(paramPtr,scanHndl)
register XCmdBlockPtr paramPtr;
Ptr *   scanHndl;
{
        paramPtr->inArgs[0] = (long)scanHndl;
        paramPtr->request = xreqScanToReturn;
   (*paramPtr->entryPoint)();
}
```

ScanToZero.c

```c
#include "HyperXCmd.h"

/* Move the pointer scanPtr along a zero-terminated
   string until it points at a zero byte.
 */
pascal void
ScanToZero(paramPtr,scanHndl)
register XCmdBlockPtr paramPtr;
Ptr *   scanHndl;
{
        paramPtr->inArgs[0] = (long)scanHndl;
        paramPtr->request = xreqScanToZero;
   (*paramPtr->entryPoint)();
}
```

SendCardMessage.c

```c
#include "HyperXCmd.h"

/* Send a HyperCard message (a command with arguments) to the current card.
   msg is a pointer to a Pascal-format string.
 */
pascal void
SendCardMessage(paramPtr, msg)
register XCmdBlockPtr paramPtr;
StringPtr       msg;
{
        paramPtr->inArgs[0] = (long)msg;
        paramPtr->request = xreqSendCardMessage;
   (*paramPtr->entryPoint)();
}
```

SetFieldByID.c

```
#include "HyperXCmd.h"

/* Set the value of the field whose ID is fieldID to be the zero-
   terminated string in fieldVal. The contents of the Handle are
   copied, so you must still dispose it afterwards.
 */
pascal void
SetFieldByID(paramPtr,cardFieldFlag,fieldID,fieldVal)
register XCmdBlockPtr paramPtr;
Boolean cardFieldFlag;
short   fieldID;
Handle  fieldVal;
{
        paramPtr->inArgs[0] = (long)cardFieldFlag;
        paramPtr->inArgs[1] = fieldID;
        paramPtr->inArgs[2] = (long)fieldVal;
        paramPtr->request = xreqSetFieldByID;
   (*paramPtr->entryPoint)();
}
```

SetFieldByName.c

```
#include "HyperXCmd.h"


/* Set the value of field fieldName to be the zero-terminated string
   in fieldVal. The contents of the Handle are copied, so you must
   still dispose it afterwards.
 */
pascal void
SetFieldByName(paramPtr,cardFieldFlag,fieldName,fieldVal)
register XCmdBlockPtr paramPtr;
Boolean cardFieldFlag;
StringPtr       fieldName;
Handle  fieldVal;
{
        paramPtr->inArgs[0] = (long)cardFieldFlag;
        paramPtr->inArgs[1] = (long)fieldName;
        paramPtr->inArgs[2] = (long)fieldVal;
        paramPtr->request = xreqSetFieldByName;
   (*paramPtr->entryPoint)();
}
```

SetFieldByNum.c

```
#include "HyperXCmd.h"

/* Set the value of field fieldNum to be the zero-terminated string
   in fieldVal. The contents of the Handle are copied, so you must
   still dispose it afterwards.
 */
pascal void
SetFieldByNum(paramPtr,cardFieldFlag,fieldNum,fieldVal)
```

```
register XCmdBlockPtr paramPtr;
Boolean cardFieldFlag;
short   fieldNum;
Handle  fieldVal;
{
        paramPtr->inArgs[0] = (long)cardFieldFlag;
        paramPtr->inArgs[1] = fieldNum;
        paramPtr->inArgs[2] = (long)fieldVal;
        paramPtr->request = xreqSetFieldByNum;
   (*paramPtr->entryPoint)();
}
```

SetGlobal.c

```
#include "HyperXCmd.h"

/* Set the value of the specified HyperTalk global variable to be
   the zero-terminated string in globValue. The contents of the
   Handle are copied, so you must still dispose it afterwards.
 */
pascal void
SetGlobal(paramPtr,globName,globValue)
register XCmdBlockPtr paramPtr;
StringPtr       globName;
Handle globValue;
{
        paramPtr->inArgs[0] = (long)globName;
        paramPtr->inArgs[1] = (long)globValue;
        paramPtr->request = xreqSetGlobal;
   (*paramPtr->entryPoint)();
}
```

StringEqual.c

```
#include "HyperXCmd.h"

/* Return true if the two strings have the same characters.
   Case insensitive compare of the strings.
 */
pascal Boolean
StringEqual(paramPtr,str1,str2)
register XCmdBlockPtr paramPtr;
unsigned char * str1;
unsigned char * str2;
{
        paramPtr->inArgs[0] = (long)str1;
        paramPtr->inArgs[1] = (long)str2;
        paramPtr->request = xreqStringEqual;
   (*paramPtr->entryPoint)();
        return (Boolean)paramPtr->outArgs[0];
}
```

StringLength.c

```
#include "HyperXCmd.h"

/* Count the characters from where strPtr points until the next zero byte.
   Does not count the zero itself. strPtr must be a zero-terminated string.
 */
pascal long
StringLength(paramPtr,strPtr)
register XCmdBlockPtr paramPtr;
StringPtr       strPtr;
{
        paramPtr->inArgs[0] = (long)strPtr;
        paramPtr->request = xreqStringLength;
   (*paramPtr->entryPoint)();
        return paramPtr->outArgs[0];
}
```

StringMatch.c

```
#include "HyperXCmd.h"

/* Perform case-insensitive match looking for pattern anywhere in
   target, returning a pointer to first character of the first match,
   in target or NIL if no match found. pattern is a Pascal string,
   and target is a zero-terminated string.
 */
pascal Ptr
StringMatch(paramPtr, pattern, target)
register XCmdBlockPtr paramPtr;
StringPtr       pattern;
Ptr     target;
{
        paramPtr->inArgs[0] = (long)pattern;
        paramPtr->inArgs[1] = (long)target;
        paramPtr->request = xreqStringMatch;
   (*paramPtr->entryPoint)();
        return (Ptr)paramPtr->outArgs[0];
}
```

StrToBool.c

```
#include "HyperXCmd.h"

/* Convert the Pascal strings 'true' and 'false' to booleans.
 */
pascal Boolean
StrToBool(paramPtr,str)
register XCmdBlockPtr paramPtr;
Str31   str;
{
        paramPtr->inArgs[0] = (long)str;
        paramPtr->request = xreqStrToBool;
   (*paramPtr->entryPoint)();
        return (Boolean)paramPtr->outArgs[0];
}
```

StrToExt.c

```c
#include "HyperXCmd.h"


/* Original comment:
   Convert a string of ASCII decimal digits to an extended long integer.
          Instead of returning a new extended, as Pascal does, it expects you
          to create myext and pass it in to be filled. */

/* My comment: extended, as far as I know, is an 80-bit double, not a
   long integer. Since LSC doubles are 80-bit, I've changed myext to
   a pointer to a double */
pascal void StrToExt(paramPtr, str, myext)
register XCmdBlockPtr paramPtr;
Str31   str;
double *        myext;
{
        paramPtr->inArgs[0] = (long)str;
        paramPtr->inArgs[1] = (long)myext;
        paramPtr->request = xreqStrToExt;
   (*paramPtr->entryPoint)();
}
/*      FUNCTION StrToExt(str: Str31): Extended;
VAR x: Extended;
BEGIN
 WITH paramPtr^ DO
  BEGIN
   inArgs[1] := ORD(@str);
   inArgs[2] := ORD(@x);
   request := xreqStrToExt;
   DoJsr(entryPoint);
   StrToExt := x;
  END;
END;  */
```

StrToLong.c

```c
#include "HyperXCmd.h"

/* Convert a string of ASCII decimal digits to an unsigned long integer.
 */
pascal long
StrToLong(paramPtr, strPtr)
register XCmdBlockPtr paramPtr;
Str31   strPtr;
{
        paramPtr->inArgs[0] = (long)strPtr;
        paramPtr->request = xreqStrToLong;
   (*paramPtr->entryPoint)();
        return (long)paramPtr->outArgs[0];
}
```

StrToNum.c

```
#include "HyperXCmd.h"

/* Convert a string of ASCII decimal digits to a signed long integer.
   Negative sign is allowed.
 */
pascal long
StrToNum(paramPtr, str)
register XCmdBlockPtr paramPtr;
Str31   str;
{
        paramPtr->inArgs[0] = (long)str;
        paramPtr->request = xreqStrToNum;
   (*paramPtr->entryPoint)();
        return paramPtr->outArgs[0];
}
```

ZeroBytes.c

```
#include "HyperXCmd.h"


/* Write zeros into memory starting at destPtr and going for longCount
   number of bytes.
 */
pascal void
ZeroBytes(paramPtr, dstPtr, longCount)
register XCmdBlockPtr paramPtr;
Ptr     dstPtr;
long    longCount;
{
        paramPtr->inArgs[0] = (long)dstPtr;
        paramPtr->inArgs[1] = longCount;
        paramPtr->request = xreqZeroBytes;
   (*paramPtr->entryPoint)();
}
```

ZeroToPas.c

```
#include "HyperXCmd.h"

/* Fill the Pascal string with the contents of the zero-terminated
   string. Useful for converting the arguments of any XCMD to
   Pascal strings.
 */
pascal void
ZeroToPas(paramPtr,zeroStr,pasStr)
register XCmdBlockPtr paramPtr;
unsigned char  *zeroStr;
StringPtr               pasStr;
{
        paramPtr->inArgs[0] = (long)zeroStr;
        paramPtr->inArgs[1] = (long)pasStr;
        paramPtr->request = xreqZeroToPas;
   (*paramPtr->entryPoint)();
}
```

Appendix G

Bibliography

Apple Computer, Inc. *Inside Macintosh,* Volume I. Reading, Mass.: Addison-Wesley, 1985. $24.95.

Apple Computer, Inc. *Inside Macintosh,* Volume II. Reading, Mass.: Addison-Wesley, 1985. $24.95.

Apple Computer, Inc. *Inside Macintosh,* Volume III. Reading, Mass.: Addison-Wesley, 1985. $19.95.

Apple Computer, Inc. *Inside Macintosh,* Volume IV. Reading, Mass.: Addison-Wesley, 1986. $24.95.

Apple Computer, Inc. *Inside Macintosh,* Volume V. Reading, Mass.: Addison-Wesley, 1988. $26.95.

Apple Computer, Inc. *Inside Macintosh X-Ref.* Reading, Mass.: Addison-Wesley, 1988. $9.95.

Apple Computer, Inc. *Programmer's Introduction to the Macintosh Family.* Reading, Mass.: Addison-Wesley, 1988. $22.95 (HC).

Apple Computer, Inc. *Technical Introduction to the Macintosh Family.* Reading, Mass.: Addison-Wesley, 1987. $19.95.

Chernicoff, Stephen. *Macintosh Revealed,* Volume I: *Unlocking the Toolbox,* 2nd edition. Indianapolis: Hayden, 1987. $26.95.

Chernicoff, Stephen. *Macintosh Revealed,* Volume II: *Programming with the Toolbox,* 2nd edition. Indianapolis: Hayden, 1987. $24.95.

Goodman, Paul. *Advanced Macintosh Pascal.* Indianapolis: Hayden, 1986. $19.95.

Knaster, Scott. *How to Write Macintosh Software.* Indianapolis: Hayden, 1988. $24.95.

Knaster, Scott. *Macintosh Programming Secrets.* Reading, Mass.: Addison-Wesley, 1988. $24.95.

Smith, David E., ed. *The Best of MacTutor, The Macintosh Programming Journal,* Volume 1. Placentia, California. 1985. $24.00.

Smith, David E., ed. *The Complete MacTutor, The Macintosh Programming Journal,*
    Volume 2. Placentia, California. 1986. $24.00.
West, Joel. *Programming with Macintosh Programmer's Workshop*. New York:
    Bantam, 1987. $29.95.

A good C language reference is:

Kernighan, Brian W., and Ritchie, Dennis M. *The C Programming Language,* 2nd
    edition. Englewood Cliffs, N.J.: Prentice-Hall, 1988. $29.95.

Index

Macintosh Programming Primer: The Disk!

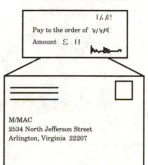

For a complete set of Macintosh Programming Primer applications, resources, and projects send the coupon on this page (or just send your name and address), along with a check for $25.00 to:

M/MAC
2534 North Jefferson Street
Arlington, Virginia 22207

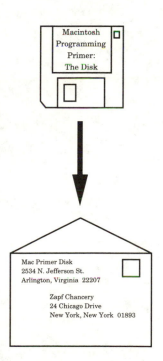

Here's my $25!
Send me the Primer Disk, quick!!! Mail the disk to:

Name_____

Company_____

Address_____

City_____ State____ Zip_____

Virginia Residents Please Add 4.5% Sales Tax
No Credit Cards, Please!